QUEERING THE SOUTH ON SCREEN

THE SOUTH ON SCREEN

EDITED BY R. Barton Palmer AND Matthew H. Bernstein

QUEERING THE SOUTH ON SCREEN

Edited by ▸ *Tison Pugh*

THE UNIVERSITY OF GEORGIA PRESS ATHENS

Athens, Georgia 30602
www.ugapress.org

Set in 10/14 Warnock Pro by Kaelin Chappell Broaddus

Most University of Georgia Press titles are
available from popular e-book vendors.

Printed digitally

Library of Congress Cataloging-in-Publication Data

Names: Pugh, Tison, 1970– editor.
Title: Queering the South on screen / edited by Tison Pugh.
Description: Athens : The University of Georgia Press, 2020. |
Series: The South on screen | Includes bibliographical references and index.
Identifiers: LCCN 2019032320 | ISBN 9780820356532 (hardback) |
ISBN 9780820356723 (paperback) | ISBN 9780820356525 (ebook)
Subjects: LCSH: Southern States—In motion pictures. | Gender identity in
motion pictures. | Identity (Psychology) in motion pictures. | Queer theory. |
Culture in motion pictures.
Classification: LCC PN1995.9.S66 Q84 2020 | DDC 791.43/65875—dc23
LC record available at https://lccn.loc.gov/2019032320

To Barry Sandler, who made the movies
so much queerer than they were before,
and to Dawn Trouard, who leaves all other
steel magnolias trembling in her wake.

Contents

QUEERING THE SOUTH ON SCREEN

Introduction ▸ Five Ways of Looking at the Queer South on Screen

TISON PUGH

Scene 1: "What degenerate produced this abortion?" thunders Ignatius J. Reilly in John Kennedy Toole's *A Confederacy of Dunces*, as this filmgoing lunatic returns obsessively to his local theater only to denounce the perversity of its offerings. "Just look at those smiling morons! . . . Thank God that scene is over," he sighs after a musical's chorus number, and then, following its love scene, pronounces disgustedly of the actors, "They probably have halitosis. . . . I hate to think of the obscene places those mouths have doubtless been before."[1]

Scene 2: Rita Mae Brown concludes her *Rubyfruit Jungle* with heroine Molly Bolt deciding, as she muses over the marginalization of southern lesbians, that she will dedicate her life to her artistic and cinematic vision: "Damn, I wished the world would let me be myself. But I knew better on all counts. I wish I could make my films. That wish I can work for."[2] Envisioning self-actualization through film, Bolt views cinematic narrative as a means of artistic expression and thus of southern queer expression, of breaking down the heteronormative biases of culture and society.

Scene 3: In Tennessee Williams's short story "The Mysteries of the Joy Rio," protagonist Emiel Kroger enjoys the decadent and furtive opportunities afforded in "the mysterious upper galleries of the Joy Rio . . . a sort of fiddler's green where practically every device and fashion of carnality had run riot in a gloom so thick that a chance partner could only be discovered by touch."[3] The audience members care little what plays on the screen but instead direct their attention to who sidles into the adjacent seat so that they may concentrate on blindly physical, rather than narratively visual, pleasures in the dark.

As these three brief literary scenes attest, queer southerners have long expressed their desires through their relationships to the cinematic and other screens: Ignatius Reilly denouncing its purported perversities while masochistically, obsessively repeating the filmgoing experience; Molly Bolt seeking to portray on film lesbian lives rendered virtually invisible throughout much of cinema's history; and Emiel Kroger preferring erotic sensations in the dark over narrative actions on the screen.[4] By way of contrast, these queer characters enjoy markedly different pleasures, perversities, and possibilities through their relationships to the screen than does Binx Bolling, the eponymous protagonist of Walker Percy's *The Moviegoer*, who stands as the definitive exemplar of the straight, white southern moviegoer—yet ironically so, for his story line progresses out of the theater and into marriage, thus allowing him to escape the existential angst that his moviegoing symbolizes.[5] One cannot extrapolate conclusively from the brief examples of Ignatius Reilly, Molly Bolt, Emiel Kroger, and Binx Bolling, yet their diverging story lines provocatively hint at the need to think seriously about the ways in which queer southerners relate to and are depicted on screens large and small. At the very least, it is virtually impossible to imagine Binx Bolling transposed into the story lines of Ignatius Reilly, Molly Bolt, and Emiel Kroger, and so their collectively queer relationships to the screen point to the dreams and discontents of southern LGBTQ+ moviegoers.

Yet within the realm of U.S. culture and its construction of its citizenry, geography, and ideology, who are southerners and who are queers, and what is the South and what is queerness? Such labels are ostensibly transparent in their demarcation and are often simply affirmed as core and constitutive factors of an individual's identity—southerners live in the U.S. South, queer people pursue nonnormative expressions of gender identity and erotic desire—yet both terms are reflective of and complicit in individual, regional, and national fantasies dependent upon the construction of an Other for the overlapping yet discrete regimes of American normalcy to function. As Jennifer Rae Greeson discerns in her study of the multiple purposes of the mythic South, "What remains constant across U.S. history is the conceptual structure provided to us by our South: it is an *internal other* for the nation, an intrinsic part of the national body that nonetheless is differentiated and held apart from the whole."[6] The United States of America has long defined itself through the South as its internal Other, and in a further twist of the screw, queer people serve as the internal Other for the citizens of the South. In this light the figure of the Southern Queer—a phantom identity etched on real and desiring bodies—incarnates the contradictions and paradoxes that inevitably arise in cultural scapegoating, in the social need for some to define themselves not by who they are so much as by who they are not.

"The South": these words appear to represent a monolith, yet without immediate clarification it remains impossible to determine precisely what any person might mean by this term. Michael Bibler succinctly dismisses this geographic specter, stating bluntly that "there's no such thing as a solid South."[7] Indeed, it is generally agreed within critical circles that "the South" does not exist as an amalgamated whole, for its contingent constructions jockey specific states and subcultures in and out, as circumstances demand. The nebulousness of the construction of "the South" is hazily apparent through its border states—Texas, Oklahoma, Missouri, Kentucky, Maryland, Florida—each of which could or could not be counted within its geographic purview. One might otherwise consider the South to be the "solid South" of the U.S. political commentariat, or the Civil War's Confederate States, or the agrarian South, or the gothic South, or the Deep South. There is no one way of viewing the South, and a kaleidoscopic vision of the region illuminates the various rhetorical circumstances that necessitate creating the region in its contradictory enactments. Any hypothesis of the South, through its inevitable occlusions, must fail to define it, and yet there emerge purposeful, provocative insights from this taxonomical failure embedded in virtually every study of the region.

A curious irony in the construction of the South as internal and cultural Other to the United States arises in the contrasting critical reception of its literary and cinematic works. The term "southern literature" conjures for many readers a mix of canonical authors (Flannery O'Connor, Zora Neale Hurston, William Faulkner) and tropes (gothicism, race relations, plantation life), while the very branding of "southern literature" delimits writers within a particular tradition yet concomitantly establishes parameters of reception conducive for their art to flourish. As John Bassett observes, in noting numerous historical efforts to define the realm of southern letters, "It seems a curious burden writers in the South bear. . . . they often find it devilishly hard to write without first being confined in a readerly box called 'Southern literature.'"[8] Notwithstanding these pressures and regional prejudices, few would deny that the South "punches above its weight" in terms of literary production, an artistic phenomenon most evident in the celebrated years of the Southern Renaissance. Still, the region and its authors simultaneously bear the scars of marginalization because the very need of a renaissance ironically heightens the cultural fantasy of a preternaturally benighted landscape.[9]

Just as southern literature haunts and inspires the United States' aesthetic imagination, it is likewise apparent that southern films function contrapuntally in its cinematic imagination. The western stands as one of Hollywood's key genres, a distinctly American narrative tradition that celebrates the nation's values through heroic and frequently violent styles, story lines, and themes,[10] but the "southern" registers much less as a defining mode of cinematic storytelling, even though hundreds of films take the South as their setting. Warren French, noting the momentous importance of D. W. Griffith's *The Birth of a Nation* (1915) and Victor Fleming's *Gone with the Wind* (1939) to film history, observes that "neither fostered a genre of imitative films that became a backbone of the industry. The legendary South gave way to the legendary West."[11] Indeed, in their *Hollywood's Image of the South: A Century of Southern Films*, Larry Langman and David Ebner announce their ambition to "establish the 'southern' as a legitimate film genre" and marshal scores of specimens to buttress their argument.[12] Despite this abundance of evidence, the "southern" is rarely discussed as a discrete film genre, with the various films that might be so labeled often blurring into predefined genres such as romance (*Something to Talk About, Sweet Home Alabama*), comedy (*Miss Firecracker, Girls Trip*), musical (*Show Boat, Hairspray*), suspense (*Cape Fear, Hush . . . Hush, Sweet Charlotte*), horror (*Angel Heart, The Skeleton Key*), drama (*Steel Magnolias, Eve's Bayou*), history (*The Tuskegee Airmen, Rosewood*), biopic (*Coal Miner's Daughter, Cross Creek*), civil rights films (*Mississippi Burning, Selma*), and literary adaptations (*A Streetcar Named Desire, I Know Why the Caged Bird Sings*). The contrasting fortunes of the western and the "southern" are also apparent in television history, where numerous westerns brought this genre's themes to the small screen (*Gunsmoke, Bonanza*), whereas programs set in the South (*The Dukes of Hazzard, Designing Women, Atlanta*) are seldom referred to as "southerns." The distinction between the "southern" as an unrealized genre and the many films and television programs set in the South highlights the vagaries of genre construction, an ill-defined and amorphous taxonomy of art forms that distorts some perspectives while enhancing others. It should be noted as well that many southern films rely on hackneyed stereotypes of the South's citizenry, thus questioning the possibility that Hollywood and other corporate media entities can see the region on its own terms.[13]

Recent studies of the South and its cinematic, televisual, and pop-culture representations agree that the South is continually constructed anew while its mythic tropes are often unquestioningly bolstered. Deborah Barker and Kathryn McKee, in their *American Cinema and the Southern Imaginary*, explore the "various ways in which the southern imaginary is constitutive of American cinema and of the ways in which the makers of movies . . . have imagined the 'South' both to construct and to unsettle national narratives."[14] Likewise, in *Small-Screen Souths: Region, Identity, and the Cultural Politics of Television*, Lisa Hinrichsen, Gina Caison, and Stephanie Rountree examine "how the televisual South speaks to national and transnational transformations, including changing modes of conceptualizing race, class, gender, and regional identity itself."[15] Additional volumes focusing on media depictions of the South include Jack Temple Kirby's *Media-Made Dixie: The South in the American Imagination*, Allison Graham's *Framing the South: Hollywood, Television, and Race during the Civil Rights Struggle*, Andrew Leiter's *Southerners on Film: Essays on Hollywood Portrayals since the 1970s*, R. Bruce Brasell's *The Possible South: Documentary Film and the Limitations of Biraciality*, and Susan Courtney's *Split-Screen Nation: Moving Images of the American West and South*.[16] These volumes focusing on film, television, and media complement the work of such scholars as Tara McPherson and Karen Cox. In *Reconstructing Dixie: Race, Gender, and Nostalgia in the Imagined South*, McPherson examines various nostalgic depictions of the South, searching for "new ways of feeling southern that more fully come to terms with the history of racial oppression and racial connection in the South,"[17] and Cox, in *Dreaming of Dixie: How the South Was Created in American Popular Culture*, examines "how perceptions of southern identity have been shaped from outside of the region" in a variety of popular-culture forms, including sheet music, radio, film, literature, and the tourist trade.[18] As this brief overview of the scholarly conversation elucidates, the South's construction—from both inside and outside of its borders—jockeys back and forth between past and present, between internal and external voices, and between myth and reality. *Queering the South on Screen* expands this discussion by focusing on the ways in which queerness is similarly constructed, serving as a site both of contention and of self-determination in visual media.

The cinematic, televisual, and pop-cultural South is a mutable fantasy, one that remains ever open to negotiation about its narrative and cultural meaning. And so while *Queering the South on Screen* takes as one of its foundational premises the necessity of investigating the South as a discrete regional fantasy of the United States' collective imaginary, one might well wonder whether "the South" as a marker of geographical and regional identity continues to matter in an increasingly interconnected world. Indeed, regional studies and regionalisms bear the potential for a retrogressive, even dangerously nostalgic, myopia—a longing for the past as the "good old days" irrespective of the depravities and injustices fostered alongside. The threat of a nostalgic view of regionalisms in general, and of the South in particular, is mitigated through the introduction of queer perspectives: that is to say, the union of regional and queer studies can result in analyses that encourage us to see yesterday's truths and ideologies differently and thus to perceive the very meanings of regionalism and identity anew. Anjali Arondekar and Geeta Patel propose that "the coupling of area [studies] and queer" can be both "generative and confounding," as they call for critics to ponder "new queer idioms of the geopolitical" through sharper focus on regionalisms—even if such microanalysis can never truly achieve lapidary precision.[19] Engaging micro and macro levels of cultural critique, putting them into dialogue rather than shunting one aside in favor of the other, enhances the insights derived, and so to focus on southern regionalisms as reflected in the cinema and on television is not to reify the fantasy of the South as much as it is to demonstrate the creation and continual re-creation of this fantasy and to query its cultural work—which could well influence the world beyond the South's porous borders. In other words, we might find additional meaning in the old activist chestnut admonishing one to "act locally, think globally" by reorienting its chiasmus in favor of "think locally, act globally." In this new world of interconnectivity, by thinking locally, we might indeed affect, even effect, global action—with repercussions for queers worldwide.

As "the South" proves intransigently difficult to define but necessary to explore for its ideological work and contradictions, so too does "the queer," for its many permutations across histories, countries, and cultures render it manifold in its enactments and malleable in its meaning. Queerness subverts facades of erotic normativity in striking ways across the globe, and Pippa Holloway tersely avows: "*The South is a unique space that generates diverse queer identities.*"[20] Eve Kosofsky Sedgwick lyrically defines "queer" as "the open mesh of possibilities, gaps, overlaps, dissonances and resonances, lapses and excesses of meaning when the constituent elements of anyone's gender, of anyone's sexuality aren't made (or *can't be* made) to signify monolithically."[21] The same act—sodomy, to take the exemplar par excellence—can register as normative in ancient Greece yet as transgressive in the modern South—and then shift again, if not quite overnight then nevertheless following a series of watershed moments. Such a transhistorical construction of queerness has become evident in the circumstances resulting in the U.S. Supreme Court's 2003 *Lawrence v. Texas* decision that struck down sodomy laws in Texas—and by extension, in the other states, many southern, that still held them in their legal codes—but only after humiliating the plaintiffs with state arrest for private sexual acts. And so as illiberal pockets of the South mosey through their resistant, recalcitrant acquiescence to modernity, sodomy may too be viewed within their range of the normative, particularly in the aftermath of the 2015 *Obergefell v. Hodges* decision legalizing gay marriage across the United States. Nonetheless, as much as homosexuality may indeed become inculcated within the South's new normal, queerness will likely persist, for even without ideological policing—if such a utopian vision could be granted—the possibility of sexuality in all of its enactments signifying neutrally remains difficult to conceive. And in the South, the issue of queerness is often complicated—productively so, in their joint challenges to regimes of normativity—with issues of race.[22] Sara Ahmed posits that "Queer pleasures put bodies into contact that have been kept apart by the scripts of compulsory heterosexuality"—with scripts of compulsory heterosexuality often interlinking with scripts of whiteness's cultural invisibility and power.[23]

Even in dismantling the cultural force of normativity's regimes, caution is warranted: as much as queerness and queer theory might appear to be necessary antidotes to the totemic weaponry of heteronormativity, Gary Richards rightly admonishes that "*queer* ironically threatens to reinforce a binarism of normative/queer and thus the notion that there is a stable, finite, knowable normativity."[24] A key risk of queer theory is the reinforcement of identities based on a tired binary, with queerness conscripted to serve as the Other to normativity yet simultaneously reinforcing the cultural scripts that depend upon Othering. The South's troubled history can be traced through a long string of binaries—black/white, female/male, gay/straight, slave/master, poor/rich—and so a misuse of queer theory would potentially arise in its facile deployment as an integral counterweight of a regressive regime rather than as an escape from the binary logic that necessitated it.

From these converging perspectives, southern queers reflect a truth of individual identity conflated with the fantasy of an ideological order that requires southern queers, and so when southern queers appear in films and on television, and when southern queers watch films and television, the inherent contradictions of this cultural fantasy reveal the fault lines of gender, geography, and desire that constitute the endless possibilities of southern life. While this insight informs the interventions offered in *Queering the South on Screen*, I would concomitantly like to acknowledge a key point: no single volume could adequately cover all forms of queerness experienced in the South, and this volume does not achieve such an unachievable ambition. Envisioning this project, I anticipated a collection explicitly engaging with a wider range of identities and texts representative of the fully intersectional nature of queer southern life. In skimming the table of contents, one might see a focus on white, cis-gendered, gay male life to the exclusion of other queer identities and communities—although reading the individual chapters would then reveal a deeper engagement with issues of race and transgender identity than the essay titles suggest. Anyone who has edited an anthology knows that one can invite, but not summon, a more fully intersectional range of essays. To such an end, I aspired to deeper coverage of lesbian narratives and stars, including such subjects as Tig Notaro's *One Mississippi*, or Ellen Degeneres's southern star persona, or the sitcoms *Golden Girls* and *Designing Women*, as well as more content featuring black narratives and stars, including such topics as Tyler Perry's corpus, or the Academy Award–winning *Moonlight*, or Steven Spielberg's adaptation of Alice Walker's *The Color Purple*. I also acknowledge that *Queering the South on Screen* does not include essays on significant screen genres, including such reality television programs as *The Real Housewives of Atlanta* (2008–) and *Love and Hip-Hop: Atlanta* (2012–). Documentaries are also absent, including such wonderful works as Parris Patton's *Creature* (1999) and Kate Davis's *Southern Comfort* (2001), which illuminate aspects of transgender life in the South. I would have warmly welcomed essays on these and other such topics. Editing a volume involves a curious mix of actively soliciting and patiently awaiting proposals, and then curating the resulting contents to the best of one's abilities.[25] *Queering the South on Screen* will, I hope, initiate further scholarly and cultural examinations of its subject, offering a preliminary foray upon which many more critics will build in various directions, thereby facilitating the further study of cinematic and televisual texts left unaddressed in these pages. Readers and critics will push beyond these gaps so that we can see the true intersectionality of the South and its queer inhabitants in all our stunning variety and individuality.

Given these conditions, the chapters included in *Queering the South on Screen* focus on five narrative and thematic modes of queerness—adaptation, gothic, homosocial anxiety, kinship, and camp—rather than on identity categories. These five modes illuminate repeated tropes found in the queer South and its narrative traditions, and thus point to pertinent intersections of queerness, regionalism, and identity. On the whole, these intertwining threads construct much of the queer South on screen and its accompanying desires and discontents, even as they can only be considered through unique case studies that collectively contribute to an overarching vision of the field.

This volume's first unit, "Queer Adaptations of Southern Authors," examines cinematic adaptations of two of the South's leading authors—William Faulkner and Tennessee Williams—and thus ponders as well the shadow of the region's literary traditions on its cinematic depictions.[26] In "The Redneck Prince and the Queen of Sheba: Labor and Queer Desire in Martin Ritt's *The Long, Hot Summer*," D. Matthew Ramsey explores the queer performances of masculinity on display in this adaptation of Faulkner's *The Hamlet*, most notably in the casting of Paul Newman as the object of multifaceted desire. Surprisingly, male queerness in this film acts not to valorize a preferred version of heteronormativity but to instigate the female characters' realization of their own agency; in a very real sense, queered southern men create empowered southern women. David Markus's chapter, "'The Prison of Our Skin': Orpheus and Antinormativity in *The Fugitive Kind*," analyzes the cinematic adaptation of Williams's *Orpheus Descending*, probing the intersection of Marlon Brando's star persona and the antinormativity key to his role as Val Xavier. Val's attempts to metaphorically shed the skin of his past collide with the male power structures of the small Mississippi town where he finds himself, aligning him with the women who similarly desire to escape the strictures of southern gender. In these striking readings, Ramsey and Markus demonstrate the ways in which complex versions of gender, as staged in film adaptations, cannot help but engage with the authors of their source texts, pointing to the intersecting axes of gender and sexuality that render adaptation itself a queer genre.[27]

In the volume's second unit, "The South's Queer Gothicisms," essayists ponder the long-standing vision of the South as a nightmare land of freakish characters, dead mules, and twilit sorrows. In her influential musings on the southern gothic, Ellen Glasgow famously wondered, "Has Southern life—or is it only Southern fiction—become one vast, disordered sensibility?"—a sentiment expressed and reified in the masterpieces of Faulkner, Flannery O'Connor, and Truman Capote, among numerous others.[28] This antiquated view of the region may be in need of mothballing, yet any tradition that inspired Faulkner and his kindred is illuminating nonetheless. Such dynamics are similarly evident in the ways in which film and television narratives deploy the tropes of the haunted South to allow new ways of viewing queer sexualities and telling queer tales—or simply to remain trapped by them. This unit begins with R. Bruce Brasell's "'Mass Production of Degeneracy': Queer Genre-ship and Southern Gothic Film," in which he analyzes the genesis of southern gothic films not as a preconceived Hollywood genre but as a response to journalistic and popular-press conversations addressing literary, theatrical, and cinematic works. For Brasell, the southern gothic is an inherently queer genre both for its story lines and for the ways in which it was perversely conceived through disruptions to prevailing codes of cultural reproduction, as he further notes the genre's interest in degeneracy as a primary trope of queer antisociality. In "Revolting Queers: The Southern Gothic in Queer Horror Film and Television," Darren Elliott-Smith analyzes the role of homosexuality in the subgenre of southern horror. In such works as Lucio Fulci's *The Beyond* (1981), Tim Sullivan's *2001 Maniacs* (2005), Alan Ball's *True Blood* (2008–14), and Alan Rowe Kelly's *A Far Cry from Home* (2013), the antiquated horror metaphor of the monstrous queer is reimagined both to depict the fundamental normativity of homosexuality and to expose the true horror of the ostensibly heteronormative. Within this reframing of the genre's codes, the bloodied human bodies of these films, in their representation of Deleuzian queer becomings, register the semiotic and thematic shifts evident in recent southern horror.

The chapters of "Southern Homosociality and Queer Anxieties," the third section of *Queering the South on Screen*, consider the ways in which southern men's relationships with one another are often undermined, if not threatened, by the fear of homosexuality "infiltrating" homosocial bonds, as well as, by way of complementary contrast, the ways in which the South fosters homosociality. Jessica Walker, in her chapter "'We Getting Engaged?': Toxic Masculinity and the Louisiana Marriage in *True Detective*," examines the necessity for homosociality to cure heteronormative ills within this series's gothic Louisiana landscape. Reading *True Detective* through its temporal setting in the 1990s and early 2000s, Walker proposes that its gothic vision of eroticism paradoxically sets the stage for the metaphoric construction of a homosocial "Louisiana marriage" that liberates men from predatory visions of sexuality otherwise dominant in southern culture. Male homosocial desire can also provide an escape from the emasculating effects of the southern labor economy, as Ted Atkinson demonstrates in "Working toward a Southern Erostocracy: The Wages of Homosocial Labor in the *Magic Mike* Films." These movies, which depict a troupe of male strippers continually preparing for their next big show, flirt with homosexuality via the "bromance" of homosociality, displaying the power of the desired male body to create ripples of agency in a working landscape inhospitable to the individual. In "Perversion on the Plantation: Quentin Tarantino's *Django Unchained* and Other Queer Antebellum Fantasies," Scott Combs explores the nexus of race, masculinity, and repressed desires on a southern plantation. Tarantino's film depicts the African American hero Django seeking to free his beloved Broomhilda from enslavement at the plantation Candyland, only to discover it to be a hotbed of unacknowledged homoerotic desire that exposes the South as a repressed land in need of a violently cathartic purging. In these homosocial environs of the South, from a gothic Louisiana landscape to strip clubs to a decadent plantation, men negotiate their relationships with one another alongside the phantom possibility of queer desire emerging.

The fourth unit of *Queering the South on Screen*, "Queer Families and Southern Kinship," examines southern families and communities as contrasting sites of queer identity formation and of ideological conformity. Quite frequently, queer children are born and bred in otherwise normative social structures, resulting in sharp tensions that query the depth of blood and community ties. Such queer infiltrations of southern families necessitate reappraising the meaning of kinship in a southern culture often inhospitable to deviations from the erotic norm. At the same time, one need not be family to enjoy kinship with others, and in "The Backward South: Temporal Traversals and Queer Necropolitical Kinships in *Dallas Buyers Club*," Joe Edward Hatfield discusses the ways in which the AIDS crisis forges kinship between the lead characters of the film, Ron (a straight man) and Rayon (a transgender woman). Fighting the tyranny of time, homophobic indifference, and the threat of death, Ron and Rayon instead employ the clichéd backwardness of the South as a resistant strategy for preserving their lives and expanding their communities. In "Queer Native Southern Transmissions in Randy Redroad's *The Doe Boy*," Eric Gary Anderson details the ways in which the formation of one's identity necessitates negotiations vis-à-vis one's family, a particularly fraught process for families framed by intersecting cultural traditions. In this film of a young Cherokee man seeking to understand himself, his culture, and his desires, director Redroad theorizes transmissions within the family as multiple and contradictory, with his protagonist seeking to resolve his conflicting senses of ethnic, geographic, and sexual identity. Jeff Solomon explores how queer children learn to be gay in his "Down South at Peckerwood: Mom, Anti-Mom, and Queer Pedagogy in *Auntie Mame*," theorizing the ways in which this film, as well as the novel upon which it is based, establish its glamorous eponymous protagonist as a queer instructor to her orphaned nephew. The South is critical to this education, as it is here that Mame models, in her pursuit of a wealthy suitor, the performances of gender that allow one to transgress otherwise rigid social codes.

This collection's final section, "Camp and Comedy with Southern Queers," proves the cliché that those who laugh last laugh best, as essayists ponder the meanings of queer southern humor in film and television. Facing vicious prejudices, queers have a long history of laughing at the cultural forces that would otherwise denigrate our lives and desires; the South, too, has long generated unique comedic sensibilities that further establish its singular place in American culture.[29] Given these conditions, queer southern laughter often reflects a rebellious stance against cultural norms, humorously bucking traditions with the serious aim of overturning prevailing erotic mores. In my contribution to this volume, "Southern Manners and Camp Cannibalism in Tennessee Williams's *Suddenly, Last Summer*," I analyze the unfavorable critical reactions to Williams's play and its cinematic adaptation, discussing the ways that both contemporary reviewers and Williams and his screenwriting partner Gore Vidal failed to identify the camp at the heart of the story line. A decadent southern comedy of manners in its film version, *Suddenly, Last Summer* exposes the ways in which southern etiquette bears within it the seeds of its own destruction, as well as the ways in which Williams's outré symbolism could not withstand the transition from stage to film. In the chapter "'Vienners' at Odum's: DeAundra Peek and the Atlanta Televisual Drag Scene," Margaret T. McGehee celebrates the camp performances of Atlanta drag queen DeAundra Peek, analyzing how her appearances on local access television expanded the reach of an authentically queer southern voice throughout her city (and, to some degree, throughout the rest of the United States). An icon of the Atlanta drag community, DeAundra Peek illustrates the political potential of camp, in the daring decision simply to enjoy one's self and one's sexuality in an otherwise conservative locale.

Of course, it should be noted that these five primary narrative and thematic modes of analysis and organization for *Queering the South on Screen*—again: adaptation, gothic, homosocial anxiety, kinship, and camp—overlap one another. For example, Brasell's essay on the southern gothic addresses issues of cinematic adaptation; Walker's essay on *True Detective,* while paying keen attention to the homosocial relationship between its lead detectives, also probes the series's gothic setting; Solomon's essay on kinship and family in *Auntie Mame* revels in the film's campy humor; and so on. The table of contents is organized so that the first essay of each unit could have been included in the unit preceding it and the last essay of each unit could have been included in the unit following it, which demonstrates the fluidity among the categories. As with the vast majority of attempts to classify art by genre and theme, these categories assist in clarifying deep patterns in visual narratives, yet they bear the potential to obfuscate as well, if trusted too implicitly. One should always approach generic and thematic classifications with caution.

Also, as these chapters tacitly illustrate, it is not the goal of *Queering the South on Screen* to stake out exclusive parameters for this field—an unnecessarily prescriptive endeavor that would ironically blanche the queer South of much of its diversity—as much as it is to explore these five key areas of engagement, along with their contradictions and possibilities. Within the array of visual narratives under examination in this volume, the essayists agree on the mutability of the South and the divergence of its manifold voices, each of which expresses desires unique and true to the individual that almost inevitably conflict with the region's strict cultural codes. But the South is changing, and the chimerical vision of a postsouthern South posits an intriguing possibility that tomorrow's South might be unrecognizable to today's.[30] As Michael Kreyling memorably muses in this regard, "Maybe you can't get to the South from here-and-now ever again, 'here' being the postsouthern position of infinite (or almost infinite) simulacra."[31] Films and television multiply such infinite simulacra even more infinitely, and the cinema and television screens of America reflect the shifting meanings of southern queerness in the past and along the path forward into the future. Within these images, we see ourselves anew and askew, absent and present, through truths and through lies. To get to this new postsouthern South, as always, much work remains to be done.

NOTES

1. John Kennedy Toole, *A Confederacy of Dunces* (1980; New York: Wings, 1996), 67–68.

2. Rita Mae Brown, *Rubyfruit Jungle* (1973; New York: Bantam, 1977), 246.

3. Tennessee Williams, "The Mysteries of the Joy Rio" (1954), *Collected Stories* (New York: New Directions, 1985), 99–109, at 103.

4. Of course, this is not to suggest that lesbianism specifically or homosexuality more generally was ever completely absent from the screen but rather that many films have occluded homoerotic desires at the very moment of depicting them. Vito Russo's masterful *The Celluloid Closet: Homosexuality in the Movies* (New York:

Harper & Row, 1987) remains an essential introduction to the issue of Hollywood's representation of queer lives. See also Patricia White, *Uninvited: Classical Hollywood Cinema and Lesbian Representability* (Bloomington: Indiana University Press, 1999), for her consideration of the occlusion of lesbian characters and desires.

5. Walker Percy, *The Moviegoer* (New York: Knopf, 1961). Deborah Barker and Kathryn McKee open their *American Cinema and the Southern Imaginary* (Athens: University of Georgia Press, 2011) by citing Binx Bolling and proposing that "the movies tell people who they are and where they are" (1). Their provocative analysis prompted me to ponder the narrative trajectories of Binx Bolling's queer counterparts.

6. Jennifer Rae Greeson, *Our South: Geographic Fantasy and the Rise of National Literature* (Cambridge, Mass.: Harvard University Press, 2010), 1 (italics in original).

7. Michael Bibler, "Introduction: Smash the Mason-Dixon! or, Manifesting the Southern United States," *PMLA* 131.1 (2016): 153–56, at 153.

8. John E. Bassett, ed., *Defining Southern Literature: Perspectives and Assessments, 1831–1952* (Cranbury, N.J.: Associated University Presses, 1997), 19. Bassett catalogs a range of attempts to define the field of southern literature, often as markedly distinct from American literature.

9. On the Southern Renaissance, see Richard H. King, *A Southern Renaissance: The Cultural Awakening of the American South, 1930–1955* (New York: Oxford University Press, 1980).

10. On the tropes of the western and a reappraisal of this genre's ostensible conservatism, see Douglas Brode, *Dream West: Politics and Religion in Cowboy Movies* (Austin: University of Texas Press, 2013).

11. Warren French, ed., *The South and Film* (Jackson: University Press of Mississippi, 1981), 3. See also Edward D. C. Campbell Jr., *The Celluloid South: Hollywood and the Southern Myth* (Knoxville: University of Tennessee Press, 1981).

12. Larry Langman and David Ebner, comps., *Hollywood's Image of the South: A Century of Southern Films* (Westport, Conn.: Greenwood, 2001), ix.

13. On media stereotypes of the South, see Alison Slade and Amber Narro, "An Acceptable Stereotype: The Southern Image in Television Programming," *Mediated Images of the South: The Portrayal of Dixie in Popular Culture*, ed. Alison Slade, Dedria Givens-Carroll, and Amber Narro (Lanham, Md.: Lexington, 2012), 5–20.

14. Barker and McKee, *American Cinema and the Southern Imaginary*, 1.

15. Lisa Hinrichsen, Gina Caison, and Stephanie Rountree, eds., *Small-Screen Souths: Region, Identity, and the Cultural Politics of Television* (Baton Rouge: Louisiana State University Press, 2017), 3.

16. Jack Temple Kirby, *Media-Made Dixie: The South in the American Imagination*, rev. ed. (Athens: University of Georgia Press, 1986); Allison Graham, *Framing the South: Hollywood, Television, and Race during the Civil Rights Struggle* (Baltimore: Johns Hopkins University Press, 2001); Andrew B. Leiter, ed., *Southerners on Film: Essays on Hollywood Portrayals since the 1970s* (Jefferson, N.C.: McFarland, 2011); R. Bruce Brasell, *The Possible South: Documentary Film and the Limitations of Biraciality* (Jackson: University of Mississippi Press, 2015); Susan Courtney, *Split-*

Screen Nation: Moving Images of the American West and South (New York: Oxford University Press, 2017).

17. Tara McPherson, *Reconstructing Dixie: Race, Gender, and Nostalgia in the Imagined South* (Durham, N.C.: Duke University Press, 2003), 8.

18. Karen L. Cox, *Dreaming of Dixie: How the South Was Created in American Popular Culture* (Chapel Hill: University of North Carolina Press, 2011), 6. See particularly her chapter "Dixie on Film," 81–105.

19. Anjali Arondekar and Geeta Patel, "Area Impossible: Notes toward an Introduction," *GLQ* 22.2 (2016): 151–71, at 166.

20. Pippa Holloway, "Manifesto for a Queer South Politics," *PMLA* 131.1 (2016): 182–86, at 185 (italics in original).

21. Eve Kosofsky Sedgwick, "Queer and Now," *The Routledge Queer Studies Reader*, ed. Donald E. Hall and Annamarie Jagose (London: Routledge, 2013), 3–17, at 8 (italics in original).

22. For insightful analyses of the intersections of race, sexuality, and queerness, see Sharon Patricia Holland, *The Erotic Life of Racism* (Durham, N.C.: Duke University Press, 2012), and Kathryn Bond Stockton, *Beautiful Bottom, Beautiful Shame: Where "Black" Meets "Queer"* (Durham, N.C.: Duke University Press, 2006). Of course, the necessity of investigating the intersection of race and sexuality is not limited to the South.

23. Sara Ahmed, *The Cultural Politics of Emotion*, 2nd ed. (Edinburgh: Edinburgh University Press, 2014), 165. On the invisible yet intransigent power of whiteness, see Mike Hill, ed., *Whiteness: A Critical Reader* (New York: New York University Press, 1997).

24. Gary Richards, *Lovers and Beloveds: Sexual Otherness in Southern Fiction, 1936–1961* (Baton Rouge: Louisiana State University Press, 2005), 2. See also Michael P. Bibler, *Cotton's Queer Relations: Same-Sex Intimacy and the Literature of the Southern Plantation, 1936–1968* (Charlottesville: University of Virginia Press, 2009).

25. Beyond posting announcements of the volume to such websites as the University of Pennsylvania's Call for Papers (call-for-papers.sas.upenn.edu), I emailed more than a hundred scholars in a range of fields and subspecialties related to southern narrative and media studies to apprise them of the volume and to solicit their interest, support, and essays. I deeply appreciate the many kind and supportive responses. Editing a volume is an inherently unpredictable affair. I originally did not intend to include an essay of my own, but when three contributors unexpectedly withdrew rather late in the process, necessity once again became the mother of invention—in this instance, by my adapting and expanding a previously published essay.

26. Faulkner's and Williams's preeminent positions in Southern Studies serve as something of a blessing and a curse: a blessing for the richness of their oeuvres, a curse for their outsized influence on the field. As Gary Richards notes, "contemporary southern sexuality studies remain[s] limited in scope and influence" owing to a "tendency to fetishize a disturbingly narrow set of southern texts centralizing sexuality, most of which is associated with twentieth-century literary production"; see "Tennessee Williams and the Burden of Southern Sexuality Studies," *The Oxford Hand-*

book of the Literature of the U.S. South, ed. Fred Hobson and Barbara Ladd (New York: Oxford University Press, 2016), 310–26, at 312.

27. On the queerness of adaptation, see Pamela Demory, ed., *Queer/Adaptation: A Collection of Critical Essays* (New York: Palgrave Macmillan, 2019).

28. Ellen Glasgow, "Heroes and Monsters," *Saturday Review of Literature* 12.1 (4 May 1935): 3–4, at 3. On the intransigence of the gothic as a defining trope of the South, see Susan V. Donaldson, "Making Darkness Visible," *Undead Souths: The Gothic and Beyond in Southern Literature and Culture*, ed. Eric Gary Anderson, Taylor Hagood, and Daniel Cross Turner (Baton Rouge: Louisiana State University Press, 2015), 261–65.

29. On the South and the politics of queer laughter, see my *Precious Perversions: Humor, Homosexuality, and the Southern Literary Canon* (Baton Rouge: Louisiana State University Press, 2016), esp. 1–18.

30. On the possibility of a postsouthern South, see Suzanne W. Jones and Sharon Monteith, eds., *South to a New Place: Region, Literature, Culture* (Baton Rouge: Louisiana State University Press, 2002), and Martyn Bone, *The Postsouthern Sense of Place in Contemporary Fiction* (Baton Rouge: Louisiana State University Press, 2005). For the postsouthern South and film, see Jay Watson, "Mapping Out a Postsouthern Cinema: Three Contemporary Films," *American Cinema and the Southern Imaginary*, 219–52.

31. Michael Kreyling, *The South That Wasn't There: Postsouthern Memory and History* (Baton Rouge: Louisiana State University Press, 2010), 194.

PART I

QUEER ADAPTATIONS OF SOUTHERN AUTHORS

Chapter 1 ▸ The Redneck Prince and the Queen of Sheba: Labor and Queer Desire in Martin Ritt's *The Long, Hot Summer*

D. MATTHEW RAMSEY

This is, in part, a call to arms. Forget *Cat on a Hot Tin Roof* for a moment. Forget about the box office success, the notoriety, the six Academy Award nominations of that Richard Brooks film, Tennessee Williams's status as a gay man, and the controversy surrounding the adaptation from Broadway to the screen. The Hollywood melodrama from 1958 that provides a richer, more compelling opportunity to explore southern queerness is Martin Ritt's *The Long, Hot Summer*. At first glance, two striking aspects of Ritt's film—Paul Newman's presence as the potential object of bisexual desire and the vintage Hollywood happy ending with three happy heterosexual couples, two of whom are headed to the altar—seem to be at odds: the former would apparently destabilize the latter's complicity with Hollywood's standard heteronormativity. Yet examining the layers of meaning that accrue around Newman's presence and the particulars of his role as protagonist Ben Quick makes available a more complicated understanding of the film's ending, one that does less to reassert a norm than to open other, less normative possibilities. The film's handling of male sexuality and masculinity unlocks a greater appreciation of female sexuality, desire, and self-fulfillment. Queered southern masculinities, in this instance, give rise to female agency.

In *The Long, Hot Summer*, queerness is not so much a characteristic of an actor as a lens through which to consider a critique of identity—an analytical concept or way of reading texts to explore a wide spectrum of interpretive possibilities. Even an acknowledgment of the film's sympathetic and complex handling of southern masculine archetypes—the new-money patriarch, the upper-class "mama's boy," the weak heir, and the lower-class figure of virility—can limit queer reading to an attempt to catalog the instances of instability in masculine identity within the film. The multiple intersecting texts and contexts involved in the production and reception of *The Long, Hot Summer*, which bring with them their own queer resonances, include the film's relationship to its Faulknerian source material; its setting; its actors, writers, and director; the overlapping film genres it evokes; and its muted but significant engagement with race and class structures. Being open to a broader sense of how queerness intersects with southern discourses allows for a fuller exploration of the complexity of sexual dynamics and, especially, how the fractures made visible by a queer reading of the film suggest there is a space for authentic male and female desires, for straight and queer pleasures, in its reception. Such a reading also brings us back to the source texts, compelling an ongoing exploration of the political valences of this adaptation, the critical spaces it opens up, and the nonnormative desires it nevertheless leaves unexamined.

Hollywood's typical version of heteronormativity is destabilized not just by Newman's Ben Quick but by Joanne Woodward's Clara Varner, and indeed by the needs and desires of various other characters. In her analysis of lesbian sexuality in William Faulkner's *Absalom, Absalom!* Jaime Harker notes, "The South is usually imagined as 'grounded,' a 'fixed' space immune to the changes, materialism, and moral relativism of modernity. 'Sense of place' brings with it any number of clichéd ideologies: family, stability, morality, tradition." Harker asks for a reimagining of the South as "a crossroads, a fluid, intersecting, unfinished trajectory of narratives."[1] *The Long, Hot Summer*, a film whose origins lie in not just one but three Faulkner texts, offers just such a crossroads.

Hollywood's Production Code and South-sploitation

Just as Faulkner's texts provide one recognizable, limited version of the South, so did 1950s Hollywood add more layers to the idea of southernness that the film develops. By no means unique in its preoccupations, *The Long, Hot Summer* is one of a number of Hollywood films from the late 1950s that constructed a southern mythology grounded in the tension between a repressive social code and the transgressive nature of the sexuality it shapes but only partially contains. Examples include Elia Kazan's *Baby Doll* in 1956, Anthony Mann's *God's Little Acre* in 1958, and in 1959 both *Suddenly, Last Summer* from Joseph L. Mankiewicz and *The Sound and the Fury*, another Faulkner adaptation directed by Ritt. Even though the Production Code Administration barred direct references to transgressive sexuality ("perversion"), there was in the late 1950s much discussion of a "movement," an opening up of Hollywood films to more adult, controversial content. Walter Lowe's syndicated newspaper piece from March 1959, titled "Hollywood Defies Critics, Goes 'Adult,'" notes:

> The word "taboo" no longer exists in Hollywood's dictionary. What 10 years ago would have raised eyebrows, and 20 years ago would have scandalized the audience, today is considered almost normal in the movies. Dope addiction, homosexuality, prostitution, adultery, sex and sex talk marked "ultra-frank," miscegenation, even incest—there's nothing left any more that the screen won't touch. It's all part and parcel of Hollywood's new "adult" approach to life, which some call a welcome widening of the horizons and others castigate as the by-product of a desperate struggle for survival.[2]

Also writing in 1959 about what he termed the "New Hollywood," Robert Brustein observed that something "unusual" was happening on the screen, including "artiness," "radical new developments," and "harsh truths."[3] Many of these late 1950s melodramas adopted a serious approach to conveying more realistic representations of sexual identity and relationships, as Brustein further noted: "the realistic film-makers are dedicating themselves to the exposure of the unsavory truth behind the manufactured dream. With suggestions of incest in *Desire Under the Elms*, sadism in *Baby Doll*, adultery in *God's Little Acre*, and homosexuality in *The Strange One*, the realistic movie works manifold variations on conventional sexual themes."[4]

The Long, Hot Summer, however, stands out in its handling of potentially transgressive male sexuality—specifically, *white* southern masculinity—as a way to understand and articulate a wide range of female desires (albeit white, largely heteronormative ones). Ritt often worked with the husband-and-wife writing team of Irving Ravetch and Harriet Frank Jr., and despite all three being non-southerners, their joint projects often featured (decidedly Hollywood-inflected) southern settings. These collaborations include *The Sound and the Fury* (1959), *Hud* (1963), and *Conrack* (1974). James Crank considers *The Long, Hot Summer* a prime example of what he terms "South-sploitation": "In films such as *Baby Doll* (1956) and *The Long, Hot Summer* (1958), cinematic representations of southerners showed a people afflicted with not only a deep, racial anxiety but also a primitive, combustible and overpowering sexuality. The 'lust-under-the-magnolias' clichés that permeated American cinematic portrayals of the South from the 1950s to 1970s suggested the South as a land of sexual taboo, a place where unquenchable homosexual, interracial and even interfamilial sexual desires were explored behind closed doors."[5]

Producer Jerry Wald, fresh off his 1957 success with the scandalous *Peyton Place*, added to the expectations of an exotic, mythic South, writing of *The Long, Hot Summer*: "it's a comedy about appetites, about love and sex, courtship and mating, ebullient young men and brainy young ladies, the yearning of parents for their children. It departs in fact, but not in faith, from William Faulkner's attitude."[6] More Erskine Caldwell and less William Faulkner, in other words, with Faulkner still receiving a writing credit.

Masculinity and Labor, from Faulkner to Ritt

Loosely based on the early twentieth-century "exploits" of the Snopes clan, *The Long, Hot Summer* transplants characters and events from Faulkner's novel *The Hamlet* (1940) and his short stories "Barn Burning" (1939) and "Spotted Horses" (1931) into the 1950s. In the film, Newman's Ben Quick stands in for three different Snopeses—Ab, Flem, and Sarty. The movie opens with a country-store trial as Quick, a tenant farmer accused of burning a neighbor's barn, is run out of the county; he then finds himself in the Mississippi hamlet of Frenchman's Bend, where his interactions with the Varner family lead to drama and romance. That a character based in large part on the cold, odious Flem Snopes appears on screen as both beautiful and charming accounts for some of the most forceful critical dismissals of the film, as do the decidedly un-Faulknerian happy plot resolutions, as in Michael Adams's assessment: "Faulkner's slimy toad of a villain Flem Snopes becomes the blue-eyed, redneck prince Ben Quick, and all conflicts are hastily resolved in an epitome of the contrived Hollywood ending."[7]

Flem's transformation is not the only factor that shifts both character and mood, however. Faulkner's practical, jocular, down-to-earth Will Varner, father to sixteen children and the most important landowner in Frenchman's Bend, becomes in Orson Welles's broad performance a blowhard patriarch and widower who tries to bully his two children into providing him with grandchildren. At the same time his "woman," Minnie Littlejohn (Angela Lansbury), presses him about marriage and respectability. Will's son Jody remains a perennial bachelor in the novel, is mocked for wearing the same suit of clothing year-round, and spends much of his time defending the honor of his aloof and enticing sister Eula from the advances of the men of Yoknapatawpha County. Perversely, in *The Long, Hot Summer* Jody (Anthony Franciosa) is married to Eula (Lee Remick), a beautiful, much admired southern belle who appears to be an outsider to Frenchman's Bend. Characters with no

Faulknerian antecedents include Jody's sister Clara (Joanne Woodward), an unmarried schoolteacher living at the Varner mansion, and the prestigious but in decline Stewart family, which includes Clara's best friend, the spinster Agnes (Sarah Marshall); Clara's longtime but reluctant suitor Alan (Richard Anderson); and Agnes and Alan's mother Elizabeth (Mabel Albertson).

The dynamics and relationships of these new and transformed characters reorient the few plot details that *The Long, Hot Summer* retains from its Faulknerian sources. In *The Hamlet,* Faulkner's Jody rents a tenant farm to Ab Snopes, a sharecropper and reputed barn burner who wanders the county with his family. Only belatedly recognizing his mistake, Jody hires Ab's older son Flem to work in the general store as an insurance policy against having his property burned down. Flem, an unscrupulous man, takes advantage of the situation and schemes his way into Will's good graces at the expense of Jody's relationship with his father, ultimately agreeing to marry Will's daughter Eula, pregnant by another man. Toward the end of *The Hamlet*—and in the primary action of "Spotted Horses"—Flem returns from his "honeymoon" with Eula to auction off, through a surrogate, wild ponies to local men, cheating them of their money when the horses cannot be caught. In the final section of *The Hamlet,* Flem plans to defraud local citizens by burying "treasure" at the decrepit mansion known as the Old Frenchman's Place and tricking them into buying the property for a hefty fee.

As in *The Hamlet,* in *The Long, Hot Summer* it is an outsider, Quick, who accepts the offer from Varner's "weak" son Jody to sharecrop on Varner land and is taken under the wing of the powerful father, moving from sharecropper cabin to the general store and eventually into the Varner mansion. Jody is "overtaken" at the expense of Quick's rise. The film covers, albeit in different detail and tone, the soiling of an expensive rug, the selling of the wild Texas ponies, and the con involving bags of money buried on the grounds of an abandoned plantation, and these events all connect to Quick's rise in status and his relationship with Clara.

Faulkner's novel is rambling, loosely structured, and full of Twain-like frontier humor and conflicts revolving around men and their trading, swapping, and dealing. *The Long, Hot Summer,* by contrast, combines Hollywood melodrama and romance. Part of the reason the film has been largely ignored may have to do with Faulkner's "shadow" and critics' sense that literary significance was abandoned for a big-budget commercial Hollywood adaptation emphasizing romance. Bruce Kawin focuses on Quick's social climbing and argues that the film turns "Faulkner's anti-capitalist black comedy into a

Horatio Alger bedtime story . . . just the kind of success story *The Hamlet* parodies." He adds, "but for all that, it's not a bad picture."[8] Edwin Arnold articulates the distinction between "value" and popularity in his introduction to the "Faulkner and Film" special issue of the *Faulkner Journal*: despite identifying the film as one of Ritt's "two bad, sometimes very bad, movie adaptations" of Faulkner, Arnold acknowledges that "it was silly as could be but entertaining nonetheless once you got away from the fact that this was supposed to be Faulkner."[9] Silly but entertaining. Much of the limited critical discussion addressing *The Long, Hot Summer* uses such language to understand the very un-Faulkneresque happy ending involving the un-Snopes-like, sanctioned social climbing of Quick and the relatively quick resolution of conflicts through the marriage (or the saving of a marriage) of three couples: Quick and Clara, Varner and Minnie, and Jody and Eula.

Paul Newman, Hollywood, and the Labor of Desire

Part of the problem, of course, is that Paul Newman is a beautiful man. Flem—described as "frog-like," impotent, and devoid of any decency—is clearly not what Newman offers in his characterization of Ben Quick. The film's queer potential is blatantly embodied by one particular image—Newman's sweaty bare chest (see figure 1.1). The image invites a consideration of the role that the eroticized male body and queer erotics play in the film, as specifically embodied by Newman. Interestingly, Newman, an actor who often played conflicted men without women—or men conflicted about women—has received little attention when it comes to queer theory. Newman championed gay rights and, as a young actor, was repeatedly compared to James Dean, Montgomery Clift, and Marlon Brando, and was subject, as those actors were, to rumors of bisexuality. He was also a practitioner of the Method and a student of Lee Strasberg's, and, of course, he was Brick in *Cat on a Hot Tin Roof*. His sexuality transcends categories and bursts forth from the screen uncontained, as testified to by Eleanor Morrow's assertion in her review of *The Long, Hot Summer* that "Newman's charm is so explosive it's all Ritt can do . . . preventing every other character in the cast from jumping his bones at any given moment."[10] Ritt's own assessment spells things out clearly while underplaying his film's emphasis on the heat suggested in Newman's sweaty image: "Paul always had that cool sexuality, what I call a great fuckability quotient, which, let's face it, is part of what makes a star. Men and women are sexually drawn

FIGURE 1.1. Ben Quick outside Clara Varner's bedroom window, looking and being looked at.

to stars."[11] *The Long, Hot Summer* explicitly stages a scene based on Newman's desirability. When Jody finds a crowd outside his father's store, a townsman explains to him, "They ain't come to do much buyin'. . . . Oh, they just come to look . . . at the new man." Certainly, many a movie ticket was sold under the same simple premise: people want to look at Paul Newman.

Although he was an Ohio native, Newman's early career was marked by representations of southern masculinity, which started with *The Long, Hot Summer* and *Cat on a Hot Tin Roof.* Newman's body of work deserves more attention than I can give it here, but briefly, his starring roles in a decade's worth of southern-themed films established a compelling continuum of masculinities: in addition to Ben Quick and Brick Pollitt, he appeared as Chance Wayne in Richard Brooks's *Sweet Bird of Youth* in 1962, as Hud Bannon in Martin Ritt's *Hud* in 1963, and as Luke in Stuart Rosenberg's *Cool Hand Luke* in 1967. In film after film we witness an exploration of masculinity celebrated and mourned. As Mark Harris writes, Newman "was unmatched at creating characters who were at once romantic and cynical, hard-bitten and yearning, idealistic and self-destructive. No American actor has ever embodied wounded, confused masculinity with more skill or grace."[12]

At this stage in his career Newman was often compared to Marlon Brando and James Dean, two Method actors renowned for their "bisexual effect."[13] As many have noted, such actors were raising questions for Hollywood cinema regarding gender and sexuality because, as Richard Maltby puts it, "Men . . . were becoming more like women. They were becoming 'feminized.' When they put down the gun, they put on the apron."[14] Such blurring of categorical lines, Virginia Wright Wexman argues, created a new type of male romantic hero that often led to associating the actors, and sometimes their characters, with homosexuality owing to the actors' portrayals of characters who were

> neurotic, alienated men, reckless and nonconforming. The cause of their alienation centered on their sense of themselves as male. Clift, Dean, and Brando were the first male stars whose legends encompassed public speculation regarding homosexual activity. Such speculation foregrounded the tenuousness of their commitment to a heterosexual regime in which a male's sexual identity was based on his ability to dominate and provide for a woman. The traditional view of heterosexual male identity involves the cultivation of male-identified characteristics that clearly delineate gender difference. The demeanor of the new rebel stars, by contrast, was marked by such "neurotic" qualities as emotional confusion, irrationality, and violent behavior, suggesting the conflicted nature of their gender identifications.[15]

Newman's early roles often conform to this description—for example, an anguished Billy the Kid with an Oedipal complex in the 1958 Arthur Penn film *The Left Handed Gun.* With his southern roles, the new romantic hero's category-confounding masculinity is placed in a context in which homosexuality is evoked to signal upper-class moral decline within a corrupting and decaying class system. That "southern" coding runs counter to, or at the very least complicates, the trends Wexman perceives in relation to Method actors and Hollywood's former tendency to equate homosexuality with questionable morals. She argues that "popular Freudianism fostered the view that homosexual behavior expressed impulses that everyone to some extent shared. . . . A confused gender identity was no longer understood as a symbol of ineradicable moral decay but rather elaborated as a developmental problem of a divided protagonist."[16] Thus Newman's sexuality in films set in the South awakens complicated responses in others; he plays the erotic interloper figure who exhibits "feminized" traits that signal the new crisis in masculinity but, because this character represents the New South and new hope, he reads simultaneously as queer and as the object of heteronormative romantic desire. Newman, as tortured Method actor and as romantic hero, brings a fluidity to masculinity that challenges norms, in particular expectations of southern sexual dysfunction.

Sweaty Men: Work and Queer Desire in *The Long, Hot Summer*

On the surface Ben Quick represents a fairly stock character—the mysterious, disruptive, but ultimately romantic stranger who shakes things up in an insular community, what Eula calls "the most nowhere place in the state of Mississippi" that "laces you in tight as a corset."[17] As the judge admits at the opening barn-burning trial, "I can't find against you, Quick. There's no proof." This ambiguity surrounding Quick runs throughout the film. But unlike Faulkner's Flem Snopes, or the outsider character found in many melodramas and romances, he isn't *actually* a puzzle to be solved. Yes, the specific details of his past that make him seem ambiguous are in question. But this mystery does not drive the narrative—rather, he is part of an overall examination of male roles and masculine performance, particularly as they involve work. *We* never doubt that he was unjustly accused of barn burning or that he will be the focus of romance. As Quick walks out of the country store and saunters down the dirt road, having been told to leave the county, lush, swelling strings begin, and the romantic song "The Long, Hot Summer" by crooner Jimmie Rodgers runs over the credits as Quick catches a barge and travels downriver. The lyrics leave no doubt as to the future of our misunderstood protagonist and obliquely point to the languorous southern setting: "The long hot summer / Seems to know what a flirt you are. / Seems to know your caress isn't mine to possess." Quick finds the road and catches a ride with Clara and Eula, who are returning from a shopping trip to Memphis. He describes himself as a "quiet living man," and Eula comments that he sounds "free as a bird." As the film soon makes clear, though, Quick cannot escape his family's reputation and the distrust it involves. The Quick family name, associated not just with "poor white trash" but also with criminal behavior, drives the plot as he becomes the focus of townfolk's speculation, and although he uses that reputation to his advantage to insinuate himself into the Varner family, it is also the heart of the apparent mystery that tortures him and adds to his melodramatic characterization.

Quick's intentions are clearly, at first, unromantic and entirely bound up in work. He wants to earn his way through gainful employment. He asks several locals lounging at the courthouse about work—"How does a man make a livin' around here?"—and is directed to the Varner mansion to inquire about renting a tenant farm. Here he encounters Clara again, who is talking with her friend Agnes. Quick's rapid rise through the social classes takes him from seeking employment to working the tenant farm, agreeing to sell horses for Will, dining at the Varner mansion, being hired to work at the general store, and ultimately moving into the mansion after agreeing, at Will's insistence, to court Clara. This movement centers several conflicts around Quick—rivalry with Jody for Will's affection as a surrogate son, rivalry with Alan for Clara's affections, and internal struggle with the rightness of his pursuit of Clara as a business transaction.

Quick develops a genuine sexual interest in Clara, but his interactions with her are initially staged as acts of salesmanship, as a conscious or unconscious exhibition, a testing of his ability to seal the deal. During their first encounters, Clara is actively hostile, whereas Quick is slightly teasing but not entirely engaged in any type of pursuit. On the day of their first meeting, and after Quick wipes his feet on a rug in the mansion after interacting with Jody, Clara and a young African American boy bring the rug to Quick's cabin, ostensibly to force him to clean it.[18] Quick, sweaty and in a sleeveless undershirt, first displays the swagger and confidence implicit in his physical appeal: "That's a lot of fuss to be makin' about a rug, lady. If it's the rug that's botherin' ya." He recognizes, or decides, that Clara represents a sexual challenge that could help his rise in status. Clara's response suggests that she does not reject Quick because he's "a stranger" but because she recognizes his brand of toxic masculinity: "Mr. Quick, you're being personal with me. I'll be personal with you. I've spent my whole life around men who push and shove and shout . . . and think they can make anything happen just by bein' aggressive. I'm not anxious to have another one around the place." Later, as Quick establishes his worth to Will by selling useless horses to the men of the town, Clara watches intently. Quick directly addresses Clara, trying to encourage the men to bid on the horses and also furthering his pursuit of her. This exchange is conducted as a public sales pitch, in a conflation of salesmanship and flirtation that highlights the homosocial aspect of the transactions: "I can see you've got 'No' written all over your face, but wait. You stop and think a minute. You can pack yourself a picnic basket and follow some woodsy trail. . . . If you see a young fellow along the way who happens to take your eye, you can put him behind you and ride double. Uh, what's your answer, Miss Clara?" Clara declines, and after the sale is concluded, the one-sided flirtation continues in the language of commerce, with Clara identifying Quick as a "pitchman." Clara obviously does not intend to buy one of her father's horses, and Quick knows that as well, emphasizing the performativity of flirtation/sexuality on offer.

What stands out is that Quick's masculine appeal arises from his ability to notice things about Clara that transcend crass commerce. He combines the aggressive charm of a successful salesman with insight and empathy, perhaps even despite himself. He breaks down Clara's defenses momentarily in the general store, where he is working late. In Newman's longest speech in the film, Quick demonstrates real understanding of Clara's frustrations: "Well, let's just examine the way you do live, Miss Clara. You drive around in that old Lincoln car of yours like it had wings, and you teach school, and you sit on your front porch with your skinny little friend drinkin' lemonade. Now, what is all that, when you see the rest of the world passing you by paired up? You're what, twenty-three? Yeah, thems are golden years, and you're bein' asked to play a waiting game. Why wait?" He and Clara kiss passionately, and the chemistry between Newman and Woodward is unmistakable.[19] But Clara is not ready to accept her feelings and slaps him. Quick loses his temper for the first time, but it takes the form of a mean-spirited (but still insightful) dig at Clara's supposed sexual frustration: "Oh, I know what's troublin' you. It's all those boys hollerin' for Eula every night. And Eula with her hair hangin' down, and Jody with his shirt off, chasin' her. And your old man at sixty and he's callin' on his lady love."

When Clara, mirroring her father, calls Quick a barn burner and runs from the store, we witness his anger and frustration to their fullest extent. In a sense, this is the first time Quick appears as emotionally vulnerable, but also the first time Will, standing outside the store, shrewdly recognizes the potency of their attraction. He decides to make a deal with Quick to court Clara for wealth and prestige. Will's intervention here reintroduces uncertainty about Quick's motives that had ostensibly been allayed as their relationship developed and followed a relatively familiar romantic pattern. From this point on, Quick's courtship becomes more aggressive and tone-deaf until the resolution, which highlights the film's complex exploration of southern masculinity as the tenuous, fraught balancing of work and sexuality. Quick is more mesmerizing to Clara when his relationship to sexual desire and work are overlapping, in balance. Once the deal is struck, Quick's attention to Clara becomes about work absent empathy or desire.

The Wrong, and Right, Kinds of Sweat

The film uses Quick to explore different aspects and versions of masculinity, but a spectrum of possible masculine positions predates his introduction into Frenchman's Bend. Jody is clearly anxious about his roles as husband to the town beauty, Eula, and as heir to the Varner empire. He is emotionally weak, jealous, and seemingly incapable of carrying out his responsibilities, but he is also resolutely heteronormative in the sense that he is oversexed, choosing recreational sex over his business interests. Unlike those of some "weak" characters in southern dramas, Jody's insecurities do not stem from sexual impotence. We first see him impatiently waiting for Eula to return from her Memphis shopping trip, and his sexual interest in her seems excessive and hornily adolescent for the middle of a hot Mississippi workday. He only partially puts on the tie his wife has bought him and chases her around their bedroom, eventually pillow fighting as "spinsters" Clara and Agnes sit outside, drinking lemonade. They overhear Eula say, "Where do you get so much energy on a day like this?" suggesting, in part, her annoyance with the never-ending attention. Jody does not lack energy—his energies are misplaced. When Quick arrives at the Varner mansion, Jody, distracted by what awaits him upstairs, makes a poor business decision to rent the tenant farm to the stranger.

On the porch, Clara mentions to Agnes the never-ending "party" going on with Jody and Eula: "The party's been going on since Papa left for the hospital." When Will returns the next day from a recuperation of several months, it is clear that Jody's sexual interest in Eula deflects the anxieties associated with his relationship to his father and their family's business interests, which are also tied to his father's obsession with grandchildren and mortality. Will asks Eula why she is not pregnant yet, and when he learns that Jody has conducted business with Quick, he explodes with anger over his son's failures in his familial duties as well. The conflation of sex and work is clear: "Quick!? Don't you keep abreast of anything except Eula? Don't you know what Quick means in this county? Hellfire! Ashes and char! Flame follows that man around like a dog! He's a barn burner." Jody frankly reveals how his father raises his anxieties, rubbing his hands together while pleading, "You want to hear something? I sweat around you. All those months you were away in the hospital, I was dry! Now I'm sweatin' again." For Jody, sweat is tied either to smoldering sexuality or to Oedipal anxieties—it is not the result of labor, as it is for Quick.

The difference between Jody's sweatiness and Quick's underscores how work and sexuality function in *The Long, Hot Summer*'s representation of masculinity. When Quick threatens Jody's position by replacing him in the general store and moving into the room next to his in the mansion, Jody stops performing his "manly" duties and stays home from work, ultimately frustrating Eula so much with his attentions that she explains to him his place within the economies of work and sexuality: "Jody, aren't you ever going to work again? You always gonna be hangin' around? I can't do my nails or fix my hair without havin' you hangin' around. Now, you take that Ben Quick. He's down at that store workin', sweatin'. He's where you ought to be." When Jody deflects and tries to convince Eula to sleep with him, she posits that his interest in sex is not "masculine" because he has disconnected it from labor or even procreation: "No, Jody! No! I sure do wish you'd find yourself some other form of recreation." Sweat becomes the signifier of labor, sex, the southern setting, and anxieties. Jody thus occupies a familiar melodramatic male role, the estranged son, the man "unmanned," but without the traditional sexual dysfunction or alcoholism that audiences might expect. When it becomes clear he has been completely "passed by" and has lost his father's love and respect, he throws himself onto a chaise longue, crying, and is attended to by his supportive sister and concerned wife. Only when he attempts to murder Will by locking him in a barn and setting fire to it, and then relents and lets him out, is Jody brought back into the fold and acknowledged by Will as a worthy son and heir. Jody has, finally, made his own father sweat—and the outcome is not only Will's recognition, as the barn burns behind them, that Jody has "hellfire and damnation" in him, but also Jody's redemption and acceptance back into the fold: "I've got me a son again!"

Jody's uncertainty in his masculinity is obviously a response to the shoes he must fill as Will's only son, which surfaces in the connections between family legacy and masculinity that define the men in the film. His father represents an exaggerated, partly tongue-in-cheek version of the Big Daddy southern stereotype: Will is a self-described "ugly redneck," a cigar-chomping, larger-than-life parvenu patriarch, and a widower obsessed with his legacy, particularly in the form of grandchildren.[20] Orson Welles was merely forty-two years old when he put on the weirdly dark makeup, ludicrous fake nose, and gray wig to play the much older Will, and this unconvincing concealment of Welles's age lends to the character a virility and sexual power that unmans Jody and challenges Quick. Before returning to his mansion from the hospital, he visits his "woman" Minnie, and it is clear their relationship is robustly, unapologetically sexual. Also, while he is careful about "appearances," Will is unconcerned with social niceties or gossip. Sexual mastery is part of the show, the performance. As he says to the ambulance driver, "My white hairs kinda had you fooled, huh?" But unlike Jody, Will puts business first, and his burgeoning relationship with Quick is predicated on recognizing in Quick a like-minded man willing to do business, legitimate and illegitimate. Of course, Will has no actual basis, beyond Quick's economic prowess and "manly" physical attractiveness, for describing Quick as a "big stud horse" as he gives Clara the ultimatum either to marry Alan or to be forced to marry Quick. Only after establishing that Quick shares his priorities regarding work does Will consider that he might be able to "seduce" Quick into courting Clara, hopefully producing heirs more like his vision of himself.

Several times the similarities between Will and Quick are vocalized—by Will, by Quick, and by Clara. Both men represent aggression, sexual prowess, and the willingness to break rules at the expense of others. At their first meeting, as Will tries to secure a guarantee that his property will not go up in flames, he says to Quick, "Son, why should I be scared of you? You're a young, dangerous man. I'm an old one." Later, surveying the Old Frenchman's Place, he tells Quick, "I been watching you. I like your push. Yes, I like your style. I like your brass. It ain't too dissimilar from the way I operate." The narrative implies that without Quick's being "taught" to value people through Clara's intervention, he would likely end up in a similar position to Varner, willing to harm his own family to achieve his legacy.[21] Will suggests to Quick that he may give the ruins to him and invites him to dinner. The film establishes the necessity for a deeper, growing relationship between Will and Quick because Jody is, until his homicidal turn toward the end, an inadequate son in both a procreative and business sense, and Clara is an unmarried, childless woman with little chance of changing these circumstances with her current suitor, Alan.

The Long, Hot Summer's fourth major male character and version of masculinity, Clara's longtime suitor Alan Stewart, on the surface occupies the familiar third part of the love triangle in the sexual economy—the unsuitable suitor. Alan also represents a blatantly southern representation of queer identity—the upper-class man of manners, part of a declining Old South family, slightly too old to be unmarried, pampered by his mother. In any 1950s Hollywood film, direct reference to homosexuality was impossible, but hints about Alan's sexuality are easy to discern, if perhaps less easy to unpack in all their complexity. He has been described by critics, often in a rather homophobic way, as "a weakling son," "a fey, genteel suitor," "a puny Mississippi mama's-boy," "a mother-dominated, tepid-spirited boyfriend," "a repressed homosexual," and "probably gay." These characterizations reduce Alan to a plot point, an expendable barrier to the final happiness of the heteronormative Quick-Clara couple. But just as a trite reading of the film's marriage-inclined ending paints over the complexities of Quick's masculinity, with its balance of work and sexual desire, in the context of Jody and Will, so too does comparison with Quick complicate a generalized reading of Alan's seemingly stereotypical queer masculinity.

From the first mention of Alan's name, it is clear that he occupies a different position not only in the film's sexual economy but in its socioeconomic system as well. On the same day that Quick arrives in town, Agnes informs

Clara that "Alan's been asking about you. He's sick in bed, bein' fed milk puddin' . . . all dreamy with temperature. Thoroughly enjoying himself. I'd give something to know what goes on in my brother's temperature dreams." Agnes's words hint that perhaps something scandalous, besides "normative" desires, might lurk in Alan's subconscious. Alan's first appearance on screen depicts him convalescing in a lounge chair outside his antebellum home as Clara visits him while his mother watches from afar. From the beginning we see in their interactions a genuine friendship and respect, but also none of the chemistry on display between Clara and Quick. As Quick's attentions increase, Alan's inadequacies as a sexual partner become apparent—something that both he and Quick recognize but that Clara only slowly accepts.

Alan also stands out, in part, because he does not work, an aspect of his identity connected to his status as Old South aristocracy. This class status, Alan suggests, fuels Will's disrespect for him and his family. He notes ruefully, "Your father refers to me as decayed gentry." Clara, who has on her end table a "volume of Jane Austen," appreciates what Alan's family represents and defends him from her father and his new-money ways. Clara says to Alan: "He would give anything in the world to have what you have. Wouldn't he just love to have your shine and polish? He can put up all those billboards and those neon signs and those filling stations, but quality is one thing he can't buy and he knows it." Alan tacitly recognizes that he represents a remnant of a South that no longer exists; that is, he conflicts not just with Varner but with *progress*: "Most people say I'm fighting the twentieth century. I suppose I oughta sell this place, put it to corn and cotton, go out and get a job like everybody else but I wouldn't be any good at it and I'd hate it and make a mess of it." Clara *seems* to support this attitude, but she is unconvincing, and in a romantic, nostalgic vein she conflates all work with scheming and conniving: "Then don't do it. There are enough hustlers around here as is. You stand for something, you hold on to it." This idealism inspires Alan's love for Clara—he tells her he loves her, praises her "quality," wants what's best for her. But he offers only a chilly, asexual love—he tells her she is a "nice, quiet, self-contained girl"—and when Clara asks him, in their last conversation, "But do you want me the way a man wants a woman?" his answer deflects her interest in sexuality: "What I want is to help you, Clara."

Prior to this conversation at the church bazaar, Clara has convincingly refused Quick because he resembles her father too strongly. Quick, for a hefty fifty dollars, has purchased Clara's time and a picnic lunch, and she is disturbed by this economic exchange. Her rejection of Quick allows her to bring herself to ask, outright, how Alan feels about her. She is then forced to refuse Alan because he does *not* sufficiently resemble her father. Clara does not want someone to "help" her. In her angry, pleading conversation with Quick after he declares that he intends to marry her, and that she'll "wake up smilin' in the mornin'," Clara articulates what makes both Quick's and Alan's versions of masculinity unsuitable for her true desires and her sense of self-worth. Whether or not she consciously realizes it, Clara describes her feelings using the language of money and economics that has driven Quick's interactions with her and that has left Alan behind:

> Mr. Quick, I am a human being. Do you know what that means? It means I set a price on myself, a high, high price. You may be surprised to know it, but I've got quite a lot to give. I've got things I've been savin' up my whole life, things like love and understanding and jokes and good times and good cooking. I'm prepared to be the Queen of Sheba for some lucky man, or at the very least, the best wife that any man could hope for. Now, that's my human history, and it's not going to be given away to any passing stranger.

This is the longest one-take in the film, more than forty-four seconds of a medium close-up on Woodward. The mention of the Queen of Sheba could be a reference not only to Clara's wealth and status but also to the legend that the queen asked King Solomon hard questions and posed riddles to test him. Quick's brief, blustery response suggests he knows that he has been caught out, that he has misread his mark, and that, perhaps, he has just figured out that her status as Varner's daughter and the road to wealth does not matter to him: "All right. Then run, lady. And you keep on runnin'! Buy yourself a bus ticket and disappear. Change your name, dye your hair, get lost. And then maybe, just maybe, you're gonna be safe from me." Alan represents sterile, "easy" safety and security, whereas Quick offers danger and passion with his more "acceptable" transgressive sexuality. As Quick finishes his warning, Alan arrives, and he gallantly intercedes in this angry moment, politely but firmly driving Quick off.[22] This confrontation gives Clara the confidence to confront Alan about his intentions, which becomes their final conversation in the film.

What's most interesting, and unusual, about Alan's characterization is that while he is established as the unsuitable mate for the heroine and is understood by many viewers as gay or asexual, the film does not condemn him. His is a complex, perhaps melancholy but not tragic relationship to sexuality and social status. The film's recognition of a spectrum of masculinities, these constellations of men relative to Clara, invites viewers to consider the spectrum of femininities (and the experience of empowered femininity) that the film also presents but does not condemn. Agnes, Alan's sister, freely articulates her desires, confounding the repressed spinster stereotype: "Oh, Clara, it's unnervin' havin' all this time on my hands. I wanna rush home and fix supper for some big, handsome man, and put kids in a bathtub and broil steak and crank ice cream, and think about what the night's gonna bring. Why aren't there enough men to go around?" Minnie, Will's "woman" and the owner of the local boardinghouse, convinces him to marry her after issuing an ultimatum and explaining simply, "Women have got to take care of themselves. That's what I done." Eula, no dumb southern belle, articulates what her role in her marriage to Jody consists of, and what part she expects him to play.

The Queen of Sheba and Possibilities for Female Sexuality

As soon as we start contemplating the varieties of male sexuality and the potentialities of masculinity, it becomes clear that not only do men's identities become complicated by issues such as class and genre but female sexuality is both illuminated and complicated as well. The film frankly addresses female sexuality, such as when Clara candidly tells her wishy-washy suitor, "No, Alan, there's no sense in pretending that girls don't think about sex. They do." Ultimately, the film focuses not on Quick but on Clara, who becomes aware of her options and expectations and her power to choose following her interactions with men. The film pivots on Clara's learning, through her experiences with Alan, Quick, Will, and Jody, that she can determine her future path. When Will learns that Alan is out of the picture (literally), he angrily tells Clara and Quick that they must wed. Before he can attempt to force them to marry, Jody's attempt to kill his father in a barn-burning intervenes. The local men conclude that Quick is the culprit, and as they come to lynch him, Clara drives to the store and rescues him. He then, in a moment of vulnerability, reveals the origin of his family's reputation as barn burners. Choking back tears, Quick tells Clara that his father had set maybe fifty fires, and that as a young boy, Quick turned his father in, an act that potentially led to his death. Clara, calling him Ben for the first time, says, "How terrible that must have been." Quick responds, "No, it wasn't. The terrible part come later. Knockin' around this whole countryside, floatin' from town to town, lookin' in on other people's kitchen windows from the outside. Boy, that man sure left his mark on me. I got his name, and I can't run away from that." Quick's masculinity is explicitly tied to his sense of familial duty, just as Alan's and Jody's and Will's are. But his lowbred origins and outcast social status create in him a sense of

FIGURE 1.2. As Quick packs to leave, Clara follows him to his bedroom and returns his words to him, making clear that she has made her choice.

inferiority that ultimately cannot be overcome by his aggressive posturing and physical stature.

Clara, who has through Will come to understand that her mother had sexual desires and "listened" when he howled at her as a young man, responds to Quick's honesty and his decision to "let you go." As he leaves her to pack and move on, he tells her, "You couldn't tame me, but you taught me," and he informs a bewildered Will that "Life's a pretty valuable thing, and it ought to be treated with a certain amount of respect. You're old enough to know that, and I'm young enough to learn it." When Quick goes to his bedroom to pack, Clara follows him and finds her voice, returning Quick's words from the church bazaar back to him: "So you run, and you keep runnin,' and you buy yourself a bus ticket and you disappear. And you change your name and you dye your hair and maybe, [pointing] just maybe you might be safe from me" (see figure 1.2). Clara's awakening, her acceptance of Quick (and thus her own desires), is the important resolution. Nevertheless, the nuances of Clara's decision-making underscore that looking closely at Quick and the complex of masculinities represented in the film reveals the spaces available, in this setting, for a broader spectrum of male and female sexualities as well. Heteronormative as the Quick-Clara pairing appears, these spectra include the potentialities for an unmarried young woman who continues to pursue her desires and for an asexual man who is content with his choices. The film in fact presents us with four pairings at the end: Clara and Quick, Minnie and Will, Eula and Jody, and Agnes and Alan.

As noted, several critics have complained that while it is entertaining enough, the film relies on familiar stereotypes and on an unearned happy ending that transforms the complexity of Faulkner's texts into consumer-driven pablum reaffirming bourgeois norms of sexual desire and coupling, whereas, according to critics such as Michael Kreyling, Faulkner's originals frequently violate the "banalities" of mass-produced entertainment and refuse the "normalization of heterosexual relations."[23] In such readings, the shadow of Faulkner's approach to gender and sexuality has obscured the very interesting, though different, challenges offered by *The Long, Hot Summer*, especially in terms of the sexual economy and queer energy in its happy ending.

In the process of drawing from, bringing together, and updating Faulkner's stories, *The Long, Hot Summer* evokes the source texts' rendering of the decline of the southern economy and the suspicion of capitalism and commercialism and then represents it within a more mainstream Hollywood (and middle-American) framework for melodrama and romance. Noel Polk convincingly argues that the world of Faulkner's *The Hamlet* is a queer one in which male homosocial bonds reject, exclude, or marginalize women: "Men who run from the feminine usually run to each other, and in Frenchman's Bend they mostly congregate on the front porch of Varner's store, talking and ogling and staying away from home. . . . The men's constant relationships with each other become sublimated into various forms of competition . . . that galvanize them into a community that does not, cannot, admit women." In Polk's reading, the most significant relationship is not heteronormative but, in fact, involves Will Varner and Flem Snopes as a "logical extension of the extreme homosocial atmosphere in the novel."[24] The film, by contrast, potentially queers Quick, but it does so in the service of female sexual potentialities. Attending to queerness in this sense requires exploring the wide spectrum of reading possibilities, challenging in a specifically southern way the norms of masculinity and femininity and sexual desire. Queering our reading of the film, attending to its explorations of alternative and unconventional sexual energies, allows us to recognize how this adaptation creates female characters who are not punished for being sexual and staying true to their values.

Ultimately, unlike *Cat on a Hot Tin Roof* and any number of other southern melodramas of the period, *The Long, Hot Summer*'s queerness does not function to reaffirm or question some "norm" or deviation from that norm but instead offers an understanding of how queerness in a southern framework is performative, something that *does* gender and sexuality rather than reflecting a fixed straight or gay identity. The film reworks Hollywood's mythic southern landscape, so often concerned with sexual "deviance," into a more probing and pleasurable experience in which more balanced and expansive relationships can exist. It presents a mid-twentieth-century updating of the southern plantation as a cultural and economic nexus, but it also transforms the "perverse" and homosocial, masculine sexual energy of the Faulknerian relationship between money, labor, and sex into something more focused on how southern women negotiate and find expression in these relationships with masculinities. Commercial and generic demands prompted a reshaping of *The Hamlet*, and that shift to Hollywood melodrama would result in the presence of a continuum of female characters, voices, and articulations of desire. Feminine voices are multiplied, and these women are concerned about sex, love, and money in ways missing, or repressed, in *The Hamlet.* Faulkner's tragic/comedic tales look back, constantly reliving the past and ruing fate. Hollywood, particularly the Hollywood of the 1950s, narrates in the present but looks to the future, to the promise of tomorrow. *The Long, Hot Summer* illuminates the ways the social and sexual economies of the source text have been reworked well beyond transforming impotent, inhuman con-man Flem Snopes into virile, misunderstood, queered Ben Quick. The much more interesting shift has to do with the choices Clara makes in her interactions with these versions of masculinity, finding agency in the confusion of southern masculinities surrounding her.

Coda: Queering, Adaptation, and Shifting Consumption

In "Barn Burning," after Ab Snopes has deliberately wiped dung on an expensive rug and been thrown out of the mansion by Mrs. de Spain and her black servant, he scrapes his boot clean on a step, looks back at the house, and says to his son Sarty, "Pretty and white, ain't it? That's sweat. Nigger sweat. Maybe it ain't white enough yet to suit him. Maybe he wants to mix some white sweat with it."[25] As we have seen, Quick also soils a rug, but otherwise the film all but removes Ab's race resentment and his astute recognition of how black sweat has built the mansion (and by extension the South). In *The Long, Hot Summer*, Quick's potential act of defiance is merely a way to continue his interactions with Clara. Still, as John T. Matthews and others note, the film does not entirely ignore race, and liberal director Ritt nods toward a fantasy of racial progress in this 1950s version of Faulkner's hamlet. Looking at both Ritt/Ravetch/Frank adaptations of Faulkner, Matthews writes:

> The issue of race relations in the South attracts no explicit attention in either *The Long, Hot Summer* or *Sound and Fury*, yet both reveal an unmarked fantasy about the achievement of desegregation at the moment of the 1950s civil rights move-

ment. Repeatedly in both movies crowds in Frenchman's Bend and Jefferson are portrayed as racially mixed: blacks and whites mingle on porch galleries, on sidewalks and in streets. . . . the unremarked ordinariness of it here suggests that Ritt was projecting a social fantasy.[26]

When Clara brings the soiled rug to Quick's cabin to be cleaned, she is accompanied by a young black boy, and Matthews reads this as a naively color-blind "family portrait of those seeking expanded rights"[27]—women, the lower classes, and African Americans.

As the adaptation of this particular interaction makes clear, for all that Ritt's film reorients stereotypical assumptions about white southern work and sexuality, its treatment of race underscores the limits of its intervention—into the South of Faulkner's fiction and into the world where filmgoers live. Elsewhere, Quick's lower-class status is paralleled with the African American experience. As he moves from his tenant farm to live in the Varner mansion, he walks past a group of black workers in the fields, and when he arrives and is shown his room, he has a discussion with Lucius, one of Will's black servants, about their similar upbringings. Quick notes, "I had five sisters and a brother, and a mother and a father and an old maid aunt, and all together we slept in a room about half this size." Lucius responds, "Same as my family." Quick then says, "And look at us now, Lucius." In conflating the lower-class white and African American experiences in the South, Ritt and his screenwriters ignore the kind of nuance the film's Faulknerian sources bring to that relationship, despite the likelihood that they are very aware of them. *The Long, Hot Summer* introduces to the world of Faulkner's texts the potential for empowered women and for a continuum of female desire—but it has nothing to say about black sexuality and desires.

This limited grappling with the intersections of race, gender, and sexuality does not diminish the empowerment the film offers up for characters like Clara, Agnes, Alan, and Quick himself. What it reaffirms, however, is the roiling complexity that so many critiques of *The Long, Hot Summer* elide: in adapting Faulkner's page-bound representations into cinematic ones, Ritt's film simultaneously intervenes in the conventions of sexual economy that Faulkner maintains *and* represses the fictions' recognition of how race shapes the landscape in which characters travel, work, and desire. Queering the film allows us to ask provocative questions about how masculinity, tied to labor and sweat, creates a space for (white) women and their desires—and recognizing how race and class limit the purview of these questions, in turn, brings us back to Faulkner's engagements with these issues. Although beyond the scope of this essay, there is much to be done, for example, with how *The Long, Hot Summer* inserts a racial component and coding into the queer relationship between Will and Quick. Polk's reading of this relationship does not address such a racial component, arguably because *The Hamlet* makes no pretense toward African American representation—the county is, in the novel, one that the black population avoids at night—and the film's seeming "blackfacing" of Will and Quick's associations with African American experience suggests potential nuances to be teased out when we return to Faulkner's source texts.

In a moment that finds Hollywood—and American culture more generally—grappling with how power dynamics hinging on race, gender, sexuality, ability, and class continue to shape the making and consumption of cinematic art, the example of *The Long, Hot Summer* surfaces useful questions about what film and literature ask of us. Queering our reading of this ostensibly conventional adaptation requires not only a reevaluation of the film's representation of plot and characters, not only an acknowledgment of the spaces it and its source texts both offer and foreclose, but also a reconsideration of how criticism itself can make space for nuance and unresolved tensions in its objects of study. Keeping these texts in dynamic conversation, allowing our reading of one to inform our examination of another, has the potential to open up the limits of our own norm-challenging interventions, as we continue to read and to write about the South and its culture.

NOTES

1. Jaime Harker, "'And You Too, Sister, Sister?': Lesbian Sexuality, *Absalom, Absalom!*, and the Reconstruction of the Southern Family," *Faulkner's Sexualities*, ed. Annette Trefzer and Ann J. Abadie (Jackson: University Press of Mississippi, 2010), 38–53, at 39 and 40.

2. Walter Lowe, Central Press Association, "Hollywood Defies Critics, Goes 'Adult,'" *Massillon (Ohio) Evening Independent* 30 March 1959: 16.

3. Robert Brustein, "The New Hollywood: Myth and Anti-Myth," *Film Quarterly* 12.3 (1959): 23–31, at 23. The term "New Hollywood" typically refers to the slightly later period of 1968 to 1980 as the studio system began collapsing and directors were given more creative control. This period is sometimes referred to as the American New Wave.

4. Brustein, "The New Hollywood," 27.

5. James Crank, "An Aesthetic of Play: A Contemporary Cinema of South-Sploitation," *Southerners on Film*, ed. Andrew Leiter (Jefferson, N.C.: McFarland, 2011), 204–16, at 205.

6. Jerry Wald, "Faulkner & Hollywood," *Films in Review* March 1959: 131–32.

7. Michael Adams, "'How Come Everybody Down Here Has Three Names?': Martin Ritt's Southern Films," *The South and Film*, ed. Warren French (Jackson: University of Mississippi Press, 1981), 143–55, at 144.

8. Bruce Kawin, *Faulkner and Film* (New York: Frederick Ungar, 1977), 53.

9. Edwin Arnold, "Faulkner Writ Large/Faulkner Ritt Small," *Faulkner Journal* 16.1–2 (2001/2002): 3–6, at 3.

10. Eleanor Morrow, "Swinging Dicks & Easy Tricks," *This Recording* 18 December 2009, http://thisrecording.com/today/tag/long-hot-summer.

11. Martin Ritt, quoted in Joe Morella and Edward Epstein, *Paul and Joanne: A Biography of Paul Newman and Joanne Woodward* (New York: Dell, 1988), 57.

12. Mark Harris, "Cinema '67 Revisited: *Cool Hand Luke*," *Film Comment* 22 November 2017, www.filmcomment.com/blog/cinema-67-revisited-cool-hand-luke.

13. James Naremore, *Acting in the Cinema* (Berkeley: University of California Press, 1988), 205.

14. Richard Maltby and Ian Craven, *Hollywood Cinema: An Introduction* (Cambridge: Blackwell, 1995), 257.

15. Virginia Wright Wexman, *Creating the Couple: Love, Marriage, and Hollywood Performance* (Princeton, N.J.: Princeton University Press, 1993), 161, 167.

16. Wexman, *Creating the Couple*, 169.

17. Dialogue taken from *The Long, Hot Summer*, dir. Martin Ritt (1958; Beverly Hills, Calif.: Twentieth Century Fox Home Entertainment, 2003), DVD. As subsequent quotations make clear, the available screenplay and transcriptions render most characters' dialogue as othered, as dialect—affirming their linguistic nonnormativity even as the characters complicate other stereotypical representations of southernness.

18. This rug-soiling episode from *The Hamlet* and "Barn Burning" establishes the conflict between Ab Snopes and a different prominent resident, Major de Spain, which leads to the burning of de Spain's barn and, perhaps, Ab's death. It also leads to Sarty's separation from his family and disappearance. The film elides the connection and, in a sense, makes Quick both Ab and Sarty when Quick describes his troubled childhood at film's end.

19. Many contemporary reviews mention the actors' chemistry, likely influenced by the publicity surrounding their marriage. Newman and Woodward wed in January 1958, three months prior to the film's release.

20. In *The Hamlet*, Will Varner and his still-living wife have sixteen children scattered across the country, Jody and Eula being the only children still living at home.

21. Although Varner ultimately gets everything he wanted—a married daughter, a worthy heir in Jody—these are achieved through means that question his methods and values. Clara and Jody achieve happiness on their own terms.

22. At this point, as Quick storms off, the Old Frenchman's Place subplot reemerges as Jody, distraught over his father's rejection, threatens Quick with a gun. Quick takes this opportunity to con Jody into sparing his life with the promise of buried gold.

23. Michael Kreyling, "The Last Faulkner: *The Reivers* on the Road to Banality," *Southern Quarterly* 54.2 (2017): 10–27, at 11.

24. Noel Polk, "Around, behind, above, below Men: Ratliff's Buggies and the Homosocial in Yoknapatawpha," *Haunted Bodies: Gender and Southern Texts*, ed. Anne Goodwyn Jones and Susan V. Donaldson (Charlottesville: University of Virginia Press, 1998), 343–68, at 347 and 355.

25. William Faulkner, "Barn Burning," *Collected Stories of William Faulkner* (New York: Random House, 1950), 3–25, at 12.

26. John T. Matthews, "Faulkner to Film in the Fifties," *William Faulkner in the Media Ecology*, ed. Julian Murphet and Stefan Solomon (Baton Rouge: Louisiana State University Press, 2015), 17–33, at 26.

27. Matthews, "Faulkner to Film in the Fifties," 27.

Chapter 2 ▸ "The Prison of Our Skin": Orpheus and Antinormativity in *The Fugitive Kind*

DAVID MARKUS

Orpheus brought all my problems to a head.
—TENNESSEE WILLIAMS,
interview, 1958

En Avant!—En Avant! En Avant!
—TENNESSEE WILLIAMS,
notebook entry, 1941

Peculiar Beauty

Although it brought together some of the period's greatest talent from cinema and the stage, Sidney Lumet's 1959 film *The Fugitive Kind*—based on Tennessee Williams's adaptation of his 1957 play *Orpheus Descending*—was by most accounts a disastrous endeavor for all involved: a misery to produce, a critical flop, a box-office bust. Affirming Williams's worst apprehensions about the commercialism of Hollywood, the film was hamstrung from the get-go by a feud between stars Anna Magnani and Marlon Brando over who should get top billing. (Brando eventually won, landing Hollywood's first million-dollar contract.)[1] For Williams, who had worried that his career was foundering, and who, following negative reviews of *Orpheus Descending,* had finally begun a long-postponed psychoanalysis, the film version of what he described as his "beautiful and true play" provided little redemption.[2] Yet much of what seemed to detract from the film on its release heightens its viewing retrospectively. Watching it today, one senses a prematurity to Williams's vision, an attempt to unfold queer complexities of art, gender, and sexuality in the contemporary South that early viewers could not help but find perplexing.

Like many early reviewers, Parker Tyler was especially struck by the peculiarity (I have chosen the term carefully) of the lead male role. "A modern, jazz-traumatized schizoid" is how he described the guitar-playing drifter Val "Snakeskin" Xavier, "a depressed and unconscious psycho-neurotic."[3] In Tyler's view, these qualities made the central character's "beauty" something "thoroughly embarrassing"—a curious statement that perhaps says as much about the expectations surrounding the actor playing Val as the role itself.[4] For audiences who had watched Brando emerge as the embodiment of gruff machismo in *A Streetcar Named Desire,* it must have come as a surprise to see the actor playing a pensive, strange-talking wanderer with a shady past "entertaining" at the Starlight Lounge—a gay hangout in New Orleans, whose name Williams opted not to alter for his script. One suspects that Williams, who had long speculated about Brando's sexuality, took pleasure in seeing his leading man transformed in his new role. In a 1954 letter to Elia Kazan, Williams remarks, "He's smoldering with something and I don't think it's [his then fiancée] Josanne [Mariani]," adding, "he's the nearest thing to Brick"—the outwardly straight but homoerotically fixated protagonist of *Cat on a Hot Tin Roof*—"that we both know."[5] Whether or not Williams's assessment of the actor was accurate, Brando in the character of Val Xavier was placed in a position to play out this perceived heteromasculine crisis. In Lumet's film, Val is at once an object of intense fascination to the male and female gaze and a figure who is desperate to break away from the existing paradigms of attraction that he has both exploited and been exploited by. He embodies a fragmented vision of manhood that is untimely to 1950s conformist American culture, if also, as James Gilbert has observed in his work on midcentury "men in the middle," hovering just beneath the surface of it.[6] Performed by an actor who remains associated first in the minds of Williams's audience with the brutish Stanley Kowalski, Val Xavier seems at times to be crawling out of his skin: all the more fitting, since it is the painful shedding of old skin that constitutes the central theme of *The Fugitive Kind.*

When Lady—the female lead, played by Magnani—asks a sulky, sauntering Val, "Why do you walk like that?" and he responds, "Like what?" he is not simply playing dumb about his seductive powers; he is registering the manner in which gesture and appearance are coded in ways from which he cannot escape. "For Val, in the person of Brando," as Tyler observes, "*is* a beauty," with the character's mere presence sufficiently captivating to create a stir among the denizens of Two River County, the fictional county in which the work is set, and, evidently, film critics alike.[7] Later in the movie, in a surge of disillusionment, Brando's character will more forcefully assert, "All we know is just the skin surface of each other. . . . We're all of us sentenced to solitary confinement inside our own lonely skins for as long as we live on this earth." Here, again, Val gives voice to the manner in which his powers of attraction have caged him in, made him an object of suspicions that threaten his very existence, even as he also articulates a bleak thesis about human relations for which much of Williams's work serves as a testing ground.

Referencing a similar line from *Orpheus Descending*, Mike Wallace once asked Williams, "How much of Tennessee Williams is talking there?" The author's response was "about ninety per cent," yet he added: "I think there are moments when we can get out of it, and those are the great moments in life. The moments we must wait for are the moments when we escape from our—the prison of our skin."[8] Given the far-reaching metaphorical significance of the corporeal in Williams's writing, such a remark might elicit reflection on a troubling number of works by the author, *The Fugitive Kind* among them, in which gay or crypto-queer protagonists are quite literally de-carnated: dismembered, cannibalized, or, in Val's case, burned alive. What I want to suggest is that *The Fugitive Kind* occupies a special place in this category of works, which includes "Desire and the Black Masseur," *Suddenly Last Summer*, and *Sweet Bird of Youth*, insofar as it subtly affirms relational possibilities that Williams was ordinarily inclined to deny.

My reading here tracks a shift in emphasis regarding the theme of Orphic dismemberment as it reverberates throughout Williams's work. In contrast to related works, *The Fugitive Kind* shows Williams distancing himself from an enthrallment—exhibited by artists from Ovid onward—with the mythical figure of Orpheus as a cipher for artistic mastery, impossible desire, and perfection in death.[9] With the figure of Val Xavier, Williams offers an Orpheus (or anti-Orpheus) whose openness to imperfect and incomplete possibilities prevails even at the moment of his destruction. In what follows, I will draw out the queer hermeneutical implications of this subtle displacement.

Orpheus and Incompletion

By this point, the most vital discussions of the interrelation between violence and queer sexuality in Williams's work have moved beyond reductive portrayals of the author as a "self-hating homosexual." As David Savran observes, at the very least, observations about Williams's conflicted relationship to queerness ought to mark "the beginning, not the end of an inquiry," because "the homosexual . . . subject" of the "deeply homophobic culture" in which Williams was brought up is "necessarily split, alienated from its own desires."[10] One of the larger aims of this chapter is to better situate Williams's recurrent literalization of the psychic cleavage perpetuated by homophobic culture in relation to contemporary debates about the political potentialities of anti-relational, death-driven desire—or what has come to be referred to as "the antisocial thesis" in queer theory.[11] On one level, the fragmented body in Williams's work, as the recurrent destiny of those whose very existence is excluded by the social order, would seem to affirm the self-avowedly "unthinkable, irresponsible, inhumane" queer ethics proposed by Lee Edelman, who advocates a radical "embrace" of the negativity ascribed to queer subjects by a society whose future is ideologically predicated upon the hetero-exclusive domain of sexed reproduction.[12] Yet a close examination of Williams's writing is just as liable to produce the antithetical conclusion that the act of dismemberment and, especially, cannibalization, actually figures, paradoxically, as a consummate reparative gesture—one that registers as, in Annette Saddik's assessment, "a yearning for wholeness—a oneness—which will put an end to fragmentation."[13]

Here Tim Dean's distinction between "normalizing" and "normative" conceptions of desire may be helpful. Dean asserts that "normalization is less a question of inculcating heterosexuality than of coordinating desire with the ego, freezing fragmented and mercurial unconscious effects into the total form of an identity."[14] Privileging a queer pedagogy over identitarian strategies, he observes that although homosexuality has historically figured as a "synecdoche for perversion," a reminder "of how desire itself remains potentially antinormative," this by no means exempts it from the sorts of "pathogenic . . . totalizing impulse[s]" that curtail desire's "contingency and ambiguity," rendering queerness all too normal in the process.[15]

An avid reader of Rainer Maria Rilke, Williams was captivated by the "assenting Angels" of the *Duino Elegies*, one of twentieth-century literature's most enduring emblems of, in Robert Hass's words, "absolute fulfillment," the fantasy of an all-consuming, never-ending "power . . . completeness and repose."[16] In "Desire and the Black Masseur" and *Suddenly Last Summer*, Williams followed Rilke in grafting his "totalizing impulse" onto one of the central elements in the Orpheus myth: the act of dismemberment, which, in Rilke's *Sonnets to Orpheus*, is conceived as a moment of artistic consummation through "pure destruction."[17] It is "only because" Orpheus is "torn and scattered through Nature," we are told at the end of the first part of Rilke's poem cycle, that the "transfigured song" of Western culture's originary artist achieves its immortal resonance.[18] A similar sense of consummation and fulfilled destiny hangs over the violent dismemberment undergone by both Anthony Burns in "Desire and the Black Masseur" and Sebastian Venable in *Suddenly Last Summer*. Ironically, although Williams's unconscious appears to have been deeply haunted by the Orpheus narrative, it was only in turning explicitly to the myth that the author was able to rearticulate his relationship to his own "totalizing" desires.

In the 1952 poem "Orpheus Descending," written in the midst of a creative crisis that would extend throughout the decade, Williams strikes an unusual tone for one accustomed to ventriloquizing Christ's "Consummatum est."[19] Envisioning Orpheus's voyage to the underworld and back, a voyage that has resonated in the imaginations of artists down the centuries, Williams writes:

> . . . it will not be completed,
> no, it will not be completed,
>
> for you must learn, even you, what we have learned,
> that some things are marked by their nature to be not completed
> but only longed for and sought for a while and abandoned.
>
> And you must learn, even you, what we have learned,
> the passion there is for declivity in this world,
> the impulse to fall that follows a rising fountain.
>
> Now Orpheus, crawl, O shamefaced fugitive, crawl
> back under the crumbling broken wall of yourself,
> for you are not stars, sky-set in the shape of a lyre,
> but the dust of those who have been dismembered by Furies![20]

It would be easy to read these lines as a weary concession to defeat, or a prelude to the failed attempts at coupling represented in *Orpheus Descending* and *The Fugitive Kind*. Nevertheless, Williams's poem could be understood instead as the author's admonition to his own fixated, half-cognized desires as embodied by the figure of Orpheus. Although the theme of dismemberment remains, it is here disentangled from the image of completion, which in another of Rilke's sonnets figures as "a constellation," "glittering" in the "pure nocturnal sky."[21] It seems as though Williams is making a concerted effort to reassess the dream of self-annihilating transcendence and instead to encounter head-on his agonizing sense of incompletion, which is similarly characterized, in "Desire and the Black Masseur," by the image of a structure with "a missing wall."[22]

The manner in which Williams describes this apparent disruption of a deeply harbored image of selfhood is suggestive of the traversal of fantasy in psychoanalysis, in the analysand's encounter, within the analytic session, of what Jacques Lacan calls "the ecstatic limit of the '*Thou art that.*'"[23] What interests me is how, in the wake of this disturbance, whose reverberations would lead the author to begin psychoanalysis, Williams articulates a notion of "decentered and fragmented" subjecthood that I follow Savran in associating with the more promising manifestations of Williams's "skittish radicalism."[24] In turning to *The Fugitive Kind*, it is important to remember that the film is ostensibly set within a heterosexual matrix, whose function as a safe enclosure for relational possibilities—and thus also as a form of political containment—should not be ignored when delineating affirmations of the interpersonal. At the same time, it remains the case that the fate of Val Xavier, whom John Clum calls a "sexually ambiguous" protagonist, results to a large degree from the manner in which he abides in a space of sketchy or deficient conformity to prescribed roles of sex and gender.[25] Ultimately, what distinguishes Val Xavier qua Orphic protagonist from characters in related works is his refusal to invest in "totalizing" fantasies of self-annihilation, and his inclination, instead, toward dwelling amid the "contingency and ambiguity" of incompletion. In this sense, to recall Dean's distinction above, the desire Val embodies is less antinormative than it is anti-normalizing.[26]

Skin and Bones

Val's "trademark," as he calls it, is a snakeskin jacket used during his entertaining days in New Orleans. He dons and removes this piece of skin to symbolic effect throughout the film, and he finally sheds it at the film's conclusion. If somewhat heavy-handed as a theatrical device, it serves as an important marker of Val's entanglement in a paradigm of spectacle and captivation, and as a reminder of his own surface-level beauty. Within the context of Two River County, the jacket also signifies Val's outsider status and the threat he poses, largely through his physical appearance, to the law of the community. "A good-lookin' boy like you is always wanted," he is told by Sheriff Talbot, one of the film's two chief emblems of white supremacist patriarchy. The implication is that simply by virtue of the skin he lives in—his status as an object of desire—Val stands in conflict with the law.

Val's threatening alterity results in him being associated, in turn, with a people whose skin is the basis of their perpetual persecution: the black community of Two River, which occupies a shadowy—and fugitive—position in the film. Upon Val's arrival in the county, he is momentarily mistaken by the sheriff's wife, Mrs. Vee Talbot (Maureen Stapleton), for "that boy," a black escapee from the county jail who is tracked down and killed by the sheriff and his grinning cronies. Val spends his first night in Two River in the lockup that had previously held the black prisoner, and for the rest of the film he faces the threat of being figuratively, if not literally, confined to the same cage as the racial other.[27]

In attempting to negotiate his way through the Hades of the rural South, Val encounters a series of women who, as Clum observes about the female characters in what he calls Williams's "sacrificial stud" plays, "offer the potential for change in the sex/gender system."[28] Carol Cutrere (Joanne Woodward) is something like the female counterpart to Val's rebellious past self. She is the outcast member of a wealthy southern family, and her drinking and public displays have led to her being "ordered to stay out [of Two River County] by the sheriff and paid to stay out by [her] brother." Carol knows Val from his hustler days in New Orleans, and she clings to an image of reckless abandon that he feels he has outgrown. For Carol, Val is proof that "there's something still wild in the country." Although he introduces himself to the people he meets in Two River as Val Xavier, she insists on referring to him by his old nickname, Snakeskin. Whereas Val is trying to turn over a new leaf, Carol sees wildness as the only available response to the corruption that suffuses every aspect of existence in the Jim Crow South. In her former life as a "church bitten reformist" protesting "the gradual massacre of the colored majority in the county," she attempted to march to the state capitol wearing a potato sack but only managed to get a few miles out of town before being arrested for "lewd vagrancy." Disillusioned but still seething with anger, she continues her protest, even though it has devolved into a quasi-subversive doubling down on the actions attributed to her by the legal system. She is a self-proclaimed "exhibitionist," who vows to "show them all just how lewd a lewd vagrant can be when she puts her whole heart into it."

Although she has given up on politics proper, Carol's flouting of conventions of dress and gesture remain compelling instances of what Savran refers to as the "destabilization of mid-century notions of masculinity and femininity" in Williams's work.[29] With its conventionally attired male and female mannequins hovering in the background of numerous scenes, Torrance Mercantile Store—where much of the action unfolds—is a bastion of accepted forms of economic and interpersonal commerce. When Carol, dressed in what looks like a men's trench coat, suspects two gossiping women inside the store of talking about her, she turns on them fiercely, holding up a pair of women's panties over her waist in a parody of "degraded" womanhood. In such moments she reveals herself as a savvy gender troubler, a figure determined, in Judith Butler's terms, to "enact and reveal the performativity of gender itself" so as to undermine its "naturalized categories."[30]

Later in the film, after Val has begun working as a clerk in the Torrance Mercantile Store, Carol chides him for replacing his snakeskin jacket with a suit and tie—in her words, "the nice blue uniform of a convict." From Carol's exhibitionist standpoint, kowtowing to the conventions of respectable appearance is tantamount to enforcing societal norms. As a figure who, in her words, "run[s] with nobody" and who is on the run from the oppressive social atmosphere into which she was born, Carol is the film's true "fugitive kind." Val may be no less out of place within Two River County, but the fugitive existence Carol represents is one he has known for too long. After years of making a living as the life of the party, he recognizes Carol's tendency to confuse her ability to make "people . . . know [she's] alive" with actually "living." Indeed, it seems her idea of "living" amounts to little more than a spiral of self-destructive desire. The path she represents is encapsulated by her invitation to Val to "go juking," which involves drinking, driving, and dancing at juke joints in succession until she can share only some form of half-conscious contact with her juking companion. Val allows himself to be led along by Carol up to a certain point, but he recognizes the cold and senseless destination to which her desires lead when she attempts a crude seduction in a cemetery—or, as Carol calls it, "the local bone orchard."

The choice of words here recalls an earlier scene in which Carol tells the black, mad "conjure man" Uncle Pleasant, who embodies a paradoxically included outsiderness in relation to the symbolic order of Two River County, to take a small bone he has found and "leave it on a bare rock in the rain and the sun . . . till every sign of corruption is burned and washed away." Like Anthony Burns in "Desire and the Black Masseur"—whose story ends only when his sucked-clean "bare white bones" are dropped beneath a "lake's quiet surface"[31]—Carol has desires that are tied to an image of self-immolative absolution. Her avowedly dissolute life, enabled by the bankroll of her wealthy family, similarly anticipates the decadence of Sebastian Venable in *Suddenly Last Summer*, whose carnal exploits take place on lavish trips around Europe, and who meets his decidedly Orphic end after being pursued by a crowd of cannibalistic young boys up a "steep white street . . . that was like a great white bone of a giant beast."[32] When Val refuses Carol's advances in the cemetery, asking her, "Who are you trying to fool beside yourself?" one senses Williams turning away from a refraction of himself—from a fantasy of death-driven completion that has hounded him throughout his life. Although Val furnishes the work's central image of fugitiveness, in his speech about "a kind of bird that don't have any wings, so it can't alight on nothing at all," he eventually tells Carol: "Fly away . . . fly away, little bird." The remark suggests an effort to shoo away a form of compulsive desire that insists on returning to peck at one's flesh.

Back to the Garden

One of the driving questions of *The Fugitive Kind* is how the desiring subject goes about challenging power in a manner that does not simply reaffirm its mandates negatively through a kind of agonistic, or indeed "antisocial," dropping out: the choice, represented by Carol and her ilk, to "run with nobody," to remain forever a fugitive. In the figures of Lady and Mrs. Talbot, the spouses of the town's two most prominent male figures, the possibility is presented for a subversion of the dominant order not through an evasion of power's domain but through the patient transformation of relational structures from within their seemingly unyielding enclosures.

If Carol is a Eurydice who identifies with the "death" of symbolic exclusion, and who would have her Orpheus follow her into that underworld, then Lady is a Eurydice capable of envisioning a future at once within and beyond Two River County—a future that would transform the hell in which the film is set into a new paradise. When we first meet Lady, however, she appears on the point of falling prey to the same death-driven resignation that has consumed Carol. "I wish I was dead," she mutters to herself as she waits on a telephone for the pharmacist who will deliver her the sleeping pills she needs to get through nights spent aiding her dying husband, Jabe, the racist, homicidal owner of Torrance Mercantile. As she waits on the phone, she is unaware that Val has entered the store to retrieve his guitar. Awakening Lady to his presence, Val responds, "No you don't, ma'am." He has just returned from his night with Carol, and the remark reaffirms his resistance to the deathly desires she represents. If Val's past life placed him among "the cold and beautiful bodies of the young" toward which Williams, in a revealing notebook entry about the limits of carnal desire, discusses being drawn, his mission moving forward will be to emanate warm life.[33] "My temperature's always a cou-

FIGURE 2.1.
Brando, one hand in pocket, the other holding his guitar, attracts Lady's gaze with his smoldering eyes.

ple of degrees above normal," he tells Lady after she observes the warmth in the snakeskin jacket he has placed around her shoulders. Val's "cold" beauty, like his jacket, which is made from the skin of a coldblooded animal, corresponds to a plane of existence from which he is committed to distancing himself. This commitment is understood within Carol's bifurcating imagination as a turn away from the "wild" and toward the decidedly *straight* and narrow. But it is more evidently part of a complex strategy of sex and gender negotiation inextricable from the one enacted by Brando in his performance of Val. To quote José Esteban Muñoz's remarks on disidentification, what is at stake here is a form of self-presentation that effectively "scrambles and reconstructs the encoded message of a cultural text"—in this case, midcentury heteromasculinity—that Brando had as much a hand in constructing as destabilizing (see figure 2.1).[34]

Val is repelled by Carol's captivation with the image she has of him, the image of him as "Snakeskin." Referring to Carol's attempts at seduction, he tells Lady, "She made a mistake about me . . . she thought I had a sign hung on me: 'Male at Stud.'" Intent on not being mislabeled again, he reveals another side of himself to Lady. He speaks about his "control" over his body, which, although it seems at first like a blatant come-on, ends up being suggestive of his sexual fluidity, his ability to redirect the pathways of his desire away from normative affirmation. "They say that a woman can burn a man down, you know? But I can burn a woman down," he tells Lady, adding, "I'm saying that I could. I'm not saying I would." When she asks, "Have they tired you out?" he responds, "No, I'm not tired. I'm just fed up."

The reference letter Val offers Lady, in hopes that she will give him a job, describes him as honest and hardworking but mentions that he had to be let go from his former employment because he was a "peculiar talker." The phrase communicates something of Val's queerness while further disassociating him from the fantasy embodied by his mythical prototype, Orpheus. In Mladen Dolar's account of the myth, when Orpheus charms the animals and the trees of Thrace, his voice figures as an emblem of "some primordial fusion . . . the core of a fantasy that the singing voice might cure the wound inflicted by culture."[35] What psychoanalysis seeks to enable, by contrast, is a "break in the continuity of 'bodies and languages'"—a disruption of the codes that penetrate our being, seeding compulsory prescriptions of sex and gender along the way.[36] It is the willingness to abide in this space of discontinuity, in peculiarity, the refusal to resolve into what Dean calls "a total form of an identity," that Val represents. The musicians with whom Val identifies—male blues singers whose signatures grace the soundboard of his guitar—bear testament not to Orphic fantasies of self-continuity and completion but to the *lived* discontinuities and travails of desiring being. When Val speaks to Lady of their names being "written in the stars," one envisions a firmament in which the music of the spheres allows a place for cosmic dissonance.[37]

Val's candor and peculiarity lead Lady to reveal aspects of her own outsiderness and to confide to him her plans for the future. "I was touched by your—strangeness, your strange talk," her theatrical counterpart tells Val in *Orpheus Descending*.[38] Following Val's monologue about "another kind" of person than "the buyers and the ones that get bought" and his description of the bird that "spends its whole life on its wings," Lady invites Val into a room at the back of the store, which she intends to transform into a "confectionery" that will allow her to "compete for the night life" in Two River. Whereas the trajectory of Carol's desires ultimately leads to the "bone orchard," Lady's fantasies revolve around the possibility for vitality and renewal. The confectionery will resemble "an orchard in spring," she tells Val. Only later will we learn the extent to which this all-too-edenic vision of futurity is tied to a dark past. Lady intends to model her confectionery on her father's wine garden: a place where "young couples would come to make love," before local Klansmen (or "vigilantes") burned it to the ground—her father with it—as punishment for serving liquor to black patrons.

If Lady is "not a big optimist," she nevertheless believes that a new, flourishing garden—tied, by way of its past incarnation, to sexual and racial liberation—can be brought into being from within the structure of oppression symbolically represented by the Torrance Mercantile Store. Heartened to encounter someone whose vision extends beyond the crude "buy and sell" stratagems that have determined her and Val's existences, and imagining that this guitar-wielding stranger might perform his music to confectionery patrons, Lady offers Val a job in the store. Although Lady insists that theirs will be simply "a good working relation," a level of intimacy develops between the shop owner's wife and the much younger drifter. For the remainder of the film, this intimacy will be threatened not only by Lady's husband, Jabe, the dying embodiment of heteropatriarchy, but also by Val and Lady's own compulsions to turn back—in an echo of Orpheus's fateful error on the path out of Hades—toward fixed notions of identity and desire.

Visual Pleasure in 1960

Of the three women who play prominent roles in the narrative, Vee Talbot, the sheriff's wife, is the one with whom Val interacts the least. Yet as the shared first letter of their names suggests, Val and Vee are bound by an enigmatic connection. Vee is the first person Val encounters upon arriving in Two River, and she offers to aid him in "turning over a new leaf" by helping him secure a job in town. In contrast to his interactions with Carol and Lady, Val's interactions with Vee seem devoid of sexuality. What the two have in common is a relationship to art. "I tell you, Mr. Xavier, since I took up my painting, my whole outlook is different. I can't explain it," Vee says. "You don't have to explain it," Val responds, "I know what you mean. It's like me when I'm playing my guitar."

Vee's amateur paintings depict her Christian spiritual visions. Val's relationship to art has primarily been defined by a very different paradigm. Relying as much on his good looks as on his abilities, he has been an "entertainer," as he dismissively calls himself when Vee asks if he is a musician. Humble and homely, Vee has inhabited a place on the other side of the footlights. Indeed, as the wife of the county's racist sheriff, she has looked at the world around her "from seats down front at the show." Practically alone in her cautious sympathy for the black inhabitants of Two River, she tells Val that she has "seen some terrible things . . . been a witness." But she has also, in Val's words, "made some beauty . . . out of this dark river county."

Given the numerous allusions to Val's physical beauty in the film, it is notable that the beauty Vee has created through her paintings comes from seeing beyond external appearances. When Val arrives in Two River, Vee has been working all night on a painting of the Church of the Resurrection. When Val asks if the church she has painted is "supposed to be blue," Vee responds, "No, that's how I felt it. You see, I paint a thing how I feel it." In the context in which the film is set—a small southern town obsessed with the color and look of people and things—Vee's "color-blind" attunement to affective intensities and to spiritual visions that literally blind her are subtle reminders of the film's broader subversion of the dominant visual paradigms represented by the town's patriarchs.

"*I want to look at you* while I run through photos of men wanted," Sheriff Talbot says to Val, after accosting him in the street for attempting to aid a blind-struck Mrs. Talbot (my emphasis). As the partial strip-search to which Val is subjected affirms, the desire expressed by the sheriff is not simply a turn of phrase but a subtle insinuation that the quasi-clinical gaze of legal authority is riven from within by homoerotic longing. "He's a beauty, Jabe. A real beauty," Sheriff Talbot later informs the store owner, whose bedbound condition has prevented him from descending from his quarters above the store to meet his new employee. Upon seeing Val for the first time, a sinister grin forms on Jabe's sweat-streaked face. "You fit the description," he remarks. "I heard you were good-looking."

Within the film's rural southern context, one prototype of these objectifying episodes is the eroticization of the racial other, whose imagined libidinal superiority is a source of violence-inducing disquiet in the white racist psyche. In the knowing look exchanged between Jabe and the sheriff at the moment Val appears before them, one detects the anticipatory excitement of a pair of Klansmen dreaming up the cruel acts they will perform on their victim. At the same time, violent intentions come to serve in this instance as an almost self-consciously flimsy "psychic management system," as D. A. Miller would call it, for the film's eroticization of its male lead. Indeed, the image of the two central representations of the county's patriarchal social order gazing intently at Val/Brando crystallizes the peculiar fact that it is the film's male protagonist, and decidedly not its de-feminized female characters, whose "to-be-looked-at-ness" is positioned as a source of "visual pleasure." *The Fugitive Kind*, in this sense, not only affirms Miller's critique of Laura Mulvey's seminal essay "Visual Pleasure in Narrative Cinema," which he accuses of erasing the classic Hollywood male star qua recipient of the (homo)erotically charged gaze; it also, radically for 1960, calls into question the "hetero-structuration of the visual field" whose internal contradictions Miller so deftly reveals in the film version of *Suddenly Last Summer*, released one year prior.[39]

Nevertheless, just as the gaze is linked to tragedy in the myth of Orpheus, where it is the musician's compulsive *look back* that famously banishes Eurydice to the underworld, so too will it play a central role in the tragic events that conclude Williams's version of the myth. Although Jabe's cynicism and his low esteem for his wife forbid him from imagining that anything more than some crude exchange of sexual favors for money is taking place under his roof, he recognizes that Lady has begun dressing and acting differently since Val arrived on the scene. From the moment he lays eyes on the "beauty" who has come under his employ until the film's end, Val and Lady find themselves carefully watched. The true threat, however, to the gradually developing relationship of the film's two protagonists arises less from outside surveillance than from their own compulsive redirection of their gazes away from the uncertain future before them and toward the struggles that have determined their pasts.

The Perhaps of the Future

In the closing lines of his introduction to one of the published versions of *Orpheus Descending*, Williams offers an insight into his own life experiences that is equally relevant to the characters in his script. "The future is called 'perhaps,'" he writes, "which is the only possible thing to call the future. And the important thing is not to allow that to scare you."[40] In contrast to his invocations of Rilkean completion, his words here suggest not an attachment to fantasy-born conceptions of futurity but rather an avowal of uncertainty amid the travails of becoming. One antecedent to the statement is a sort of Beckettian cry of perseverance that appears at various intervals throughout Williams's journals. In a notebook entry from 1942 he writes: "Always the outlook appears to be finally tragic—but clears. Clears as we go.—Or darkens. Well—at any rate it changes." In need of encouragement, he pens the words "*En Avant!*"[41] It is a phrase that will accompany him through the more darkened outlooks of the next fifteen years. Despondent about his inability to "create with power and certainty as I have at rare times when I was loved by the gods," he exhorts himself, "En Avant."[42] Broke, threatened with the "contingency" that a check from his agent might be the last, and left with "no answer" to his dilemma, his response is "*En Avant*!—*En Avant*! *En Avant*!"[43] Burnt out from work, sex-crazed, but "too nervous for any social composure," feeling like a "frantic little caged beast"—once again, all he can tell himself is: "En Avant!"[44]

If this refrain is at times tinged with hopefulness for one or another object on the horizon, it is more often, and more characteristically, an expression of the will to proceed onward precisely in the absence of any clearly defined hope. Although it conjures a radical mode of insistence in the face of the dissolved supports of subjectivity, this is not a matter, as Edelman would have it, of embracing the inhuman pulsations of the death drive at the expense of all positive ascriptions. Rather, it is closer to what Lauren Berlant, in her illuminating debate with Edelman on the value and limits of antisocial queer ethics, describes as "bearing the unbearable encounter with the unfinished business of being."[45] Casting the experience of the unbearable in Hegelian terms, Mari Ruti proposes that "such tarrying with the negative" is perhaps "the greatest of human achievements, for it transforms the terrors and midnights of the spirit into symbolic formations, imaginative undertakings, and sites of delicate beauty."[46] I have suggested how Williams's efforts to refigure the Orpheus theme and, with it, his own investments in the fantasies it expresses, constitute an exemplary instance of tarrying with the "midnights of the spirit." I would like to conclude by showing how, at the expense of his usual recourses to fantasy, Williams's insistence in the face of the negative ultimately comes to be expressed in *The Fugitive Kind*.

The final events of the film unfold in the aftermath of Palm Sunday mass. The confectionery at the rear of the store—a labor of love and creativity between Lady and Val—nears completion. The future looks bright. On the day the confectionery is to open, however, Jabe finally manages to descend the stairs to inspect Lady and Val's handiwork. His rage upon realizing that Lady has effectively rebuilt her father's wine garden under his roof leads him to the exclamatory confession that he was among the vigilantes who helped murder her father. Tragically, this revelation solidifies Lady's resolve to avenge her father before Jabe's eyes, at any cost. Jabe's repeated refrain, "Boy, I sure married a live one!" ominously foretells the events that will unfold, as Lady, like Carol before her, becomes more interested in exhibiting that she is alive than in living. Although Val, who has been told to leave the county or risk his life, urges Lady to delay opening her nightclub, she will not be dissuaded. "I want that man to see the wine garden come open again while he's dying tonight," she tells Val. "Nothing can stop it. It's just something got to be done to square things away. To be not defeated. I won't be defeated, not again in my life, you got me?"

Compounding matters, Carol has returned to town and poisoned Lady's mind with the thought that Val is going to make her his Eurydice and drive her across the county line. Although Val insists that Carol is mistaken, he does, in fact, intend to leave the county that evening. Val tries to hold Lady close to him, telling her of the "true love" that he feels for her—"something I never told anybody"—and promising that he'll wait for her just outside the county. But Lady's capacity for patiently abiding in the space of "contingency and ambiguity"—in the "perhaps" that is the only name for the future—has expired. In her eyes, Val has in some sense already fulfilled his duties anyway. Her dream "that somebody must be coming here to take me out of this hell" has come true: she has been revitalized thanks to Val and the project they have undertaken together. "Look at me," she shouts, exhibiting her furious vitality, even as she is steadily sowing the seeds of her demise, "I'm alive once more!"

As Lady shortly learns, her most coveted squaring away of accounts—a child to replace the one she lost the summer the wine garden burned down—is also on its way to being accomplished. What the "cold eyes" of Jabe's nurse discerns, which Lady herself could not, is that she has become pregnant with Val's child. The knowing gaze that the nurse casts upon Lady before she leaves the Torrance Mercantile Store for the last time is a prelude to the film's final, damning look back. Ironically, this look will be couched in a starry eyed look ahead—the same that Edelman pithily sums up with the term "reproductive futurity." Just as "the Child as the preeminent emblem of the motivating end . . . of every political vision . . . must," by virtue of the normative couplings it underwrites, "weigh on any delineation of a queer oppositional politics,"[47] so too will its fixating power as an image of completion weigh on and ultimately crush the strange, contingent relational possibilities of Val and Lady in *The Fugitive Kind.*

Overwhelmed by the news that she will bear a child, Lady tells Val to take out the Christmas ornaments and decorate her like a tree. Draping strands of tinsel in her hair from the trellis above her, she runs through the confectionery exclaiming, "Glass bells, glass birds, and icicles . . . and tinsel. Put them on me, Val!" If "Lady's Confectionery" already seemed a saccharine compensation for past injustices, it has suddenly become more cloying than vi-

FIGURE 2.2. In these moments before avatars of patriarchal, southern, homosocial normativity kill Val, flames shoot up behind him. The subsequent shots depict Val as he struggles against the spray of an unleashed fire hose—an exaggerated metaphor for the orgasmic release of his murderers' repressed homoerotic desire.

sions of sugarplums. The impending Easter holiday, which was formerly associated, through Vee's depiction of the Church of the Resurrection, with the emancipation from dominant spectatorial paradigms, has been displaced by a Christmastime fantasy in which showy ornamentation holds center stage. The evocation of a holiday synonymous with commerce reminds us that in a literal and figurative sense we have not escaped from the Torrance Mercantile Store—that, indeed, the "boss upstairs" still rules over his domain. At the very moment Lady imagines she is celebrating her "life beginning again," Jabe leans out his upstairs window to set fire to the scenery below—the same that his nurse all-too-accurately described as "artistic as hell." In the chaos that ensues, Lady is mortally wounded by a shot from Jabe's pistol. Meanwhile, the water hoses that never arrived to aid Lady's father as he struggled to save his wine garden are directed by Sheriff Talbot and company upon Val in an explosive ejaculation of long-withheld homoerotic longing and fury. The belated sousing, which pushes Val back into the inferno where he is burned alive, completes the link between past and present (see figure 2.2). In holding too firmly to her vengeance, in refusing to "learn," as the Orpheus of Williams's poem must, "that some things are marked by their nature to be not completed," Lady has condemned Val to her father's fate.

In 1960 the image of a southern man of law directing a hose upon the outsider in his midst connects Val once more to black residents of Two River and to the civil rights movement, for which he serves as an unwitting martyr figure. It would seem that Val is "that boy" after all, the Law having succeeded in placing him back in the cage that he has spent the entire film trying to escape. *The Fugitive Kind* ends with Uncle Pleasant arriving to recover Val's snakeskin jacket from the ashes. He trades the jacket to Carol for a gold ring, and she drives away at last in her convertible after delivering the film's closing lines: "Wild things leave skins behind them. They leave clean skins and teeth and white bones. And these are tokens, passed from one to another. So that the fugitive kind can follow their kind." Carol's cold, fleshless fantasy of fugitive existence has not diminished in her own mind, although its captivating power may well have in the mind of the viewer. The self-styled wild thing, we have earlier learned, is departing to spend the rest of her life in "a Mediterranean villa" with the "limitless funds" of her brother and sister-in-law to support her. Although Carol appears to have the final word on Val and the emancipatory struggles around which the film revolves, her identification with the figure she insists on referring to by his onetime stage name remains skin deep. It is in direct defiance of Carol's desperate pleas, "Snakeskin! Snakeskin! Don't go back there," that Val—having removed his jacket in a final symbolic shedding of skin—follows Lady toward the front of the store where the vigilantes are waiting for him with their hoses. What ensures his demise is thus the very opposite of flight or fugitiveness.

Val's final gesture dramatically contradicts the actions of Orpheus, whom Plato chastised for being too cowardly to die for love. Yet if Orpheus, as an emblematic constellation of totalizing fantasies, can be said, finally, to be descending in *The Fugitive Kind*, it is no less for the peculiar tendencies that define the film's protagonist throughout his time on screen. Foremost among these are Val's disidentification with his own powers of captivation, his refusal to allow the attestation that "all we know is just the skin surface of each other" to harden him into the solitary figure he is at times in danger of becoming. In the image of Val pushed backward yet pressing onward against the rushing water, struggling against the too-powerful forces of heterosexist, southern, patriarchal Law, one grasps something not only of Brando's struggle, in this most peculiar of roles, against his own physical comportment and calcified public image, but also of the willfulness required of Williams in his effort to translate his own divided subjectivity into his work in a manner that would not once again ratify the urge, so strikingly delineated in "Desire and the Black Masseur," to "cover his incompletion."[48] Although Val is immolated in a fashion similar to previous sacrificial figures in Williams's corpus, his dogged persistence—the embodiment of the author's personal refrain, "*En Avant,* and always *En Avant*"[49]—is not toward any normalizing compensation for his unfinished existence but toward a future of queerer possibilities whose name is "perhaps."

NOTES

The first epigraph is drawn from Don Ross, "Williams on a Hot Tin Roof," *Conversations with Tennessee Williams*, ed. Albert J. Devlin (Jackson: University Press of Mississippi, 1986), 50–53, at 51; the second is from Tennessee Williams, *Notebooks*, ed. Margaret Bradham Thornton (New Haven, Conn.: Yale University Press, 2006), 285.

1. John Lahr, *Tennessee Williams: Mad Pilgrimage of the Flesh* (New York: Norton, 2014), 339.
2. Lahr, *Tennessee Williams*, 342.
3. Parker Tyler, review of *The Fugitive Kind*, dir. Sidney Lumet, *Film Quarterly* 13.4 (1960): 47–49, at 49, 48. An early chronicler of homosexuality in cinema, Tyler elsewhere disparages the sense of internal sexual conflict expressed by a number of Williams's protagonists.
4. Tyler, review of *The Fugitive Kind*, 49, 48.
5. Williams, *Notebooks*, 662.
6. James Gilbert, *Men in the Middle: Searching for Masculinity in the 1950s* (Chicago: University of Chicago Press, 2005).
7. Tyler, review of *The Fugitive Kind*, 48.
8. Mike Wallace, "Tennessee Williams," Devlin, *Conversations*, 54–58, at 55.
9. For readings of Orpheus relevant to how he figures in this essay, see Slavoj Žižek, "The Sex of Orpheus," www.lacan.com/zizekopera2.htm, and especially Klaus Theweleit, "The Politics of Orpheus between Women, Hades, Political Power and the Media: Some Thoughts on the Configuration of the European Artist, Starting with the Figure of Gottfried Benn or: What Happens to Eurydice?" *New German Critique* 36 (Autumn 1985): 133–56.
10. David Savran, *Communists, Cowboys, and Queers: The Politics of Masculinity in the Work of Arthur Miller and Tennessee Williams* (Minneapolis: University of Minnesota Press, 1992), 84.
11. Robert L. Caserio, Lee Edelman, Jack [Judith] Halberstam, José Esteban Muñoz, and Tim Dean, "The Antisocial Thesis in Queer Theory," *PMLA* 121.3 (2006): 819–28.
12. Lee Edelman, *No Future: Queer Theory and the Death Drive* (Durham, N.C.: Duke University Press, 2004), 4.
13. Annette Saddik, "The (Un)Represented Fragmentation of the Body in Tennessee Williams's 'Desire and the Black Masseur' and *Suddenly Last Summer*," *Modern Drama* 41.3 (1998): 347–54, at 348.

14. Tim Dean, *Beyond Sexuality* (Chicago: University of Chicago Press, 2000), 237.

15. Dean, *Beyond Sexuality*, 238, 237.

16. Robert Hass, "Looking for Rilke," Rainer Maria Rilke, *The Selected Poetry of Rainer Maria Rilke*, ed. and trans. Stephen Mitchell (New York: Random House, 1982), xxxv.

17. Rainer Maria Rilke, *Duino Elegies, and The Sonnets to Orpheus*, ed. and trans. Stephen Mitchell (New York: Vintage International, 2009), 133.

18. Rilke, *Duino Elegies*, 133.

19. John M. Clum observes such a Christ reference in relation to "Desire and the Black Masseur" in his "The Sacrificial Stud and the Fugitive Female in *Suddenly Last Summer, Orpheus Descending*, and *Sweet Bird of Youth*," *The Cambridge Companion to Tennessee Williams*, ed. Matthew C. Roudané (Cambridge: Cambridge University Press, 1997), 128–46, at 132.

20. Tennessee Williams, *In the Winter of Cities: Collected Poems of Tennessee Williams* (New York: New Directions, 1964), 28.

21. Rilke, *Duino Elegies*, 97.

22. Tennessee Williams, "Desire and the Black Masseur," *Collected Stories* (New York: New Directions, 1985), 205–12, at 206.

23. Jacques Lacan, "The Mirror Stage as Formative of the I Function as Revealed in Psychoanalytic Experience," *Écrits: The First Complete Edition in English*, trans. Bruce Fink (New York: Norton, 2006), 75–81, at 81.

24. Savran, *Communists, Cowboys, and Queers*, 9.

25. Clum, "The Sacrificial Stud," 140.

26. For a series of more recent discussions, and critical appraisals, of antinormativity as deployed in queer theoretical discourse, see "Queer Theory without Antinormativity," ed. Robyn Wiegman and Elizabeth A. Wilson, special issue, *Differences* 26.1 (May 2015).

27. Although it was Williams's principle to deal with social issues in an "oblique" or "allusive manner," the author considered *Orpheus Descending* among his works that most "directly" dealt with racism and civil rights (Walter Wager, "Tennessee Williams," Devlin, *Conversations*, 124–33, at 129). Still, the parallel drawn between Val's nonconformity to masculine norms and the experiences of southern blacks remains problematic. Within the scope of the present inquiry, suffice it to say that the threat posed by white supremacist patriarchy to all forms of otherness is powerfully represented in both *Orpheus Descending* and its film adaptation, even if racial politics remain underdeveloped and subordinated to issues of sexuality and gender.

28. Clum, "The Sacrificial Stud," 130.

29. Savran, *Communists, Cowboys, and Queers*, 80.

30. Judith Butler, *Gender Trouble* (New York: Routledge, 1990), 139.

31. Williams, "Desire and the Black Masseur," 211.

32. Tennessee Williams, *Suddenly Last Summer*, in *The Theatre of Tennessee Williams*, 8 vols. (New York: New Directions, 1971–92), 3:343–423, at 421.

33. Williams, *Notebooks*, 237.

34. José Esteban Muñoz, *Disidentifications: Queers of Color and the Performance of Politics* (Minneapolis: University of Minnesota Press, 1999), 31.

35. Mladen Dolar, *A Voice and Nothing More* (Cambridge, Mass.: MIT Press, 2006), 31.

36. Dolar, *A Voice and Nothing More*, 162.

37. As Angela Y. Davis observes in her work on the blues era and specifically on Bessie Smith (whom, notably, Val includes among the "immortal" figures on his guitar in *Orpheus Descending*), the blues as a genre eschews "certain resolution" and the "dominant, etherealized ideology of love" for themes of failure and brokenness that at the time were "largely banished from the established popular music culture" (*Blues Legacies and Black Feminism* [New York: Pantheon: 1998], 79, 3).

38. Tennessee Williams, *Orpheus Descending*, in *The Theatre of Tennessee Williams*, 3:217–342, at 303.

39. D. A. Miller, "Visual Pleasure in 1959," *October* 81 (Summer 1997): 34–58, at 46n6.

40. Tennessee Williams, *Orpheus Descending*, in *Four Plays* (New York: Signet, 1976), ix.

41. Williams, *Notebooks*, 285.

42. Williams, *Notebooks*, 475.

43. Williams, *Notebooks*, 245.

44. Williams, *Notebooks*, 269.

45. Lauren Berlant and Lee Edelman, *Sex, or the Unbearable* (Durham, N.C.: Duke University Press, 2014), 68.

46. Mari Ruti, "Why There Is Always a Future in the Future," *Angelaki* 13.1 (2008): 113–26, at 119.

47. Edelman, *No Future*, 13.

48. Williams, "Desire and the Black Masseur," 206.

49. Williams, *Notebooks*, 285.

PART II

THE SOUTH'S QUEER GOTHICISMS

Chapter 3 ▸ "Mass Production of Degeneracy": Queer Genre-ship and Southern Gothic Film

R. BRUCE BRASELL

Although it initially emerged out of book reviewing and literary criticism in the 1930s and 1940s, today southern gothic is a social classificatory schema as well as an artistic one, unbounded by medium specificity, and has even attained a level of trendiness within popular culture through websites and magazine articles and within the academy through entries in encyclopedias and reference guides. One can rest assured that once *Southern Living*, the upper-middle-class magazine of regional virtue as expressed in lifestyle consumption choices, is comfortable enough to include a spread on it, the label has finally been sanitized of its perversity—or, in the lingo contemporaneous with the release of the various works, degeneracy. The spread's headline reads: "Southern Gothic: This Literary Genre Celebrates Our Hauntingly Beautiful and Mysterious Region."[1] It includes a list of the usual literary suspects: William Faulkner, Carson McCullers, Eudora Welty, and Flannery O'Connor. A "memorable quote" is provided from a book by each author, but in keeping with the magazine's commodification of American regionalism, the spread prioritizes photographs of the covers of those books, with blurbs promoting them. The spread sutures this historically contentious (and often pejorative) label into the magazine's "editorial policy of presenting the positive aspects of the South" by redefining the literature as not only "beautiful and mysterious" but concerned with "quirks" and "eccentricity" rather than the grotesquery—much less degeneracy—with which it was historically associated.[2] While the term "southern gothic" is routinely invoked, as Margie Burns noted as far back as the early 1990s, it is a term that "almost nobody attempts to scrutinize," an observation that remains true today, although there have been a number of insightful and important auteur-oriented works about artists affiliated with it.[3] My interest in this classificatory schema lies in its historical formation and initial queerness, which *Southern Living* normalizes through the framework of eccentricity, and more particularly in its evolution into a transmedia phenomenon and spectral filmic form.

Use of the word "gothic" to refer to the texts of certain artists whose works engage with the southeastern United States was historically often meant as a slur. Similarly, "queer" was meant to be an insult when it was shouted at gays, lesbians, and transgender people prior to their reappropriation of the word in the late 1980s and early 1990s. But the connection between the artistic expressions aligned with southern gothic and the theoretical concepts aligned with queer theory runs deeper than just this superficial similarity. In the decades since queer theory blasted onto the academic scene in the early 1990s, it has continued to develop, an important line of flight its engagement with temporality.[4] But for my purposes it is the initial configuration of queer theory and its concern with the normal that I find productive for theorizing southern gothic. When using a contemporary theory to assist in understanding a phenomenon that occurred before the theory existed, one always runs the risk of a forced imposition on that past. But in this case, the earlier cultural phenomenon is a manifestation within the historical social continuum that informed the present that queer theory was addressing upon its appearance and why some of these texts make appearances in the writings of some queer theorists who are unconcerned with southern gothic or the southern United States per se. Queer theory was not intended to be synonymous with lesbian, gay, bisexual, and transgender studies. Although individual theorists may work in both arenas, the two areas operate from very different suppositions. Many queer theorists reject the idea of identity politics that typically informs LGBTQ+ studies, countering that queer is defined not in relation to heterosexuality but to the normal. According to David Halperin, queer "demarcates not a positivity but a positionality vis-à-vis the normative—a positionality that is not restricted to lesbians and gay men but is in fact available to anyone who is or who feels marginalized because of her or his sexual practices."[5] Early queer theorists such as Eve Kosofsky Sedgwick and Michael Warner pushed this concern further than just gender and sexuality, claiming it is a theory about "resistance to regimes of the normal" within society because everyday political "contests over sexuality and its regulation are generally linked to views of social institutions and norms of the most basic sort."[6] As a result, a queer understanding challenges "the common understanding of what gender difference means, or what the state is for, or what 'health' entails, or what would define fairness, or what a good relation to the planet's environment would be." In other words, queerness protests "not just the normal behavior of the social but the *idea* of normal behavior," thereby providing a dose of skepticism "to the methodologies founded on that idea."[7] Queerness offers a strategy to denaturalize the disciplinary regimes of the normal that operate within society, a description apropos of the cultural work performed by southern gothic and why it is a queer genre. Southern gothic is a queer genre not because works aligned with it include representations of homosexuality and other nonheteronormative sexualities on their pages or within their prosceniums or frames but rather, as will be demonstrated, because the discourses historically accompanying the circulation of these works framed the genre as, first, sired through perverse parentage (the lineage of a same-sex literary coupling) and, second, concerned with degeneracy. After a general overview of the emergence of southern gothic as a cultural genre, this essay focuses on these two matters, the latter one taking us back to an engagement with 1990s queer theory to assist in understanding how the genre socially functioned during the classical Hollywood period. This is a historical investigation, and while, yes, the past informs the present, it makes no claims regarding whether the genre continues to function similarly today.

While culture critics typically approach books for the words between their covers and films for the sounds and images within their recorded scenes, they can also be approached as cultural objects that circulate within society. This flow is typically accompanied—especially upon initial release—by retail displays, newspaper advertisements, magazine reviews, artist interviews, and face-to-face gossip. In a 1959 *Harper's Magazine* article on book reviewing, Elizabeth Hardwick observed that "some publishers have concluded that *Time* readers, having learned *Time*'s opinion of a book, feel that they have somehow already read the book, or if not quite that, if not read, at least taken it in, *experienced* it as a 'fact of our time.'"[8] Extratextual material enables individuals who have not read a book or attended a play or seen a movie to become familiar with its content. In other words, one need not have read Erskine Caldwell's novel *Tobacco Road* or seen its stage or film adaptation to hold a familiarity with it, because such awareness can be acquired from advertising, press coverage, and personal conversations. And this cultural terrain that surrounds the material circulation of books within society rather than the texts themselves is the cultural space out of which southern gothic as a classificatory schema emerged, initially within the cultured classes, thereafter onto the popular landscape.

As I have argued elsewhere, southern gothic emerged as a genre through journalism rather than through industrial production processes or the education system, with this manifestation in the press preceded by personal conversations within the New York literary scene. Book reviews in magazines and newspapers (and to a limited extent on radio and television) aimed at the educated professional classes were the primary mechanism of its genesis, although literary criticism and author interviews contributed as well. Its initial incarnation was conjured through three different operations that were enacted in these book reviews: first, the invocation of the names of other authors and the titles of their works that were considered similar to the work under review (thereby forming an authorial family tree for the genre); second, the recurring incantation of particular words and concepts to describe the work under review (thereby providing a definition of the genre); and, third, the use of a genre label to classify the work (thereby offering a title for referencing the authorial family tree and definition). The first operation constructed the skeleton of the genre, while the second offered the muscle and flesh to be attached to those bones and the third a name for referring to it. While individually these three elements cannot form a genre, their mutual interaction solidified as one. I refer to genres formed through this peculiar means as "genre-ship" because it emerges out of authorship.

Although the concepts of auteurism and genre are typically assumed to be competing and antagonistic classificatory approaches, in the particular situation of southern gothic, authorship was a key ingredient in its formation. Building on Foucault, the authorial function of various artists can be interwoven into a larger collective authorial function that is a genre.[9] Although the citation of other artists and their works was intended to provide readers with an overall sense of the particular work under review, it created a chain of associations that connected various author personas and artistic works into a genre. While any particular review might reference a range of authors, certain ones recurred synchronically across them for a particular work and diachronically across the works of the related artist. The cumulative effect of exposure to these repetitions is that the isolated references fall by the wayside while the consistently recurring names form a web of connections, a map much like a family tree or corporate organizational chart that provides the foundation of genre-ship. In the terms of contemporary theory, one could call this an assemblage, à la Gilles Deleuze and Félix Guattari.[10] Culture critics, most of whom were part of or had close ties to the literary scene in New York, the epicenter of U.S. publishing, collectively operated from an unspoken and, to a certain degree, unconscious master text for evaluating and apprehending this literature, and the faint contours of this apparition are traceable from the ghostly residue left behind in the reviews. Prior to the 1960s, reviewers and critics were more likely to conjure southern gothic indirectly through citation of certain authors, titles, and descriptive terms rather than by hailing the explicit label. As a result, the genre often seemed translucent, more felt than seen. A certain irony exists in the use of the label "gothic," which implies the supernatural, to refer to a group of works that are not about the supernatural per se but rather were received as part of a genre that operates as a specter. In other words, the genre was a phantom ideal that haunted the reception of a certain group of texts within American society, with this specter materializing in the reviews through the means outlined above. In practice, of course, some works conformed more closely to this archetype than others. Lack of proximity did not disqualify any particular text from being considered southern gothic, because what ultimately made a textual object "southern gothic" was not fidelity to a list of prescribed criteria but the assignment of the label to it by users, be they industry producers, marketing distributors, retail and exhibition providers, journalists, audiences, or, more routinely today, academic scholars. In practice, however, users typically justified their classification by referencing such criteria, and those justifications by users rather than a textual analysis of the works themselves provide the historical conceptualization of southern gothic proffered here, one that attempts to re-create the framework through which the works were initially presented to the cultured classes for consumption—that of abnormality, degeneracy, and grotesquery.

While this is a historical argument about the formation of a particular genre, other American genres have emerged out of journalistic criticism as well, the most famous being film noir. The classification of certain American films as film noir occurred during the immediate post–World War II period in France, entering the American lexicon only decades later when its existence was perpetuated by the academy (through the incorporation of film into university curricula) and journalism (through concern with film as art worthy of intellectual engagement similar to literature). Initially these films were neither conceived by the studios and filmmakers nor received by American audiences as film noir. Instead, they were seen as melodramas and crime films, perceived as film noir only when they were subsequently screened, discussed, and written about several decades after their initial release. Following this retro-application, New Hollywood filmmakers began to consciously make films in the form, which studios then marketed and audiences received as such.[11]

Southern gothic's emergence as a film genre took a more meandering route than that of film noir. One of the earliest formulations of southern gothic was by Ellen Glasgow in the mid-1930s. She used the phrase to describe the literary works of William Faulkner and Erskine Caldwell, whom she christened purveyors of the "mass production of degeneracy in our fiction."[12] Southern gothic blossomed into an acknowledged genre within literary circles during the 1940s, followed by adaptations of these works for the stage in the 1950s along with original plays that eventually became aligned with the genre, before finally appearing on the screen as a derivative genre, with the films preceded by a life on either the page or the stage or both. Since the films functioned as reincarnations rather than adaptations, no genre specification was necessary for them to be perceived generically. In addition, because reviews of the books and plays had previously appeared in the same magazines and newspapers that were now reviewing the films, the films' categorizations were filtered through those earlier reviews. This made the film genre identifiable not through any particular inherently cinematic qualities but through the films' prior materialization in another medium that haunts their circulation.[13]

Most of the plays and novels aligned with southern gothic could not compete with the movies in popularity, and while they may not have been seen and read by a large part of the public, mass audiences were often familiar with them owing to their coverage in the press. For example, mass magazines like *Life* routinely included photo spreads of Broadway plays consumed by the cultured classes. In analyzing the role expected of a critic reviewing a film adaptation of a stage play, Robert Hatch lamented in the *New Republic*, "It is enough if he comments on the faithfulness of the adaptation, compares the dramatic merits of the two productions, and informs the mass market that it may now sample what had the New York audience by the ears in an earlier season."[14] In other words, audiences were drawn to film adaptations of certain plays because they could finally see what the hullabaloo over them was all about. While Erskine Caldwell's early-1930s novels were wildly popular, such sales were not typical of other literary works aligned with southern gothic, which were aimed at the cultured classes. As an anonymous reviewer in *Time* magazine reminded readers: "Publishers often complain that the South writes more books than it buys."[15]

Southern gothic solidified as a film genre in the late 1950s in the wake of the 1956 release of *Baby Doll*, written by Tennessee Williams and directed by Elia Kazan. In 1941 the *New York Post* film critic Archer Winston perceived William Wyler's adaptation of Lillian Hellman's *The Little Foxes* as "an antidote to all the flood of romanticism concerning the Old South" as represented by such recent films as *Jezebel* and *Gone with the Wind*.[16] As Edward D. C. Campbell has demonstrated, the major filmic representation of the American South during this period was "of a genteel southern class of [white] country squires who ruled a well-ordered, contented society devoted to an agrarian ideal and the courtly pursuits, and sustained by a large work force of adoring [black] slaves," a film type that today is commonly referred to by scholars such as Ed Guerrero as "the plantation genre."[17] Less than two decades later, the antidote to the romanticism of the plantation film had become the dominant mode, and *Baby Doll* was a major factor in demonstrating to Hollywood its potential as a profitable replacement for a depiction of the South that had become problematic in the changing times of the mid-1950s. Although southern gothic works had already been brought to the screen, among them Erskine Caldwell's *Tobacco Road* and Carson McCullers's *The Member of the Wedding*, a number of elements distinguished *Baby Doll* from these earlier releases.[18]

First, the Williams-Kazan film appeared just as the romanticization of the plantation and slavery became untenable within popular culture as the black civil rights movement moved into a new phase with the 1955 Montgomery, Alabama, bus boycott. Second, although the earlier works had sensational elements, their marketing emphasized the artistry and prestige of the source material from which they were derived. Most of these plays had won a major Broadway award such as the New York Drama Critics' Circle Award. In contrast, the marketing of *Baby Doll* centered on the salacious and sensationalist nature of the material as the primary draw, not its cultural pedigree, with most reviewers noting that the film was condemned by the Catholic Legion of Decency. In contrast to reviews in magazines and newspapers aimed at the moviegoing public, be they for the masses or the cultured classes, reviews in the industry-oriented newspaper *Variety* typically included a prognosis regarding the film's box-office success and a diagnosis of features that might make the film hard to sell. *Variety* assessed *Baby Doll* as "b.o. dynamite," conjecturing that "if sensationalism in theme and exploitation can put a picture over the top (as it has in most instances in the past), this Kazan entry should make a barrel of dough."[19] And the cultured classes perceived *Baby Doll* as a crass attempt at such commercialization. Unlike the earlier films, which were based on well-known plays, often in turn based on a highly regarded book, *Baby Doll* was an unknown textual commodity and therefore had to rely on popular associations with Tennessee Williams and Elia Kazan. The film's marketing campaign highlighted their names as well as using an image that at the time was considered sensational: the lead actress Carroll Baker lying in a baby bed sucking her thumb.

The third element distinguishing *Baby Doll* from these earlier films is that film reviewers were beginning to acknowledge the generic nature of such works, routinely invoking authors and titles from the southern gothic family tree that had formed in literary circles during the 1940s, as well as incanting descriptive words that had become aligned with southern gothic such as "degeneracy" and "grotesque." In the process, they solidified Tennessee Williams's alignment with the genre. When his early plays premiered, southern gothic was perceived as a literary genre restricted to novels and short stories, and the plays were rarely received through its prism, although Williams was socially linked to Carson McCullers, the two sharing a 1951 photo spread in *Vogue* magazine in which the caption under her photograph teased the reader: "Frail, tall, and pallid, there are moments when Miss McCullers seems rather like the young girl of Mr. Williams' play, *The Glass Menagerie*."[20] Although the play had not been aligned with southern gothic when it appeared in 1945, here it is reconfigured as such with one of its key characters presented as embodying the heart of an author whose works had been labeled "southern gothic" and whose personal life had been alluded to in the same way. Such occurrences heralded the splicing of Williams and his works into the southern gothic lineage in the wake of *Baby Doll,* his conscription coming primarily through the reception of the cinematic reincarnations of his stage works during the 1950s, as well as through the invocation of his name and his works' titles in the reception of other artists' works, rather than through the initial reception of his own plays.

After *Baby Doll,* film critics began routinely to use the relational reviewing practice popular since the 1940s with book reviewers to invoke genreship. The absorption of these literary concepts into the practice of film reviewing during the mid-1950s can be seen as an attempt to lift film criticism to an equal status with literary criticism at a time when film was beginning to be approached as an artistic form, not just an entertainment commodity, and European art cinema was becoming popular in the United States with the cultured classes.[21] While it was clear that book reviewers were citing other literary works, an ambiguity typically arose as to whether film reviewers were referring to the novel, play, or film form of the work being summoned for comparison. Bosley Crowther of the *New York Times* began his review of *Baby Doll* thus: "It looks as though the ghost of Tennessee Williams' *Streetcar Named Desire* has got bogged down in the mud of Erskine Caldwell's famous *Tobacco Road* in the screen play Mr. Williams has written for Elia Kazan's *Baby Doll*."[22] At the time of Crowther's writing, *A Streetcar Named Desire* existed as a play, film, and ballet, while *Tobacco Road* existed as a novel, play, and film, and which manifestations he is referring to is unclear, although the inclusion of the authors' names before the titles implies the initial incarnations of, respectively, play and novel. And finally, the earlier films had all been staged as Broadway plays, even those that were initially novels, but with *Baby Doll* the field of adaptable material moved beyond Broadway to include plays from other venues and novels that had never received a stage adaptation.

In the wake of the phenomenal success of *Baby Doll* in 1956, there appeared a plethora of film adaptations of literary and stage works aligned with southern gothic, including Tennessee Williams's *Cat on a Hot Tin Roof*, Erskine Caldwell's *God's Little Acre*, and the William Faulkner stories that inspired *The Long, Hot Summer*, all in 1958. Bosley Crowther identified these films as representative of a new trend, leading him to refer to *The Sound and the Fury* in 1959 as the "most recent Hollywood look-in on a decadent family in the South, boiling in sullen sex urges and stewing in alcohol," a trend he perceived still to be going strong after five years with *Toys in the Attic* in 1963.[23] The literary genre that had solidified during the early 1940s within the cultured classes was transformed through filmic reincarnations during the late 1950s into a resolutely popular one for a mass audience. Whether within cultured circles or popular culture, the use of explicit genre labels became prominent primarily when the style that had initially been praised for its artistry began to proliferate and assume a level of predictability. Unlike traditional genres within popular culture such as the western, southern gothic emerged out of the cultured classes. Because of the spectral nature of the genre, the works often oscillated between the cultural spaces of the prestigious and the popular, depending on the user, slipping between low, middle, and highbrow, a proto-formation of the conceptual terrain that informed pop art and its siblings of the 1960s.[24] While New York intellectuals such as Dwight MacDonald held them in disdain, for the general populace they signified sophisticated culture. Studios and independent producers were thus able to take advantage of the novels' and plays' prestigious status to justify the presence of degeneracy (nay, perversion) on the screen. Such adaptations were produced just as Hollywood's ever-weakening Production Code finally allowed the last of such tabooed behaviors to appear on screen.[25]

During the 1940s and 1950s, literary critics routinely invoked the names of William Faulkner and Erskine Caldwell as their reference point when reviewing a current work they perceived to align with a certain type of literature set in the southeastern United States. As a result, these two authors retrospectively became positioned as the founding fathers of southern gothicism, the same-sex parents who sired the literary genre. Ironically, these two resolutely heterosexual men can be viewed as propagating a school of writing dominated by predominantly childless women—most of whom were also unmarried—and gay men. It is fitting that the joint fruit of their literary loins is associated thematically not only with degeneracy, which will be discussed shortly, but also with individuals considered degenerate at the time: women who refuse to bear children and men who have sex with other men. This is a lineage based on discourse, not on interpersonal relationships or mentoring, for rarely did Faulkner or Caldwell nurture the writers whom reviewers identified as their progeny. Whether their distance from these younger writers was due to misogyny and/or homophobia is something that can only be speculated about. This distance, however, stands in stark contrast to the deep friendships that developed among writers who emerged in their shadow. Although these writers could be catty toward one another, they typically publicly supported each other, forming a number of tight childless women/gay men pairs such as Carson McCullers and Tennessee Williams, Harper Lee and Truman Capote, and Eudora Welty and Hubert Creekmore. In other words, while the media promoted a discourse of hierarchical artistic reproduction, albeit one of same-sex parentage, in practice the lines were horizontal. So southern gothic is a queer genre not because of the perverse parentage attributed to it by reviewers but because, as an artistic endeavor practiced predominantly by childless women and gay men, its creative context enabled new forms of queer sociability. Although the discursive formation of the genre produced through the practice of book, stage, and film reviewing in the press on the surface appears to be queer because it positions Faulkner and Caldwell as siring the genre, it assumes the social relations reproducing the genre are heteronormative, occurring in a vertical pattern of descent from one generation to the next. In contrast, the social practice of many authors reproduced the genre in a horizontal fashion. It is this social practice of the writers, not the discursive one of the reviewers, that makes the genre queer.

When southern gothic solidified as a popular film genre in the aftermath of *Baby Doll*, film critics attributed its parentage not to William Faulkner and Erskine Caldwell, as literary critics had done before them, but rather to Faulkner and Tennessee Williams. For example, when reviewing *The Fugitive Kind* for the *Saturday Review* in 1960, Hollis Alpert expressed the frustration many reviewers experienced in the wake of the explosion of such films (although Alpert displaces it onto an implied movie audience): "The deep South, as any faithful movie-goer knows, has had enough time already in other Tennessee Williams movies and in reconstruction of Faulkner novels, but it has never been painted so dreary as this."[26] Along similar lines, a reviewer claimed that same year that *Desire in the Dust* might "remind one of Tennessee Williams or William Faulkner but it is a mere superficial resemblance."[27]

The artistic reputations of these three authors during the 1950s contributed to this shift. In the 1930s, Erskine Caldwell was widely known, commercially profitable, and critically praised, while William Faulkner was neither a household name nor financially solid and considered a secondary writer. During that decade, one book reviewer claimed that since Faulkner "has abandoned his more shocking themes, he is compelled to distinguish himself from the generality of authors by employing one of the most complex, unreadable and uncommunicative prose styles ever."[28] The very thing for which he would be praised a decade later initially brought condemnation. During the 1940s, their commercial and literary reputations reversed. Caldwell became perceived as a commercial hack, with one critic lamenting in 1950 that he "used to be a serious, talented writer."[29] Some scholars attribute the 1946 publication of *The Portable Faulkner* as the initiator of this reevaluation of Faulkner as an original modernist, which solidified with the award of the 1949 Nobel Prize for Literature and with Pulitzer Prizes for fiction in 1955 and, posthumously, in 1963. In a 1964 interview Malcolm Cowley, the editor of *The Portable Faulkner*, reminisced: "There were a great many novelists and critics who deeply appreciated Faulkner, but the public at large had been told that he was only a master of southern gothic horrors."[30] Paralleling Erskine Caldwell's toppling and William Faulkner's elevation, Tennessee Williams emerged as an acclaimed dramatist, popular with critics and audiences alike, receiving numerous New York Drama Critics' Circle Awards, and in the late 1950s his pending decline had yet to register on the radar of popular perception, although theater critics were beginning to speculate whether Williams was capable of creating another major work. While in literary circles Caldwell and Faulkner represented two different stylistic approaches within the genre—humorous horror versus tortured (gothick) sentences, sociological inflection versus modernist tendencies—from the perspective of film, Faulkner and Williams represented the two sources of adaptable material, novels and plays. And this intertwining of book and stage authors and/or works became common in film reviews after the success of *Baby Doll* in 1956. Unlike book and play reviewers, who prior to the 1970s kept their comparisons within their respective fields, movie reviewers did not, thereby playing a significant role in unmooring southern gothic from medium specificity.

Besides citing other writers considered similar, critics writing for the cultured classes also conjured southern gothic through coded descriptors such as "grotesque" and "degeneracy," two words commonly used to describe the supposedly abnormal characters in these works and the environment in which they lived. The use of such descriptors was a safe means to invoke genre without having to openly acknowledge its existence, given genre's association at the time with popular culture and entertainment rather than art. Although reviewers routinely framed the materializing genre as prioritizing mood over narrative, some recurring plot elements became closely associated with the genre. When Calder Willingham's southern gothic satire *Eternal Fire* was published in 1963—when film critics, if not audiences, had tired of the genre just as literary critics had in the late 1940s—the basic conventions of the genre had become such a part of American popular culture that his parody was easily understood by a wide audience. Book reviewers routinely listed these plot and character conventions. For example, the *Atlantic* observed that "Mr. Willingham draws out nearly all the stops in Southern Gothic fiction: lots of lurid sex, incest, blackmail, a rigged trial, a prostitute mother, a feebleminded dwarf, and several killings," while the *Commonweal* reviewer noted: "By the time [Willingham] has exhausted his imagination we have been hauled the length of the gamut: alcoholism, lechery, satyriasis, voyeurism, idiocy, homosexuality, sadism, masochism, lunacy, nymphomania, incest—a parody, and catalogue in short, of the netherside of Southern Gothic."[31] To the above lists can be added miscegenation, suicide, financial bankruptcy, racial lynching, self-mutilation, rape, and insanity. What connects these character traits and story components to the genre is not the particular elements themselves but rather a common characteristic they share, that of decline, in other words degeneracy, for degeneracy is not a static state but an active process of downward spiral.

Although culture reviewers had previously attributed greater weight neither to "degeneracy" nor to "the grotesque," during the 1960s, the use of the former term gradually receded as the latter became institutionalized through the academy as the appropriate conceptual framework for approaching artists associated with southern gothic. Some scholars even followed Flannery O'Connor's personal preference and referred to the genre as "southern grotesque" rather than the more common "southern gothic."[32] Although the concepts of the grotesque and degeneracy are similar, they are not identical. As highlighted by the definitions in the *Oxford English Dictionary*, "grotesque" deals with distortion or fantastical combinations, while "degeneracy" refers to a decline from a higher state. While the grotesque aligns with incongruence, degeneracy evokes degradation. So unlike the static state implied by the grotesque's juxtaposition, degeneracy refers to an active process of deterioration.[33] While historically the press's culture critics—through whom I am arguing the genre was formed and entered into public discourse—associated the genre with both degeneracy and the grotesque, one of the ramifications of the academicization of criticism was the reduction of southern gothic to the equivalent of the grotesque. After all, most culture critics are part of the educated professional cultured class.

As audiences tired of the genre during the 1960s, preferring more youth-oriented films such as *The Graduate* and *Bonnie and Clyde*, both from 1967, film critics became freer with the explicit label "southern gothic," its usage increasing steadily as the decade proceeded. A contributor to this freedom could be that some of these 1960s films were received as camp. Susan Sontag's 1964 *Partisan Review* article "Notes on 'Camp'" introduced camp into the lexicon.[34] Released the year after the article's publication, *Hush . . . Hush, Sweet Charlotte* was one of the films received by some critics through this lens. *Newsweek*'s reviewer combined it with auteurism, contending that director Robert Aldrich "wallows in Gothicism and plays for camp," while the *New Republic*'s Stanley Kauffmann appealed to the audience, declaring, "To enjoy this flaccid grotesque, one needs intense devotion to that lately hailed sensibility, 'camp.'"[35] By the early 1970s, southern gothic fell off the radar as a classificatory schema for films, although a number of movies appeared during the 1970s that easily could have been received through its lens, in particular *Deliverance* in 1972 and *Mandingo* in 1975. Except for the isolated case of John Huston's 1979 film adaptation of Flannery O'Connor's 1952 novel *Wise Blood*, use of the schematic remained dormant among film critics until the late 1980s and 1990s, when it reappeared with a bang, the genre that had emerged during the classical Hollywood period now reconfigured as a New Hollywood genre. The reception of *Wise Blood* stands as a testament both to the widespread embrace of the label "southern gothic" and to the abandonment of the concept of degeneracy.[36] Of the close to three dozen film reviews I found, few critics failed to mention "grotesque" or "gothic" either in reference to the novel or the film, while none referred to "degeneracy" or to any of its other signifiers such as "decadence" and "decay." The earlier common association of southern gothic with degeneracy had been eliminated, leaving only the grotesque as the paradigmatic descriptive characteristic. *Wise Blood*, along with Beth Henley's play *Crimes of the Heart*, which was popular at the same time as the film's circulation, signifies the normalization of the label "southern gothic" and the acceptance among journalism's culture critics of the academic view. The privileging of the grotesque over degeneracy, in effect, de-queered the genre.

"Degeneracy" historically referred not only to the individual but also to the group, encompassing fields ranging from biology and medicine through the social sciences to politics and theology and of course the arts. As a concept, degeneracy found a home both in the natural sciences and in the humanities. Although theories of degeneracy are thought to have emerged in the wake of Darwinism as its dark inverse—the deterioration of biological/social organisms rather than their advancement—and are closely associated with the apocalyptic tenor of the nineteenth-century fin de siècle, their influence on American society continued into the mid-twentieth century. In the pre–World War II era with the rise of the eugenics movement, to be labeled a degenerate was a serious matter; it could have disastrous results such as institutionalization and/or sterilization. Prior to such "biologizing of social theory," degenerate inflections appeared in the political theory of such writers as John Stuart Mill and Thomas Jefferson.[37] So degeneracy can occur not only in individuals and social groups but in the nation itself.

Today it has become common among new Southern Studies scholars to frame the region as the nation's internal—and, typically, abject—other. And on a certain level the approach presented here represents a similar move. But I believe there is one key difference: the concern with movement is not about separation per se—the expelling, the rejecting—but rather about the descending.[38] So unlike the grotesque, degeneracy is similar to perversion, both being about a downward movement from the normal, a decline rather than an enhancement. According to Jonathan Dollimore, the perverse is perceived as "utterly alien to what it threatens, and yet, mysteriously inherent within it" and, if this paradox is not displaced, repressed, or disavowed, it "reveals the potential for transformations inherent in all social orders as a consequence of their own structure and developmental logic." In other words, the perverse is an "inherent aspect *of* the dominant or the conventional rather than what it would exclude or define itself against."[39] Perversion, like degeneracy, has historical associations with politics as well as sexology. An assumption routinely accompanies southern regionalism that it is a perversion of the national ideal because of its linkage to the Confederacy's failed attempt at nationhood. This configuration of the American South emerges from a regime of the normal that discursively positions it as perverse, that is, queer. The region's association with deviancy allows it to function as a fissure within the American national fabric that "reveals the potential for transformations inherent in all social orders as a consequence of their own structure and developmental logic."[40] Dollimore's conceptualization of perversion, however, proceeds further than just revealing instabilities in the norm, for the proximity of the perverse to the dominant normal "enables a tracking-back of the 'other' into the 'same,'" a process he calls "transgressive reinscription," a return of the displaced that intensifies the "internal instabilities within repressive norms," thereby "turning them against the norms."[41] Because the region emerges from within the nation, it cannot be written off as foreign except through an act of repression, displacement, or disavowal on the part of the nation in order to thwart transgressive reinscription. While this may be the case with many discursive configurations of the American South, its manifestation as southern gothic functions as a cultural site for just such a return.

Southern gothic is a generic site that allows the nation to discuss its many ills under the guise of a regional problem, thereby providing the emotional distance necessary to engage constructively with issues considered by American society as deviations from the (supposed) normal, that is, controversial matters involving decline. Although this generic site is about regional deterioration, its circulation through American society results, paradoxically, in the production of discourses about prohibited matters, enabling a social negotiation with them. In contrast to America's ascension captured by the western in the form of dime-store novels or Hollywood movies, southern gothic provides a site for public negotiation with acts of descension, be they physical, mental, sexual, financial, social, racial, moral, or spiritual. In other words, while the western deals with—to borrow a word from the title of one of Richard Slotkin's famous books—regeneration, southern gothic focuses on degeneration.[42] The genre speaks not about the perversion itself, the region, but what the perversion derives from, the nation. Similarly, as argued on behalf of the gothic in general, southern gothic is not fettered sociopolitically to either a progressive or regressive cause; it can be either. When transgressive reinscription blocks repression or disavowal of the paradoxical perverse, southern gothic functions as a critique of the nation. Fred Botting holds that the primary conventions of gothic are excess and transgression, arguing: "Gothic excesses transgressed the proper limits of aesthetic as well as social order in the overflow of emotions that undermined boundaries of life and fiction, fantasy and reality. . . . The terrors and horrors of transgression in Gothic writing become a powerful means to reassert the values of society, virtue and propriety: transgression, by crossing the social and aesthetic limits, serves to reinforce or underline their value and necessity, restoring or defining limits."[43] While the concept of degeneracy can be viewed as transgressing the normal and is, therefore, a type of excess, it does so only in the direction of decline. A superman transgresses the normal too, but it is a different kind of excess. Southern gothic is ultimately not about exceeding the normal but perverting it. As a result, unlike Botting, who holds that the gothic reinforces and restores social limits, I hold that southern gothic routinely fails to contain the havoc it wreaks, especially in terms of spectator affect. Of course, many gothic studies scholars consider southern gothic not *really* to be gothic and ignore it.

As J. Edward Chamberlin and Sander L. Gilman highlight, rather than a movement "toward a more advanced state," degeneration is a movement "toward death."[44] Because degeneracy (that is, perversion) moves toward death, it is an antisocial concept similar to queerness in that it too is a threat to the social because it does not reproduce the social in a familiar, much less familial, form. It is an imperfect reproduction—indeed a perversion—that therefore must be expelled if the purity of the social order is to be maintained. During the past decade, the antisocial strain of queer theory has come under critical scrutiny.[45] Part of the debate centers around the role of the future: does queerness produce no future (that is, death) or new forms of sociability? As Tim Dean reminds us, "the antisocial thesis proper begins with neither [Lee] Edelman nor [Leo] Bersani but rather with Guy Hocquenghem . . . [for whom] the shattering of the civilized ego betokens not the end of sociality but rather its inception."[46] While my purpose is not to engage this debate, degeneracy as the conceptual framework for approaching southern gothic is a queer antisocial one, but not one inherently antagonistic to the articulation of new forms of sociability because of its focus on the active process of decline, not the static condition of death. Where Guy Hocquenghem differentiates between horizontal homosexual production and hierarchical heterosexual reproduction, my concern is with the intersection of these two modes of sociality.[47] Degeneracy does not produce itself but rather is a consequence of the reproductive process of the normal. In other words, degeneracy, the abnormal, is a normal component of normal reproduction, but society has chosen to disavow its origin. As the normal reproduces itself, sometimes the act of repetition fails to duplicate exactly, resulting in a so-called degraded version. Because the normal and the abnormal are parts of the same reproductive system, the distinction between them derives from where the line to separate them has been drawn within society. Degeneracy is that element of the normal that has been expelled and labeled abominable to ensure that it does not defile the body politic. This terrain is what southern gothic as a genre formation negotiates and why its genre-ship is queer. And southern gothic film is a site where this negotiation materializes in narrative emplotment and, on occasion, in audiovisual aesthetics.[48]

NOTES

1. "Southern Gothic: This Literary Genre Celebrates Our Hauntingly Beautiful and Mysterious Region," *Southern Living* 46.10 (October 2011): 16.

2. Amy J. Elias, "Postmodern Southern Vacation: Vacation Advertising, Globalization, and Southern Regionalism," *South to a New Place: Region, Literature, Culture*, ed. Suzanne W. Jones and Sharon Monteith (Baton Rouge: Louisiana State University Press, 2002), 253–82, at 261. In addition to Elias's chapter, for more on *Southern Living* see Tracy Lauder, "The *Southern Living* Solution: How the *Progressive Farmer* Launched a Magazine and a Legacy," *Alabama Review* 60.3 (2007): 186–221, and Diane Roberts, "Living Southern in *Southern Living*," *Dixie Debates: Perspectives on Southern Culture*, ed. Richard H. King and Helen Taylor (New York: New York University Press, 1996), 85–98.

3. Margie Burns, "A Good Rose Is Hard to Find: Southern Gothic as Signs of Social Dislocation in Faulkner and O'Connor," *Image and Ideology in Modern/Postmodern Discourse*, ed. David B. Downing and Susan Bazargan (Albany: State University of New York Press, 1991), 105–23, at 107. Two such books within film studies are R. Barton Palmer and William Robert Bray, *Hollywood's Tennessee: The Williams Films and Postwar America* (Austin: University of Texas Press, 2009), and Tison Pugh, *Truman Capote: A Literary Life at the Movies* (Athens: University of Georgia Press, 2014).

4. See Elizabeth Freeman, *Time Binds: Queer Temporalities, Queer Histories* (Durham, N.C.: Duke University Press, 2010).

5. David M. Halperin, *Saint Foucault: Towards a Gay Hagiography* (New York: Oxford University Press, 1995), 62.

6. Michael Warner, introduction to *Fear of a Queer Planet: Queer Politics and Social Theory*, ed. Michael Warner (Minneapolis: University of Minnesota Press, 1993), xiii.

7. Warner, introduction, xiii, xxvi, xxvii.

8. Elizabeth Hardwick, "The Decline of Book Reviewing," *Harper's* 219.4 (October 1959): 143.

9. See Michel Foucault, "What Is an Author?" *The Foucault Reader*, ed. Paul Rabinow (New York: Pantheon, 1984), 101–20.

10. See Gilles Deleuze and Félix Guattari, *A Thousand Plateaus: Capitalism and Schizophrenia*, trans. Brian Massumi (Minneapolis: University of Minnesota Press, 1987), 88–91, 503–5.

11. The scholarship on film noir is expansive and includes such works as J. P. Telotte, *Voices in the Dark: The Narrative Patterns of Film Noir* (Urbana: University of Illinois Press, 1989); R. Barton Palmer, *Hollywood's Dark Cinema: The American Film Noir* (New York: Twayne, 1994); E. Ann Kaplan, ed., *Women in Film Noir*, rev. ed. (London: British Film Institute, 1998); Kelly Oliver and Benigno Trigo, *Noir Anxiety* (Minneapolis: University of Minnesota Press, 2003); and James Naremore, *More Than Night: Film Noir in Its Contexts*, 2nd ed. (Berkeley: University of California Press, 2008).

12. Ellen Glasgow, "Heroes and Monsters," *Saturday Review of Literature* 4 May 1935: 3–4, at 3.

13. Of the films released between 1940 and 1970 that were aligned with southern gothic, only one was not based on a previously published work or performed play. That film, *Hush . . . Hush, Sweet Charlotte* (dir. Robert Aldrich, 1964), was based on an unpublished short story.

14. Robert Hatch, "Old Hit, New Venture," review of *A Streetcar Named Desire*, dir. Elia Kazan, *New Republic* 8 October 1951: 21.

15. Review of *Reflections in a Golden Eye*, by Carson McCullers, *Time* 17 February 1941: 96.

16. Archer Winston, "*The Little Foxes* Opens at Radio City Music Hall," unidentified newspaper review, Performing Arts clipping file "*The Little Foxes* (Film)," New York Public Library.

17. Edward D. C. Campbell Jr., *The Celluloid South: Hollywood and the Southern Myth* (Knoxville: University of Tennessee Press, 1981), 14; Ed Guerrero, *Framing Blackness: The African American Image in Film* (Philadelphia: Temple University Press, 1993), 10.

18. Erskine Caldwell's novel *Tobacco Road*, published in 1932, was adapted for the stage in 1933 and for the screen in 1941. Carson McCullers's 1946 novel *The Member of the Wedding* was adapted for the stage in 1950 and for the screen in 1952.

19. Review of *Baby Doll*, dir. Elia Kazan, *Variety* 5 December 1956: 6.

20. "Incessant Prize-Winners," *Vogue* 15 April 1951: 84.

21. See Tino Balio, *The Foreign Film Renaissance on American Screens, 1946–1973* (Madison: University of Wisconsin Press, 2010).

22. Bosley Crowther, "Screen: Streetcar on Tobacco Road; Williams-Kazan 'Baby Doll' Is at Victoria," review of *Baby Doll*, dir. Elia Kazan, *New York Times* 19 December 1956: 40.

23. Bosley Crowther, "Screen: Down South; 'Sound and the Fury' Opens at Paramount," review of *The Sound and the Fury*, dir. Martin Ritt, *New York Times* 28 March 1959: 11. See Crowther, "Southern Accent: Films of Family Fights Set in the South," *New York Times* 21 September 1958: II-1, and "Old Familiar Faces and Farces: New Films Manifest the Difficulty of Making Them Look New," *New York Times* 11 August 1963: II-1.

24. Many gothic studies scholars hold that traversing high and low culture is a common characteristic of the gothic.

25. On film censorship during the classical Hollywood period, see Francis G. Couvares, ed., *Movie Censorship and American Culture* (Washington, D.C.: Smithsonian Institution Press, 1996); Matthew Bernstein, ed., *Controlling Hollywood: Censorship and Regulation in the Studio Era* (New Brunswick, N.J.: Rutgers University Press, 1999); Thomas Doherty, *Hollywood's Censor: Joseph I. Breen and the Production Code Administration* (New York: Columbia University Press, 2007), and various articles on the topic by Richard Maltby.

26. Hollis Alpert, "Orpheus Descended," review of *The Fugitive Kind*, dir. Sidney Lumet, *Saturday Review* 23 April 1960: 28.

27. Review of *Desire in the Dust*, dir. William F. Claxton, *New York Herald Tribune* 12 October 1960.

28. Harold Strauss, "Mr. Faulkner Is Ambushed in Words," review of *Absalom, Absalom!*, by William Faulkner, *New York Times Book Review* 1 November 1936: 7.

29. Chandler Brossard, "Another Caldwell," review of *Episode in Palmetto*, by Erskine Caldwell, *New York Times Book Review* 17 September 1950: 28. When Caldwell's *God's Little Acre* appeared on the screen in 1958, Stanley Kauffmann in the *New Republic* reminded his readers of this truism common among the cultured classes to which he and his readers belonged: "we have come to regard him as the source of a staple product rather than a literary creator"; see "God's Belittled Acre," review of *God's Little Acre*, dir. Anthony Mann, *New Republic* 30 June 1958: 21.

30. L. L. Graelle, "An Interview with Malcolm Cowley (1964)," *Conversations with Malcolm Cowley*, ed. Thomas Daniel Young (Jackson: University Press of Mississippi, 1986), 42–52, at 44.

31. William Barrett, "Passions Hot and Cooled," review of *Eternal Fire*, by Calder Willingham, *Atlantic* 211.2 (February 1963): 132; Saul Maloff, "Passing Sparks," review of *Eternal Fire*, *Commonweal* 77.19 (1 February 1963): 497.

32. See Flannery O'Connor, *The Habit of Being: Letters*, ed. Sally Fitzgerald (New York: Farrar, Straus & Giroux, 1979), 501.

33. Although the creation of an incongruent juxtaposition or distortion results from a process, the concept of the grotesque typically focuses on the incongruent juxtaposition or distortion itself rather than that process. In contrast, degeneracy is intrinsically about the process—moving from a higher state to a lower one. While distortion entails a twisting of the normal, it is more like that of a fun-house mirror, without the negative value judgment always associated with the decline from the normal innate to degeneracy.

34. Susan Sontag, "Notes on 'Camp,'" *Partisan Review* 31 (Fall 1964): 515–31. See as well Tison Pugh's essay in this volume on the camp valence of Williams's *Suddenly, Last Summer*.

35. "Swamp Pie," review of *Hush . . . Hush, Sweet Charlotte*, dir. Robert Aldrich, *Newsweek* 15 March 1965: 98; Stanley Kauffmann, review of *Hush . . . Hush, Sweet Charlotte*, *New Republic* 20 March 1965: 27.

36. *Wise Blood* was a quirky low-budget film in the spirit of the then-emerging independent film scene that eventually became closely associated with the Sundance Film Festival. The film was directed, ironically, by a senior statesman from the classical Hollywood era. A significant bifurcation occurred in the genre when it reappeared during the late 1980s in the New Hollywood era. While dramas continued to be produced as in the classical Hollywood period, an explicitly comedic variation appeared that previously did not exist, although historically many culture critics in the press held that southern gothic had a humorous underpinning to its drama—albeit typically a dark one—that could easily go unnoticed by the undiscerning textual user. The introduction of this explicitly comedic version within film can be traced back to trends in the 1970s New York theater scene that culminated in Beth Henley's play *Crimes of the Heart*, which became wildly popular in the early 1980s.

37. David Trotter, *The English Novel in History, 1895–1920* (New York: Routledge, 1993), 114.

38. Julia Kristeva, in *Powers of Horror: An Essay in Abjection*, trans. Leon S. Roudiez (1980; New York: Columbia University Press, 1982), holds that the "abject is related to perversion" (15), but she defines abjection with terms such as "separate," "exclusion," "breaking away," "rejecting," and "repelling" (13, 17). While her classic definition of abjection includes the concept of movement, it does not specify a particular direction of that movement other than away from. While the concepts of degeneracy, abjection, and the grotesque intersect in many ways—for example, they all deal with the normal, so therefore are related—my concern is with how degeneracy, notwithstanding these points of commonality, differs from abjection and the grotesque.

39. Jonathan Dollimore, *Sexual Dissidence: Augustine to Wilde, Freud to Foucault* (New York: Oxford University Press, 1991), 121, 125.

40. Dollimore, *Sexual Dissidence*, 125.

41. Dollimore, *Sexual Dissidence*, 33.

42. See Richard Slotkin, *Regeneration through Violence: The Mythology of the American Frontier, 1600–1860* (Middletown, Conn.: Wesleyan University Press, 1973).

43. Fred Botting, *Gothic* (New York: Routledge, 1996), 4, 7.

44. J. Edward Chamberlin and Sander L. Gilman, "Degeneration: An Introduction," *Degeneration: The Dark Side of Progress*, ed. Chamberlin and Gilman (New York: Columbia University Press, 1985), ix–xiv, at xiii.

45. Two key texts in the antisocial debate are Lee Edelman, *No Future: Queer Theory and the Death Drive* (Durham, N.C.: Duke University Press, 2004), and José Esteban Muñoz, *Cruising Utopia: The Then and There of Queer Futurity* (New York: New York University Press, 2009). Also see Robert L. Caserio, Lee Edelman, Jack [Judith]

Halberstam, José Esteban Muñoz, and Tim Dean, "Forum: The Antisocial Thesis in Queer Theory," *PMLA* 121.3 (2006): 819–28.

46. Tim Dean, "The Antisocial Homosexual," *PMLA* 121.3 (2006): 826–28, at 827.

47. See Guy Hocquenghem, *Homosexual Desire*, trans. Daniella Dangoor (1976; Durham, N.C.: Duke University Press, 1993), 109.

48. While this article does not address the aesthetics of southern gothic, for a discussion of them in relationship to the concept of degeneracy, see R. Bruce Brasell, "Southern Gothic and Film Noir: The Commingling of Genre and Cinematic Stylistics," *Detecting the South*, eds. Deborah E. Barker and Theresa Starkey (Baton Rouge: Louisiana State University Press, forthcoming).

Chapter 4 ▸ Revolting Queers: The Southern Gothic in Queer Horror Film and Television

DARREN ELLIOTT-SMITH

> A revolution of southern queers recruits kindred spirits to subvert gender, create intersections, celebrate assorted sexual identities, insist on all kinds of diversity, and critique the violence of poverty and injustice.
>
> —PIPPA HOLLOWAY

Pippa Holloway's "Manifesto for a Queer South Politics" encourages southern queers to rise up, or to revolt, in celebration of their difference. She continues that it is via this embrace of queer sexual miscellany, alongside longstanding cultural associations of deviance, abnormality, and subversion, that queer subjects from the South can highlight the inequality, prejudice, and violent acts meted out to generations of queer individuals throughout U.S. history. These anxieties and celebrations are often metaphorically played out in the form of southern gothic texts in literature, theater, film, and television. Here the metaphorical values of the gothic horror offer a symbolic space both for queers who revolt and for *revolting* queers. By queering the traditionally conservative formula of certain horror film subgenres (here slasher horror and survival/backwoods rural horror), and in rendering explicit the queerness already inherent in the figures of the vampire and the zombie, queer creators and audiences can engage in a process of telling familiar stories anew from a contemporary perspective that allows for a critique of the past and a projection of current anxieties felt by LGBTQ+ communities in the twenty-first century. More specifically, some of the most potent critical voices can arguably be found in queer-authored depictions of sexual Otherness in recent southern gothic–inspired queer horror film and television.

Southern gothic traditions often depict a contemporary world that is constituted and textured by the past and yet is also agitated by present turmoil. There is a sense that the southern gothic is frenetically layered with ghosts and past cultural traumas that have never truly been laid to rest. Christopher Lloyd paints the contemporary South as a world where "cultural memories . . . are . . . engaged within gothic form and transformed in the process; dark traumas from the region's past are lodged in and substantiate culture."[1] Eric Savoy posits that "the gothic registers a trauma in the strategies of representation as it brings forward a traumatic history toward which it gestures but can never finally refer."[2] The South can be considered an "oppositional" space, one that is often thought to be out of time, disjointed against the rest of the United States. This notion of the haunting of the present by the past rings true in many queer horror texts that represent, as David Punter and Glennis Byron put it, a "gothicized version of the American South" with a notable portrayal of "madness, decay, and despair, and the continuing pressures of the past on the present, particularly with respect to the lost ideals of a dispossessed southern aristocracy and to the continuance of racial hostilities."[3] Teresa Goddu argues that the region "has often been depicted in gothic terms" because it is a "benighted landscape, heavy with history and haunted by the ghosts of slavery."[4]

In relation to the queer potential present in the southern gothic, Lloyd further suggests that "the South has long been depicted as the nation's other, an aberrant space within America's borders."[5] In depicting Othered spaces, moving-image representations of the South in horror clearly connect with Robin Wood's concept of the Other in his seminal article "Introduction to the American Horror Film," in which he offers a reading of the monstrous metaphors that represent cultural fears and anxieties, many of which center on differences of gender, class, race, and sexuality.[6] The Other serves not only to symbolize that which either the individual or the dominant culture designates as different, but it also represents "that which is repressed (but never destroyed) in the self" and is then "projected outwards in order to be hated or destroyed."[7] Wood's figure of the queer monstrous Other here can also, by extension, be seen to represent the queer spaces and individuals of the South. Goddu's consideration of the South as an oppositional, ghettoized space therefore offers it as a means through which the "normative United States" can cleanse itself of any abject relations: "The South's gothic excesses and social transgressions [have] served as the nation's safety valve: as the repository for everything the nation is not, the South purges contrary impulses."[8]

Horror scholars such as Robin Wood, Harry Benshoff, Ellis Hanson, and Jack Halberstam have written extensively on depictions of the symbolic Other in the horror genre as representative of sexual difference (typically, homosexuality or bisexuality).[9] What is perhaps most notable about their considerations of the queer Other in the horror genre is that both the monster and the homosexual are permanent residents of shadowy spaces. To elucidate, these "closeted" queer horror films' treatment of the sexual Other often results in representations of queerness that remain metaphorical. Conversely, in my recent work I provide further insight into contemporary queer horror film and television texts in which the monstrous metaphor of queerness is rendered explicit by queer-identified directors and producers and by narratives and characters that are "out" in their presentation of sexual difference.[10] I wish to continue along such a line of analysis in this chapter's consideration of southern-oriented queer horror by stating that when monstrousness as a metaphor for the threat that homosexuality poses to heteronormativity ceases to be coded and instead becomes open, it then operates to turn the focus of fear upon itself, its own communities and subcultures. It projects contemporary anxieties *within* queer subcultures.

Michael Bibler writes that for scholars working in Southern Studies, the possibilities of operating via a queer methodology are often overwhelming. Taking a queer approach allows for an understanding of "the complex deployments of gender, desire, and eroticism both prior to the invention of homosexuality as a category and in relation to the region's culturally diverse topographies, where the labels 'lesbian' and 'gay' may seem foreign or anachronistic, including rural and Appalachian spaces as well as Southern African American, ethnic, Native, and poor white communities."[11] Bibler also warns against an idealistic, umbrella-style categorization whereby differences within queer communities can be "drained" and "anything Gothic can be interpreted as Queer," as would any analysis of southern regionalism that suggests it "as an aberration of, or deviation from, national normativity." Instead Bibler recommends that any attempt to "queer the region" should take into consideration "historical differences" and should appreciate the ways that "non-normative expressions of gender and desire" are negotiated with "concepts of nation and . . . race and class." Bibler's point that is perhaps most relevant for this chapter's analysis of southern-oriented queer horror is that "queering the region is more a matter of taking a particular methodological approach to Southern literature and culture than of building . . . a ready archive of texts."[12] To that end, as I have argued in my previous work, the central concern of queer horror film and television is a focus on supposed aberrations of eroticism, sexuality, and gender. These in turn work to expose and highlight the hypocrisies and inconsistencies within seemingly normative power structures, and draw attention to the failure to maintain imaginary boundaries and borders that demarcate "normalcy" from "deviancy." Southern queer horror therefore also reveals certain cultural shifts and certain queer subjectivities that will not fit comfortably into what Bibler calls "narratives of region."

The recent edited collection *Undead Souths: The Gothic and Beyond in Southern Literature and Culture* similarly seeks, as its central project, to "resist and dismantle inherited master narratives about the region," looking instead to "pose in good postmodern fashion, the possibility of multiple micro-narratives splintering off from the region's boundary-bound master narrative of loss, death, and mourning [by] venturing into the Caribbean, Native American Studies, critical race theory, and redefinitions of horror, haunting, and affect in the aftermath of trauma."[13] Christopher Lloyd's latest study of the U.S. South in literature and culture extends this project via a consideration of the ways in which the histories of racial violence are manifest in representations of the body, arguing that "again and again, southern culture returns to the body; it is obsessed with corporeality's vicissitudes."[14] Jay Watson also notes that cultural representations of the South "are abundantly peopled with remarkable bodies: physically excessive, or deficient bodies; sexually contradictory bodies; moving, morphing, volatile bodies; diseased, disabled or disfigured bodies; disappeared or spectral bodies; commodified bodies; bodies out of place; disciplined and punished bodies; labouring bodies; aestheticized, ethereal or otherwise exemplary bodies."[15]

This chapter's analysis of southern queer horror also seeks to demonstrate the ways in which the southern queer body is displayed as transgressive, borderless, disorganizing, de-territorializing, and shown to embrace a fluid state of "becoming." It will do so first by analyzing blurred sexual and gendered identities and bodies/subjectivities that are not fixed in space or time in Lucio Fulci's surreal Louisiana-set zombie horror *The Beyond* (1981), in the spectral southern hospitality of the cannibal townsfolk of Pleasant Valley in Tim Sullivan's "gaysploitation" horror sequel *2001 Maniacs* (2005), and in Alan Ball's nostalgic-queer vampires in the HBO series *True Blood* (2008–14). Second, I will turn my attention to the importance of fluidly performative subjectivities (gendered, racial, and sexual) as seen in the postmodern parody present in new queer horror film and television that deconstructs "postsouthern" identities. This postmodern play is where Bibler suggests that "writers play with claims of truth and authenticity by self-reflexively referencing the images, tropes, signs and symbols of southern culture from earlier works."[16] This can be seen most clearly in the textual reflexivity that exists in the simultaneous gender and genre play in Ball's *True Blood* and more recently in Alan Rowe Kelly's *A Far Cry from Home* (2013), a backwoods horror pastiche that queers the subgenre to posit a critique of oppressive right-wing Christian homophobia. The chapter will conclude by considering the literalization of the fluid queer body using Patricia MacCormack's concept of the "squishy" body, Halberstam's notion of queer "bodies that splatter," or, in more Deleuzian terms, the "body without organs." This is represented in the dilapidating, decomposing, rotten, and melting bodies of the zombies and victims from *The Beyond*; in the soft, splattering, pliant, and queered flesh of Sullivan's *Maniacs* sequels; and in the liquefying, gloopy corpses of *True Blood*'s vampires and vampire queers.

Pleasant Valley Revisited: Queer Maniacs and the Return of the Queer Repressed

Lucio Fulci's cult supernatural zombie film *The Beyond* is perhaps an unlikely choice to pave the way for a consideration of southern-gothic-inspired queer horror narratives. While not explicitly queer in its treatment of sexual identities, *The Beyond*'s queer potency lies in its collapse of temporal and spatial boundaries, in its opening representation of a historical lynch mob, and in its depictions of the messily corporeal zombie body as queer. Fulci's film opens in Louisiana, 1927, in a sepia-tinted sequence. We are introduced to a torch-bearing posse rowing a makeshift raft laden with rifles and shackles across a lake toward a careworn hotel isolated in a shroud of mist. One of the hotel's residents, the artist Schweik (Antoine Saint-John), is putting the final touches on a painting of an unclear, otherworldly landscape strewn with gray blobs that at a glance appear as corpses. Bursting in on Schweik, who is clearly depicted as a nonnormative, marginalized, queer figure persecuted for his deviancy in practicing the "dark arts," the mob accuses him of witchcraft. Without hesitation, they beat and chain Schweik and take him to the hotel's cellar, where they crucify him, pour acid over his head, and watch him in the throes of agony as his face dissolves. This opening sequence reveals that, as is written in the Book of Eibon (a fictional book of the occult that contains ancient prophecies), the hotel is one of the seven sacred gateways to hell. Upon this revelation, Schweik is walled up alive in the cellar by the baying crowd. The importance of this sequence of mob rule does not lie simply in the beating and torture of Schweik, which is arguably evocative of a queer-phobic fear of the Other, but in the film's return to Schweik's painting in its final moments. Fulci's two protagonists, Liza (Catriona MacColl) and Dr. John McCabe (David Warbeck), having endured and escaped a dreamlike, dizzying spatial journey via portals leading to various parts of Louisiana, from soft-focus, clammy swamplands to booze-infused depictions of French Colonial–style quarters, all the while being pursued by shambling zombies, finally find themselves back at the hotel, trapped in a hell-like landscape that bears an uncanny resemblance to Schweik's painting. Soon it is clear to the spectator that the painting does not depict hell—it *is* hell.

The film's disruption of temporal order is of interest to this chapter's consideration of the southern gothic aesthetics of queer horror. The film's original Italian title is *E tu vivrai nel terrore—L'aldilà*, which translates as "And you shall live in terror—The beyond" and, as Michael Grant suggests, refers to "the notion of a future that is conditional on the past—a terror beyond, beyond the grave, beyond the end and before the beginning, in which you shall live."[17] Patricia MacCormack also draws attention to *The Beyond*'s final statement inscribed on the screen in intertitles—"and you will face the sea of darkness, and all therein that may be explored"—positing that "Baroque waves in a sea replace finite territories of organised, signified corporeal social space and chronological causal time."[18] *The Beyond*'s queering of temporality and spatiality allows for the tortured, queer-coded Schweik to enact his revenge from "beyond" death and across time. The walling-up of Schweik can be read as an obviously queer signifier of the enforced closeting of the queer marginality that he represents, which refuses to be imprisoned or silenced and thus haunts the present in the form of the film's numerous decaying, reanimated corpses and its intangible supernatural forces. Schweik's queer-coded revenge operates as a "return of the repressed" and is projected into the present as a monstrous persecution of the heteronormative couple Liza and John.

The southern gothic trope in which revenants from the South's troubled past haunt the present returns as the central concept of "Godfather of Gore" Herschell Gordon Lewis's *Two Thousand Maniacs!* (1964). Lewis's film is perhaps the most infamous B-movie horror film to articulate certain clichés and stereotypes of the Deep South. Partly inspired by the Broadway musical *Brigadoon*, Lewis utilizes the same "return of the repressed" motif, shifting its fantastical Highlands setting to the South and replacing the genre conventions of the musical with those of the slasher subgenre. *Two Thousand Maniacs!* centers on a group of young Yankees traveling through the rural South who find themselves stranded in a backwoods part of Georgia called Pleasant Valley while on the way to Atlanta. They are welcomed by the townsfolk with true southern hospitality—and invited by the town's leader, Mayor Buckman (Jeffrey Allen), to take part in the upcoming centennial festivities. Slightly wary of the townsfolk's Confederate flag–waving enthusiasm, the group is charmed by the mayor's cordiality and agrees to stay. Soon it becomes clear to the spectator, and to some of the guests, that the quaint southern town of Pleasant Valley is not quite all it seems. One by one the guests are lured away to various events in the town's fair to be murdered in increasingly elaborate ways, from dismemberment to drawing-and-quartering to being rolled down a hill in a spiked barrel.

The story surrounding the town is eventually revealed. Toward the end of the Civil War, Pleasant Valley was destroyed by Union forces (ironically, only an "army" of six Yankees) and the ghosts of the town have reappeared on the hundred-year anniversary of the atrocity. Its townsfolk are bent on avenging the massacre by ritually murdering six lost Yankee travelers with northern license plates who follow a detour sign to the town. Lewis's comedy-horror Deep South clichés include southern lotharios, "white trash" hicks, and a banjo-playing bluegrass troupe called the Pleasant Valley Boys, whose recurring tune "The South's Gonna Rise Again" feeds into the concept of unburied trauma resurfacing in spectral form. William Matthew McCarter considers the regional Othering in Lewis's film as perhaps unrepresentative of racial unrest in the region from the past and indeed from the time in American history in which the film was made. He notes, "Although the film was released in the midst of America's Civil Rights movement, there is no mention of race relations in the South or of the segregated South. . . . By focusing on the 'centennial celebration' of Pleasant Valley and the destruction by Union troops, Lewis is able to make implicit claims about the South. . . . The redneck ghosts of the Confederacy's ritualistic acts of revenge represent the South's obstinate refusal to desegregate the South during the Civil Rights movement."[19] Anthony Szczesiul suggests that Lewis's film exaggerates its clichéd southern character types to comment ironically on already-present stereotyped views of southern hospitality: "The film's ironic parody of Southern hospitality highlights the performative nature of the discourse. Here the possibility of Southern hospitality is transformed into a cruel joke: the visitor becomes victim."[20] Indeed, part of the enjoyment for queer spectators in their engagement with Lewis's film arises in what Harry Benshoff states is the "immense pleasure . . . available in offering a queer reading of seemingly 'normative' horror texts,"[21] whereby the queer spectator rereads the text's intricacies via an already present historical conflation of monstrousness with homosexuality, and the part that the film's excessively performative enactment plays is key in this formulation.

Indeed, the cult appeal of *Two Thousand Maniacs!* for queer audiences is evidenced in "out" gay director Tim Sullivan's sequels *2001 Maniacs* (2005) and *2001 Maniacs: Field of Screams* (2010), both of which take Lewis's original plot and cast of characters and update them, intensifying the original's presentation of camp textuality and performativity. Sullivan utilizes the concept of ghostly reincarnations to develop more explicitly queer characters made possible by these films' productions in a more permissive postmillennial period. Both sequels follow Lewis's original twist of the long-gone town and its inhabitants supernaturally reappearing to avenge their deaths by picking off groups of young Yankee travelers on their way to spring break in Florida. In Sullivan's films, the Yankee group contains one closeted gay male character, biker Ricky (Brian Gross) in *2001 Maniacs* and Falcon (Trevor Wright) in *Field of Screams*.

Sullivan's sequels also feature a recurring queer-oriented antagonist as a somewhat sympathetic Other among the Pleasant Valley townsfolk. Mayor Buckman (played by Robert Englund and Bill Moseley, respectively) has a son, Rufus (Brendan McCarthy and Christopher McDaniel), portrayed as a closeted hillbilly who, in several scenes, is encouraged to indulge his repressed desires by the aforementioned gay male characters Ricky and Falcon, only to succumb to overwhelming guilt and shame, which brings about the outrageous deaths of the seducing males. Rufus's attempts to indulge his homosexual desires with both Ricky and Falcon are discouraged by his homophobic father, and instead such erotic desires are comically projected into sex/death murder sequences. For example, as part of the town's festivities, the now outed queer character Ricky is captured by Rufus and tied to a log-cutting bench where he is comically and fatally sodomized with a large spike by two beautiful young women—incestuous "kissing cousins" who themselves represent the town's perverse sexuality—while Rufus looks on. The slapstick impaling of Ricky (which Mayor Buckman laughingly exclaims is "Ricky on a Sticky") ends with the spike emerging out of his gaping mouth (see figure 4.1).

Such queer southern gothic narratives operate as a means for the traumatic past to inhabit the present and for seemingly distant cultural anxieties to remain firmly lodged in the subconscious of the contemporary South

FIGURE 4.1. "Ricky on a Sticky" from *2001 Maniacs* (2005).

presented on screen. Certain apprehensions remain obvious and carry across with ease from the stereotypical performativity of Lewis's film, including racial tensions around slavery and rather base depictions of abject, backward white trash. While Lewis's film does not confront alternative sexual orientations and queerness explicitly, Sullivan's films clearly do. In their inclusion of gay male characters as both monsters and victims, *2001 Maniacs* and its sequel offer a critique of outdated traditional views of homosexuality belonging to old-fashioned and uncivilized folk from the South and comically point toward the dangerous repercussions that occur in the repression of alternative sexual orientations.

Southern Queer Vampires: "We are nothing like you. . . . We are . . . immortal. Why would we seek equal rights?"

Alan Ball's *True Blood* is perhaps the most literal of the queer horror texts discussed in this chapter to utilize the southern gothic trope of the past haunting the present. In *True Blood* there is a blurring of temporality whereby multiple undead voices, subjectivities, and anxieties from the past continue to speak to the present day. The show's central monster—the immortal vampire—allows for the transcendence of temporal limitations. Queer vampires from various points in American, and indeed global, history remain "un-living" in the present, interacting with characters from the contemporary South. These include Eric (Alexander Skarsgård), a centuries-old bisexual Viking, his bisexual progeny Pamela De Beaufort (Kristin Bauer van Straten), and Eric's bisexual vampire maker, the ancient Godric (Allan Hyde), who is more than two thousand years old. Older still, the vampire king of Mississippi and would-be queer terrorist Russell Edgington (played by "out" gay actor Denis O'Hare) was "made" in the Carpathian Mountains more than three thousand years ago, in a time before the coming of Christ. The existence of queer vampires thus extends across lengthy timelines, yet the symbolic haunting of the southern past into the present is not limited to queer "return of the repressed" *metaphors*; rather, the show's explicit depiction of vampires as queer monsters is more complex than operating merely as a cipher for a wealth of sexual difference.

In "God Hates Fangs: *True Blood*, Black Queer Agency, and Appropriations of the History of Racial and Sexual Violence in the Deep South," Joanna Davis-McElligatt criticizes as "too simplistic" creator Alan Ball's robust dismissal of the vampire as a queer metaphor. Ball accuses interpretations of "vampires-as-queer, or vampire-as-black" of being instances of "weak historical interpretation." Instead, Davis-McElligatt inquires into Ball's "misapprehension" of both historical and contemporary twentieth- and twenty-first-century black and queer cultural politics to focus mainly on the black genderqueer figure of Lafayette. She concludes that as a result of the show's "appropriation of narratives of resistance by the oppressed,"[22] radically queer characters like Lafayette fail to be recognized or represented in the show as a fitting experience of the struggles "faced by black queer southern men outside the world of the television show." She suggests instead that the show is indicative of a "new postracial, colorblind, and posthomophobic temporal landscape where subjects of derision, scorn, and oppression are not now, and in the future will not be, black and queer."[23]

While I agree that, for the most part, the portrayal of Lafayette is somewhat assimilated into the narrative as a character whose struggles become less about his gendered, class, or racial status and more driven by plot complexity, I suggest that this is perhaps due to the show's appropriation of the (queer) uncanny, returning the initially radical, edgy figure of Lafayette as a familiar-unfamiliar subject. Indeed, where Davis-McElligatt concludes, "In the context of the show, vampires are structured as incomplete metaphors or representations of black and queer people, but the presence of Lafayette ultimately hinders the success of those metaphors,"[24] this is precisely *because* the typical tropes of the gothic uncanny are "queered." If the show stands to represent a critique of anything, it comes from its reflection of the white, cisgender, queer male at the top of a hierarchy of queerness, in its presentation of middle/upper-class white male vampires. This is something that Davis-McElligatt concurs with in her interpretation that "vampires are routinely coded as the most dangerous magical creatures in the universe, not only because of their extraordinary power, but because of their desire to upset the social order of the South by living openly as vampires."[25] What occurs instead, consciously or not—as Ball seems to indicate that the only possible interpretation of a monstrous symbol is one that is consciously encoded—is a complex portrayal of the various queer subcultures in the real world that exist in disharmony.

True Blood's metaphorical placing of the vampire as a figure of Otherness bears a double effect. The show's representation of the vampire as a metaphor for Othered minorities (ethnic, gendered, class-based, and sexual) is clear, yet their wish to "come out" and live openly alongside humans also questions what happens to the vampire-as-metaphor (for homosexuality) in a text in which homosexuality, and indeed queerness, is rendered so explicit.[26] In an essay I have written on this subject, I conclude that, in the case of *True Blood*, the figure of the vampire critiques queer subcultures by highlighting the dead "homo-ness" of a (non)conformist gay culture in an age of assimilation.[27] *True Blood*'s approach to queerness is largely celebratory, excessive, and outrageously multiple in its depiction of faeries, maenads, witches, werewolves, were-panthers, and vampires as subcultures of difference. In *True Blood*, abject Otherness is both assimilated and reveled in. Chief among its Others, the vampire not only stands as a metaphor for homosexuality but is also literalized in the plethora of outed and closeted gay vampire, witch, faerie, shape-shifter, and human characters. In representing an assimilative homonormativity, the show ceases to offer the same essentialist threat to heteronormativity that the metaphorical vampire-as-homosexual might once have done. Moreover, in its ever-increasing continuum of Othered subjectivities, the show offers up a varied selection of queer "becomings."

The series's multiple, overlapping, and blurred sexual and monstrous/nonmonstrous identities arguably distort any attempts at classification; furthermore, the show dismisses any attempts to categorize its queer Others as an absurdist pursuit. Nevertheless, the show's explicitly queer creatures offer critiques of specific subcultural difference and confront queer experiences of pride, shame, and guilt around seemingly assimilated alternative sexualities. *True Blood*'s representation of the homonormative encodes subcultural tensions within gay (vampire) subcultures. It highlights the psychical traumas of "fitting in" to a subculture defined by materialism, promiscuity, gym body cultivation, youth obsession, and self-indulgence. For example, the withdrawn gay vampire Eddie Gauthier (Stephen Root) from season 1 is portrayed as a closeted, couch-surfing creature who is reclusive not only because of his vampiric and/or homosexual impulses but because, being middle-aged and overweight, he does not fit into a world in which bodily perfection is revered. He then resorts to using escorts to feel loved.

This complex stratification of difference and fluid sexual Otherness is compounded by *True Blood*'s southern locale, the central location of Bon Temps (meaning Good Times) in the swampy, often fecund bayous of Louisiana. The show's opening titles depict an American South that is part-steeped in the murky waters of rotting wetlands, with dense vines clouding the semi-submerged camera, with wildlife and vegetation shown in stop-motion decomposition as it is becoming mulch. Brigid Cherry and Caroline Ruddell offer a vibrant description of the various settings from *True Blood* as "anchored in the lush vegetation and humid wetlands of the Deep South. . . . In the humid, subtropical climate, the lush woodlands, swamplands and bayous clothe and conceal the contours of the land beneath. . . . It is in vegetation (not shadows) that monsters hide."[28] Cherry and Ruddell continue that "Bon Temps is an ideal location for barely concealed prejudices, buried secrets and damaged relationships."[29] Yet their work suggests that, while *True Blood* can clearly be placed as part of a southern gothic subgenre of texts, it is an ironic and self-reflexive portrayal that is more akin to a performative play with southern gothic textualities, aesthetics, themes, and characters: "The parodying of excess in *True Blood* is central to understanding its [queer] remediation of the Gothic. . . . The setting provides a particularly southern context where the Gothic is negotiated and remediated within a contemporary environment."[30] Returning to Lloyd's consideration of the South as America's "Othered space," when *True Blood*'s depiction of southern spaces serves as a *home* to those Othered species, the supposed aberrant space and the radical potency that is implied becomes tamed, domesticated—by queering the *unheimlich*, it becomes *heimlich*. Both the vampire and the Othered space of the South become commodified by the outsider, assimilated into an industry of experience and commercialization. For example, the vampire bar Fangtasia, first seen in "Escape from the Dragon House" (season 1, episode 4), is visualized as a theme venue that attracts human customers wishing to experience the novel thrill of vampire culture. Here the presence of human tourists, "fangbangers" (those who participate in vampire sex without becoming vampires themselves) and "V-addicts" (those who seek a druglike high experienced by drinking vampire blood), foregrounds and celebrates the accessibility of the vampires' alternative sexual otherness and offers up "vampirism," and therefore queerness, as performative. In applying such an interpretation, I deliberately reference both the theatricality within Fangtasia and vampire tourism per se (that is, merchandising that extends to false vampire incisors marketed in actuality and in the fictional show) and Judith Butler's concept of gender "performativity" in relation to an excessively theatricalized sexual subjectivity. Butler argues that the supposed biology of binary gender is constructed via the repetition of acts and behaviors in which social performance creates gender, a performance that imitates culturally prescribed and impossible ideals.[31]

"Fluid" sexuality is represented in the show's use of orally sharing/drinking blood as a means of opening up bisexual and homoerotic relations for those seemingly essentialist heteronormative characters like Jason Stackhouse (Ryan Kwanten) and Sam Merlotte (Sam Trammell). The über-straight Jason, after having been healed by feeding from the vampire blood of both Eric Northman and the part-faerie-part-vampire Macklyn Warlow/Ben Flynn (Rob Kazinsky) (season 6, episode 4), proceeds to have erotic dreams in which his subconscious desires for both men are satirically depicted. In close-up, Jason is shown in a steamy mirror in his bathroom, his face partially lathered in shaving cream; the camera slowly tracks back to reveal another male's hand shaving him with a razor. The hand belongs to Ben/Warlow, who sensually offers to let Jason shave him in return. Jason complies, and the two shirtless men are seen in a two shot, surrounded by the suggestive steam of the bathroom. When Jason accidentally cuts his partner, he is erotically drawn to lick the trickling blood that oozes from the wound. The camera pulls in, capturing Jason's lustful urge, only to cut away to him sitting bolt upright in bed, having woken disturbed by the events of his erotic dream. The show plays with this "conversion" of its seemingly straight characters in several erotic dream sequences, including another of Jason's homoerotic nightmares, this time involving Eric (season 7, episode 2), and one involving the shape-shifter Sam's shower-set homoerotic desires for Bill Compton (Stephen Moyer) after having been healed by the ingestion of his blood (season 3, episode 1). *True Blood* suggests that the passing of blood can cause repressed queer desires to come to the fore, and this can be seen in examples such as the comical "turning" of staunch anti-vampire religious zealot Steve Newlin (Michael McMillian) into an "out" gay conservative American vampire who then declares his love for Jason Stackhouse, and in the case of Tara Thornton (Rutina Wesley) who, having been made a vampire by Pam, indulges in lesbian relations thenceforth.

The introduction of vampire king Russell Edgington and his long-term male partner Talbot (Theo Alexander) as the "civil-partnered" rulers of Mississippi reinforces a stereotypical portrayal of privileged homonormativity that arguably harks back to the capitalistic, landowning, consumerist vampires of the Old World. Edgington's southern gothic antebellum mansion is steeped in references to an era of colonialism and the slave trade upon which his fortune rests. As an openly gay vampire couple, Talbot and Russell's partnership resembles bourgeois monogamy, yet they remain promiscuous: Talbot seduces Eric after a disagreement with Russell, and Russell's desire for power leads him to undertake a marriage of convenience with Sophie-Anne, the vampire queen of Louisiana, in order to resolve her debts and to expand his empire.

True Blood's knowing reflection of homo-conformism encompasses the inevitable failure of monogamy between the Edgingtons, leading to Talbot's death. In an act of vengeance, the omnisexual Eric provides Talbot with the experience of "the true death": first luring him with the promise of sexual penetration, he then impales him from behind with a wooden stake. Upon Talbot's explosively fluid death, Russell suffers a mental breakdown and descends into a crazed and vengeful rampage. The trajectory of Russell Edgington from materialistic aesthete to crazed *homme fatal* perpetuates the cliché of a psychotic, murderous gay love. Despite his obvious white privilege, Edgington stands in opposition to the American Vampire League (AVL) and represents an antiassimilationist southern vampire/queer terrorist. During his reign of terror, Edgington bursts in on a live television news report on the AVL. Appearing suddenly behind the anchorman, he rips the spine from the fellow, pulling out a blood-clotted section as the newscaster slumps out of frame. Edgington takes his place and makes an impassioned, if campy, speech to the American public:

> We are nothing like you. . . . We are . . . immortal [laughs] because we drink the true blood. Blood that is living, organic, and human. [He licks his hand, blood-slicked from the insides of the newscaster.] That is the truth the AVL wishes to conceal from you because, let's face it, eating people is a tough sell these days—so they put on their friendly faces to pass their beloved VRA [Vampire Rights Amendment]. But make no mistake: mine is the true face of *vampires*. Why would we seek equal rights? You are not our equals. We will eat you, after we eat your children. Now time for the weather—Tiffany?

Edgington becomes the recurring antagonist of season 3 and season 5. As an enraged, politicized, queer vampire protester, his outrageous attempts to bring down the conformist ethos of the AVL are eventually thwarted by the more cultist Vampire Authority group. In the show, Edgington can arguably be seen as a hysterically camp protest against the acceptance and normalization of the vampire race, but extratextually the argument clearly resounds in the contemporary United States in which queer *difference* runs the risk of being lost in the attempt to strive both for acceptance and for equal rights, which ultimately requires some assimilation into prevailing cultural norms. In essence, *True Blood* is a problematic queer text, in the sense that its various representations of queerness exist to trouble or upset efforts to conclude anything about the show's sexual-political standpoints, suggesting instead that queer subjectivity is anything but fixed, essentialist, and *true*. Instead, the series possesses a polymorphously perverse pride in the presentation of its multiple, often incompatible, queer identities.

Queering the Backwoods Horror

Alan Rowe Kelly's *A Far Cry from Home*, a short section from the 2012 anthology horror film *Gallery of Fear*, directed by Kelly and Anthony G. Sumner, taps into contemporary cultural unease surrounding the recent acceptance of LGBTQ+ rights into the U.S. mainstream. The film features a queer couple who, in true survival horror tradition, unwittingly stumble into the world of religious and Republican fanaticism in the backwoods South and find themselves tortured and slaughtered by stereotypical rednecks. Setting its story in the southern Appalachians, the film offers a queer twist on the backwoods horror subgenre. *A Far Cry from Home* inverts traditional survival horror's dynamic of heteronormativity (as represented in the heterosexual couple and/or the nuclear family) threatened by marginalized, transgressive, and often symbolically queer Others. Instead, religiously conservative, oppressive, and southern-coded heteronormativity is turned monstrous and threatens a queer-oriented couple at the center of its narrative. The backwoods horror has long configured its monsters as veiled queer antagonists. In John Boorman's *Deliverance* (1972), physically grotesque, sodomizing, inbred families threaten an adventuring troupe of macho outdoors enthusiasts from the city. Tobe Hooper's *The Texas Chain Saw Massacre* (1974) depicts the post–Industrial Age, cannibalizing Sawyer family, who threaten to consume the next generation of white privilege, along with the complexly gendered character Leatherface (Gunnar Hansen), who is seen wearing the faces of women and men. Kelly's film develops the well-trodden tropes of the conservative horror film narrative, positing the religious right and moral conservatism as the monstrous Other and depicting queerness as the normativity placed under threat.

A Far Cry from Home centers on Lane, a typically *Final Girl*–style protagonist with a gender-neutral name, a forty-something androgynous queer figure with long, feminine hair and subtle traces of drag makeup (played by director/actor Alan Rowe Kelly, known for undertaking female roles), and Lane's twenty-something lover Kayle (Don Money), who appears more typically masculine. The couple decide to escape for a weekend's antiquing to share some quality time. Stopping off at a dilapidated junk store in the Appalachian Mountains called Hung by a Thread, they encounter a family of southern Christian rednecks led by a clichéd preacher who claims that they are "God's warriors put on this pitiful planet to rid it of all its abominations." While not an outright parody, the film utilizes pastiche in that it clearly alludes to southern-set backwoods survival horror, such as the porcine references in sodomy-obsessed *Deliverance* and the grotesquely mutated, literally nuclear family of *The Hills Have Eyes* (1977).[32] It also pays visual homage to both *The Texas Chainsaw Massacre*'s and *The Skeleton Key*'s mise-en-scène in the junk shop's animal skins, rickety furniture, dried bone ornaments, toy skeletons, grotesque Mardi Gras masks, and pickled vegetables and human organs in jars, and parallels such primal collectables with Christian objets d'art, including crucifixes and figurines of the Virgin Mary.

A Far Cry from Home also mirrors Tobe Hooper's film's narrative trajectory in that, while Lane smokes a joint outside the shop, Kayle disappears, leaving the feminine-masculine central character to endure extended torture at the hands of the monstrous family, *Final Girl*–style. The family, consisting of Aunt Idella (Katherine O'Sullivan) and her grown nephews Otis (Benzy) and Buster (Jerry Murdock, who is introduced squealing offscreen as a Leatherface-like brute), receive dubious religious guidance from the equally monstrous Preacher (Terry West), who legitimizes their crusade against "certain debased, debauched humanity," declaring that "sodomites will be sent straight to hell!" The Preacher encourages the slaughter of homosexuals, particularly effeminate gay men, who he claims "fuel the fires of Satan!" before further quoting from I Corinthians 6.9–10: "Be not deceived, neither fornicators, nor idolaters, nor adulterers, nor effeminate, nor abusers of themselves with mankind . . . shall inherit the kingdom of God." In one scene Lane's liminal, fluid, feminine masculinity is shown as the main target of hatred for the family, and is, arguably, a source of anxiety for both homosexual and heterosexual characters. Lane asks to use the store's telephone and is quickly cornered by the threatening but intrigued Otis and Buster. The grotesquely simplistic duo become confused as to Lane's gender. Both Otis and Buster exclaim: "Do you smell pussy? I smell pussy"; "Well, I smell cock!" before concluding "You look like a girl!" Director and actor Alan Rowe Kelly comments on his decision to keep Lane's gender fluid: "I kept Lane sexually ambiguous. Viewers needed to look at Lane the same way as the rest of the characters in the film look at him/her—with confusion, curiosity, and apprehension."[33]

After being tortured, Lane escapes the family and, fleeing into the woods nearby, discovers in a clearing a collection of tents, each of which contains the rotting corpses of previously murdered gay couples. Lane finds Kayle strung up and barely alive, tied between two trees and posed crucifixion-style, complete with a crown of thorns and nails driven into his wrists. Lane stumbles into a trap, falling onto spikes driven into the ground and piercing both hands. The trap then literally rips Kayle in two and, kneeling beneath his body, Lane is orgasmically sprayed with arterial blood and innards. Kayle's flesh here eases apart rather than being riven with force, further evidencing the fluid pliability of queer flesh.

Tracked down, Lane is captured and forced to repent. The Preacher and the two brothers prepare to kill Lane, who reveals the palm wounds, which the fanatically religious pursuers interpret as (queered) stigmata (see figure 4.2). Tricking them further by appearing to speak in tongues, Lane dispatches Buster with his own axe before being shot and killed with a crossbow by the Preacher. Lane's dead body is dragged into the tent circle. In the film's final shots, a mixed-race straight couple arrive at the junk shop, much to the bigoted annoyance of Aunt Idella, with the film hinting that the narrative repeats itself.

A Far Cry from Home is one among many pointing toward a trend in recent queer horror film and television texts that focus on one of the primal fears of LGBTQ+ identified subjects: someone wanting to kill them precisely *because* they are queer.[34] *A Far Cry from Home* manifests a very real, violently homophobic reaction encouraged by religious fundamentalism and right-wing family values, seen localized in the rural regions of the more "traditional" South, that is exacerbated by the increasing assimilation of homosexuality into the mainstream. Gaysploitation horrors such as Kelly's are significant in that they

FIGURE 4.2. Lane (Rowe Kelly) and his "queer stigmata."

depict seemingly heteronormative America, here comically symbolized by the inbred southern family, as their monsters, and suggest that repressed homosexuality lies at the root of homophobia.

Splattering Southern Bodies and Swampy Queer Subjectivities

In conclusion, I would like to suggest that the queer bodies on display in southern gothic queer horror film and television can be said to represent a breaking down, a deconstruction and reconstruction, of enforced essentialist structures that would seek to fix sexuality in place through conformity to a set of norms. The texts analyzed in this chapter all show interesting configurations of perversions and queerness that renegotiate the way queer bodies and pleasures become disorganized and challenge traditional corporeal and sexual paradigms. They do this with their appropriation of gothic traditions, including the collapse of temporal and spatial borders in their spectral storytelling; their portrayal of a multiplicity of excessive, self-reflexive, queer identities; and their depiction of a literalizing of the fluid subjectivities seen in the physical breakdown of queer corporeality.

There are clear parallels between the queer fluidity in southern gothic horror and Deleuze and Guattari's "body without organs," which they describe as "permeated by unformed, unstable matters, by flows in all directions, by free intensities or nomadic singularities, by mad or transitory particles."[35] This fluid substratum is what Deleuze calls the "body without organs." In a general sense, this can be seen in the abject, dilapidating zombie bodies in Fulci's *The Beyond*; in the pliably soft flesh of the victims of violent acts that see bodies burned, broken apart, and melted in gaysploitation horror; in the bloody, orgasmic pools that the vampire body is "reduced" to in *True Blood*; and in the fluid performativity of genre styles, gender traits, and queer identities found in queer horror film and television texts.

Returning full-circle to *The Beyond*, Patricia MacCormack considers the queer potential of Fulci's zombie films. She applies the concept of "the body without organs" to Fulci's recurring zombie figure, and writing specifically about *The Beyond*, she argues that the representation of corporeal violence does not serve to destroy identities, but instead suggests that such "acts of violence are acts of corporeal experimentation, not destruction."[36] The swampy environs of Fulci's films exist not only as spaces that conceal rotting, decaying bodies but also as places of rebirth and re-creation with a focus on queer libidinal energies. MacCormack concludes by listing *The Beyond*'s inventive scenes of bodies in torment: "crucifixion, melting by acid, a face is eaten by spiders, another wrenched off, a throat torn out and handyman Arthur . . . has his eyes squelched out and kills his wife in an equally gruesome way in a marital parody, showing interest in corporeal reconfiguration (the body, literally "beyond"). . . . Death creates self through larval flesh. Zombies desire bodies without organs and as their libidinal acts are ones of infection rather than copulation they create other bodies without organs, open up and fold back."[37] The queer bodies depicted in southern-set queer horror can be understood as reorganizing bodies that are perpetually shifting in state. This is especially relevant of the death/rebirth seen in the orgasmically explosive "deaths" of *True Blood*. The show's iconically gloopy death scenes depict the vampires' bodies liquefying into a comically visceral mess upon receiving the "true death" by stake. It is in this sense that the notion of fluid sexual Otherness and queer subjectivities are rendered literal in the orgasmic symbolism of the vampire's melting body. However, in the episode "Save Yourself" (season 5, episode 12), there is an interesting extension of *True Blood*'s lore of vampire death. Having grown tired of living the apologetic life of an assimilationist vampire, Bill drinks the blood of Lilith (the progenitor of the vampire race) to assume her godlike powers. He begins to bleed out from various orifices—eyes, ears, nose, mouth—and eventually he bursts apart in a postcoital explosion, liquefying into a pool of blood. The spectating Sookie and Eric look to leave, only to see the naked, reborn Bill rise and re-coagulate from the pool of vampire viscera as an all-powerful phallic god. Bill's white cisgender male displacement of Lilith as vampire god further cements my earlier point about *True Blood*'s critique of queer culture's own hierarchical problematic.

Rather than representing the body's breakdown and messy visualization of the vampire's "true death," these explosively sticky, orgasmic moments from *True Blood* stand out as temporary, comic, gross-out depictions of Deleuzian queer "becomings" in which characters move from one status to another, one identity to another. This outlines the southern gothic's propensity to present a contemporary, nonessentialist, queer, fluid identity that is literally in flux, visualized in rotting and abject bodies and, more symbolically, in queer horror's multiplicity of shifting, inconsistent, continually changing, and performative subjectivities.

NOTES

The epigraph is from Pippa Holloway, "Manifesto for a Queer South Politics," *PMLA* 131.1 (2016): 182–86, at 186.

1. Christopher Lloyd, "Southern Gothic," *American Gothic Culture: An Edinburgh Companion*, ed. Joel Faflak and Jason Haslam (Edinburgh: Edinburgh University Press, 2016), 79–91, at 81.

2. Eric Savoy, "The Face of the Tenant: A Theory of the American Gothic," *American Gothic: New Interventions in a National Narrative*, ed. Robert K. Martin and Eric Savoy (Iowa City: University of Iowa Press, 1998), 3–19, at 11.

3. David Punter and Glennis Byron, *The Gothic* (Malden, Mass.: Blackwell 2004), 116–17.

4. Teresa A. Goddu, "The Ghost of Race: Edgar Allan Poe and the Southern Gothic," *Criticism and the Color Line: Desegregating American Literary Studies*, ed. Henry B. Wonham (New Brunswick, N.J.: Rutgers University Press, 1996), 230–50, at 230.

5. Lloyd, "Southern Gothic," 79.

6. In addition to the queer horror films set in the South discussed in this chapter, see, for instance, *Frogs* (1972), *The Texas Chain Saw Massacre* (1974), *Eaten Alive* (1977), *Interview with the Vampire* (1994), *Candyman: Farewell to the Flesh* (1995), and *The Skeleton Key* (2005).

7. Robin Wood, "Introduction to the American Horror Film," *Movies and Methods*, ed. Bill Nichols, 2 vols. (Berkeley: University of California Press, 1976–85), 2:195–220, at 198.

8. Teresa A. Goddu, *Gothic America: Narrative, History, and Nation* (New York: Columbia University Press, 1997), 76.

9. See, for instance, Wood, "Introduction to the American Horror Film"; Ellis Hanson, "Undead," *Inside/Out: Lesbian Theories, Gay Theories*, ed. Diana Fuss (London: Routledge, 1991), 324–40; Jack [Judith] Halberstam, *Skin Shows: Gothic Horror and the Technology of Monsters* (Durham, N.C.: Duke University Press, 1995); Harry M. Benshoff, *Monsters in the Closet: Homosexuality and the Horror Film* (Manchester: Manchester University Press, 1997).

10. See my *Queer Horror Film and Television: Sexuality and Masculinity at the Margins* (London: Tauris, 2016).

11. Michael Bibler, "Queering the Region," *The Cambridge Companion to the Literature of the American South*, ed. Sharon Monteith (New York: Cambridge University Press, 2013), 188–203, at 188.

12. Bibler, "Queering the Region," 188–89.

13. Susan Donaldson, "Making Darkness Visible," *Undead Souths: The Gothic and Beyond in Southern Literature and Culture*, ed. Eric Gary Anderson, Taylor Hagood, and Daniel Cross Turner (Baton Rouge: Louisiana State University Press, 2015), 261–65, at 264.

14. Christopher Lloyd, *Corporeal Legacies in the US South: Memory and Embodiment in Contemporary Culture* (Palgrave Macmillan, 2018), 5.

15. Jay Watson, *Reading for the Body: The Recalcitrant Materiality of Southern Fiction, 1893–1985* (Athens: University of Georgia Press, 2012), 9.

16. Bibler, "Queering the Region," 188.

17. Michael Grant, "The 'Real' and the Abominations of Hell: Carl-Theodor Dreyer's *Vampyr* (1931) and Lucio Fulci's *E tu vivrai nel terrore—L'aldilà* (*The Beyond*, 1981)," *Kinoeye* 3.2 (February 2003); Web.

18. Patricia MacCormack, *Cinesexuality* (London: Routledge, 2008), 112.

19. William Matthew McCarter, "Regional 'Othering' in Herschell Lewis's *Two Thousand Maniacs!*" *Steel Toe Review* 10 August 2011; Web.

20. Anthony Szczesiul, "Re-mapping Southern Hospitality: Discourse, Ethics, and Politics," *European Journal of American Culture* 26.2 (2007): 127–41, at 132.

21. Benshoff, *Monsters in the Closet*, 16.

22. Joanna Davis-McElligatt, "God Hates Fangs: *True Blood*, Black Queer Agency, and Appropriations of the History of Racial and Sexual Violence in the Deep South," *Small-Screen Souths: Region, Identity, and the Cultural Politics of Television*, ed. Lisa Hinrichsen, Gina Caison, and Stephanie Rountree (Baton Rouge: Louisiana State University Press, 2017), 99–114, at 100.

23. Davis-McElligatt, "God Hates Fangs," 101–2.

24. Davis-McElligatt, "God Hates Fangs," 115.

25. Davis-McElligatt, "God Hates Fangs," 109.

26. The show builds on a cinematic and literary history of southern queer vampires, most famously in Neil Jordan's 1994 film *Interview with the Vampire*, adapted from Anne Rice's *Vampire Chronicles* series. Rice's novels and Jordan's screen adap-

tation, with its depiction of more explicitly queer vampirism, arguably paved the way for *True Blood*'s postmillennial presentation of a plurality of "out" queer vampires.

27. Darren Elliott-Smith, "The Homosexual Vampire as a Metaphor for . . . the Homosexual Vampire? *True Blood*, Homonormativity, and Assimilation," *True Blood: Investigating Vampires and the Southern Gothic*, ed. Brigid Cherry (London: Tauris, 2012), 139–58.

28. Brigid Cherry and Caroline Ruddell, "More Than Cold and Heartless: The Southern Gothic Milieu of *True Blood*," Cherry, *True Blood*, 39–58, at 42.

29. Cherry and Ruddell, "More Than Cold and Heartless," 42.

30. Cherry and Ruddell, "More Than Cold and Heartless," 53.

31. Judith Butler, *Gender Trouble: Feminism and the Subversion of Identity* (New York: Routledge, 1990). See a more detailed discussion of how integral Butler's work is to an informed understanding of queer horror texts in my *Queer Horror Film and Television: Sexuality and Masculinity at the Margins*.

32. It is interesting to note here that contemporary queer horror films clearly take ownership of the queer-phobic sodomy references that originate cinematically in Boorman's *Deliverance*. Sullivan's *Two Thousand Maniacs!* sequels, Ball's *True Blood*, and Rowe Kelly's *A Far Cry from Home* all feature scenes where the fear of sodomy is turned into a gross-out, often absurdist, comic element that arguably defuses homosexual panic.

33. Alan Rowe Kelly, quoted in Sean Abley, *Out in the Dark: Interviews with Gay Horror Filmmakers, Actors, and Authors* (Maple Shade, N.J.: Lethe Press, 2012), 230.

34. For example, see *Bite Marks*, dir. Mark Bessenger (2011); *The Gay Bed and Breakfast of Terror*, dir. Jaymes Thompson (2007); *Bloody Bloody Bible Camp*, dir. Vito Trabucco (2012).

35. Gilles Deleuze and Félix Guattari, *A Thousand Plateaus* (London: Bloomsbury, 1987), 40.

36. MacCormack, *Cinesexuality*, 111.

37. MacCormack, *Cinesexuality*, 111.

PART III

SOUTHERN HOMOSOCIALITY AND QUEER ANXIETIES

Chapter 5 ▸ "We Getting Engaged?": Toxic Masculinity and the Louisiana Marriage in *True Detective*

JESSICA WALKER

In the first season of HBO's 2014 anthology series *True Detective*, the protagonists, homicide detectives Marty Hart (Woody Harrelson) and Rust Cohle (Matthew McConaughey), justify being "bad men," prone to infidelity, violence, and substance abuse, as necessary to keep "other bad men from the door"—namely, the cult of murderous pedophiles they seek over a timeline spanning from 1995 to 2012 (LR).[1] After eight episodes of violent posturing, however, they overcome the toxic masculinity that has tainted their lives in a southern gothic landscape. The last episode concludes with their symbolic marriage in the parking lot of the hospital where they are recovering from injuries after stopping the serial killer. Marty presents Rust with what looks like a telltale blue Tiffany box. "We getting engaged?" Rust jokes, opening the box to reveal a pack of his favorite cigarettes (see figure 5.1).

This metaphorical homosocial engagement unexpectedly concludes a narrative consumed with heteroerotic violence, set in rural Louisiana in the years before the legalization of same-sex marriage. Historically, the South has resisted LGBTQ+ rights more than other regions of the United States: for instance, it was more likely to have passed antisodomy laws and slower to retract them.[2] While overt homophobia is largely absent from *True Detective*, homophobia in its most literal sense—a terror of partnership based on *sameness*—pervades the series.[3] As a same-sex partnership, Rust and Marty's symbolic marriage rejects a social hierarchy that relies on male supremacy over women and children; as a union of men, however, it avoids perpetuating oppression but does not truly disrupt it. A "Louisiana marriage," it symbolizes the contemporary South: inextricably bound to a troubled, gothic past, yet moving gradually forward.

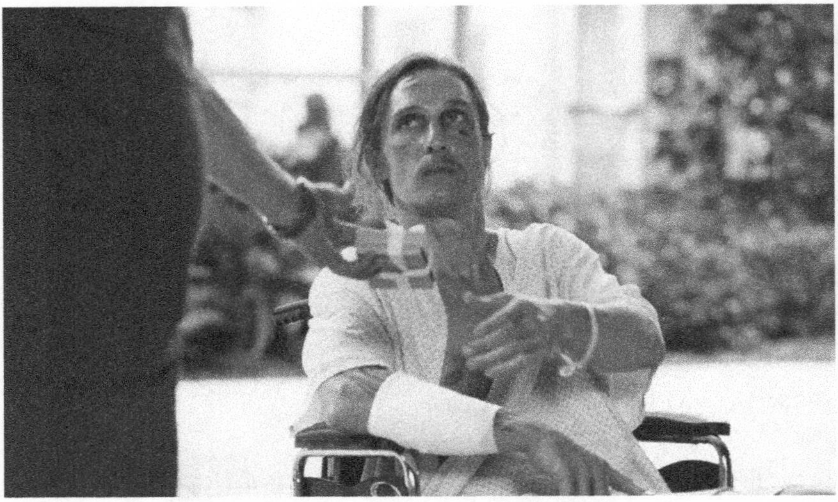

FIGURE 5.1. Marty presents Rust with a pack of cigarettes in a blue Tiffany box, with this iconic imagery suggestive of their union.

The surprisingly conventional imagery surrounding their relationship, as not just a working partnership or friendship but a marriage, underscores the paradoxical continuum demonstrated by the southern gothic tradition to which *True Detective* belongs: the most traditional heteropatriarchal values pushed to their extreme, manifested in the strange, dangerous, sexually deviant acts of the series's chief antagonists, the Tuttle cult. The cult's practices—luring children and young women to be raped and murdered as part of their folk rituals—clearly violate mainstream sexual values. The cult's roots, however, are found in the aristocratic plantation culture of antebellum Louisiana; its members include men of wealth and influence, and their sadistic acts uphold patriarchal, economic, and religious ideologies, revealing the "complicity and phallic rewards of what might be called 'deviant sexualities' within patriarchal and heterocentric power relations."[4]

These heteropatriarchal values extend their insidious influence beyond the Tuttle cult's practices, shaping not only sexuality but family life, race relations, politics, and religion. What I call "heteropatriarchy" here does not exclusively denote heterosexuality, as these values reveal themselves in both heterosexual and homosexual acts, both heteroerotic and homoerotic desires. Rather, the term refers to the power structure at work in the cult's activities: only men are aggressors in these acts, and the cult targets children and socioeconomically marginalized women (particularly sex workers), never adult men.

Here the same root cause—men's economic, political, and social power over women and children—manifests as both hyper-normative and hyper-deviant sexualities: heterosexual marriage and murderous cult sacrifice.[5] While occupying opposite ends of a spectrum of acceptability, these practices emerge as equally destructive, gothic manifestations of an inherently southern, and specifically Louisianan, heteropatriarchal violence. Consequently, the protagonists' queer partnership at the series's end, founded in mutuality rather than hierarchy, subverts the show's negative associations with marriage to symbolize their rejection of their culture's toxic masculinity.

"It's supposed to help me": Eroticized Inequality in Heterosexual Marriage and Southern Heteropatriarchy

While some have criticized *True Detective* as a misogynistic text,[6] it could also be considered a radical feminist one, its story line driven by the belief that heterosexuality is a "non-egalitarian, oppressive, violent" means by which "patriarchy maintains itself."[7] The series is cynical about marriage, an institution that has "reflected and shaped the core values of southerners," from the "legal, political, and social subordination of white wives to husbands" to the role of antimiscegenation laws as "an important tool for the social order in the postbellum South."[8] "[S]harp divisions between males and females"[9] have shaped family life in what has been "historically the region of the United States most resistant to changes in the role of women," reluctant to ratify the Nineteenth Amendment and the Equal Rights Amendment; this resistance largely stems from the notion of "sexual equality as contrary to biblical teachings."[10]

Most relationships in *True Detective*—between parents and children, teachers and pupils, cops and criminals—are characterized by attempts to assert one's control over someone lower in the social hierarchy, but no relationships so consistently and overtly as those between men and women, particularly marriage. Negativity about heterosexual partnership pervades the series, as expressed in such dialogue as "Men, women, it's not supposed to work except to make kids" (WGT) and "what always happens between men and women—reality" (SF). In the few marriages that do not end in divorce, participants regard the institution with world-weary cynicism: "I know what it's like to be married to a man" (ST); "Still on the first [wife]" (HH). Marriage's stated role is to uphold patriarchy and produce children: "It's supposed to help me" (ST), Marty says of his family life, while Rust considers children "the only reason for this whole man-woman drama" (WGT). Marty reminisces about his "Donna Reed type" mother and expects his home to be "the one place where there's supposed to be peace and calm" (ST). In their other relationships, both personal and professional, the protagonists manipulate and intimidate women to satisfy their desires for sex, narcotics, or information.

Their need to assert power in their relationships is not isolated from the story's larger plot of two homicide detectives seeking a serial killer; rather, their personal problems reflect the evils perpetrated by their culture, and Rust and Marty simultaneously perpetuate and seek to curb such ills. Much of the violence historically associated with the South, such as feuding, vigilantism, police brutality, and white supremacy, supports its social hierarchies; as the "nation's most homicidal region," the South has historically "defend[ed] . . . racial hierarchy" and "demonstrate[d] masculine prowess" through murder.[11] Much of this violence occurs in Louisiana, whose high rural murder rates date from the 1870s.[12] As homicide detectives, the protagonists battle heteropatriarchal violence as they attempt to restore order to an environment where victims, perpetrators, and witnesses participate in sex work, pedophilia, exhibitionism, and other such deviant practices. The detectives use their authority to extract information from these socially marginalized figures, yet this authority is constantly undermined and reversed, pushing them to greater displays of hypermasculinity, such as when Rust reacts to Marty's aggression by beating an informant with a toolbox and when Marty reacts violently to the humiliation of being handcuffed as foreplay, forcing his way into his mistress Lisa's apartment and pulling his badge on her date (LR).

This tension between traditional norms and dark undercurrents reflects the complex sexual culture of a region strongly associated with gothic degeneracy. As Benjamin Wise argues, while "the intensely regulated norm was an ideal of white, reproductive, monogamous, heterosexual sex within the context of marriage," in truth "interracial sex, homosex, pre-marital sex, rape, extramarital sex, and commercial sex took place every day in the South."[13] Therefore, as Wise notes, "using the broadest notion of 'queer' as that which is different from the norm, most sex throughout southern history has been queer."[14] This troubled boundary between normative and deviant heteropatriarchy emerges in the narrative's central conflict, the detectives' pursuit of a murderous cult along the rural coast. At this group's center stands the powerful Tuttle clan, whose members include a state senator, Edwin Tuttle, and a prominent evangelist, Billy Lee Tuttle. The area from which the Tuttles hail "used to be a pirate hideout, then turned into plantations and whatnot" (AYG). This passing reference to piracy and plantations connects the violence and greed that shaped early southern colonialism to the use of slave labor supporting its agricultural economy, and finally to the cult's exploitation of economically marginalized women and children. Southern patriarchy "has been attributed to slavery" in that the patriarch "maintain[ed] control of the peculiar institution" by publicly controlling his family.[15] As the power of the colonial-era planters waned, there emerged "an increasing self-consciousness about their patriarchal role" that emphasized "family and kin loyalty, . . . a deep attachment to the land, and complete control in managing [their] slaves, servants, kin, and various hangers-on."[16] Exploitation is bred into the landscape itself, and the connection between dominating the land and dominating others runs throughout the series: Billy Lee Tuttle's ministry takes advantage of zoning regulations along the rural coast to promote his schools, while Errol Childress and his father exploit their landscaping jobs for access to victims. Hurricanes and flooding make evidence disappear.

The image of Dora's body, posed by her murderer and encircled by police, reappears throughout in a series of tableaux, always scrutinized by investigators: a curious arrangement of dolls put in place by Marty's daughters; a photograph of Dora as a child, surrounded by mysterious men on horseback; Rust's beer-can men during his interview with Papania and Gilbough. These images and symbols demonstrate the link between culture and cult: while the southern society objectifies women, the cult transforms them into actual objects, fetishes necessary to its rituals but holding no more inherent value than the relics found at the crime scenes. The Tuttle family's servant, Delores, describes the household in terms of patriarch Sam Tuttle's ownership: "People kept their own back then. I mean, a man's house was his own. Mr. Sam? He had lots of children. All types" (AYG). Tuttle's sexual partners and their children appear only as (re)producers of the patriarch's vision: the cult's abuses are essentially procreative, serving to grow their ranks either through biological reproduction or through recruiting converts and victims, to be discarded and replaced as the cycle continues. Just as Marty loses sexual interest in his wife after she bears children—"I haven't been fucked like that since before the girls" (HH)—and replaces her with a "young Maggie" (WGT), the family patriarch Sam Tuttle "didn't like a woman . . . once she had it done to her" (AYG). Women's and children's roles in upholding the cult's power echo Marty's and Rust's parallel assumptions about heterosexual marriage: "it's supposed to help me" (ST); "it's not supposed to work except to make kids" (WGT).

The counterintuitive parallels seen here between traditional marriage and cult sexual abuse reflect the South's paradoxical reputation as simultaneously prudishly conservative and sexually deviant, grounded in a white supremacist patriarchy that reveres the traditional family while exploiting enslaved women and sex workers. As Sharon Sharp observes, "From early southern history on, sexuality was intertwined with issues of not only race but also gender and social class, within an emerging hierarchical, patriarchal society."[17] This is particularly true of Louisiana, historically associated with both the slave trade and sex tourism; New Orleans's "reputation as the South's Babylon sprang from its reputation as a center of tolerated prostitution and its position as the region's largest slave market."[18] Rape has historically been "part of the complex system of social control that maintained the racial, gender, and class hierarchies that structured the southern social order."[19] Women and children, Rust observes, "[get] no press, the way things in the bayou get no press," and Tuttle's subordinates "didn't do nothing" about sexual abuse at his schools (HH). Throughout the series, the vulnerable body of the abused child surfaces repeatedly as a symbol of this theme, often in ways unconnected to the main narrative.[20] The show's central victim of cult violence, Dora Lange, was molested by her father; Beth, a sex worker with whom Marty later has an affair, was similarly abused by a male relative. Marty implies that his father was physically abusive (ST). Charmaine Boudreaux, a woman investigated by Rust and Marty at the series's midpoint, murders her three children (HH). *True Detective* reflects the unfortunate reality of the mistreatment of children in Louisiana, which in 2009 ranked forty-ninth among U.S. states in child wellbeing.[21]

"A regular-type dude with a big-ass dick": The Queer Contradictions of Southern Masculinity

The respectful homoromantic partnership that develops between the protagonists differs significantly from the series's earlier instances of homosexual encounters and homoerotic desire. Throughout the series, erotic desire is inseparable from issues of dominance and control; it is always heteropatriarchal, even when not heterosexual, and so homoerotic desire does not represent a rejection of oppressive structures. Sexual activity between members of the same sex is never presented as a healthy relationship between equals; rather, it is always tied to cult abuse and unbalanced power dynamics.[22] The male cult members molest boys; when addressing the abuses suffered by two of these boys, the series implies that they have gone on in adulthood to pursue same-sex encounters. In the first instance, the ambiguously gendered Toby Boelert, a.k.a. Johnny-Joanie, recounts being molested by Errol Childress while a student at one of Billy Lee Tuttle's private church-run schools; like Dora Lange, the series's central victim, Boelert grows up to become a sex worker arrested for prostitution. Childress, as he lures Rust and Marty to their final confrontation, implies that he had a sexual relationship with fellow cult members Reggie and Dewall Ledoux, linking their relationship directly to an ongoing cycle of violence in which he is both victim and perpetrator: "You know what they did to me? What I will do to all the sons and daughters of man. You blessed Reggie, Dewall. Acolytes, witnesses to my journey, lovers. I am not ashamed" (FV).

Similarly, for the series's protagonists, homoerotic tension is always rooted in the need to establish authority over other men by controlling one's own masculinity. These moments of queer eroticism and queer anxiety emerge at the places where contrasting, competing ideals of southern masculinity come into tension, threatening one's control over his own manhood. Judith Butler argues that "gender hierarchy" and "compulsory heterosexuality" manifest through "*a regulated process of repetition* that both conceals itself and enforces its rules precisely through the production of substantializing effects," but that "these ontological locales are fundamentally uninhabitable," a performance whose requirements shift constantly.[23] These unstable norms often contradict one another: southern masculinity requires embodying both the "chivalrous southerner . . . [devoted] to family [and] tradition" and the hypermasculine figure characterized by "violence, hard-nosed football, stock car racing, militarism, and hawkish attitudes."[24] Much of the protagonists' internal and external conflict stems from their inability to reconcile these competing masculinities—to be, as Marty describes himself, "a regular-type dude with a big-ass dick" (LBD). Both men express a desire to be "steady": for Marty, this word entails monogamous, patriarchal heterosexuality (LBD); for Rust, a failed husband and father, it signifies a stoic, asexual devotion to his work (LBD). This desire wars with the urge to indulge in aggressive masculinity, which manifests for Marty as infidelity (a desire for "something wild" [WGT]) and for Rust as risky behavior in his undercover work ("wild man junkie" [ST]). The tension between these "steady" and "wild" selves becomes a queer-coded locus for eroticized control, and loss of control, over one's own masculinity and that of other men.

Marty constantly fears losing the upper hand in his relationship with his wife and daughters, regarding them as possessions who reinforce his patriarchal power, as he repeatedly stresses: "You are not gonna break up *my fucking family*"; "I am having a private conversation with *my wife*" (WGT); "I'm talking about *my teenage daughter*" (SF; emphases in original). At the same time, his desire for sex makes him unable to truly control himself, and he eroticizes what he perceives as his own emasculation. While his marital sex life (as his wife implies) is dully procreative, his heterosexual adultery is sodomitic (anal, oral, or manual sex). In relating a cop-and-coed anecdote straight out of *Penthouse* to his fellow policemen, Marty recalls how his tenuous authority as a young officer ("third day on the job") is symbolically stripped from him ("I got my uniform around my knees"), his desire undermining his professional vigilance ("I'm occupied, so I don't hear anything"). Reduced to a submissive, penetrated position ("She stuck her finger up my ass"), he is helpless against his own sexual needs ("Ruined me. Now I can't do without it" [ST]). His inability to resist sexual temptation earns him not the admiration of his male colleagues but, rather, nicknames like "the human tampon" (HH).

Indicating how deeply toxic masculinity runs through this culture, not only does Marty use homophobic language in an attempt to emasculate other men, but the women in his life do the same to him. Desperate to reinforce his status after learning Lisa is seeing other men, Marty assaults her date, threatening to "have some Ninth Ward prison queen wearing your face for a condom" (LR). Likewise, Maggie calls Marty "chicken shit" (ST) and a "coward" (HH), while his nine-year-old daughter Audrey seems critical of her father's failure to shoot anyone (LBD). The exchange between Marty and Lisa following his violent behavior against her and her date demonstrates how both men and women are invested in the paradoxical requirements of southern manhood. She criticizes Marty's hypermasculinity ("you think it's okay to treat your wives the way you do") and lack thereof ("you fucking wet-noodle, whiskey-dick faggot fuck"), while he veers between paternal traditionalism ("I have children . . . you fucking whore") and hypermasculine violence ("I will skull-fuck you, you bitch" [WGT]).

In a culture so consumed with the need to control, the only way to retain control over the self without controlling women is to avoid them, and the character most obsessed with self-control practices an almost monk-like abstinence.[25] Rust is a rugged Texan, skilled in hunting and tracking, his masculinity rooted in a singular focus on work and a disdain for both homosocial bonding and heterosexual companionship. As Ben Morgan notes, "Beneath

Rust's fervent masculinity lies an insecurity, but unlike Marty, Rust does not fear poor performance or an inability to be deeply masculine, he fears the feminizing effect of the body."[26] Controlling his physical desire—for both sexual contact and mind-altering substances—is key to maintaining the career so central to his masculinity, ultimately resulting in utter self-destruction when Marty's wife, Maggie (Michelle Monaghan), manipulates him into a drunken sexual encounter (HH).

Marty immediately feels threatened by the presence of a man whose stoic independence throws his own lack of self-control into sharp relief, and he attempts to reestablish masculine dominance by characterizing Rust's reserved behavior as a perversion, with such memorable lines as "Not everybody wants to sit alone in an empty room beating off to murder manuals"; "Getting him near your lap is gonna be the challenge"; and "I thought for a minute you just liked looking at pictures of dead people" (LR). Fearful of losing control over his wife and mistress, Marty becomes paranoid about Rust seeing or even speaking about Maggie, leading to two violent, erotically charged confrontations in which he attempts to assert his sexual dominance over Rust (ST, LR). In the first instance, Marty interprets Rust's snide remark about Marty's infidelity as interest in Maggie, pinning him up against a locker and warning Rust, "You don't say fuck-all about my wife. Don't say her name" (ST). Later, he comes home to find Rust has mowed the Harts' lawn in return for borrowing their mower. Confronting Rust, Marty demands: "What the hell do you think you're doing, man, at my house when I'm not here? . . . You mow *my lawn*? . . . I just don't ever want you mowing my lawn, all right? I like mowing *my lawn*" (LR).

Because Marty's desire is so closely tied to his control of, and loss of control over, women, he finds himself drawn to Rust's carefully crafted image of masculine self-control. Rust's masculinity lies, paradoxically, in his awareness that masculinity itself is a performance: while men like Marty are pulled between competing masculinities, Rust deftly navigates these roles, manipulating others' perceptions of him to achieve his professional goals. This power makes him the focus of queer desire, particularly in the fourth episode, when he transforms into his undercover persona, Crash, in hopes of infiltrating a biker gang to solve their case. Marty, staying with Rust after having been rejected by both wife and mistress, embodies the male gaze before whom Rust reveals a footlocker filled with guns, grenades, and whiskey; exposes his bullet-scarred torso and arms covered in fake track marks; and does pull-ups in his apartment. As Rust "constructs himself into hyper-masculine Crash," demonstrating his "heroic, military masculinity," he becomes the eroticized subject of Marty's envious gaze, "a construction [Marty] can't hope to emulate or out-perform."[27]

This same episode demonstrates Rust's ability to pass as both extremes of masculine behavior, the rough outlaw and the buttoned-down servant of the law. Rust, as Crash, meets with Ginger, a biker gang leader from whom he hopes to gain information. Placed in an uncomfortable position between his cop and criminal personas when Ginger asks him to join in a robbery, Rust asserts power over the exchange not by hiding his duplicity but by drawing attention to it:

> GINGER. You get neutered down South? I embrace the outlaw life. Now, you dress the part still. That just an act?
> RUST. When in Rome, brother. But I do clean up real fucking pretty. (WGT)

The other men in this episode can only ever perform at one end of the steady/wild continuum of southern masculinity: Marty's laughable attempt at going "undercover" (wearing a trucker hat and a Pink Floyd T-shirt) gets him kicked out of the biker bar, while the plan by Ginger and his fellow bearded, tattooed gang members to don police uniforms to infiltrate the projects proves ineffective. Rust's reframing of Ginger's emasculating insult about being "neutered" as a boast about his ability to "clean up real fucking pretty" when the situation demands it underscores the power that his body, able to adapt to multiple masculinities, gives him over men who cannot live up to society's demands.

"There's this place down south where all these rich men go to devil-worship": Deviant Sexuality and Louisiana Politics

Rust's and Marty's need to dominate both others and oneself is rooted in the heteropatriarchy and upheld by white supremacy that shapes southern culture from private relationships to public politics. The occult practices they are investigating, however hidden, soon become linked to public power and influence: "There's this place down south where all these rich men go to devil-worship" (WGT). The Tuttle family's authority originates in the antebellum era, when plantation owners built economic and political power through family connections and local government. This hierarchical, paternalistic power structure, supported by slavery, engenders a dark, gothic underbelly—especially in Louisiana, a state with a long history of sex scandals involving the same power structures at work in *True Detective*: politicians, educators, and clergy. Billy Lee Tuttle has numerous real-life counterparts, the most famous being Jimmy Swaggart, the Louisiana televangelist whose affairs with prostitutes sparked a 1980s scandal. The conspiracy surrounding Tuttle's ministry also recalls the sex abuse scandals that have shaken the Catholic Church in recent decades. One of the first publicized cases involved Gilbert Gauthe, a priest in Lafayette (where the series is set) who was exposed in 1986 at the center of a cover-up involving hundreds of victims.[28] Tuttle's schools as a source of victims also recalls Louisiana's "bad reputation for inappropriate relationships between school staff and students: in 2014, it ranked third in the United States, counting both convictions and arrests."[29]

Louisiana's dysfunction is evidence not of a system that has failed to work but of a system that, in aiming to help powerful white men pursue their financial and sexual desires, works all too well; its public servants are notorious for avoiding the consequences of political corruption and sexual deviancy. Even repeated public scandal is no deterrent for Louisiana's most infamous, and most successful, politicians; as in *True Detective*, abusive power persists from one generation to the next. David Vitter was reelected to the U.S. Senate in 2010 despite a history of patronizing prostitutes; neither an "open affair" with a burlesque performer, Blaze Starr, nor a stint in a mental hospital prevented Huey Long's brother, "Uncle Earl" Long, from serving three terms as governor in the late 1930s through the early 1960s. Perhaps the "most outrageous political career in a state known for outrageous politicians" is four-term governor Edwin Edwards, who famously bragged before his 1983 victory that "the only way I could lose this election is if I'm caught in bed with a dead girl or a live boy."[30] After a decade in prison for fraud, extortion, racketeering, and money laundering, Edwards, then in his late eighties, continued to seek public office. In *True Detective*'s Louisiana, as in its nonfictional counterpart, this "ain't what kind of world" (FV) where such wrongdoing is brought to justice.

"Things like that didn't happen in these parts when I was young": Southern Identity and Same-Sex Marriage

This paradoxically hyper-conservative deviancy contributes to the South's strange status within the United States. In its identity as a region different from the rest of the nation, the South represents a deviation from American norms, a willful "perversion of its national ideal."[31] While "[d]eviancy is typically thought of as a negative characteristic," queer theory "provides a means to move beyond this simple divide between good and bad."[32] The South's status as a unique region is a vital part of southern identity. As with queerness, asserting one's southernness arises from a need to define one's place *outside,* but *not less than,* the norm: "one's cultural goals as a queer person and as a Southerner might be connected, in that queers and Southerners ask the same questions, such as *What is special and distinct about us, our culture, heritage, and traditions?* and, *Do we really want to be just like you?*"[33] Paradoxically, the South is considered perverse because of its adherence to social norms, and its history of defining the "normal" and discriminating against the "other" has made the region a scapegoat for the nation's racism, sexism, homophobia, religious extremism, and other such ills.

Maggie's father, Jake, as a mouthpiece for southern conservatism, expresses anxiety that the breakdown of traditional gender roles jeopardizes marriage: "Things like that didn't happen in these parts when I was young. People said 'ma'am' and 'sir.' Families stayed together" (ST). This scene takes place in 1995, amid the "culture wars," a period that began with the religious right's "stern calls for a return to schools and homes with clear parental authority"[34] and developed into "ideological warfare [that] continues to center on the issue of racial and cultural diversity."[35] "So you're telling me the world isn't getting worse?" Jake demands. "Everything's sex. Clinton!" (ST). Andrew Manis suggests that at this time, Bill Clinton's name served as a shorthand for challenges to traditional sexuality: "In this era, Bill Clinton, a southerner so liberal as to flout traditional sexual ethics in both his public policy (Gays in the Military) and private life (the Lewinsky scandal), became the Antichrist to many in the Religious Right."[36]

In the midst of these changes, opposition to homosexuality and same-sex marriage became central to southern identity and male identity. Jake nostalgically recalls an earlier time when "[e]veryone wasn't out in the street, yelling about their rights" (ST). While he does not specify *whose* rights are at stake, LGBTQ+ rights became a particularly prominent issue in the 1990s as the movement's focus shifted to legal issues such as adoption, marriage, and military service. The period during which *True Detective* takes place witnessed the passing of Louisiana state laws forbidding both same-sex marriage (1988) and the recognition of such unions from other states (1992);[37] the U.S. Defense of Marriage Act, which defined marriage as exclusively between a man and woman (1996); city benefits extended to same-sex partners in New Orleans (1997);[38] the legalization of same-sex marriage in Vermont (2000) and Massachusetts (2003); the nationwide decriminalization of sodomy with the U.S. Supreme Court's 2003 *Lawrence v. Texas* decision; and the "[p]assage of constitutional amendments prohibiting gay marriage in many southern states in 2004."[39] This period witnessed a telling development in regional attitudes toward same-sex marriage. In the late 1980s, only about 12 percent of Americans favored marriage equality; at the time, factors such as gender, level of education, church attendance, or political affiliation had little effect on one's stance.[40] As acceptance of marriage equality rose nationwide over the next decade, opposition "became more localized to specific subgroups," including men and southerners.[41]

Rejection of same-sex marriage is frequently rooted in conservative ideas about gender; its opponents often frame it as a threat to "traditional" marriage, while support of same-sex marriage corresponds to changing beliefs about marriage in general. In 2005, a decade before the Supreme Court's ruling to legalize same-sex marriage throughout the United States, Stephanie Coontz argued that the possibility of marriage equality stemmed from "the previous revolution in heterosexual marriage. It was heterosexuals who had already created many alternative structures for organizing sexual relationships or raising children and broken down the primacy of two-parent families based on a strict division of labor between men and women."[42] Acceptance of same-sex marriage, therefore, relies on the breakdown of harmful structures at work in both the failed marriages and the deviant abuses portrayed in *True Detective*. In its final two episodes, the show symbolically enacts Rust and Marty's rejection of toxic masculinity: they must defeat Errol Childress, the serial killer who embodies the cultural sins of which Rust and Marty themselves are guilty, before they are free to celebrate their same-sex union. To effectively establish Childress as this symbol of southern heteropatriarchal deviance, the show turns to the conventions of the southern gothic in its final episodes.

"I'm police. I could do terrible things to people with impunity": Subverting the Lynching Trope

The southern gothic is one of many genres that inform *True Detective*, and for the first six episodes, its tropes surface primarily through images of the rural landscape and hints about the "big people" (SF) involved in Dora's murder. Corrupt, powerful men motivated by "pride in their own family line" or "in their own ability to manipulate and victimize others" are a familiar type of southern gothic villain.[43] Overall, the series shows relative restraint, avoiding stereotypes of the genre by portraying the South with complexity and exploring the modern economic and environmental factors responsible for the region's ills. In the final two episodes, however, the show abruptly turns to the most clichéd southern gothic tropes. An elderly black house servant's ranting of the unspeakable horrors of "Carcosa" leads the detectives to the crumbling, vine-choked mansion that Childress shares with his mentally feeble sister/wife, whom he brings to orgasm while she tells the story of their grandfather raping her in the cane fields (FV). They then discover the decaying body of Childress's abusive father tied up in a small building—likely a slave shack—behind the house and, farther back, Carcosa itself, a Civil War fort filled with the skeletal remains of decades' worth of victims.

Nothing about Childress's brief, unremarkable first appearance in the third episode hints at such horrors; he emerges as a full-fledged southern gothic villain when he is needed to clearly contrast with Rust and Marty, who have been chastened by time and regret. The appearance of an inbred villain lurking in his stereotypically southern gothic home links Childress to the historical oppression from which his family derives its power. The southern gothic replaces the medieval castle of its gothic forebears with "plantations, often sprawling and in varying degrees of decrepitude"; within this setting, a "symbolic reference to a fallen aristocracy," secret rooms serve as sites of torture, particularly against slaves.[44] This stereotypical southern depravity appears only in the two episodes that occur entirely in 2012, when the protagonists have reunited to solve the case; older and wiser, they endeavor to reject the toxic southern masculinity that led to the destruction of Marty's marriage and their friendship. In killing Childress, they rid society not just of a dangerous criminal but of the show's symbol of southern deviancy, a heteropatriarchal monster whose defeat symbolizes the weakening of that structure.

But just as the South serves as America's scapegoat for ills found throughout the nation, Childress bears the weight of sins endemic to his whole culture, sins of which Rust and Marty also have been and, to an extent, continue to be guilty—a "blurring of the line between villain and victim" characteristic of the southern gothic.[45] The circumstances surrounding Childress's death (as earlier with the deaths of Ledoux and Dewall), in which he is likened to a lynching victim and the detectives to vigilantes, demonstrate the difficulty Rust and Marty face in opting out of this oppressive system. No longer employed as police (and repeatedly warned against pursuing the case by those who are), they investigate and ultimately execute Childress with no legal authority (AYG, FV). This is the last in a string of extrajudicial killings: earlier in the series, viewers learn that Rust killed a drug user who had been poisoning his daughter (ST), and Marty shoots Reggie Ledoux when he discovers the children held captive (SF). Like lynching victims, these men are suspected of harming weaker members of society but never tried in a court of law, killed by prominent white men who are praised for the acts rather than punished for ignoring protocols.

Whereas vigilantism in various forms was found throughout the country following the Civil War, lynching in particular "became a southern phenomenon that was used most often to enforce white supremacy."[46] The myth of the black rapist reinforced racial and gender supremacy among white men, whose "rhetorical promises of protection came only in return for white women's promise of obedience and adherence to the dictates of middle-class respectability."[47] Long before his identity is revealed, Childress serves as a scapegoat for his culture's crimes against women, allowing Marty to shift the blame away from his own misogyny by invoking the unknown serial killer to discourage his mistress from seeing other men and to end an argument with his wife (ST). The pursuit of Childress can be read as an inversion of the "southern rape complex," in which "the innocent white victim is transformed into a symbol of a threatened southern culture" and "the white male is thereby sanctioned by the 'code of honor' to seek revenge in the form of lynching."[48] Childress is both the lynched rapist and the "symbol of threatened southern culture"—here, an oppressive culture whose time has come to an end.

However well-intentioned Rust and Marty's attempts at curbing criminal activity, police brutality has roots as a "crucial tool for white southerners in their attempt to reinforce white supremacy." Many of the slave patrols that "used means of physical coercion and violence to deter slave rebellions and capture fugitive slaves" later developed into southern police forces.[49] The protagonists use manipulation, intimidation, falsehood, and violence to pursue their professional goals, particularly against women: Marty asserts his dominance over Lisa and Maggie by flashing his badge (LR and WGT), while Rust extorts information and Quaaludes from Lucy, a sex worker. "Of course I'm dangerous," he tells her, "I'm police. I could do terrible things to people with impunity" (ST). They are, of course, lone men risking their lives and careers to defend helpless children, and viewers will likely consider Childress and his ilk deserving of their fates; on the other hand, vigilantes "take the law into their own hands to reinforce existing power relationships, not to subvert them."[50] These morally ambiguous heroes are also men with judicial and social power asserting this authority over those on society's fringes; their actions cannot help but make viewers uneasy, particularly when Childress's fictional death occurs the same year as Trayvon Martin's real one.

In aligning Rust and Marty with vigilantism, the series reminds viewers of the impossibility of eradicating heteropatriarchy; there is no cure for the evils committed against women and children, no possibility for healthy heterosexual partnership or a happy nuclear family in a culture where men hold all the power. To keep from undergoing further harm in the series's final scenes, therefore, women must be erased entirely. Unlike in the confrontation with Ledoux and Dewall in 1995, there is no victim to save (other than Rust and Marty themselves, rescued from their own southern heteropatriarchal pasts by the series's only significant black characters); all the cult's known victims are dead or intractably insane. Women and children continue to disappear in the final scenes. When Maggie visits Marty's bedside with their daughters, only Audrey speaks. Her words, "How are you?," keep the focus on Marty as the camera pulls in on his weeping face, forcing the women out of frame (FV). Rust is treated to the same closeup when he describes a vision of his long-dead daughter "fading out" (FV) as he struggles to let go of his grief. The hierarchies of southern culture are so deeply entrenched that the only possibility that the series offers for a relationship built on mutual respect is between two men.

"All this time, you two, and just like that?": *True Detective*'s Queer Marriage

Given this context, the relaxed humor of the two former policemen's engagement joke, after so much internal and external conflict over masculinity and marriage, serves as a gesture of the troubled heterosexual unions of earlier episodes giving way to a same-sex partnership that displays the trappings of traditional courtship and marriage without its implicit hierarchies. Comparisons of their partnership to a marriage surface throughout the scenes taking place in 2012. In the first episode, Marty twice says "together" to describe his time working with Rust, a word that elsewhere refers to heterosexual partnership (LBD). His assessment of the end of their work partnership sounds more like the description of a breakup: "People change. Relationships change" (LBD). The series spans seventeen years, the same length as Marty and Maggie's marriage. While the show's other partnerships occur within either a nuclear family or an uncontrollable, uncharted "sprawl" (AYG) of "all the branches" (FV)

FIGURE 5.2. Amid the gothic gloom, Marty cradles the injured Rust, with the lighting accentuating both the purity of their relationship and the horrors they have endured.

of Tuttles, Rust and Marty are most often portrayed as a pair, alone in a car and isolated from those toxic networks. Even as single men, parallel flashbacks show them living the same lives in different places (AYG).

The hierarchy-enforcing homoerotic tension of earlier episodes ultimately gives way to the conventions of romance, fitting the familiar phases of courtship narrative: an initial dislike that changes to affection when the two face challenges together; the appropriately timed seven-year itch of 2002; a subsequent breakdown in communication, leading to infidelity and breakup; reunion and reconciliation in 2012, leading Maggie to marvel, "All this time, you two, and just like that?"; and the trappings of engagement and wedding, with an emphasis on the monogamous image of a couple entering the world together (AYG). When Rust descends into Carcosa for his final confrontation with Childress, his gleaming white shirt (one of many visual parallels between Rust and Christ in this scene) suggests both a sacrificial lamb and a wedding gown: "Take the bride's path," the unseen Childress urges. After Rust is injured, Marty cradles him in the *Pietà* pose and calls him "my friend," a designation he had previously rejected (FV; see figure 5.2). The final scene shows an open exchange of emotion, as the previously self-centered Marty is attentive to the heretofore stoic Rust's grief.

Among the more obvious trappings of engagement and wedding ceremonies—the cigarettes in a Tiffany box, Marty kneeling beside Rust's wheelchair, the image of Rust carried away over the threshold in a white gown—another moment, early in the series, foreshadows this symbolic marriage. Rust, questioned about his decision to return to work as a homicide detective, paraphrases a biblical passage that reads: "the body is not made up of one part but of many . . . there are many parts, but one body" (1 Cor. 12:14, 20 NIV). He explains that he was "just trying to stay a part of the body"—that is, to reintegrate into society following four years of isolation while working undercover (ST). Recounting the story in 2012, nearly two decades after the events in question, Rust is in the process of repeating this journey, having returned from "off the grid" to reunite with Marty and solve the case.[51] The chapters in which these verses appear—1 Corinthians 12–13—recall the protagonists' struggle to overcome their culture's upholding of toxic hierarchies.[52] Taken as a whole, 1 Corinthians 12 asserts the value of all members of the body of Christ, regardless of status: "those parts of the body that seem to be weaker are indispensable . . . that there should be no division in the body, but that its parts should have equal concern for each other" (1 Cor. 12.22, 25). Paul then offers to show the reader "the most excellent way" (1 Cor. 12.31), leading to the next chapter, well known as a staple of wedding ceremonies: "Love is patient, love is kind" (1 Cor. 13.4).

The message of 1 Corinthians 12, which urges respect and sympathy toward the weaker members of society, runs directly counter to the oppressive heteropatriarchy of *True Detective*'s southern gothic culture. Over the course of the series, the protagonists come to recognize that "those parts of the body that seem to be weaker are indispensable, and the parts that we think are less honorable we treat with special honor" (1 Cor. 12.22–23). Not only do they no longer seek to dominate the weaker members of society, they now value the more vulnerable, less stereotypically masculine parts of their selves.[53] The subsequent chapter, so deeply associated with wedding ceremonies, lists the faults they have overcome in order to find peace and contentment in their partnership: "It does not envy, it does not boast, it is not proud. It does not dishonor others, it is not self-seeking, it is not easily angered, it keeps no record of wrongs" (1 Cor. 13.4–5). It suggests love can overcome all worldly evils, even the seemingly unstoppable corruption of the Louisiana political machine: "Love does not delight in evil but rejoices with the truth. It always protects, always trusts, always hopes, always perseveres. Love never fails" (1 Cor. 13.6–8).

This outlook runs counter to the cynicism pervading *True Detective* even in its final scenes, which reveal that most of the Tuttle cult escape justice. Yet the closing moments of the show offer cautious hope. "Where I wanted them to go in their journeys wasn't a point of redemption or conversion or even closure," states show writer Nic Pizzolatto, "but a point of deliverance. They are not healed, but now, for the first time, you can imagine a future where they are healed."[54] The "Louisiana marriage" between Rust and Marty is, like all marriages, an imperfect one; it bears the scars of their culture's gothic toxicity, just as both men bear literal scars from their fight with Childress. The damage that patriarchy has inflicted on the cult's victims, and on the protagonists' relationships with women, cannot be undone, but it is not too late for them to step into the future in hopes of being better men. Three years after the conclusion of *True Detective*'s first season, the city of New Orleans began, amid great controversy, to remove Confederate monuments from city property. Mayor Mitch Landrieu called these statues "an affront to our present, and a bad prescription for our future. We should not be afraid to confront and reconcile our past."[55] Louisiana, like all the South, is a place with a vibrant and troubled past, struggling to learn from its history and move to a more inclusive future. Slowly but surely, the light, as Rust says in the show's closing moments, is winning.

NOTES

1. *True Detective*, dir. Cary Fukunaga (HBO, 2014), DVD. The eight episodes of the first season are cited parenthetically: "The Long Bright Dark" (LBD), "Seeing Things" (ST), "The Locked Room" (LR), "Who Goes There" (WGT), "The Secret Fates of All Life" (SF), "Haunted Houses" (HH), "After You've Gone" (AYG), and "Form and Void" (FV).

2. Sharon Sharp, "Sexuality," *The New Encyclopedia of Southern Culture* (hereafter *NESC*), ed. Charles Reagan Wilson, 24 vols. (Chapel Hill: University of North Carolina Press, 2006–13), vol. 13, *Gender*, 257–62, at 261; John Howard, "Gays," *NESC*, 13:122–26, at 122.

3. Because of *True Detective*'s anthology format, I will use "the series" throughout to refer to the first season.

4. Elizabeth Grosz, "Experimental Desire: Rethinking Queer Subjectivity," *Supposing the Subject*, ed. Joan Copjec (New York: Verso, 1994), 133–58, at 154.

5. I use the word "heterosexual" throughout to mean sexual relationships between men and women, not to suggest that the participants are necessarily heterosexual.

6. Emily Nussbaum, "Cool Story, Bro: The Shallow Deep Talk of *True Detective*," *New Yorker* 3 March 2014, Web.

7. Nikki Sullivan, *A Critical Introduction to Queer Theory* (New York: New York University Press, 2003), 123, 122.

8. Lorri Glover, "Marriage and Courtship," *NESC*, 13:173–78, at 173, 176, 177.

9. Orville Burton, "Fatherhood," *NESC*, 13:106–10, at 106.

10. Marjorie Spruill, "Feminism and Antifeminism," *NESC*, 13:110–14, at 110, 112.

11. Michael Pfeifer, "Homicide," *NESC*, vol. 19, *Violence*, 74–78, at 78, 74.

12. Pfeifer, "Homicide," 76.

13. Benjamin E. Wise, "Sideways, Backwards, and Queer: Toward a New Southern Studies," *Journal of American Studies* 48.3 (2003): 719–22, at 721.

14. Wise, "Sideways, Backwards, and Queer," 721.

15. Burton, "Fatherhood," 106.

16. Daniel Smith, "Family Dynasties," *NESC*, 13:101–4, at 103.

17. Sharp, "Sexuality," 257.

18. Alecia Long, "Prostitution (New Orleans)," *NESC*, 13:342–44, at 343.

19. Lisa Dorr, "Rape," *NESC*, 13:227–31, at 227.

20. *True Detective*'s medium impacted viewers' reading of such symbols. The series was created by a prose fiction author/creative writing professor and directed by a filmmaker; both writer Nic Pizzolatto and director Cary Fukunaga had little to no prior experience in television, and the show's emphasis on symbolism, intertextuality, and character development reflects its creators' literary and filmic roots. As a week-to-week serial whose plot ostensibly concerned a murder investigation, however, *True Detective* (perhaps unintentionally, as interviews with Pizzolatto suggest) invited audiences to focus on the mystery of Dora Lange's fate. Symbolic echoes of the Tuttles' abuses were read as "clues" to the mystery, while Rust and Marty's personal lives were often dismissed as mere subplot, and many viewers were sorely disappointed with an ending that emphasized character development over conspiracy.

21. William O'Hare, Annie E. Casey Foundation, and Vicki L. Lamb, "Ranking States on Improvement in Child Well-Being since 2000," 18 March 2009, aecf.org/m/resourcedoc/AECF-RankingStatesOnImprovementInChildWellBeing-2009-Full.pdf.

22. This choice certainly sends a disturbing message, implying that same-sex desire is inextricable from deviant sexuality and sexual abuse, and I do not wish to dismiss the harm such stereotypes cause. Within the context of the series, however, it is worth noting that relationships between men and women hardly fare any better. Other than the fact that we know nothing, either good or bad, about Papania's marriage or Maggie's implied remarriage, heterosexual relationships on *True Detective* are uniformly presented in a negative light.

23. Judith Butler, *Gender Trouble* (New York: Routledge, 1990), 185, 186 (emphasis in original).

24. Burton, "Fatherhood," 106.

25. For more on the role of monasticism and asceticism regarding Rust, see my essay "'I contemplate the moment in the garden': Medieval Sainthood in *True Detective*," *True Detective: Critical Essays on the HBO Series*, ed. Scott F. Stoddart and Michael Samuel (Lanham, Md.: Lexington, 2018), 101–20.

26. Ben Morgan, "Spiraling Masculinity: The Postmodern Trajectory of the Hero in HBO's *True Detective*" (presentation, Popular Culture Association/American Culture Association National Conference, New Orleans, 1–4 April 2015), 4.

27. Morgan, "Spiraling Masculinity," 7.

28. Madeleine Baran, "Betrayed by Silence," Minnesota Public Radio 21 July 2014; Associated Press, "Pedophile Ex-priest Gilbert Gauthe Out of Texas Jail," NOLA.com 26 April 2010.

29. Danielle Dreilinger, "What's with Destrehan High? Three Teacher-Student Sex Cases in Two Years," NOLA.com 15 January 2016.

30. Mark Jacobson, "Edwin Edwards Will Live Forever," *New York Magazine* 16 July 2014, Web. Edwin Tuttle's name is likely an homage.

31. R. Bruce Brasell, "'The Degeneration of Nationalism': Colonialism, Perversion, and the American South," *Mississippi Quarterly* 56.1 (2002–3): 33–54, at 33.

32. Brasell, "'The Degeneration of Nationalism,'" 49.

33. Pippa Holloway, "Manifesto for a Queer South Politics," *PMLA* 131.1 (2016): 182–86, at 183.

34. Ted Ownby, "Family," *NESC*, 13:91–97, at 96.

35. Andrew Manis, "Culture Wars," *NESC*, vol. 10, *Law and Politics*, 177–81, at 177.

36. Manis, "Culture Wars," 180.

37. CC89 and CC3520, Louisiana State Legislature, 14 March 2016.

38. "New Orleans Same-Sex Partner Benefits Protected," *Lambda Legal*, lambdalegal.org/publications/new-orleans-same-sex-partner-benefits-protected.

39. Sharp, "Sexuality," 262.

40. Dawn Baunach, "Changing Same-Sex Marriage Attitudes in America from 1988 through 2010," *Public Opinion Quarterly* 76.2 (2012): 364–78, at 368.

41. Baunach, "Changing Same-Sex Marriage Attitudes," 364, 375–76.

42. Stephanie Coontz, *Marriage, a History: From Obedience to Intimacy, or How Love Conquered Marriage* (New York: Viking, 2005), 274.

43. Bridget M. Marshall, "Defining Southern Gothic," *Southern Gothic Literature*, ed. Jay Ellis (Ipswich, Mass.: Salem, 2013), 3–18, at 8.

44. Marshall, "Defining Southern Gothic," 6, 7.

45. Marshall, "Defining Southern Gothic," 10.

46. Robert Ingalls, "Vigilantism," *NESC*, 19:185–89, at 187.

47. Dorr, "Rape," 230.

48. Deborah E. Barker, *Reconstructing Violence: The Southern Rape Complex in Film and Literature* (Baton Rouge: Louisiana State University Press, 2015), 1.

49. Silvan Niedermeier, "Police Brutality," *NESC*, 19:130–32, at 130, 131.

50. Ingalls, "Vigilantism," 185.

51. The phrase "off the grid," used elsewhere to describe the Tuttle cult's activities, underscores how Rust's rejection of society is as toxic as the cult's rejection of societal standards of decency.

52. The series does not quote from the other parts of 1 Corinthians 12–13, but given how closely it fits these themes, as well as how densely the series was packed with textual references and how ardently its viewers scrutinized them, it is conceivable that viewers may have noticed the verse's connection to such a well-known chapter as 1 Corinthians 13, or that Pizzolatto may have intended the verse to be read in the context of the surrounding passages.

53. For more on Rust's developing sense of compassion for the victimized, see my essay "'I contemplate the moment in the garden,'" 107–10.

54. Jeff Jensen, "*True Detective* Post-mortem: Creator Nic Pizzolatto on Happy Endings, Season 2, and the Future of Cohle and Hart," *Entertainment Weekly* 10 March 2014, Web.

55. Madison Park, Keith Allen, and Jason Hanna, "New Orleans Begins Removing Second Confederate Monument," CNN 11 May 2017, Web.

Chapter 6 ▸ Working toward a Southern Erostocracy: The Wages of Homosocial Labor in the *Magic Mike* Films

TED ATKINSON

It's Reigning Men: Performing a Southern Erostocracy

When the film *Magic Mike*, directed by Steven Soderbergh, was released in 2012, it enjoyed a combination of box-office profits and critical acclaim not often seen in an era of cinematic universes populated with larger-than-life figures. In those realms, the hard bodies are superheroes who don elaborate costumes to perform feats of strength and prowess, usually to save the world from destruction. In the more grounded domain of *Magic Mike*, however, the costumes inevitably come off in performances designed to exploit the objectifying gazes of straight women, gay men, or anyone looking to invest in the economy of playful desire and masculine fantasy that defines the industry known as male entertainment. The framing of the highly stylized and choreographed performances creates a feast of visual consumption that seats the customers depicted in the film at the table and leaves moviegoers once removed by way of voyeurism. *Magic Mike* was so successful that a sequel, *Magic Mike XXL*, was released in 2015; it was directed by Soderbergh protégé Gregory Jacobs and hewed closely to the established formula of the backstage drama while widening the expanse by taking the show on the road. The second film built on the accomplishments of the first, garnering a larger haul at the box office and becoming one of those rare examples of a sequel generally regarded as better than the original. The question of why these films were successful would seem to call for an easy answer derived from a bare minimum of reflection on how screen and skin combine to produce abundant visual pleasure, if not profound narrative cinema. For all of the superficial (sex) appeal, though, the *Magic Mike* films operate on another frequency—one more deeply attuned to the mode of social consciousness and commentary that informs Soderbergh's body of work.[1]

That the films are set in the U.S. South—Tampa, Florida, and various locales along the southern Atlantic seaboard—might seem incidental in a cursory viewing. It is reasonable to assume that the generous tax breaks some southern states have enacted to entice filmmakers had a hand in the choice of locations. The regional setting is more pronounced in the sequel than in the original. Still, in each case the filmmakers draw from a southern imaginary defined by Deborah Barker and Kathryn McKee as "an amorphous and sometimes conflicting collection of images, ideas, attitudes, practices, linguistic accents, histories, and fantasies about a shifting geographic region and time." This approach means that the films extend a historical pattern in which the South in American cinema has served "as a repository for the nation's unresolved problems and contradictions."[2] Specifically, the conditions of being a man laboring under late capitalism find representation in the *Magic Mike* films. A central concern is the precarity that working men in an economy shaped by the dual forces of globalization and neoliberalism endure as a fixture of daily life. For the most part, Mike and his fellow performers turn to male entertainment in response to precarity, hoping to find some measure of stability, agency, and solidarity through the homosocial labor they perform. That work involves the strategic unsettling of heteronormativity and queering of rigidly constructed masculinity to project fantasies in which idealized male bodies in choreographed motion express the problem of alienated labor and the desire for autonomy and satisfaction in working life. The performances, including simulated consensual sex acts, model customer service relations in which the depersonalized exchanges of the neoliberal marketplace vie with the magical possibilities of eros. In both films, images and terms associated with nobility become part of the act, serving as figurative means of envisioning what can be termed an erostocracy, as the male entertainers fashion themselves a noble clan (often in blue-collar drag) and pledge devotion to customers heralded as regal and worthy of service regardless of body type (stipulation: as long as they are flush with dollar bills). Here again, the southern setting provides a fitting backdrop: the historical fixation on aristocracy in the southern imaginary adds symbolic weight to the fantasy of an erostocracy, the thrust of which is to stage buoyant performances of social mobility that are hard to come by for real.[3]

The critical reception of the original film shows the recognition that much of its magic comes from the capacity to deliver pointed commentary on matters of pressing social and economic concern in an entertaining package. Film critics in the popular press aligned *Magic Mike* with an emergent trend in film and television responsive to the devastation of the Great Recession. Keith Phipps, in a review for the *A.V. Club,* calls *Magic Mike* "an of-the-moment film about life in a down economy, so much so that it would play like a bait-and-switch if it didn't just as thoroughly deliver as a film about stripping."[4] In a *New York Times* review of *Magic Mike XXL,* A. O. Scott casts the original as "a musical fable for a moment of economic anxiety," adding that the secret to the sequel's greater success lies in dispensing with such overt themes to revel in the pure fun of spectacle.[5] It is true that the plight of the post–Great Recession precariat gets explicit treatment in *Magic Mike.* But it goes too far to say that those concerns are absent from the sequel. Looking back to the culture of the Great Depression is helpful for illustrating the point. The heavy doses of soberness and the overt commentary in *Magic Mike* are reminiscent of the "social problem" films prevalent during the 1930s, while the frivolity of *Magic Mike XXL* recalls the escapism that audiences craved—as in, say, Busby Berkeley's musicals. Another analogy that springs to mind is Preston Sturges's *Sullivan's Travels* (1941): Soderbergh strikes notes similar to those of the protagonist, Sully, a limousine liberal director who seeks to produce a timely film to dramatize the plight and extol the virtues of the common man. Jacobs infuses *Magic Mike XXL* with metacommentary on the value of escapism and the mechanics of the entertainment industry to deliver its brand of social consciousness, striking a similar balance to the one Sturges achieves in *Sullivan's Travels.*

As entertainment that explores relations between economic distress and performances of masculinity, the *Magic Mike* films fit into a broader cultural history of American manhood traceable in popular culture and expressed in terms of crisis. In *Manhood in America: A Cultural History,* Michael Kimmel draws a timeline from the nation's founding to the cusp of the new millennium. Through analysis of various cultural artifacts, he pinpoints the emergence of the self-made man as a mythic construct in the eighteenth century and traces its influence over time. It was most influential at moments when (white) men who understood self-making as their American birthright sensed that it was in jeopardy, whether precipitated by economic downturns or by the sweeping social changes championed by women's-rights and civil-rights activists. Kimmel identifies a more pernicious threat in a "cultural malaise" that is engendered by industrialization and modernization and characterized by "empty anxiety that sprang directly from the blind pursuit of marketplace masculinity."[6] This anxious pursuit, Kimmel argues, found expression in the idealized male forms on display in the mid-twentieth-century magazines purportedly devoted to bodybuilding but likely consumed as soft-core porn. In the industrial era of manufacturing jobs, the rugged, muscular physiques on exhibition embodied the ideal of potent production in the factory and reproduction in the household.

As the *Magic Mike* films attest, the symbolic value of male musculature has changed with the decline of manufacturing jobs and the growth of a neoliberal economy dominated by the service sector. The physiques of the men in these films, like those of the famous exotic dancers known as the Chippendales, appear not so much rugged as stylized. Crafted and commodified, bronzed and waxed, the male entertainers in the *Magic Mike* films are ready to serve themselves up in specular displays of eroticism and athleticism that appear to spare no effort. They work hard for the money. Like their predecessors in the bodybuilding magazines, these men both embody and transcend the economic conditions they experience, though in noticeably redefined terms. As Linda McDowell observes, working for wages or tips in a service economy "involves the establishment of social relationships, albeit typically transitory, with customers." The resulting "co-presence of workers and purchasers" is enacted through the close proximity of bodies during the process of exchange: "In these consumer-driven, service-dominated economies, individuals' bodies—as the producers and objects of exchange—have become absolutely central in a way that differs from the embodied labour power driving manufacturing industries. The physical attributes of the body providing a service are part of the exchange that occurs."[7] On one level, the *Magic Mike* films stage the literal enactment of such transactions, extending the logic of the service sector to an extreme. On a deeper level, they express the desire for empowerment sufficient to overcome the depersonalization and emasculation that come from the reduction of human interactions to base economic transactions.

Bad Bromance: Testing the Limits of Homosocial (Be)longing in *Magic Mike*

In the opening sequence of *Magic Mike*, the protagonist is introduced not on center stage but in the quotidian routine of an average workday. Mike Lane, as played by Channing Tatum, drives away in his pickup truck past a white van emblazoned with a "Mike's Mobile Detailing" placard visible in the frame. The implication is that Mike works at least two jobs. When Mike arrives at work, a construction site, he learns that the foreman has once again used a Craigslist classified advertisement to assemble a group of haggard day laborers. Mike is a crew leader in charge of laying roof tile in a pattern that requires an experienced hand. After voicing displeasure to the foreman, Mike is met with a sharp rebuke: "I can't have fucking union guys around here balking about benefits and shit!" Apparently even Florida unionism, dealt a virtual death blow in the late 1960s when the state jumped on the antilabor bandwagon with the passage of right-to-work legislation, is too restrictive for the company whose bottom line is the foreman's main concern. The scene establishes the precarity and exploitation experienced by contingent labor as a key theme, with the construction site calling to mind the housing bubble that burst and sent the Great Recession into overdrive, leaving scores of homeowners and construction workers in dire straits.

In addition to serving as a thematic foundation, the construction site is the setting for a budding bromance between Mike and one of the day laborers, Adam (Alex Pettyfer), who is called The Kid for most of the film.[8] On a rooftop and ready to start the tile job, Mike discovers that The Kid gives new meaning to the term "unskilled labor," having never worked in construction before. The scene functions as a "meet cute," the popular term for that moment in a rom-com when the leads first connect. As a brom-com variation, the rooftop encounter establishes a rapport "between men," to borrow the main title of Eve Kosofsky Sedgwick's landmark study of male homosociality in English literature. Sedgwick argues that societal changes registered in malleable constructions of homosocial desire such that "the emerging pattern of male friendship, mentorship, entitlement, rivalry, and hetero- and homosexuality was in an intimate and shifting relation to class."[9] Sedgwick's theory is applicable given the conditions of working-class struggle that precipitate homosocial bonding between Mike and The Kid.

Not surprisingly, The Kid is not long for the construction business. It becomes clear that the sagging economy is a factor in his poor job prospects, but so is an inflated ego held over from his time as a promising college football recruit. That aspiration foundered because he failed to adhere to the coach's program, evincing a problem with authority that continues to shape his outlook on life and work. When his sister, Brooke (Cody Horn), confronts him about losing yet another job and urges him to consider making his way onto the professional track, he dismisses the idea with a reminder that he does not wear ties. "You know my rules," The Kid tells Brooke, who is allowing him to live with her despite the fact that he does not contribute much, if anything, to the rent and household expenses. There is obvious room for improvement in The Kid—a project that Mike, a striver with entrepreneurial aspirations and a perception of himself as a man with a plan, is willing to undertake.

Although Mike believes his sense of purpose sets him apart from his aimless protégé, the unfolding bromance reveals that Mike is in a state of denial about his own arrested development. A key factor in this realization is the feelings that Mike develops for Brooke, who resists his advances by prolonging her relationship with an obnoxious corporate executive. The dynamic involving Mike, The Kid, and Brooke enacts the theory of triangulation that Sedgwick describes when she notes the homoerotic bonds that form between men as they vie for the attention and affection of a woman.[10] The arrangement is fraught with psychological implications for Mike's ego, as the bromance with The Kid becomes the freewheeling domain of the id and the romance with Brooke delivers the normalizing influences of the superego.[11] The bromance starts to flourish amid the gigs, clubs, and marathon parties to which Mike introduces The Kid. This Adam is cut from the mold of the mythic "American Adam," acting as the purportedly innocent figure who braves the new world—or, better yet, the underworld of Tampa nightlife—with a lack of knowledge and experience that makes him highly impressionable.[12] While Brooke does visit the underworld, partly out of curiosity but mostly in an effort to rescue her brother, she is clearly on the up and up, maintaining a respectable day job as a Medicaid claims specialist and professing values in keeping with an ethos of "legitimate" work as a measure of character.

The stable domestic sphere of Brooke's quiet apartment is far removed from the revelries of the Tampa underworld, where Mike dazzles audiences on the strength of raw sex appeal and natural dancing talent. The Kid's tutelage involves an entrée into the XQuisite Male Dance Revue with Dallas (Matthew McConaughey) at the helm and Big Dick Richie (Joe Manganiello), Ken (Matt Bomer), Tito (Adam Rodriguez), and Tarzan (Kevin Nash) on the bill with the headlining Magic Mike. The backstage drama component of the film comes to the fore when The Kid first visits the XQuisite. The scene unsettles the masculine/feminine gender binary with shots of Richie using a sewing machine to make alterations to his costume and Tito shaving his legs with a pink razor while the banter, peppered with "bro" deployed as a term of endearment, flows freely. Whether backstage, on stage, or in social settings, this cohort plays a game of alternately transgressing and reinforcing heteronormativity such that performing a fluid form of masculinity is an essential qualification for becoming an XQuisite man.

The first sequence of performances brings the issue of fluid masculinity literally and figuratively to center stage. In the opening number, the full revue performs a choreographed routine to "It's Raining Men," a 1983 disco hit by the Weather Girls that famously became a gay anthem. While the audience in the club is composed entirely of women screaming in delight and waving dollar bills, the song selection is an appeal to gay men—an important target audience for both installments of *Magic Mike*. The men perform a series of suggestive gestures and poses with umbrellas, transforming them into phallic symbols of potency to whet the appetites of customers and to attract a shower of dollars. Magic Mike's first performance is in keeping with the conventions of blue-collar erotica, a staple of male entertainment—and pornography for that matter. Dancing on screen, Tatum evokes the athleticism of Gene Kelly melded with the robotic pop motions and smooth gliding that distinguish the hip-hop aesthetic.[13] Dressed in construction garb, Mike reconstructs the terms of his unfulfilling day job and takes inspiration from his dream of becoming a custom furniture maker and small business owner. To paraphrase W. B. Yeats's famous poetic figuration, it is difficult to separate the dancer from the dance as Mike channels the frustration of alienated labor and thwarted aspiration into bodily expression of the desire for autonomy and a meaningful vocation.

On his first night at the XQuisite, The Kid is enlisted to perform when Tarzan becomes incapacitated from imbibing too much of a narcotic elixir concocted for performance enhancement. The plot twist involving the neophyte who is suddenly catapulted from behind the scenes to center stage is a common feature of the backstage drama. In this instance The Kid, wearing the same jeans and ill-fitting hoodie he had on earlier at the construction site, gets a push from Mike and finds himself in front of the cheering throng wanting to see some skin. The lack of a gimmick becomes his gimmick: his inhibition makes for a slow burn of a striptease that eventually heats up, much to the delight of the customers thrilled by his boyish good looks and physical attributes. As part of the improvised number, performed to Madonna's "Like a Virgin," he allows a young woman whom he met earlier at a club to crown him with the tiara she has been wearing in celebration of her twenty-first birthday (see figure 6.1). Later, The Kid wears the tiara again in a stylized sequence in which the camera pans down in close-up to reveal the young woman's hands

FIGURE 6.1. In a reversal of the conventional gender roles performed in a lap dance, The Kid (Alex Pettyfer), clad in a tiara, delivers attentive customer service during his coronation as an XQuisite man.

unzipping his jeans, then moves to her friend and Mike reflected upside down in a mirror as they kiss. The positioning of the actors and the lighting obscure the two women and highlight The Kid and Mike, yielding the visual implication of a homoerotic bond between men. The implications of this connection become clear the next morning when The Kid says to Mike during a swim, "I think, um, we should be best friends," essentially taking the bromance to the next level. The Kid's coronation and the strengthening of his homosocial bond with Mike are the culmination of his initiation into the XQuisite erostocracy.

After The Kid's impromptu debut, Dallas clearly recognizes his potential to make a contribution to the revue and, of course, to the club's bottom line. He gives The Kid notes on his performance, stressing that a solid routine relies on not allowing reality to compromise the fantasy. Serving the customer with pleasure should involve the illusion of availability but not intimacy so as to achieve the maximum effect. "Never kiss the girls," Dallas advises, before stating a key provision of the standard XQuisite employment contract: "Every man keeps every dollar he makes on that stage." Dallas's grand showman shtick, which he performs with aplomb on the stage and off, entails self-fashioning as a benevolent leader of the band—one of the guys but also *the* one who defines the path for the enterprise by dreaming big enough for the men to see where he wants to take them. In this role, Dallas competes with Mike for influence in the effort to shape the novice into an XQuisite man—competition that increases a tension between the leader and the headliner that apparently has been brewing for some time. Accordingly, the easygoing scene in which Mike takes The Kid shopping "for a look" marks another step forward in their budding bromance, standing in contrast to the scene in which Dallas provides intensive instruction in a dance rehearsal hall by modeling gyrating moves in a mirror for The Kid and molding him with a literally hands-on pedagogy of hard-body homosociality.

The Kid enthusiastically immerses himself in the culture of male entertainment, adopting the requisite clothing and grooming habits and contending with what this means for his understanding of masculinity. When Brooke finds his stash of costumes and catches him shaving his legs with one of her razors, she offers reassurance: "I don't care what your preferences are." The Kid's rapid response, fueled by homosexual panic, evinces a need to set the record straight, in every sense of the word, by emphatically asserting his heterosexuality. It is clear that the rules of the bromance between Mike and The Kid and the homosocial bonding in the revue dictate compliance with compulsory heterosexuality. Love between men does enjoy freedom of expression, but it dare not do more than speak its name. A late-night party at Dallas's McMansion on Fourth of July weekend demonstrates how the rules apply in practice. On this festive occasion, Dallas announces that the markets have hit a "sweet spot" such that his plan to expand to Miami can come to fruition, paving the way for the "cock-rocking Kings of Tampa" to be crowned the "cock-rocking Kings of Miami." While the kings, save for a skeptical Mike, are high on believing, they also feel the effects of alcohol and drugs—not least doses of Molly (MDMA, or Ecstasy) that provide social lubrication for homosocial affection. One such exchange occurs through yet another instance of triangulation, as the The Kid goes into a room where Ken and a topless woman are lying on a bed. Noticing that The Kid is eyeing the woman's breasts, Ken gets her consent to let his friend feel her up. While The Kid caresses her breasts, he and Ken remain locked in eye contact as they express bro-therly love. Rather than serving the woman, as they do on stage, the men require the woman to serve as heteronormative protection against the "danger" of homosociality giving way to homosexuality. But the erotic appeal is more complicated than that, taking into account that Bomer is an openly gay actor and that his interaction with Pettyfer is another wink to gay men in the audience.

The wild nights of sex, drugs, and alcohol send The Kid into a downward spiral of self-destructive behavior. When he ruins a gig at a sorority house, Mike berates him for being irresponsible and reckless—a charge that gains further justification when Mike discovers that The Kid has lost a stash of Ecstasy, which he agreed to sell as part of a sideline scheme to earn extra cash, and is now on the hook with a dangerous kingpin to the tune of ten thousand dollars. Mike loses the moral high ground, though, when a series of disappointments influence him to join The Kid in steering into the skid of reckless behavior. Unable to secure financing for his custom furniture business, Mike feels chronic frustration and gives in to the temptation of an all-night bender. In a surreal morning-after scene, Brooke bursts into Mike's house frantic with worry about her brother, only to find him unconscious on the floor in a pool of vomit, which is now breakfast for a small pet pig belonging to Nora, an enigmatic woman established earlier as a Siren figure. Having broken his promise to Brooke to protect her brother, Mike endures a wrathful scolding and falls further into the despair of self-loathing and failure.

For Mike, this wake-up call brings the realization that the wages of homosocial labor are woefully inadequate to sustain meaningful connections. An inevitable clash with Dallas brings the issue to a head. When Mike threatens to quit, hoping to expose Dallas as a greedy manipulator by jeopardizing the grand Miami plan, the showman calls his bluff. "You gotta deal with what you got," Dallas says. "You are worth the cash you pry out of their purses, and you know that better than anybody." This dose of reality exposes the magic trick as an illusion, reducing the noble (customer) service of the erostocracy to a degrading transaction that figures Mike's body in terms of monetary value. The choice presented in the triangulated relationship with The Kid and Brooke now becomes crystal clear, and Magic Mike, the king of the "cock-rocking Kings of Tampa," decides to abdicate his XQuisite throne to pursue a relationship with Brooke. When she initially rejects him, declaring, "I see you. . . . You are a bullshit thirty-year-old male stripper," Mike counters with an appeal to authenticity and aspiration: "I'm not my lifestyle. Am I Magic Mike right now talking to you? I'm not my goddam job. . . . It is what I do, but it's not who I am. I want to own something." The passion Mike expresses to Brooke contrasts with the hollowness of his last meeting with her brother. "I have freedom, thanks to you," The Kid tells Mike, clearly having learned nothing from his recent brushes with death. The Kid knows that Mike has spent the startup money for his furniture business to bail him out of the drug-dealing debacle, but all he has to offer is a meaningless toast (with Mike's beer) to "bright futures" and an empty promise to repay the money. "Kid's in. Mike's out," Dallas later declares, bringing an official end to the bad bromance and punctuating the film's conservative turn to heteronormative romance once Brooke learns who saved her brother's life with a transaction that reveals the soul of Mike Lane beneath the skin of Magic Mike.

Bro Time: The Return of the Kings in *Magic Mike XXL*

The opening sequence of *Magic Mike XXL* is similar to the one in the original, only this time the impression is that a dream must have come true. As Mike and another man carry a piece of furniture, a placard emblazoned with "Mike Lane Custom Designs" is visible on the side of the truck. The dialogue, however, reveals that living the dream is not easy for Mike, who cannot afford the retail space he needs to expand his small business enough to secure its viability. Insufficient capital remains a drain on the creative and entrepreneurial spirit that Mike longs to express in its fullness. In a plot twist that signals the film's engagement with representations of the South in American culture, Mike receives a call that evokes the famous Faulknerian observation that the past is never past. Calling from Miami, Tarzan breaks the news that Dallas has died and that he and the other members of the revue will be in Tampa. When Mike arrives at their hotel wearing a black suit in anticipation of a wake, he finds instead that a raucous pool party is in full swing and that he has been tricked. Dallas is not dead; rather, he has left with The Kid to pursue a business opportunity in China. This self-serving move shows that Mike was right about Dallas all along. As the contemplative Big Dick Richie explains, the betrayal by their ringleader prompted the collective decision to undertake a "pilgrimage"—the return of the kings to the annual male stripper convention in Myrtle Beach, South Carolina, where they once reigned supreme. "If I'm going down," Richie declares, "I'm going down in a fucking tsunami of dollar bills." All this weary band of bros needs now is for Mike to find his magic again and join them in the quest for renewal and redemption.

At the end of the first film, Mike is determined to escape the hedonism of male entertainment for the stable domesticity he believes a relationship with Brooke will afford. Initially, Mike toes the line in the sequel by declining the invitation to join the pilgrimage. "I'm just happy to be running my own show for once," he says, figuratively underlining the notion that he has shed the skin of his stage persona. But Mike remains a consummate performer: his claim of newfound autonomy, success, and satisfaction in work and life masks the precarity he is actually experiencing. He is not only struggling to keep his business afloat but also hurting after a difficult split with Brooke when she declined his marriage proposal for reasons he does not fully explain when he finally opens up to his buddies.[14] Given these disappointments and the prospect of a trip to Myrtle Beach, Mike is hard pressed to keep his past from intervening in his present. In the first dance sequence in the film, Mike is alone in his carpentry shop working on a piece of furniture while music plays in the background. When the opening chords of Ginuwine's "Pony" blare from the speaker, Magic Mike is resurrected in a tantalizing display of skill, agility, and strength on Tatum's part. The choreography blends the showmanship of male entertainment with the craftsmanship of furniture making, using the tools of both trades to craft a sublime bodily expression of desire for unalienated labor. In this self-made performance, Mike embodies the mythic figure of, in Michael Kimmel's words, the "Heroic Artisan, characterized by the Jeffersonian virtues of the yeoman and the autonomous shopkeeper."[15] On this count, the film indulges in the well-worn American practice of defining the South against a future-oriented national temporality calibrated for technological progress and, consequently, as an optimal site for preserving cultural traditions and practices in an amber of historicity that resonates with "authenticity."[16]

The refrain of "Pony" ("If you're horny, let's do it, ride it, my pony. My saddle's waiting, come and jump on it") serves as a motivational call to Mike and a signal to the audience that he is now up for the quest. Mike joins the crew just as they are poised to take off in the ice cream truck Tito and Tobias (Gabriel Iglesias), the former manager of the XQuisite club, have purchased with the goal of starting a business selling frozen yogurt—or, as Tito puts it, "artisanal probiotic fro-yo." The narrative assumes the familiar episodic structure of a road movie as the men make their first stop at Mad Mary's, a strip club in Jacksonville, where a drag queen named Miss Tori Snatch (Vicky Vox) is "host for this evening of good ol' swamp country debauchery" and emcee for a contest to name the Best Amateur Queen. The initial contestants take to the stage, performing runway walks and dance moves reminiscent of those captured in the acclaimed documentary *Paris Is Burning* (Jennie Livingston, 1990), which centers on New York drag ball culture in the 1980s. They eventually cede center stage to the professionals, and each king takes his turn as an amateur queen. The scene injects the film with a dose of camp, as the men vogue and vamp in an effort to emulate the house style. For Richie, Mike's performance is more than mere camp: it is a pact made as a genuine show of commitment to the journey they have undertaken. When the scene shifts from the camp of Mad Mary's to a campfire setting, the process of homosocial bonding becomes even more ritualistic as Mike is brought further back into the fold through a playful "gladiator show" and pledges of bro-hood that harken back to the mythopoetic philosophy of the 1980s men's movement. The juxtaposition of the two camps follows the established pattern in the

Magic Mike films of unsettling and then restoring heteronormative constructions of masculinity and of using experiments with queerness as mechanisms for homosocial bonding.

Although the comic tone signals that the earnest investment in the notion of self-actualization derived from men's movement philosophy is all in good fun, there is an undercurrent that continues the engagement with the serious concerns that *Magic Mike* explicitly raises. The journey to Myrtle Beach is fueled by a longing for solidarity, personal integrity, and dignity in work. There is a desire for the self to be actualized through authenticity that the men (strip)tease out by trying on different stage personas and performances in search of one that naturally fits. One of the standout scenes in the film is a case in point. The men take doses of Molly in an effort to unleash creativity, and the desire to break out of conventional molds becomes a focal point. For Richie, this means doing away with the safety net of his standard fireman act in favor of something more expressive of his true aspirations. When he confesses self-doubt, arguing that his dancing talent is limited, Mike intervenes. "Look at you," he says. "You're a fucking Greek god. You just have to be you." Mike then throws down the gauntlet, affirming Richie's natural endowments (besides the one advertised in his stage name) and insisting that he can prove himself by bringing a smile to the dour face of a convenience store clerk who is caught in a smartphone trance. To the nondiegetic sound of "I Want It That Way" by the Backstreet Boys, Richie performs an improvised routine that makes use of Cheetos (a clever nod to the gleeful cheesiness on display, perhaps) and bottled water as props to simulate ejaculation. As Richie, Manganiello cuts the figure of a marble statue sprung to life, transforming the dead zone of the fluorescent-lit store into a makeshift platform for posing. For much of the scene, the clerk remains detached, indifferent to the hard body's hard work to coax the winning smile. When it does finally appear, it makes for a moment of mutual appreciation and human connection charged with eros and contrasted with the alienating transactions that routinely take place in such corners of the service economy in the name of convenience.

From the nondescript setting of the convenience store, the two subsequent legs of the journey take the men into more conspicuously southern locales by Hollywood standards. When Tobias passes out at the wheel and the fro-yo truck careens into a wooded area, Mike feels compelled to seek refuge at a place near Savannah he once haunted. When they arrive at Domina, the domain of the imperious Rome (Jada Pinkett Smith), it becomes apparent that the haunting is not confined to the past given that Rome immediately likens Mike to a ghost. After Mike introduces the crew as "what's left of the Kings of Tampa," he and Rome retire to her suite, where he responds to her query about his mysterious return by claiming that he was only in the neighborhood "to borrow a cup of brown sugar." The mise-en-scène of Domina marks the dramatic interruption of the established racial scheme in the *Magic Mike* films: the prevailing whiteness momentarily gives way to an aesthetic of blackness. The proprietor has remade a house built in the southern-plantation style into a "Roman" empire—a den of female pleasure devoted to the worship of beauty as an inherent virtue possessed by all and codified in the principle that every woman in the club is regal. "There's always a queen up in here who must be reminded how beautiful she is," Rome declares to her customers. The male entertainers on the bill—Augustus (Michael Strahan), Malik (Stephen Boss), and Andre (Donald Glover)—deliver reminders in performances that range from raunchy to sweet but have in common a show of reverence for the queen in question. At Rome's behest, Mike joins the act, answering the call to revive his old stage persona, White Chocolate, and to treat the queens to his trademark magic. Drawing from the Roman Empire and the southern plantation, the fantasy of Domina evokes oppressive histories marred by rigid caste systems, slave labor, and misogyny even as it imagines a new order of eros. Rome's decree of woman-worship appropriates and revises the raced and gendered terms of the repressive gyneolatry that W. J. Cash defined as a feature of the dominant southern social order since its inception.[17]

The bacchanalia of Domina seems a far cry from the quiet stateliness of the Davidson home, where the men make their way next in search of the young women from Savannah whom they met at a party following the contest at Mad Mary's. But the grand plantation-style house where the widowed Nancy Davidson (Andie McDowell) lives with her daughters connects the two settings, as does the adherence to the female pleasure principle that Rome professes. The episode at the Davidson home unfolds as a parody of gendered propriety. "Thank you for your hospitality, ma'am," Ken says, affecting southern charm after Nancy welcomes the men into the parlor to join a small gathering of her girlfriends. "Quit that proper shit," Nancy says, eager to dispense with burdensome social graces. As the expensive wine flows freely, Nancy and her friends open up, describing their marriages as rote, unsatisfying, and passionless. The men respond by tending to the women's needs. Ken serenades one of Nancy's friends with an earnest rendition of Bryan Adams's "Heaven," the song she and her husband once claimed as their own in passionate youth but that has now morphed into a melancholic reminder of the way they were. Richie lets Nancy "check under the hood" when she comments on the perfection of his body—a prelude, as it happens, to a night of mutually gratifying sex. The kings provide a customized service to their queens for a night by performing a variation on the role of the southern gentleman, playing the gentle man who is attentive so as to know precisely how to satisfy the desires of the individual woman rather than acting on a man's idea of what a woman wants.

The emphasis on performance speaks to the limitations of the *Magic Mike* films evident on the stage and off. Although the kings profess to serve their queens—or even show a willingness at times to act like queens—the prerogatives of female desire, or of a black aesthetic, or of queerness remain circumscribed. In the end, the man's self-image and the homosocial bonds among men sanctioned by compulsory heteronormativity and whiteness are what matter most to the fantasies projected in this cinematic realm of male entertainment. Fittingly, the climax of *Magic Mike XXL* is useful for driving home this point. When the travelers finally reach their destination, they find that Rome, Andre, and Malik are waiting for the return of the Kings of Tampa to Myrtle Beach. In a montage sequence, Rome oversees the transformation of the costumes and routines from stock material to tailored originals. When the time comes to take the stage, Rome breaks up the huddle the men have formed, declaring, "It's not bro time. It's showtime!" A seasoned emcee, Rome primes the large crowd of women with a tantalizing call to order: "Are you ready to be worshipped? Are you ready to be exalted?" One by one, the Kings of Tampa take the stage, performing new numbers that enact self-sacrificing reverence of the queens but project idealized images of male self-actualization. Apparently showtime *is* bro time. The queens who ascend to the stage, selected either by Rome or by one of the kings, wind up in a variety of compromising positions: hoisted in the air, dragged on the floor, bound in a sling, or doused with chocolate sauce and whipped cream like human sundaes. This is all part of the show and presented as what the women want, but it complicates the credentials of *Magic Mike XXL* as a paean to female desire—a "feminist film," as some critics lauded it. As Tasha Robinson observes in a thoughtful review that considers the film's gender politics, "There's a whiff of irony to the feminist label in this case, considering how often women in this film are used as dance props."[18] But Robinson adds the caveat that the film is remarkably successful by Hollywood standards in trying to have it both ways: foregrounding the men while giving female pleasures due time in the spotlight.

FIGURE 6.2. Mike and Malik perform as mirror images in a stylized routine that reflects the film's interest in representing racial diversity at the surface level.

The notion of a southern erostocracy is helpful for framing the fraught gender politics not as a discrete element but as an indicator of the diversity that the *Magic Mike* films project on the surface. In the final dance number, Mike shares the stage with Malik in a routine that creates a frame within a frame (see figure 6.2). In the cinematic frame, Mike and Malik stand on opposite sides of a large decorative frame positioned onstage as a faux mirror. Their identical costumes and similar-sounding names enhance the effect of mirror images. Rome taps Nancy's daughter Zoe (Amber Heard) as Mike's queen, while Malik randomly selects another young white woman from the audience. The number is a choreographed staging of reflections in which the women are alternately caressed and manhandled in synchronized simulations of foreplay and intercourse. But the homosocial bond between men is the key to the compelling number. A medley of songs concludes with R. Kelly's "Cookie," the lyrics conjuring an Oreo cookie through precise visual imagery that focuses the racial optics of the number. On the surface, the aesthetic effect appears to defy what Tara McPherson identifies as a "lenticular logic" underwriting "a racial economy of visibility" in American culture that is capable of representing black *and* white but remains limited by a tendency to think only in terms of black *or* white.[19] Although presented as mirror images, Malik and his queen are there to enhance Mike's performance with Amber, serving as shadow figures in an act of quadrangulation—an adapted form of Sedgwick's model. "Looks like somebody got their smile back," Mike says to Amber, in a callback to an earlier scene in which Mike notices her despondency after a professional setback and suggests that she look for her smile. The politics of race and gender in this scene make it possible to read Mike, regrettably, as a southern gentlemen of the old school. Granted, the stage at a stripper convention seems a poor substitute for the proverbial pedestal, but it works in a similar fashion in that the woman is there so that her faithful admirers can try to figure out what it means to be a man. Nevertheless, it seems that Mike has reached some level of understanding—at least for a fleeting moment when male fantasy defers the inevitable return to precarity that awaits him and his fellow travelers. Strutting their stuff on the boardwalk, as a Fourth of July fireworks show begins, the Kings of Tampa are ready to reign supreme, if only for the night. A close-up of Mike, accompanied by DJ Khaled's "All I Do Is Win," captures the lights of the fireworks dancing on his face as he revels in bro time and finds his smile as if by magic.

NOTES

1. Although Soderbergh did not direct *Magic Mike XXL*, he was the cinematographer of both films (credited as Peter Andrews). For this reason, among others, they bear his signature stamp.

2. Deborah Barker and Kathryn McKee, "Introduction: The Southern Imaginary," *American Cinema and the Southern Imaginary*, ed. Barker and McKee (Athens: University of Georgia Press, 2011), 1–23, at 2 and 5.

3. Although an extensive discussion falls beyond the scope of this essay, I do want to note that the concept of a southern erostocracy is applicable to other works on screen. For instance, the HBO television series *True Blood* (2008–14) relied on aristocratic tropes refitted for the purpose of queering binary oppositions rooted in race, class, gender, sexuality, and corporeality. Where homosocial bonding in the *Magic Mike* films comes from the effort to endure and the desire to escape the material conditions of estranged labor and economic precarity, the queer dynamics of the southern erostocracy in *True Blood* occur in a setting where the natural and supernatural realms bleed (pun intended) into each other to destabilizing effects for the established social order.

4. Keith Phipps, "*Magic Mike*," *A.V. Club* 28 June 2012; Web.

5. A. O. Scott, "Review: *Magic Mike XXL*, Fleshing Out a Sequel with Heart as Well as Pecs and Abs," *New York Times* 30 June 2015.

6. Michael Kimmel, *Manhood in America: A Cultural History* (New York: Free Press, 1996), 266.

7. Linda McDowell, *Working Bodies: Interactive Service Employment and Workplace Identities* (Malden, Mass.: Wiley, 2009), 8.

8. The term "bromance" originated in the mid-1990s; it was coined by David Carnie, editor of *Skateboard* magazine. Wider circulation came in 2005 after the release of Judd Apatow's film *The 40-Year-Old Virgin*. Michael DeAngelis explains that a bromance involves "an emotionally intense bond between presumably straight males who demonstrate an openness to intimacy that they neither regard, acknowledge, avow, nor express sexually" (*Reading the Bromance: Homosocial Relationships in Film and Television* [Detroit: Wayne State University Press, 2014], introduction). Recent work in masculinity studies has explored the phenomenon of the physical bromance, introducing additional terms such as "dudesex" or "bud sex" to denote sex between males who identify as straight. See Jane Ward, *Not Gay: Sex between Straight White Men* (New York: New York University Press, 2015).

9. Eve Kosofsky Sedgwick, *Between Men: English Literature and Male Homosocial Desire* (New York: Columbia University Press, 1985), 1.

10. Sedgwick, *Between Men*, 21–27.

11. It is worth noting that triangular relationships proliferate in *Magic Mike*. Mike and Joanna (Olivia Munn), a psychology graduate student, have a sexual relationship that involves their proclivity for jointly seducing women to engage in a ménage à trois. When Mike meets Brooke, she and Joanna represent to him the options of respectability and hedonism—essentially the same dilemma he faces in the triangular relationship with Brooke and The Kid.

12. See R. W. B. Lewis, *The American Adam: Innocence, Tragedy, and Tradition in the Nineteenth Century* (Chicago: University of Chicago Press, 1955).

13. The comparison to Gene Kelly took shape with Tatum's breakthrough film, *Step Up* (2006), and it was mentioned in reviews of the *Magic Mike* films. It turned meta with the release of Joel and Ethan Coen's *Hail, Caesar!* (2016), a film in which Tatum plays a studio-era movie star and leads a troupe of dancing sailors in a loving parody of such Kelly classics as *Anchors Aweigh* (1945) and *On the Town* (1949) that stages a return of the homoeroticism that the early films repressed. See Aisha Harris and Daniel Hubbard, "Is Channing Tatum Our Gene Kelly?" *Slate* 4 February 2016; Web.

14. Brooke, The Kid, and Dallas are absent from the cast of characters in *Magic Mike XXL*. Allegedly Alex Pettyfer and Channing Tatum had a falling out on the set of the original film. Although the reviews of *Magic Mike* were mostly positive, Cody Horn's performance as Brooke was not well received, drawing charges that she had landed the role through nepotism since her father, Alan Horn, was the president and COO of Warner Bros., the studio that produced the *Magic Mike* films, when she was cast.

15. Kimmel, *American Manhood*, 266.

16. See Leigh Anne Duck, *The Nation's Region: Southern Modernism, Segregation, and U.S. Nationalism* (Athens: University of Georgia Press, 2006) for a discussion of how a "backward" South serves as a regional repository of cultural traditions valued by the nation.

17. W. J. Cash, *The Mind of the South* (New York: Knopf, 1941), 87–89.

18. Tasha Robinson, "Female Pleasure Looks Mighty Odd in *Magic Mike XXL*," *Dissolve* 6 July 2015; Web.

19. Tara McPherson, *Reconstructing Dixie: Race, Gender, and Nostalgia in the Imagined South* (Durham, N.C.: Duke University Press, 2003), 26.

Chapter 7 ▸ Perversion on the Plantation: Quentin Tarantino's *Django Unchained* and Other Queer Antebellum Fantasies

SCOTT COMBS

In the middle of Quentin Tarantino's *Django Unchained* (2012), two black men wrestle half-naked while a parlorful of white slaveholders, white slave dealers, and black slaves drink cocktails and look on in a Greenville, Mississippi, room decorated with a bust of Nefertiti. The spectacle—Mandingo fighting—amounts to a blood sport for white amusement ("a good bit of fun," one onlooker offers) but also for a few invited black spectators. Present are two housemaids, a bartender, and the courtesan Sheba. That the venue is named the Cleopatra Club anoints Sheba and Nefertiti in a female triumvirate of African beauty, but the real spectacle is the male body. Django (Jamie Foxx) relays and indeed authorizes our gaze at the interlaced black bodies by refusing to look: he walks past uncomfortably as he momentarily submits himself to the event. He is willing to do so—to play the role of a black slaver, which he earlier explains is "lower than the head house nigger, and boy that's pretty fucking low"—only so that he might gain an invitation to Candyland, the plantation owned by Calvin Candie (Leonardo DiCaprio), hoping he might find his lost wife Broomhilda (Kerry Washington), whom he believes to be a "comfort girl" there. This act of passing is one of the movie's many instances of role-playing as well as projections of black spectatorship into the scene of antebellum violence. As the victorious Mandingo Fred breaks his competitor Luigi's arm and manually pierces his eyes, one of the black maids drops colorful edibles on the ground in a reference to Candie that can only be read as an orgasm—but whose? Because the camera frames the fighting separately as an object of the room's white male gazers (Django keeps his head turned, and the other black spectators are not seen looking), it is also the first in a series of white-black substitutions for heterosexual pleasure. The question of whose hunger the Mandingo fight satiates looms large.

Django Unchained is resolutely devoid of heterosexual couplings. Its narrative hinges on rescue, but Django's saving his wife occasions only the briefest moment of expressed intimacy. What stands in for relational happiness is a series of visual exchanges that stage the black body as an object of the white male gaze, a body that is not threatening as long as it lacks history and cannot be imagined as part of a reproductive lineage. The Mandingo scene repeats and introduces other fetishistic displays of the black male body, far more central than any arrangement between male lookers and female bodies. The erotic jealousy these bodies elicit raises the specter of a homosexual desire that must remain permanently deferred, even as it seems to be the source of the South's regeneration. This chapter places Tarantino's film in the context of the plantation melodrama—where lurks a violent sexual desire—to expose its various projections of a decadent South outside of history. Through Mandingo fighting, through the separation of slave men from slave women, and through slavery's absorption by the white underclass, the film would seem to insist that the absence of heterosexuality is the condition of the plantation's perpetual recycling of black bodies and its deferral of the future.

Sexual Desire and the Plantation Fantasy

The foundational films of the Hollywood plantation melodrama often invert ideological assumptions of prior texts. Sexual violence in this setting often switches from historical fact to mythical explanation for white innocence, a purity so virtuous it reads as sexually undeveloped or repressed, thus connecting to other forms of sexual repression or deficit. In D. W. Griffith's awful milestone *The Birth of a Nation* (1915), the historical cruelty of the white plantation master is flipped into the sexually violent acts committed by freed slaves—most notably Gus, who wants to "marry" white women—and as suffered by Flora, who jumps from a cliff to save herself and dies below in her brother's arms. Inspired by his sister's death and a new garb for disguise (the sheet he earlier puts over himself to hide, only to find it startles black children because they believe they see a ghost), the Little Colonel narrows his fury by mobilizing a white militia, the Ku Klux Klan, to enact revenge on the sexually errant black body. As Michael Rogin argues, the historical record of white violence against slaves—acknowledged by Harriet Beecher Stowe's novel *Uncle*

Tom's Cabin (1852) but inverted by Thomas Dixon Jr.'s *The Clansman: A Historical Romance of the Ku Klux Klan* (1905), the basis for Griffith's film—becomes black rape of white women. In *The Birth of a Nation*, this theme is further developed in the mulatto character Silas Lynch, who accedes to a throne of miscegenation—first by employing the renegade black militia in the South to take over land and elections, and second by forcing Elsie Stoneman (Lillian Gish) to become the queen of his empire. Silas Lynch retains the initials of his negative predecessor Simon Legree, carrying in his name the trace of white lynching in what amounts to a cultural *Verneinung*, or negation.[1] In fact, what freed slaves seem to want most in *The Birth of a Nation* is to rape white women.

In Victor Fleming's *Gone with the Wind* (1939), we find a reworking of the southern plantation's racial melodrama and an antecedent of sorts to *Django Unchained*. Here the belle elicits sympathy when she longs to return to an idealized version of the plantation, one that includes Mammy waiting for her. Linda Williams discusses this transition in Margaret Mitchell's novel as a way to rework the plantation as a mental rather than a physical space. Barely relatable, Scarlett redeems herself through relationships with women. First, she realizes her best (and perhaps only) friend Melanie has sacrificed for her and remained steadfast in her loyalty; and second, she returns to Mammy and her lost plantation Tara on her way back to her Boston home in an idealized version of both. "Mammy and Tara are thus the means to an end that Scarlett has been seeking and, in spite of herself, achieving, all along," Linda Williams argues, "a middle-class female agency rooted in the ideology of the rural southern home but overreaching its confines."[2] In the film version, Mammy disappears from a nonetheless nostalgic notion of the plantation as home and hearth of female agency.

Both these plantation fantasies—Griffith's idyllic Piedmont, *Gone with the Wind*'s desire to return to the idealized past in a home run by women—project the southern home as a lost origin to which uprooted characters wish to return, a veritable "space of innocence" in Peter Brooks's sense.[3] The fact that Scarlett does not return home in the movie version, but instead defines it as part of an epiphany that highlights her own moral achievement, suggests that the plantation fantasy need not be ostensibly set "on" the plantation or "in" the antebellum South. In her wish to return, Scarlett also steps away from female tradition: unlike the culture of domesticity represented by her mother, Scarlett's embrace of the land preserves her father's legacy instead. She will work the "red dirt," thus returning without husband or child to preserve a lineage that precedes and outlives her.

The plantation beckons a fantasy of lost origin reconciled through a character's attachment to an imagined future and completed, once and for all, by rebuilding a home undone by historical chaos as a bastion for white heterosexual coupling. This fantasy can continue to be traced in the western, even if the setting seems far from Griffith's blooming cotton fields or Scarlett's red earth. In a later film like John Ford's *The Searchers* (1956), Ethan Edwards's struggle to rescue his niece Debbie from Native possession plays out beside the parallel creation of the new couple Marty and Laurie. In the final image, the freshly formed duo enters the household, along with Debbie, whose belated homecoming compensates for the violently interrupted and sexually defiled homestead of her parents where the movie begins. The home once surrounded by the desert's scenic bounty is restored by the film's final image in a double frame: Ethan flanked horizontally by Monument Valley (the image of his errant homelessness, the promise of future adventure, the openness of the frontier), and the doorframe of the newly established family (the next generation promised by Marty and Laurie, and the end of Debbie's captivity narrative and her return to white sexuality). Much like *The Birth of a Nation*, *The Searchers* imagines that threats to the "white male subject" are both racial and sexual. Susan Courtney sees these threats as forming the central theme of the film: "we repeatedly find that the white male subject's encounters with his racial and sexual others seem indeed to be the moments which most threaten to rupture the cohesion of his phallic identity."[4] Here plantation motifs drift westward. I thus do not agree with Warren French's claim that the southern film died out after *Gone with the Wind*.[5] Rather, I would argue the western has continued to disseminate the semantic elements of the plantation narrative, that the two genres often overlap.

Demonstrating this point, in *The Searchers* Ethan hails from the Confederate Army; his brother lives in Texas; they struggle to maintain their home in the face of a racialized threat; the home is the hearth for heterosexuality—each datum neighbors on, or squarely fits, the plantation formula. The link between the southern film and the western can be glimpsed in Griffith, whose parallel-edited chase sequences pit whites against both Native Americans and African Americans, and it also appears in the work of early black filmmaker Oscar Micheaux, whose pioneering text *The Homesteader* (novel 1918, film 1919), as Jacqueline Najuma Stewart tells us, combines "references to Micheaux's own early adult life in the West with an interracial love story," and who soon turns briefly from North-South melodramas to westerns.[6] Although the frontier would come to be the stage for racialized contests, early for Micheaux it offered nearly the opposite, a space unbounded by the antebellum politics and tropes of racial melodrama. But both frontier and plantation films tend to focus on the growth or regeneration of a family, usually through a white household enduring an attack by nonwhites. Always, sexual desire is projected onto the outsiders: Piedmont's antebellum home is noticeably presexual, filled with diminutive characters like the Little Colonel and the Pet Sister, who later confront the "renegade" black rapist Gus and the mulatto would-be rapist Silas Lynch; and in *The Searchers*, the unseen and unspoken attack on Martha is implied to be a sexual one.[7] In both, the future of the white family adheres to a notion of sexual innocence—a desire so virtuous it must project its opposite to clarify itself.

The Birth of a Nation and *Gone with the Wind* imagine a white American home open to the hospitality of faithful slaves while expelling all others, including other slaves and poor whites—a home that points to a future because reproductive norms are maintained. *The Birth of a Nation*'s racist construction of freed slaves as rapists makes obvious the black threat to this home; in *Gone with the Wind*, race drops out of the picture momentarily for class to step in. In the Mitchell novel, a freed slave attacks Scarlett on the road in a nod to the "traditional 'plantation legend' role of the white woman victimized by the 'black beast,'" as Williams describes it.[8] But in the film, he is replaced by a figure Michael Rogin describes as "dirty, lower-class, white trash."[9] In the poor white figure of Scarlett's Reconstruction assailant, the film replaces the novel's politically unacceptable scapegoat with a more palatable object of derision. The switch to white trash and its set of visible and audible stereotypes has long been the course for films invested in even the vaguest multicultural politics, and it is not new for Tarantino. In the central scene of sadomasochistic rape of *Pulp Fiction* (1994)—Maynard and Zed's attack on Marsellus in their shop littered with Confederate icons—our white and black male protagonists join in a common heroic defense against the white-trash act of sodomy.[10]

Of course, sex must enter the picture somewhere. The fantasy of white "asexual" regeneration in earlier plantation narratives contrasts sharply with more recent versions, such as *Django Unchained*, in which black suffering is foregrounded and the white home is the source rather than the target of sexual degeneracy. Like Tarantino's earlier *Pulp Fiction*, *Django Unchained* projects sexual otherness onto poor whites, especially the itinerant laborers outside Candyland, but to some extent onto Candie himself, whose relationship with his house slave Stephen (Samuel L. Jackson) is noticeably threatened by the possibility of others' heterosexual happiness. The effect is another inversion of the plantation myth: a negative, ghostly plantation emerges, one barely located in the South, in which what was formerly either patrilineal (an adherence to the father's teachings or a brother's protection) or matriarchal (an idealization of Mammy) becomes queer. By "queer" I mean to suggest not only a projection of unspoken desire between men, mainly between Candie and Stephen, near a maternal or female absence, but also a characterization of southern masculinity as vaguely perverse and thus negatively connoting gay. It is often the case that in Hollywood cinema homosexuality becomes visible in its omissions and substitutions. It remains an unspoken connotative fact beyond verification and therefore, as D. A. Miller argues about Alfred Hitchcock's *Rope* (1948), an extremely furtive projection: "Yet if connotation, as the dominant signifying practice of homophobia, has the advantage of constructing an essentially insubstantial homosexuality, it has the corresponding inconvenience of tending to raise this ghost all over the place."[11] As if the film needs to replace the figure of Griffith's hypersexualized Gus, one potentially recalled by Django's admired masculine frame, with a new phallic danger, it draws our attention to the giddy violence of Candie's white-trash farmhands, including one notably interested in Django's genitals, and then again to Candie, whose relationship with Stephen plants the seed of an unspoken sexuality. The secret that remains untold—the hint of what might be happening, or of what could happen at any moment—effectively endorses Mandingo fighting as its cover-up. *Django Unchained* throws into relief an image of a decadent plantation whose queer relations become part of its survival.

Django's Missing Gaze

Corroborating Tarantino's favored phrase "nigger on a horse," *Django Unchained* is a kind of western-plantation hybrid in its visual topography and action sequences. On one hand, the movie spends significant time watching Django prepare for his rescue of Broomhilda by assisting the white German bounty hunter, Dr. King Schultz (Christoph Waltz), who shoots wanted assailants mostly in the West for a price. Their journeys are backgrounded by the Rockies and its foothills, and Django is bought by King in 1858 Texas, a setting more common to westerns than to southern movies. On the other hand, it features two pivotal sequences set on southern plantations—the first, in Tennessee, owned by Big Daddy Bennett and foregrounding Django's desire for revenge; the second, in Mississippi, the lengthier sequence with Candie and Broomhilda. "Hybrid" hardly does justice to the stylistic contrast between the film's two settings: the pastel-touched austerity of the western sequences paints a fantasy of mobility from which we awake for the cyclical, indeed traumatic, episodes in the South. Nonetheless, the film's generic bifurcation points to its two ostensible inspirations—Richard Fleischer's 1975 plantation film *Mandingo* and the earlier Sergio Corbucci spaghetti western *Django* from 1966. Tarantino's titular hero takes his name not from the Mandingo tradition but from the gunfighter one, where his predecessor, a white gunman, fights a group of southern Klansmen. As contemporary Django's emancipation is bought by the white German Schultz, his namesake and legacy are likewise white—not so gratifying for a politics of uplift. And to be clear, Dr. King Schultz is himself an inversion of the historical civil rights figure Dr. Martin Luther King, a kind of white man's fantasy equivalent who preaches not so much racial equality as an aversion to slavery (and whose character makes quite literal the German-ness of Martin Luther).

Mandingo paves the way for Tarantino's assault on the South. In this antebellum film, the Mandingo spectacle is directly connected to dysfunctional heterosexuality. When the would-be belle, aptly named Blanche, tells her brother Charles that she will marry the protagonist Ham—son of plantation master Maxwell—he threatens to tell Ham about "what we did." The secret of incest hovers again when, in New Orleans on honeymoon, Ham and Blanche fight over his suspicion that she is in fact not a virginal bride. In disgust he storms out to a brothel to pick up his newly bought Mandingo fighter Mede, whom in fact he purchased the day he proposed to Blanche. It is hard not to notice the displacement. The Mandingo is to the slave owner as the monster is to Dr. Frankenstein. Where there are problems of intimacy, the monster lurks about. A sexual gaze at the black male body has been enjoyed by the white owner, and no one can admit it. Twice the film draws attention to a black penis: first, when a slave is hung upside-down for whipping and a slave boy staring at his front side says, "You look funny upside down"; and second, when Mede is examined by potential buyers and a German woman appraises his penis. (A third may be indicated by Blanche's screams during intercourse with Mede). These references work to access, if ultimately to repress, the historical record of white slave owners' lynching of the black male body, and the black penis as the centerpiece of lynching-as-castration.[12]

The sexual interest in the Mandingo's body is disavowed the moment Mede appears. When Ham purchases him, he must outbid the German woman who literally feels Mede's penis at the public auction. Ham seems rattled by this breach of gender etiquette. Soon we learn how fragile his masculinity really is when he finds that his wife has had sex with Mede; he is unable to tolerate his wife's having a relationship equivalent to what he enjoys with his "bed wench" Ellen. When Blanche gives birth to Mede's baby, the plantation breaks down. Here the Mandingo conjoins the threats of gender and race: the much-appraised black body is a badge of prestige as long as it is domesticated within a white patriarchal structure—working, fighting, suffering, dying for a white family. Otherwise it threatens to render impotent the white male progenitor. Ham poisons both the baby and Blanche, and a slave Agamemnon shoots the patriarch Warren. In other words, the young Ham is left without a wife and a father, and the plantation is destroyed because it has no reproductive link to the future. Katherine Henninger argues that *Mandingo*'s undoing of the race-based sex slavery in *Gone with the Wind* and *The Birth of a Nation* creates an image of "perverse sexual desire," that is, incest.[13] Here I underscore this perversion's dependency on hierarchies and gradations of whiteness and on an imbalance of gender. It is the first-generation Warren, the European woman who fondles the slave's penis, and finally the plantation belle who carry the banner of blame. Mede's sexual relations remain normal when compared to Ham's wife's past relations with her own brother.

In so many plantation films, it seems that sexual reproduction cannot be imagined as a healthy part of antebellum southern life. There are child deaths in *Gone with the Wind* and the "modern" *Mandingo*; parents die in both. For good reason: the plantation melodrama must invert or repress the historical record of white-on-black rape, a convolution that brings to the fore its own omissions, as it is also haunted by a history of lynching whose culmination was often rendering the black penis inanimate. The fear of black male sexuality raises the question of the ascription of desire—whose want is elicited and thus threatened by the Mandingo figure? Of course equating black sexuality with rape can only be forgotten in the face of something worse—white incest, as *Mandingo* would suggest. Likewise for *Django Unchained,* where the unspoken possibility of a homosexual desire is much more loudly unspoken, and incest takes on a new form.

In a typical act of displacement, *Django Unchained*'s first suggestion of a repressed homosexual desire comes entangled in clichés of the white underclass. This is not that surprising for a film whose titular "hero" is neither Silas nor Mede but Django, the gunner who assails the white-trash clan in the original *Django*. From the opening moments when we see a chain gang of slaves walking through landscapes of red rocks and desert, beautifully pastel in twilight, the film places the visible origins of slavery in the West, a generic "semantics," or visible form, of the western's production of settler progress and social mobility.[14] Throughout the film, in fact, the western functions as the backdrop of white revenge on other whites—Dr. King Schultz is a bounty hunter—in which Django himself is soon invited to participate. In voiceover at the film's conclusion, King posthumously names Django the "fastest gun in the South," effectively joining the two generic traditions. Here King equates the "peculiar institution" to his job as a bounty hunter—"like slavery, it's a flesh for cash business." And in Tarantino's narrow universe, revenge authorizes everything, despite the fact that the equation between King's heroism and white brutal treatment of black slaves continues to haunt, and I would suggest undermine, the film's apparent celebration of black autonomy. For one, this comment posits a false equivalency between slavery and white murder. Also, it further reduces the slave to a corpse, suggesting a living black body and a living white body are roughly exchangeable (more on this later). In any event, the narrative function of the accent-heavy, polysyllabic, ironic, German, white outsider to slavery would seem to mark the path for our identification with Django—very much an insider to and victim of slavery—as he wreaks violent revenge on whites.[15] On the marginal presence of Django in the film, Ishmael Reed writes "[Jamie] Foxx serves as a buffer between the producers and the wrath of blacks. . . . The real stars of *Django Unchained* . . . are [Christoph] Waltz and Leonardo DiCaprio."[16] For that matter, the black body that suffers virtuously is most often not Django's—we see the slaves Broomhilda and D'Artagnan memorably violated and harmed, in relation to which Django appears like an action hero. Even so, his agency is first enabled by the white doctor, who publicly treats the ex-slave as something like an escort, calling him his valet.

On their first visit to a plantation, King brings Django to Gatlinburg to identify the three fugitive Brittle brothers. Earlier he says he wants "to make this slavery malarkey work" to his "benefit," employing Django as a vengeful ex-slave to identify his former owners (who, in flashback sequences, are seen lashing Broomhilda and him). Django arrives in regal blue, permitted by his white employer to ride. The camera locates the scene's focal point in the white plantation owner Big Daddy Bennett, from whose downward gaze we see Django and King. After the German introduces Django as his valet ("a fancy word for servant," he earlier explains to Django) and announces his intention to buy a female slave, he asks if one of Big Daddy's slaves can give Django a tour of the plantation. Big Daddy tells Betina to treat Django as a free slave and not like "the other niggers around here," to which she quizzically responds:

BETINA. You want I should treat him like white folks?
BIG DADDY. No. That's not what I said.
BETINA. Then I don't know what you want, Big Daddy.
BIG DADDY. Yes, I can see now. What's the name of that peckerwood boy from town that works with glass? His mama work over in the lumber yard.
HOUSE SLAVE. You mean Jerry.
BIG DADDY. That's the boy named Jerry. You know Jerry, don't you, sugar?
BETINA. Yes'm, Big Daddy.
BIG DADDY. Well, that's it then. You just treat him like you would Jerry.

The middle term of translation here, and the category not spoken, is coded as poor white—not "white," not "slave," but an intermediary position, one that can be exchanged for the equally intermediary status of Django as "free nigger" or "nigger on a horse."

The unseen Jerry character becomes quite visible during the second plantation sequence, at Candyland. Here we find white trash in full force—the tagalongs who accompany Candie on business trips and feed off the Mandingos who are no longer equity because they are no longer either physically or mentally able to fight. These white accomplices are toothless, physically offensive, and verbally ungrammatical. They embody a whiteness that must appear a step below the literate whites who traffic in black bodies. Their illiteracy contrasts with Django's ability to read, demonstrated in the scene in which King asks him to read a bounty bulletin for one Smitty Bacall. They are the scavengers for white slave owners' sacrifice of the Mandingo, the "one in 10,000," feeding on the leftovers and keeping alive the black corpse within the social economy of the plantation. Thus we cannot think of Mandingo fighting without the figures of white poverty who devour its victims.

The trip through Candyland's outskirts introduces us to the runaway Mandingo D'Artagnan, who has been chased up a tree by the dogs of the bordering white-trash laborers. Django stops King from saving D'Artagnan ("we ain't payin' a penny for that pickaninny, we ain't got no use for him"), thus authorizing Candie's disposal of his property. Candie unleashes the dogs that encircle and devour D'Artagnan, but forming a close second circle around the sacrifice are all the poor whites. Through their dogs, they dismember the dis-

FIGURE 7.1. Positioned above and yet aligned with these lower-class men, the viewer witnesses the violent depravity of repressed desires on Calvin Candie's plantation, as well as the ways in which Django modulates the viewer's gaze.

carded black male. This *sparagmos* scene inverts the earlier one in the Cleopatra Club in which Django averts his gaze from the Mandingo fighters, thereby authorizing the white spectator's view of the spectacle as the camera looks for him. Here he insists on the violence, projecting onto poor whites the visual pleasure of watching black pain (see figure 7.1).

Those members of the white underclass participating in the black *sparagmos* belong to a popular tradition of poor white invaders. They are present in what Carol J. Clover has called the "urbanoid" strand of modern horror film, in what I have described elsewhere as a facet of post-Vietnam multicultural cinema critical of war, and in popular culture before and beyond. For Clover, offensive country whites populate horror films marked by city guilt, and their horror tropes stick close to them. These "country dwellers are disproportionately represented by adult males with no ascertainable family attachments," she writes; they "snort when they breathe, snore when they sleep, talk with mouths full," and might commit sadistic acts at any moment. The projection of white trash as a sexual threat absolves the privileged of guilt. If poor whites—uncouth, uncivilized, sexually aberrant—are seen to enact a horror that jars the senses, then the "normal" whites visiting them are justified in their retaliation, no matter the form, thus permitting them to continue enjoying the benefits of the poor's disenfranchisement. "The scenario to which city/country horror obsessively returns," Clover explains, "is one in which the haves, the civilized urbanites, are separated from the system of supports that silently keeps their privilege intact," and the resulting drama exposes this privilege.[17] If rape/sadism figures as the avengeable deed performed by mountain dwellers in the most austere example of this tradition, John Boorman's *Deliverance* (1974), it is because rape is how the four middle-class male protagonists imagine the violation executed by the "power company" on the rural area—"we're gonna rape this whole goddamn landscape," says Lewis (Burt Reynolds).

There is a particular instance of white uncivility that sets into motion the sexual ambivalence of the Mandingo scenes, and thus the film's queering of the plantation. While Django struts through Candie's entourage, one member of the posse, credited as Billy Crash (Walton Goggins), approaches Django in what can only be coded as a gay threat:

BILLY CRASH. Oh, now you are one lucky nigger.
DJANGO. You better listen to your boss, white boy.
BILLY CRASH. Oh, I'm gonna go walkin' in the moonlight with you.
DJANGO. You wanna hold my hand?

Django's response presents prior knowledge of male sexual desire for, if not rape committed against, the black male. The gay subtext leaves little room for doubt—homosexuality, real or fantasized, is linked to antebellum sadism, and near the top of the culprit list are white-trash laborers who feed on Mandingo corpses. After the exchange, Django hallucinates Broomhilda walking beside him in the woods. It is the threat of homosexual desire—first clearly introduced by Billy Crash—that above all else justifies Django's conquest of the plantation, for that victory must be won over both whites and blacks who endorse the Mandingo sport, a spectacle of black males that "celebrates" (disavows) their physical attributes.[18] Even though Candie ostensibly manages the Mandingo circuit, the white trash Billy Crash brings to the surface the homodesirability of Django as a further threat to his attempt to find Broomhilda. He will not become a Mandingo, for to become one is to become the passive object of a white male gaze that is, we must also say, positioned as queer. His willingness to play the part of black slaver ensures that he will not bear the troublesome burden of defending himself against becoming a fetishized object, even though the movie decides twice to reveal its action hero's ripped back, scarred with the marks of the whip.

The collusion of white poverty with "unusual" or unspoken sexuality is as old as the scapegoating tradition itself. The point of Henry Goddard's 1912 study of the Kallikak family—in which falsified photographic evidence was mounted to inculcate the impression that white genetic deficiency resulted from incest—was to warn against the sexual practices of the poor.[19] Stephen

J. Gould revealed these representations as fraudulent, and anthropology has since disavowed its roots in eugenics, but nonetheless these images persist in American cinema and popular culture, from *Gone with the Wind* to *Deliverance* to *Pulp Fiction*.[20] *Deliverance* seems the parent text here, for Billy Crash one-ups sodomy as the violent crime (male rape) when he later reveals his desire to cut off Django's genitals. This sadistic act attempts to cover over the explicit horrors performed by the otherwise articulate and palatable character of Candie, and to fill in for the implicit violence espoused by the main house-slave Stephen, whose later diatribe on male castration is nearly unbearable. (In a few sequences, however, Django seems to be positioned as Candie's equal, or at the very least immune to the niceties of the aristocratic South.) The film's thread of unspoken homosexual desire weaves from the Mandingo to Billy Crash and finally to the relationship between Candie and Stephen. Django's hero role becomes a defense against the unpoliced homoerotics of the plantation.

The Male Mammy and His Master

In the corpse-devouring scene on the outer edge of Candyland, King averts his gaze as Django looks on. What is effected is a series of passings—Django as slave-hating black, King as Mandingo-trading racist, Candie as patriarchal white master. However, the erotics of the earlier Mandingo spectacle continue inside the plantation in the charged intimacy between Candie and Stephen. On his arrival, Django arouses Stephen's jealousy ("Who this nigga up on that nag?" he asks Candie). When Broomhilda and Django make eye contact in the middle of the dinner scene, Stephen is preternaturally quick to seize on the male gaze and later tells Candie that they know each other. Stephen's adoration of Candie, and his fidelity to the plantation system and Mandingo sport even when it means sacrificing others of his own race, has sparked some commentators to read him conservatively—best by Ishmael Reed, who writes "Samuel L. Jackson, who starred in Tarantino's *Pulp Fiction*, plays himself."[21] But Stephen's protection of Candie distinguishes their relationship from all heterosexual couples, raising the connotative "ghost" inside the plantation.

The last third of the film—and the final standoff for the future of Candyland—focuses on Stephen and Django. Stephen's frame dominates the picture as King and Django arrive at the plantation, suggesting he has replaced Big Daddy as the overseer of tradition. His first few words make clear tradition prevails despite his race, as he insults Django on the nag, and then says to

Candie: "I miss you like a baby miss Mammy's titty." His switch from Django to Mammy raises the possibility of a queer relation to Candie. Stephen's intense servitude to his master is queered through linguistic and visual connotations. First, when Stephen and Candie disappear from the dinner table and Candie returns much later, his sister Lara Lee says the company were "about to think you and that old crow run off together." Needless to say, Candie's name itself signifies a feminine presence with its spelling and sugarcoats black slave labor with its omission of "cotton." He is the flower of the field, complete with the boutonniere he wears throughout the dinner scene. Aptly described by James Crank as a "vicious southern dandy-villain," Candie is drenched in decadence and taboo.[22] The person he seems most excited to see (after Stephen, that is) is his sister, whom he twice kisses on the lips. There is neither Mammy nor wife here, rendering Stephen's comment about Mammy's "titty" all the more disturbing—not only is Mammy not part of the reproductive economy of the plantation, she is in this case not even present.[23] With the perversion of the Mammy fantasy (what "baby" could be sucking other than a white one), the film substitutes for the belle-Mammy relationship a love between two men, Candie and his male mammy Stephen. Rather like the atemporal black female matriarch whose body becomes static evidence of white reproduction, Stephen fortifies Candie's link to his forefathers in a womanless, male-enclosed, indeed queer history.

Stephen is meta-slavery, more Candie's bodyguard than house slave. As such, he delights in Mandingo fighting and complements Candie's indifference to heterosexual bonding. Later he is involved in the emasculation of a competitive black male. His actions seem rooted more in sexual jealousy than in a will to preserve plantation hierarchy. His suspicion of black-black heterosexual coupling suggests that his unspoken bond with Candie covers over an even deeper desire—not just to protect his standing in white society, but to erase another black male as (sexual) competition. In his speech on the skull of "Old Ben," Candie recounts how this slave, bearing the cranial mark of subservience that conforms to the rhetoric of Dalton's phrenology, "took care of my daddy and my daddy's daddy," and himself, "till he up and keeled over one day." (Is this Ben not the ideological inversion of Ben Cameron, the scion of the white southern plantation in *The Birth of a Nation*?) It is a matter of covering up a cover-up: as the film makes us believe that it reveals the cover of slavery—in Candie's blindness to his repression, in his not knowing that Alexander Dumas was part black, or in whatever other unknowing lack gets projected onto him—the real cover it insists on, the ease with which we separate the South as a place of closeted sexual perversity, remains untouched.

Once Django seeks revenge, he performs a series of castrations that would effectively undo historical violence on the enslaved black male. First Django shoots one of the white trash inside the house several times in the penis while defending himself, then he shoots one of the *sparagmos* clan in his (exposed) penis. The threat on his sexuality posed by Billy Crash is thus avenged *on* Billy Crash's white-trash penis, warding off slavery's homosociality, figured in this film in at best a regressive version of Leo Bersani's "two-ness," a relationship between men across class that allows for momentary equality, and at worst the usual crypt of secret gay desire.[24]

Stephen as the male mammy, and in his conflation with Old Ben, is more like the male mummy: he is undead, timeless, outside of history. Slave narratives and abolitionist tracts have punctured the image of white virtue associated with the plantation. Most scholarly considerations of the plantation as a queer space have been devoted to moments of fleeting homoeroticism in otherwise straight-focused texts. Michael P. Bibler's study of plantation narratives from 1936 (*Gone with the Wind*) to 1968 finds queerness in relationships "between white men of the planter class, between white plantation mistresses and black maids, and between black men," but the potential slave/master black/white pairing has been hard to find.[25]

It is no surprise that such interactions have come to light in the service of a view of American history that insists the South is static and unable to regenerate—that is, queer. Starting from the film's final image of a plantation facade burning by Django's hand, James Crank works through *Django Unchained*'s "queer melancholies," or visual and narrative moments of sexual contact, as a way to grasp the film's projection of an unfinished past. Rather than ending, Crank argues, with the western hero riding away, the film holds to an image of the "unkillable, zombie-like, still-burning body of the plantation house."[26] That image reanimates with vigor the supposedly dead plantation, and like its undead inhabitants whose sexual desire must never come wholly into the light but must haunt the borders of what can be said and seen, it can be neither fully absent nor fully present. The "flaming" edifice burning in spectrality culminates the film with the promise of starting another film. As the cyclical, serial logic of horror demands that it continue to repeat a prior traumatic event, Django's plantation is the dead villain the audience knows will rise again.

To take class out of this picture would be to remove Tarantino's favorite scapegoat and structural support for his racial fantasy and his gothic queerness.[27] The silenced erotics of the plantation—beginning with the Mandingo image and resumed here with the slaver's relationship with his servant—is a lineage that has always mobilized clichés of regional whiteness. Once again we have a homestead devoid of maternal influence: Maxwell in *Mandingo* and Candie in *Django Unchained* are both imagined to be Mandingo traders because they are womanless. In Stephen and Candie's dialogue, it becomes clear that Stephen's stewardship long precedes his fidelity to Candie. His service to the white plantation is intergenerational to gothic effect: on one hand, his servitude enables white patriarchy to protect itself against the black phallus; on the other hand, it characterizes the plantation as static, unable to beget a future. Stephen has observed generations of white plantation owners, defending heterosexual relations against the threat of a sexual desire he cannot articulate. As long as plantation owners are seen as one step from white trash and thus blamed for all manner of evils, they will always be easy to separate from "us," deferring the conversation about racism, slavery, and sexual violence. And the closet becomes a disturbed crypt: the plantation emerges as a queer projection, one whose constituents must remain in the dark like ghosts.

NOTES

1. Making the women weak allows the male characters to defend and rescue them, regaining masculine authority that seems to have been lost in earlier Griffith films. This feminized suffering thus performs a gender work as important as the film's racist discourse. See Michael J. Rogin, "'The Sword Became a Flashing Vision': D. W. Griffith's *The Birth of a Nation*," *Representations* 9 (1985): 150–95, at 163.

2. Linda Williams, *Playing the Race Card: Melodramas of Black and White from Uncle Tom to O.J. Simpson* (Princeton, N.J.: Princeton University Press, 2001), 202.

3. Peter Brooks, *The Melodramatic Imagination: Balzac, Henry James, Melodrama, and the Mode of Excess* (New Haven, Conn.: Yale University Press, 1976).

4. Susan Courtney, "Looking for (Race and Gender) Trouble in Monument Valley," *Qui Parle* 6.2 (1993): 97–130, at 102. See also her *Split-Screen Nation: Moving Images of the American West and South* (New York: Oxford University Press, 2017).

5. See French's collection *The South and Film* (Jackson: University Press of Mississippi, 2008).

6. Jacqueline Najuma Stewart, *Migrating to the Movies: Cinema and Black Urban Modernity* (Berkeley: University of California Press, 2005), 220.

7. Susan Courtney argues that Scar—the indigenous perpetrator—and Ethan are in fact doubles for one another, reading the invasion scene not as "Ethan's failure to

protect Martha, but instead, as Scar's double, as an opportunity for him to rape and kill her" ("Looking for (Race and Gender) Trouble," 107).

8. Williams, *Playing the Race Card*, 195.

9. Michael Rogin, *Blackface, White Noise: Jewish Immigrants in the Hollywood Melting Pot* (Berkeley: University of California Press, 1996), 164.

10. See my essay "The Screen Kallikak: White Trash for White Guilt in Post-Vietnam American Film," *Southerners on Film: Essays on Hollywood Portrayals since the 1970s*, ed. Andrew B. Leiter (Jefferson, N.C.: McFarland, 2011), 106–22, at 106–7.

11. D. A. Miller, "Anal *Rope*," *Representations* 32 (1990): 114–33, at 119.

12. See Matt Brim, *James Baldwin and the Queer Imagination* (Ann Arbor: University of Michigan Press, 2014), 141–45. Brim undoes the idea that castration should be understood as the absence of a visible penis, making room for a discussion of cultural and social castration.

13. Katherine Henninger, "The *Mandingo* Effect: Slavery, Sex, and Contemporary Cinema," *Sex and Sexuality in Modern Southern Culture*, ed. Trent Brown (Baton Rouge: Louisiana State University Press, 2017), 161–84.

14. See Rick Altman, "A Semantic/Syntactic Approach to Film Genre," *Cinema Journal* 23.3 (1984): 6–18.

15. Although Django first appears to the sound of a theme song bearing his name, the song is itself a citation of 1970s cinema and television, quite a contrast in style to the bare backs of the slaves full of slash marks.

16. Ishmael Reed, "Black Audiences, White Stars, and *Django Unchained*," *Wall Street Journal* 28 December 2012.

17. Carol J. Clover, *Men, Women, and Chain Saws: Gender in the Modern Horror Film* (Princeton, N.J.: Princeton University Press, 1992), 125.

18. Not all critics find the film as regressive as does Ishmael Reed. Adilifu Nama, for example, argues that the film goes further into race than other ostensibly critical slavery films, like *12 Years a Slave* (Steve McQueen, 2013), because of its fantastical element, and claims the Mandingo sport featured in the film criticizes the white exploitation of black bodies in professional sports; see his *Race on the QT: Blackness and the Films of Quentin Tarantino* (Austin: University of Texas Press, 2015), 98.

19. Henry Herbert Goddard, *The Kallikak Family: A Study in the Heredity of Feeble-Mindedness* (New York: Macmillan, 1912).

20. Combs, "The Screen Kallikak," 109.

21. Reed, "Black Audiences, White Stars."

22. James Crank, "The Plantation Is Burning: Queer Melancholies, Violent Intimacies, and Plantation Camp in *Django Unchained*," *Global South* 10.2 (2016): 99–114, at 99. See also Crank's discussion of the film's camp aesthetic, its "grossly over-exaggerated, and therefore, ultimately detached style," in the same essay.

23. Lara Lee contributes only the suggestion of incest. I do not mean to collide queerness with incest, but in the project of visualizing southern whiteness as perverse, it should come as no surprise that both are called to order.

24. See Leo Bersani, *Homos* (Cambridge, Mass.: Harvard University Press, 1995), 145–47.

25. Michael P. Bibler, *Cotton's Queer Relations: Same-Sex Intimacy and the Literature of the Southern Plantation, 1936–1968* (Charlottesville: University of Virginia Press, 2009), 26–28.

26. Crank, "The Plantation Is Burning," 100.

27. Unlike Crank, I do not see the queer white abuse of the black body and Django's tactile, genital revenge on poor whites (and complicit company) to map onto each other so seamlessly—queer for queer.

PART IV

QUEER FAMILIES AND SOUTHERN KINSHIP

Chapter 8 ▸ The Backward South: Temporal Traversals and Queer Necropolitical Kinships in *Dallas Buyers Club*

JOE EDWARD HATFIELD

In the 2013 motion picture *Dallas Buyers Club*, Matthew McConaughey stars as Ron Woodroof, a cowboy who earns his living as an electrician and spends his spare time riding bulls at rodeos and womanizing at strip clubs. Set in Dallas, Texas, the film promises the "true story" of the now deceased Woodroof. It chronicles how he took matters into his own hands after contracting HIV in the South in the mid-1980s, a period when popular discourses surrounding the deadly virus construed it as a "gay disease" most rapidly impacting homosexual men in coastal metropolitan areas of the United States.[1] For the rest of the film, audiences witness Ron, an HIV-positive homophobe, navigate a now distant historical context where the virus largely existed as a justified side effect of queer lifestyles. Ron struggles to understand his social position amid a climate of such rampant homophobia. Against all odds, he eventually forms a "buyers club," or an underground network of paying members who test experimental HIV/AIDS medications illegally imported from outside the United States. Unlike other popular representations of the first and second waves of the HIV/AIDS crisis, which often depict New York City and San Francisco as the primary American cities affected by the emerging epidemic, the film spotlights the South—Texas in particular—as a geographical locale where the disease ravaged both queer and straight lives. The film also makes visible the period's dearth of effective medication to treat HIV patients, and the strict standards of the U.S. Food and Drug Administration (FDA) regarding the dispensing of AZT (zidovudine), one of the few drugs tested on human HIV/AIDS patients at the time.

Immediately following the film's release, critics widely celebrated the film's depiction of Ron's business partnership and subsequent friendship with the character Rayon. Jared Leto, a cisgender actor, performs the role of the fictional Rayon, an HIV-positive transgender woman whom Ron relies on to sell club memberships to queer people of Dallas. Leto won the Oscar for best supporting actor at the 86th Annual Academy Awards ceremony, while McConaughey won the coveted best actor prize. Their awards added to a recent slew of accolades bestowed by the Academy of Motion Picture Arts and Sciences on straight actors for performances as queer characters.[2] However, not all filmgoers were as generous as the Academy in their appraisals of the film. Several queer commentators lamented the casting of Leto in the role. In the article "Don't Applaud Jared Leto's Transgender 'Mammy,'" *Time* contributor Steve Friess compares the flawed representation of Rayon to the stereotype perpetuated by Hattie McDaniel's performance as Mammy in *Gone with the Wind*.[3] Just as the Mammy trope in U.S. popular culture marginalizes and objectifies black women, Leto's performance relies on macabre and overreproduced assumptions about transgender women. Friess describes Rayon as "a sad-sack, clothes-obsessed, constantly flirting transgender drug addict prostitute, of course. . . . She's an exaggerated, trivialized version of how men who pretend to be women—as opposed to those who feel at their core they are women—behave."[4] In an editorial in the *Independent*, Paris Lees succinctly asks, "Why can't we cast trans people in trans roles?"[5] These critiques suggest the film pushes Hollywood standards for transgender representation in a backward direction because it reproduces harmful stereotypes and reinforces established precedents for casting cisgender actors in transgender roles.

Critical appraisals of backward representations tend to map a negative value onto cultural logics and temporalities that cut against the grain of the supposed linearity of liberal progress. Heather Love argues that contact with stigmatized histories of trauma or shame that disrupt queer progress narratives can induce backward feelings.[6] If faced with the "bad gay past," queer scholars often try to resignify negative histories so they more neatly fit as catalysts in a radical story line of queer political advancement.[7] Yet this recuperation of shame and its normalization requires a refusal to acknowledge the ways antiprogressive queer politics and history persist in the present in meaningful ways, especially in geographic locations, such as the South, where queer-rights rhetoric has never perfectly coordinated with that of the North. Because of its representational faults and its reckless indulgence of the arguably most injurious aspects of queer history, the film is indeed a backward text, but it is complex enough to challenge paranoid readings that declare it simply *too problematic* to ever be considered a site of queer politics or agency. Rather than recover or negate its shameful impurity, I want to allow the backward feelings it incites to linger alongside my reading of *Dallas Buyers Club*.

In its position as a 2013 cultural artifact, the film's historical content foils the mollifying effects of queer progress narratives and also queers normative temporal schema in the process. The film contains backward performances of the past, and these theatricalizations resemble what Elizabeth Freeman calls "temporal drag," or the performative means by which one embodies history's excesses in the present and viscerally disrupts the habituated flows of chrononormativity.[8] The film's temporal drag—specifically its display of anachronism and the backward effects thereof—illuminates the present-day messiness of doing queer historical representation in popular media, especially in portrayals of region-specific periods of deprivation, where survival and trauma unite and evade proper aesthetic capture.

Popular media representations of the South already map backwardness onto the bodies of southerners to render those who dwell in the South as ideologically opposed to the ideal of a progressive, industrialized, and overwhelmingly metropolitan North. In the film, backwardness comes into focus as a uniquely southern resistance to the cultural impingements of U.S. modernity and progress, especially as backwardness manifests in response to the failure of modern institutions to sufficiently respond to those living with HIV/AIDS across the nation and particularly in the South. When read in context as contingent modes of everyday life in relation to anti-queer centralizations of power, backwardness indicates a queer temporality produced by inhabitants of the South, a region that, in the words of E. Patrick Johnson, is "always already queer."[9] Both a mode of worldmaking and of world shattering, backwardness functions as a regionalized mode of embodied survival in a queer necropolitical landscape. Southern backwardness is both a queer temporality and a site of affective kinship, which bonds deeply flawed (indeed, extraordinarily *backward*) characters together under dire conditions exacerbated by the early stages of the HIV/AIDS epidemic in the United States.

Dallas Buyers Club in Context

Near the film's beginning, Ron and his rodeo pals gamble with a deck of cards atop a newspaper dated July 25, 1985. Between shots of flying aces and crinkled ten-dollar bills, the scene cuts to the paper's headline: "Rock Hudson in Paris Hospital with AIDS." Hudson was the first major celebrity to reveal his diagnosis, sending moral ripples through a nation that remembered him best as Hollywood's leading man in films of the 1950s and 1960s. Hudson died in October the same year. Although HIV/AIDS had already gripped the audiences of national news outlets since its first written appearance in the *New York Times* in 1981, the fall of 1985 also marked the first time President Ronald Reagan uttered the word "AIDS" in public. Moralistic attitudes and pervasive homophobia created sex panics around the virus, and despite the best efforts of activist groups like the Gay Men's Health Crisis (which formed during the first year of the crisis) and ACT UP (which initiated a famously unapologetic second wave of AIDS activism in 1987), HIV/AIDS was either ignored or further stigmatized by both the mainstream media and the general public. Those living with HIV/AIDS in the South were disproportionately affected, because non-southern epicenters of the epidemic received the majority of what little media coverage and funds for prevention resources existed. Today the South, with only one-third of the nation's population, carries 44 percent of all HIV/AIDS cases, an unfortunate residual effect of the media and funding disparities during the crisis's first and second waves.[10]

The film attempts to capture the precarity of contracting HIV/AIDS in the South during the late 1980s. When blood tests reveal Ron's HIV-positive status after a drunken accident on his day job, he immediately harangues his doctor, "I ain't no faggot, motherfucker. Alright? I don't even know any fuckin' faggots. Look at me! What do you see? Goddamn rodeo is what you see." Needless to say, the diagnosis shocks Ron, who shares the widespread assumption the virus affects only "faggots." He is quickly shunned by his former friends when they discover he might have "faggot blood" coursing through his veins. These cultural responses are indicative of just how little was known about HIV/AIDS at the time, especially in areas with relatively few recorded cases of the virus. Although much of the film takes place during 1987, Dallas County recorded just 1,647 AIDS cases in a populace of nearly two million by 1989; of those cases, 1,032 had died.[11] In 1988, by comparison, a reported 22,231 AIDS cases came from New York City alone.[12]

Information about HIV/AIDS was also difficult to retrieve in the South during this period. The film references this plight when a recently diagnosed Ron reads a pamphlet on a microform at the Dallas Public Library. In this scene Ron learns about AZT trials, and afterward he visits Dr. Eve Saks (Jennifer Garner) to request the medication. Saks informs Ron that AZT is available only to those enrolled in a clinical trial of the drug. Left to his own devices, Ron bribes a member of the hospital staff to steal the drug for him. Still

Ron's condition worsens. During a last-resort visit to a Mexican hospital, Dr. Vass, an unlicensed American doctor, informs Ron that using AZT can destroy critical cells in the body. Dr. Vass prescribes zalcitabine and peptide T, both illegal in the States under FDA regulations. The film shows Ron transporting the drugs across the U.S.-Mexico border in hopes of selling them to other HIV/AIDS patients. For the fictionalized Ron, the drugs represent both a pathway to self-care and an extremely profitable business venture. Thus the Dallas Buyers Club is born.

Despite Hollywood's interpretation of an acquisitive Ron, historical data tell another story. A 1989 *Dallas Morning News* article titled "Club Offers Latest Drugs for AIDS" features the non-fictionalized Woodroof.[13] Alongside an affable-looking photo of the Dallas Buyers Club president pictured with his prized experimental HIV/AIDS treatments, the article reads, "But the arrangements are not profit-making ventures, those involved emphasize." Woodroof himself elaborates: "We are not trying to make money on these drugs. . . . We have a 17 percent gross markup or less. It covers the basic product cost and shipping."[14] This article presents a strikingly different vision of Woodroof from the one interpreted by McConaughey. However, clearly parallel in the real and cinematic versions of the events is a sense of urgency, to which Ron responds with unwavering confidence in the face of unfavorable circumstances.

Ron's responsiveness materializes in the film as a backwardness, which signifies both his southern cultural heritage and his resistance to the impingements of a deathly temporality spurred by the HIV/AIDS epidemic in its early years. Like all characters racing against the clock, Ron subsists within a field of contextual constraints. Ron's character development is limited by his status as a cisgender straight man with little knowledge about a virus invading his corporeal existence, which until this diagnosis he has wrongly understood via popular discourse as a biomedical result of queer sexuality's deviance from heteronormative mores. Nevertheless, by erecting bonds of solidarity with queers he would have previously despised and by helping ensure their and his survival, the cinematic version of Ron moves against the chrononormativity of HIV/AIDS death worlds and performs what Jack Halberstam has called a "queer temporality," or a model of living resigned from normative modes of public timing. Halberstam defines queer temporalities as emergent conditions of postmodernity occurring "once one leaves the temporal frames of bourgeois reproduction, and family, longevity and inheritance."[15] Halberstam states queer performances of time emerge directly out of the HIV/AIDS crisis as a result of survival techniques and other alternate forms of LGBTQ+ worldmaking that occurred adjacent to a prevalently homophobic public sphere.[16] Strikingly, in viewing the film, one gains a fictive glimpse into the unevenness of queer temporal resistance when realized by dissimilar straight and transgender characters, in addition to its promise as a site of backward affective kinship formation across genders, sexualities, and even otherwise discriminatory ideologies.

Queer Temporalities and the Emergence of HIV/AIDS in the South

How does one responsibly acknowledge backward feelings about a shame-laden queer text, while still engaging its content as a performance of cultural and political struggle invested with symbolic meaning? Isaac West's development of a "queer generosity" can instruct an examination of backward texts. According to West, queer critique must not be deductively applied and/or binarily conceived as a "hermeneutic of suspicion enjoining us to the study of resistance to *or* complicity with normativities."[17] Riffing on Eve Kosofsky Sedgwick's reparative reading strategy, West urges scholars to withstand the self-satisfying temptation to reify a universalizing dichotomy between normativity and antinormativity in their judgment of queer texts and practices.[18] Approaching the film from this vantage point allows critics to contextualize the film in its broader symbolic and cultural field and recognize its incapacity to ever fully articulate a universally satisfying queer politics. If viewed with an awareness of this inevitably messy deficit, the film's temporal drag positions viewers differently in relation to the historical narrative it offers, whether through momentary visceral points of identification, equally felt sensations of exclusion, or the convergence of the two in the form of irreconcilably backward feelings.

When viewing the film generously rather than from the perspective of a paranoid skeptic, its uniqueness as a case study for unpacking the relationships among the South, the cultural logics of HIV/AIDS, and queer temporalities becomes apparent. Questions concerning the future as a horizon of queer temporal possibility come to the fore specifically. In his famous polemic, Lee Edelman lambastes the future as "kid stuff."[19] Edelman controversially equates the unquestioned politics of futurity with rhetorics of national citizenry, which collaborate to privilege acts of hetero(re)production as normal and erotically desirable. In anti-relational vibrato, Edelman claims individual acts of queerness disrupt the everyday flows of "heteroreproductive futurity," or bourgeois patriarchal expectations that normalize child breeding and heterosexual intercourse to reproductively secure the future for a dominant straight elite.[20] Edelman worries political efforts toward LGBTQ+ equality are nothing more than assimilatory campaigns seeking to repackage queer identity within the constrictive temporal boundaries of hetero-citizenship. Although Edelman has been taken to task on this premise, notably by queer scholars of color, his insights provide a useful characterization of the future as a ritualized order that privileges straight people, while queer identities tend to assume a disruptive temporal disposition—or to put it differently, a backward spatiotemporal inhabitance.[21]

Surprisingly, the backward temporality of the queer South remains unexplored by scholars of queer time and space. This omission is especially curious in light of Lisa Duggan's observations on why northerners perceive southern queer men as backward. Duggan writes, "One way of interpreting this regional difference is the familiar one of describing this mostly rural and small-town context as *premodern*, stuck in a time lag behind the faster, more progressive cities up north."[22] As emblematized by the film's southern aesthetics and story line, the South is backward because in the popular imaginary, southerners look to the past not merely as a container for memories of a time long gone but as a touchstone for embodying these traditions in the present, no matter how outdated or oppressive. Perceptions of the South's general resistance to the social and economic progress of the states of the coastal North—which have maintained their supreme stature at least since the end of the Civil War—reinforce this backward image. Despite the intentions of southerners themselves, backwardness exists as an oppositional regression against the temporality and cultural logics of the North, since southern customs, values, and traditions remain always already degraded. In many ways, the generalized construct of the premodern southerner and the nonreproductive, HIV/AIDS-ridden queer share a backward relationship to the hegemonic futurism of the broader United States, especially as the two identities intersect in the film.

Indeed, in the film backwardness contradictorily surfaces as an antifuturistic futurity, which corresponds to Ron's southern identity and his persistent survival despite his newfound relationship with the death-driven temporality of HIV/AIDS. Viewers of the film watch as Ron descends into a world no longer defined by sexual escapades or displays of macho human-animal domination at the local rodeo, but one now marked by quotidian visions of bodily degradation and impending death. Kyra Pearson observes that the HIV/AIDS crisis's temporal dimensions are "evident in its classification as an 'epidemic,' a term describing the *rapid* progression of a disease through a population."[23] Gust A. Yep takes this claim further by asserting that popularly reproduced images of AIDS deaths created "a temporalization of loss—a chronology—that establishes the discursive space for the formula 'HIV-positive = AIDS = Death.'"[24]

Prolonged by careless governmental responses and a lack of social uproar, the first decade of HIV/AIDS in the United States terrorized those affected by its spread, particularly queers and racial minorities. The nation's consistent failure to invest sufficient resources in prevention efforts, an effect of homophobic ideologies that permeated public policy, exposed its indifference to the mass deaths of vulnerable populations already excluded from many of its institutions. The broader public sphere adopted this unresponsiveness, and *Dallas Buyers Club* attempts to capture how the risk society produced by the expansion of HIV/AIDS culminated in an "everyday death world."[25] In turn, Ron's body becomes swept into the silent ticktock of borrowed time guaranteed by the state's necropolitical deployment of HIV/AIDS as a technology of population control. Achille Mbembe conceives the term "necropolitics" as encapsulating regimes of sovereignty that hold the "power and the capacity to decide who may live and who must die."[26] Ron's necropolitical position results from the rapid increase of social stigmas attached to his disease, its observable effects on his deteriorating body, and his location in a region lacking the crucial medicinal resources that might possibly have saved him. Ron's survival efforts carve an alternative future against the deathly future seemingly guaranteed by HIV/AIDS. Meanwhile, Ron's unlikely friendship with Rayon demonstrates the affective capacities of such backward temporal worldmaking, as the characters converge in intimate proximity and react together in opposition to institutions and policies designed to configure their bodies as toxic and disposable. Their necropolitical kinship envelops Ron in the fold of a queerness that looks to the future not as a heteropatriarchal ideal but as a promise of better and more just days for all.

Backwardness as Southernness

There are relatively few major motion pictures revolving around the U.S. HIV/AIDS crisis, and even fewer focus on the impact of HIV/AIDS in the South. *Dallas Buyers Club* is a distinctive release inasmuch as it breaks from films about HIV/AIDS primarily situated in San Francisco or New York City. John Howard calls this trend in queer representation a "bicoastal bias—a focus on persons and events from the East and West Coasts."[27] In its very production, the film interrupts prevailing HIV/AIDS cinema narratives predominantly unfolding in regions other than the South and depicting the lives of queer white men. While Ron is certainly white, his straightness queerly unsettles expectations regarding the kinds of bodies testing positive for HIV in the 1980s. Furthermore, Ron's cultural background as a southerner makes visible the regional impact of HIV/AIDS on states below the Mason-Dixon line.

Engaging the film's southern context and its depiction of certain southern mores also troubles standards of politically correct cinema production. A cringe-worthy example comes near the start of the film, before Ron's diagnosis, when he is working in an oil field. As Ron and his equally unreserved pals drink booze and holler profanities, one of the men asks whether Ron has considered taking an oil job in Saudi Arabia. Ron replies, "What do you wanna go work for a bunch of sand n——s for?"[28] The casually spoken line delivers a jolt in an otherwise mundane scene, revealing the ordinariness and overt expression of racism in the film's imagining of the U.S. South.

Ron's racism stands out as one of his most backward characteristics, and while one could certainly make a case that his southern heritage in no way predicts a prejudiced attitude, contextual cues throughout the film, such as prominently displayed Confederate flags as well as communally shared expressions of homophobia, transphobia, and sexism, point audiences to infer that Ron's social location has much to do with his intolerant attitudes. Importantly, those who knew the non-fictionalized Woodroof have disputed these aspects of the film's portrayal of the character, particularly his homophobia.[29] Regardless, in the film, Ron's southern backwardness—that is, his hostility toward diversity and difference—draws out the dilemma of many critical southern studies and the queer interrogation of backward texts. It raises the question of how one can stay committed to examining the South with respect to Carlos L. Dews's call for "southern critique"—an invitation to avoid conducting a genealogy of the South ending in an analysis of racism, sexism, homophobia, colonialism, or whatever ism one may feel best describes a cultural artifact.[30] After all, ending at one of these conclusions potentially essentializes the South as an inherently irredeemable space and also reproduces harmful images of southern life that marginalize the very real people of all races, ethnicities, sexualities, classes, and genders who call the South home. As Carolyn Leste Law observes, "It seems not a little disingenuous of the United States to heap all the racism, bigotry, and ignorance of an entire nation upon one region."[31]

The argument here is that the film's chauvinist characterization of Ron adds to its backwardness and its nonconformity to liberal visions of queer progress. While one could certainly acknowledge such a characterization as problematic, resolving an analysis of the film with this conclusion would be obvious and arguably reductive. A more complex analysis of the film goes beyond its most evident problems in representation to better understand how other coexisting, and even potentially liberatory, meanings reside within the text and produce its backwardness. To this end, consider the ways Ron's performed southern disposition collides with elitist and anti-southern perspectives on decorum and respectability. During one early scene after his diagnosis, Ron's backward body comes into view amid a scene of biomedical turmoil. While doctors, nurses, and other professionals attempt to discipline his regional habitudes and general outlandishness, Ron's refusal to lie on a hospital bed for treatment enables him to survive while others basically suggest he await his death.

Impressed most by Ron's brashness is Rayon. The pair first meet after Ron attempts to buy another non-prescribed round of AZT from a nurse. The nurse informs Ron the drug is no longer accessible, and in all his southern cowboy glory, a feeble Ron takes a delayed swing at the nurse that ultimately leaves him unconscious in the hospital parking lot. Soon after, Ron awakens in a hospital bed next to Rayon and is nettled by her presence in the room (see figure 8.1). Confidently Rayon examines Ron and aloofly concedes, "I guess you're handsome in a Texas hick, white trash, dumb kinda way." Ron tells Rayon, "Get the fuck outta here, whatever you are." Unperturbed, Rayon entices Ron to play a game of cards. Ron cannot resist, and after losing what appears to be a significant sum of money spread across the white hospital sheets, he attempts to unfold his crossed legs and screams in pain. Rayon tells Ron, "Breathe," and "Relax," as she begins massaging his calf muscle. In this moment Ron briefly lowers his homophobic guard, and while his body remains stiff with caution, the haptics of a trans woman's hand upon his body signals a change in his cultural reflex. The touching of the flesh between two HIV-positive people activates their affective connection. For the first time since his diagnosis, Ron is no longer alone in his reality.

Audiences witness a transformative moment in the formation of a kinship that complicates steadfast presumptions about the backwardness of southern bodies and ideologies. Through corporeal contact, Ron and Rayon enact

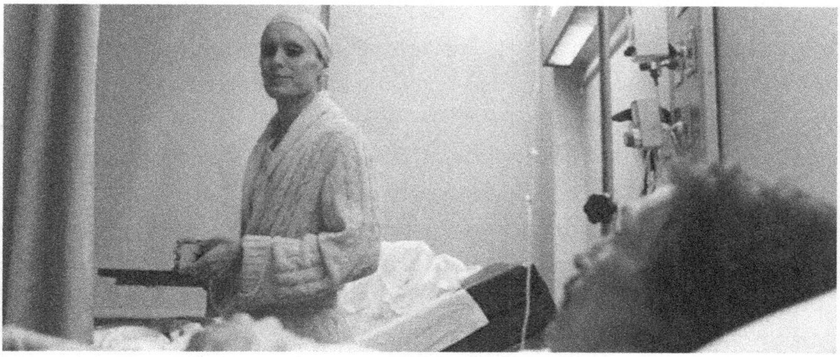

FIGURE 8.1. Rayon's catlike confidence and Ron's suspicions of the queer clash and fuse for the first time in a Dallas hospital room.

an intimacy that transfigures both of their subjectivities. Their paired bodies, one straight and the other queer, expose the malleability of southern backwardness as an expressive display of cultural habitus not predetermined by norms and traditions. The death-driven temporality of Ron's world is undone by the revelatory effect of a hand on skin, and time shifts as this affective collision refuses a historical moment when southern backwardness automatically equated to transphobia. Although he dismisses Rayon once more by reverting into himself and proclaiming his subjectivity as such—"Jesus Christ, I'm straight, okay!"—Ron finds himself born anew upon their meeting.

Backwardness as Resistance

From the beginning of the film's July 1985 setting, the timing of HIV/AIDS manifests in the forward progression of title cards, which begin when Ron first becomes privy to his HIV-positive diagnosis. Upon his abrupt exit from the hospital, a black screen appears with simple white text: "Day 1." These segues interrupt scenes and visually index various milestones in Ron's life. After his coming to terms with his prognosis in the Dallas library, "Day 7" appears. "Day 8" sees Ron bribe a nurse at the hospital and receive his first illegal dose of AZT. In the scene following his first meeting with Rayon, Ron rejects Dr. Saks's recommendation that he stay in the hospital so he can be made comfortable in what appear to be his final days. "Day 29" is when Ron drives to Mexico in search of experimental HIV/AIDS treatments. "Three months later" denotes a major passage of time, as Ron learns in the Mexican clinic that his HIV has evolved into AIDS. Looking to turn illness into a business,

Ron leaves Mexico with a trunk packed with zalcitabine and peptide T to begin the Dallas Buyers Club. The venture is largely successful, but by "March 11, 1987," the FDA bans organizations engaging in the underground trade of unapproved HIV/AIDS treatments. Consequently, Ron uses more sophisticated and covert techniques to keep the club alive, including stealing Dr. Saks's prescription pad to accumulate more doses of peptide T. "Six months later" Ron sues the FDA in a case that will ultimately be dismissed but will result in the FDA approving Ron's personal use of peptide T. The film closes as it opened: "Day 2,557" shows Ron riding a bull in the rodeo once again. The sequence of title cards ends by notifying viewers, "Ronald Woodroof died of AIDS on September 2, 1992, seven years after he was diagnosed with HIV." This chronological progression of cues throughout the film provides a captioned logic of the temporality of HIV/AIDS, a forward, linear march toward the death that one can never escape after a positive diagnosis.

In the film, the inevitability of death looms as Ron attempts to escape its grip. Ron's survival opposes the deathly outcome of a heightened futuristic progression exacerbated by cultural discourses linking HIV/AIDS to death, as well as other material circumstances including a lack of treatment options. Left to his own devices, Ron has two choices: resist to survive or die at the hands of an unrelenting illness exacerbated by the state's inaction. Throughout the film, Ron performs a backwardness—an indicator of his southern roots—in tandem with a backwardness of another kind signifying his refusal to accept the temporality of HIV/AIDS and his will to live in spite of the violent temporality of a necropolitical social economy. Notwithstanding his vehement affirmations of his heterosexuality, Ron's endurance in the film queers time and space and ultimately his sense of self.

Ron's survival operates as a backward resistance against the stifling linearity of HIV/AIDS time. Further, his actions culminate in both a regression and a transgression against the temporality of HIV/AIDS, which has become entrenched owing to callous responses from governmental institutions. Soon after peptide T is declared illegal, the FDA holds a meeting with representatives from the National Institutes of Health, the Centers for Disease Control, and ACT UP. Ron enters dragging an IV drip on wheels and clutching a fistful of informational flyers he has made to inform the attendees about the dangers of AZT. He demands, "Why'd you cut off peptide T? . . . Huh? A nontoxic drug that I got proof works, and that the National Institute of Mental Health—your own people—says is completely safe!" Ron acts as a mediator between scientists and the lay public by translating and distributing information that otherwise might have been unavailable to the HIV-positive people in the room. Ron's activism, albeit in the name of his personal profit, is a historically accurate portrayal of how those with HIV/AIDS communicated new developments in research to fellow patients without access to such resources.[32] Richard Barkley, a principal character featured throughout the film as a representative of the FDA, replies, "Mr. Woodroof, I am afraid that you are nothing more than a common drug dealer, so if you'll excuse us—" Ron cuts him off: "Oh, I'm a drug dealer? No, you're the fucking drug dealer! Goddamn, people are dying, and y'all are all up there afraid that we're going to find an alternative without you. See, the pharma companies pay the FDA to push their product . . . so, fuck no, they don't want to see my research!" Security guards remove Ron from the room.

Significant here is Ron's use of "alternative" to describe treatments other than drugs approved by the FDA. During the first decade of the HIV/AIDS crisis, those diagnosed with the virus continuously searched for alternatives, and these other possibilities extended beyond the drugs they were ingesting. Ron enacts an alternative temporality in contrast to the dominant temporality of HIV/AIDS supported by public and governmental inaction. Ron's leadership in the Dallas Buyers Club assists in the development of a new orientation to the world defined by stamina rather than resignation. Of course, Ron's backward body is made possible by his network of queer companions, including Rayon; by the end of the film they transmute his unbridled homophobia into a fresh outlook on and kinship with the lives of those estranged from normative society. Others, including Dr. Vass and Dr. Saks, help in the production of Ron's backward business by enabling the conditions necessary for his survival and the survival of his queer customers. A once uptight Dr. Saks even quits her job and lowers the doses of AZT in her patients by the film's end, proving her own resistance against the bureaucratic brutality of the FDA and the temporality of HIV/AIDS. These backward alliances prove essential for those running out of time in a world saturated by perpetual death.

Concluding Ruminations on the Queer Necropolitics of Backwardness

A signpost of both southern identity and temporal durability, backwardness also symbolizes an affective site of kinship that merges otherwise oppositional bodies into a forged state of togetherness during a period of duress.

FIGURE 8.2. Ron rejects quotidian acts of homophobia by forcing T.J. to shake hands with a startled Rayon in a public grocery store.

In the film, Ron and Rayon's backward kinship owes itself to the desperation of the moment. An exemplar of this alliance appears in the middle of the film, at a point when Ron and Rayon still share a strictly business relationship, with Ron using Rayon as a comfortable mediator between himself and his queer clientele. While Ron has certainly come a long way since his first encounter with Rayon in the hospital bed, there has been no indication from his stoic persona that he sees Rayon as anything more than a profitable resource for his business. In a pivotal scene, the duo go grocery shopping at the local supermarket. After lamenting the FDA-approved toxins in processed bologna, Ron encounters an old friend named T.J. who, like his other former buddies, has alienated HIV-positive Ron from their social circle. Awkward small talk ensues before T.J. notices Rayon and mutters, "Jesus, fuckin' faggots everywhere." Ron quickly responds, "T.J., this is Rayon." A startled T.J. refuses to shake Rayon's open hand. Before he can finish shoving his middle finger in Ron's face, Ron locks him in a chokehold. With one frail arm around his neck, Ron forces T.J. to shake Rayon's hand (see figure 8.2). "Go back to your miserable life," Ron says as he loosens his grip. T.J. furiously wipes his hand against his jeans. As he walks away, Rayon gazes at Ron with wide eyes.

Ron solidifies the backward kinship with Rayon by reversing the anti-queer disgust he once perpetuated; in effect, he strips T.J. of his choice to continue harboring unwarranted ill will toward queer bodies. By limiting T.J.'s physical sphere of agency, Ron forces him into a position where he has little control over whether he will shake Rayon's hand. Thus far, Ron has unsuccessfully attempted to reclaim power over his own body, but in this moment he achieves a role reversal. Like an HIV/AIDS patient, T.J. is now the one who cannot control the basic functions of his bodily systems, while Ron, like the homophobic public T.J. represents, presses the powerless body into a position of vulnerability. An empowered Ron forecasts his advocacy on behalf of himself and his queer companions by temporarily creating a situation where a broader societal response to HIV/AIDS can no longer be hateful apathy, but rather direct recognition. In this scene, Ron detaches himself from a group that see themselves as somehow distinguished from Rayon. In the reflection of Rayon's surprised eyes, Ron now sees himself.

From this and following scenes a sense of hope is shining through the cracks in the rubble of depravity. Ron and Rayon's backward kinship, although tumultuous at times, remains steadfast throughout the film and provides a solid foundation from which both characters can rise and face another day despite the constant barrage of obstacles they face. Viewers of the film watch Ron and Rayon's bond refuse systems of necropower that deem their queer bodies already corpses. This backward pairing illuminates the resistant potential of bonded intimacy. Such an example of this intimate backwardness comes in a scene near the film's end during a period of financial hardship for the Buyers Club. A moribund Rayon, noticeably weaker than before, visits her estranged father in a suit and tie. Once there, she requests that he sell her life insurance policy. The encounter illustrates that even in a situation as precarious as the first years of the HIV/AIDS epidemic, the direness of a relative's impending death still could not curtail transphobic attitudes in an HIV/AIDS patient's family. Rayon's father eventually grants her request, and she delivers the money to Ron. Rayon then walks back to her adjacent room in the Buyers Club's motel headquarters. Ron follows, and after Rayon tells him how she acquired the money, a noticeably shaken Ron extends his hand for a handshake. Their eyes meet. A tension fills the room. In this gap, the temporality of HIV/AIDS manifests itself and pulls their bodies away from each other. The duo briefly accept the neutrality of the handshake, a signal of normative business dealing and acquaintanceship. Closing the momentary delay, Rayon reaches out for an embrace. Ron willingly accepts. Their closeness delays their otherwise unrelenting temporal conditions, as time stops moving in its forward trajectory. Their viral bodies touch as they break the constructed poles of difference wedged against them from the beginning of the film. In a suspension of desperation, Ron and Rayon no longer yearn for explanations. Their solace in each other is the answer they have been searching for since their diagnoses. This queer necropolitical kinship temporally regresses against the timing of HIV/AIDS and provides the affective fuel for both characters to continue moving backward against the cruel world they inhabit.

Instead of preserving his unrepentant homophobia, Ron submits to the immediacy of the death world created by HIV/AIDS and adjusts his positionality in close proximity with the very queer bodies he once degraded. But Ron remains a negative figure. One can assume that had he not been diagnosed with HIV, Ron would never have defended Rayon, nor would he have partaken in queer kinship and community building through a business like the Buyers Club. Ironically, Ron's queerness comes to fruition even as he clings to his straightness and refuses to fully embrace his queer circumstances. Attempting to redeem Ron as a liberatory character is a fruitless endeavor and may leave viewers and critics feeling impossibly backward. "Backward feelings," Heather Love declares in *Feeling Backward*, "serve as an index to the ruined state of the social world; they indicate the continuities between the bad gay past and the present; they show up the inadequacy of queer narratives of progress."[33] Much like the texts Love analyzes, *Dallas Buyers Club* cannot be critically apprehended as an exemplary fictionalized account of a utopic moment in queer history. In an era of unprecedented queer assimilation in both politics and media, the backward bodies of southern queers continue to withstand conforming to totalizing gay narratives of progress. Popular representations of the necropolitical world such as the one produced by the early onset of HIV/AIDS in the South are even less likely to fit neatly into dominant understandings of queerness because these idealizations currently rely on ideas that perpetuate liberation and pride as the most desirable and productive feelings in contemporary queer life. In this historical moment and probably well into the future, Ron and Rayon's story proceeds in a backward direction against the liberal expectations of an increasingly homonormative world.

Hence, the film is an important piece of queer historical material not because it gets its history "right," but because it refuses to accept contemporary expectations of a normative queerness and its politically homogeneous cultural products. The film willingly explores the inexplicably complicated contours of the backward South and the bodies inhabiting the region during the early years of HIV/AIDS. This is especially crucial in a period when the South claims the highest rates of HIV/AIDS cases today. While the onset of HIV/AIDS fatigue in queer communities and the public sphere writ large threatens to falsely consign the ongoing epidemic to a time of the distant past, the film once again recenters the crisis in the present. But still, the film does not purport to glorify the queer future by any means; rather, it demonstrates how temporal traversals around the dominant future such as the ones performed by Ron and Rayon can result in the creation of new, otherwise unimaginable worlds that place a premium on kinship and struggle in the face of structural adversity.

Under a lens of rhetorical contingency and contextual constraint, *Dallas Buyers Club* works within the social matrix of power in which it was born. Rather than ceasing the temporality of this chapter by providing a conclusive end, I wish to suspend certainty about how the cinema *should have* represented HIV/AIDS and the South in 2013. Indeed, I want to consider the kind of world the film attempts to preserve through historical re-creation, as well as the alternatives it creates. Where do our backward feelings take us and what can they teach us about the messy convergence of queer history, media, and the priorities of capitalist entertainment industries in the United States, and in the South in particular? Let us continue to ruminate on the affective power of the film, as well as its impurities, possibilities, and inexcusable exclusions. In our suspension of queer certitude, we might find we are more backward than we ever imagined.

NOTES

1. For a brief history of the "gay disease" as a nickname for AIDS, see John-Manuel Andriote, "Reclaiming HIV as a 'Gay' Disease," *Gay and Lesbian Review Worldwide* 19.5 (2012): 28–30, at 28. See also Dennis Altman, *AIDS in the Mind of America* (Garden City, N.Y.: Anchor Press/Doubleday, 1987), 21.

2. This trend took hold prominently in the last two decades. Since 1999, some of the gay-for-pay awardees include Hilary Swank, best actress for *Boys Don't Cry* (1999); Nicole Kidman, best actress for *The Hours* (2002); Charlize Theron, best actress for *Monster* (2003); Phillip Seymour Hoffman, best actor for *Capote* (2005); Sean Penn, best actor for *Milk* (2008); and Christopher Plummer, best supporting actor for *Beginners* (2010).

3. Steve Friess, "Don't Applaud Jared Leto's Transgender 'Mammy,'" *Time* 28 February 2014; Web.

4. Friess, "Don't Applaud Jared Leto's Transgender 'Mammy.'"

5. Paris Lees, "Jared Leto in *Dallas Buyers Club*: Why Can't We Cast Trans People in Trans Roles?" *Independent* 21 February 2014.

6. Heather Love, *Feeling Backward: Loss and the Politics of Queer History* (Cambridge, Mass.: Harvard University Press, 2007), 34.

7. Love, *Feeling Backward*, 34.

8. Elizabeth Freeman, *Time Binds: Queer Temporalities, Queer Histories* (Durham, N.C.: Duke University Press, 2010), 62.

9. E. Patrick Johnson, *Sweet Tea: Black Gay Men of the South* (Chapel Hill: University of North Carolina Press, 2008), 5.

10. U.S. Centers for Disease Control and Prevention, "HIV in the Southern United States," May 2016, cdc.gov/hiv/pdf/policies/cdc-hiv-in-the-south-issue-brief.pdf.

11. Dallas County Health Department, "[Handwritten Note & Budget with Handwritten Notes: Dallas County AIDS Cases]," 14 June 1989, University of North Texas Libraries Special Collections, texashistory.unt.edu/ark:/67531/metadc854073. See also "Population Estimates of Texas Counties, 1985–89, Arranged in Alphabetical Order," Texas State Library and Archives Commission, www.tsl.texas.gov/ref/abouttx/popcnty85-89.html.

12. Perry Smith, Jaromir Mikl, Sue Hyde, and Dale Morse, "The AIDS Epidemic in New York State," *American Journal of Public Health* 81 (1991): 54–60, at 59.

13. "Club Offers Latest Drugs for AIDS," newspaper clipping, 17 May 1989, University of North Texas Libraries Special Collections, texashistory.unt.edu/ark:/67531/metadc271481.

14. Ibid.

15. Jack [Judith] Halberstam, *In a Queer Time and Place: Transgender Bodies, Subcultural Lives* (New York: New York University Press, 2005), 6.

16. Halberstam, *In a Queer Time and Place*, 6

17. Isaac West, "Queer Generosities," *Western Journal of Communication* 77.5 (2013): 538–41, at 538–39 (italics in original).

18. West, "Queer Generosities," 539.

19. Lee Edelman, "The Future Is Kid Stuff: Queer Theory, Disidentification, and the Death Drive," *Narrative* 6.1 (1998): 18–30, at 18.

20. Lee Edelman, *No Future: Queer Theory and the Death Drive* (Durham, N.C.: Duke University Press, 2004), 2.

21. Arguably the most celebrated of these critiques comes from José Esteban Muñoz, *Cruising Utopia: The Then and There of Queer Futurity* (New York: New York University Press, 2009), 11–18.

22. Lisa Duggan, "Down There: The Queer South and the Future of History Writing," *GLQ: A Journal of Lesbian and Gay Studies* 8.3 (2002): 379–87, at 380 (italics in original).

23. Kyra Pearson, "How to Have History in an Epidemic," *Remembering the AIDS Quilt*, ed. Charles E. Morris III (East Lansing: Michigan State University Press, 2011), 261–98, at 286 (italics in original).

24. Gust A. Yep, "The Politics of Loss and Its Remains in Common Threads: Stories from the Quilt," Morris, *Remembering the AIDS Quilt*, 43–68, at 54.

25. Jin Haritaworn, Adi Kuntsman, and Silvia Posocco, introduction to *Queer Necropolitics*, ed. Haritaworn, Kuntsman, and Posocco (New York: Routledge, 2014), 1–28, at 2.

26. Achille Mbembe, "Necropolitics," trans. Libby Meintjes, *Public Culture* 15.1 (2003): 11–40, at 11.

27. John Howard, introduction to *Carryin' On in the Lesbian and Gay South*, ed. John Howard (New York: New York University Press, 1997), 1–14, at 4.

28. N-word redacted.

29. They say the real Woodroof was not at all homophobic and was the fiercest advocate for the Dallas queer community's right to HIV/AIDS medication. See Sherry Jacobson, "Ron Woodroof's Isn't the Only AIDS Story Worthy of a Hollywood Movie," *Dallas Morning News* 1 November 2013.

30. Carlos L. Dews, afterword to *Out in the South,* ed. Carlos L. Dews and Carolyn Leste Law (Philadelphia: Temple University Press, 2001), 236–40, at 238.

31. Carolyn Leste Law, introduction to *Out in the South,* 1–8, at 3.

32. For a richer discussion of this history, see Valeria Fabj and Matthew Sobnosky, "AIDS Activism and the Rejuvenation of the Public Sphere," *Argumentation and Advocacy* 31 (1995): 163–84.

33. Love, *Feeling Backward,* 27.

Chapter 9 ▸ Queer Native Southern Transmissions in Randy Redroad's *The Doe Boy*

ERIC GARY ANDERSON

The Doe Boy (2001), written and directed by Randy Redroad, a Cherokee, is a coming-of-age film set in small-town northeastern Oklahoma in the late 1970s and mid-1980s.[1] Southern mainly by virtue of Cherokee historical and cultural connections to the pre-removal Southeast, the film centers on Hunter Kirk (James Duval), a mixed-blood Cherokee/white teenager entangled in his own as well as others' fears and anxieties about his masculinity, sexuality, physical health, family relationships, and future prospects. From his white father's "Sometimes I can't believe you sprung from my loins" to his own inclination to keep his uncertainties mostly to himself as he struggles to weigh and balance raw knowledge that he takes in from various sources, he finds himself buffeted by the often frustrating, conflicting transmissions he both receives and sends.

The film can be read as a narrative about adolescent growing pains and the tensions and ambiguities often associated with emerging identities. But Redroad complicates and empowers this potentially predictable coming-of-age plot by way of *The Doe Boy*'s explicit Cherokee orientation and its more implicit strain of queerness. Redroad establishes his story's Cherokeeness in a variety of ways, perhaps most obviously by assigning voiceover narration duties to Hunter's maternal grandfather Marvin Fishinghawk (Gordon Tootoosis). The first of the voiceovers establishes his colloquial omniscience: "Nobody cares how much blood runs through a deer. But everyone wants to know how much blood runs through an Indian. It's kinda hard to tell, unless you cut one of us open. And watch all the stories pour out." Throughout the film, Marvin's narration reinforces this opening assertion about the link between stories and blood. His understanding of stories as blood and blood as stories also underscores the vital importance of transmission: both blood and stories flow not only through individual bodies but also from person to person, generation to generation, and location to location. Transmission as a cultural practice is axiomatic to Native communities and to Native and Indigenous Studies. Although the term has not taken on the status of a scholarly keyword, the practice it refers to is important because it both encourages Native presence, visibility, strength, and survival and decolonizes the consequences of settler forces that ruthlessly shut down Indigenous transmissions. Set primarily in 1984 and shadowed by a growing awareness that AIDS is a public health threat, the film powerfully explores fears and anxieties associated with transmission. Relatedly, it dramatizes ways in which the anxieties fathers and sons in particular share about the transmission of normativity can frustrate and impede intergenerational relationships. *The Doe Boy* also carves out a hard-won space for queer optimism grounded in characters' willingness and emerging ability to redefine—to indigenize—the normative and to keep lines of transmission open.

But Marvin's opening voiceover lines concerning the meanings of blood are more disturbing than one might initially presume. In exposing an all-too-common conflation of human physiology (how much blood does a human body contain?) and blood quantum (how much of that blood is "Indian?"), Marvin links the transmission of stories and, by implication, culture to the sharp violence of "cut one of us open" and "watch all the stories pour out." To watch stories pour out, like blood, is to witness them seeping into the ground, drying up, and vanishing. Watching stories instead of listening to them or carefully, intentionally transmitting them signals a potentially catastrophic cultural loss. Marvin suggests, too, that sweeping generalizations ("Nobody," "everyone") serve a rhetorical purpose but ultimately need to give way to direct body-to-body personal experience ("unless you cut one of us open") and to the wisdom of his gently chiding corrective "It's kinda hard to tell."

I dwell on these lines because they help introduce what I am (and what I am not) attempting to do in bringing a queer lens to *The Doe Boy*. I do not have much to say about queer sexuality for the simple reason that the film does not focus on it, although it explores gendered identities and it shows characters suggesting that nonnormative masculinity might be "gay." Mainly, I am interested in using queerness as an analytical tool to plumb the ways characters in the film navigate their disagreements as well as their understandings of who they are, personally and culturally. I focus especially on the things that set characters apart, precisely because these tensions, often paradoxically co-created and shared, prompt characters to see one another as strange, non-normative, and potentially estranging. In other words, I want to look closely at how, where, and why differing points of view, particularly disagreements about what constitutes "normal" and acceptable behavior, construct and reveal estrangement. Reading *The Doe Boy* through a queer lens helps make anxieties about normativity more visible as obstacles to Native, and to a lesser extent southern, identity formation. The film argues in favor of disrupting and potentially transforming characters' understandings of what normative is and how it works or does not work in their lives. In so doing, *The Doe Boy* enables a queer reading that maps a subtle, fluid, often tacit space of queer possibility. Queer Native southern transmissions in *The Doe Boy* are works in progress that help reveal the contours of estrangement as well as the trajectories of hope.[2] In *The Doe Boy*, queerness patches through these tenuous and powerful spaces and gives Redroad ways of honoring the complexity of key characters' identities via the lingering presence of mistakes and losses that they have not resolved, and quite possibly never will. Queerness in this film is not always comfortable but it is dynamic, an important part of continuing processes of personal growth; it is not always articulate or articulated, let alone able to solve problems and usher characters smoothly from adolescence to adulthood. As I will argue, queerness hinges on the ways characters in the film tell stories that try, and often productively fail, to map the complexities of lives uncomfortably preoccupied with propagating, challenging, and/or redefining the normal.

In a flashback, the film roots many of Hunter's difficulties in an extraordinary, and embarrassing, event: at age eleven, he goes hunting with his non-Native father Hank (Kevin Anderson) for the first time and mistakenly shoots and kills a female deer. Hunter thus unintentionally violates both Euro-American and Cherokee notions of appropriate hunting practice. He cannot explain what happened and, as the scene is shot from his point of view and we see what he sees—a male deer before he shoots but a female deer dead on the forest floor—neither can we. But men in his family and community are happy to step up and offer their thoughts. From Hank's perspective, the killing of the doe confirms what he has suspected and feared all along: that Hunter falls short not only as a hunter but also as a man. In part because of this hunting mistake and in part because Hunter does not meet bluntly normative gender expectations in other ways, his father wonders whether he is gay. From his grandfather Marvin's point of view, the hunting mistake came about because Hank was "napping while [Hunter] shoots a woman." Marvin does not question Hunter's Cherokee identity as Hank questions his son's sexual one; in fact, Marvin understands his grandson to be the best and most promising of his Cherokee descendants. While Hank reads the situation as further evidence of something he already suspects about his son, Marvin believes that his grandson's identity is still developing and emerging. From the points of view of many of his friends, neighbors, and classmates, however, he has earned the disparaging nickname Doe Boy; the nickname sticks over the course of several years and suggests that his legacy might well be locked in and incapable of changing. Even as the film jumps from 1977 to 1984, Hunter remains what he was at the time of the accident, a boy, and he has perhaps permanently transformed into the female animal he shoots, a doe. Both of the words that make up his nickname arrest his development, while "Doe" also associates gender and species changes with mockery.

In the film's 1984 narrative present, as he works to construct a sexual identity and to parse his Cherokee and Euro-American identities, Hunter tries on a variety of masculine styles, including his father's white, borderline redneck masculinity and his grandfather's more patient Cherokee masculinity. He also learns from his Cherokee mother Maggie (Jeri Arredondo) and adopts elements of her personal and cultural identity. Although Hunter at first appears to be more allied with his father than with his mother, the father-son relationship is the more volatile and is clearly the one that most needs sorting out. During this period of uncertainty and transformation, Hunter continues to grapple with a hereditary medical condition: hemophilia. More, he learns that the only other known Indian hemophiliac in Oklahoma has died of AIDS. "That gay disease?" Hunter asks his doctor, who refutes the designation of AIDS as a "gay disease" and details how AIDS can be transmitted through infusions of blood products. This emerging mid-1980s fear of AIDS surfaces a bit more than halfway through the film and immediately shadows and haunts it, especially as Hunter awaits the results of the precautionary blood test his doctor has ordered. Yet, as I have begun to suggest and will develop in more detail, queerness in this film is more subtextual than contextual; it emerges primarily out of competing ideas about how to define normativity and nonnormativity and whether to embrace or resist it, both within and across cultures. Put another way, the film presents these conflicting notions as, potentially, a source of queer transmissions that mark, but do not always directly articulate, queerness.

Queerness upsets the tyranny of normativity in varying arenas relevant to Southern and Native Studies. In "Queer/Quare," Michael P. Bibler explains that "as a theoretical tool, 'queer' does far more than simply describe particular inflections of gender, desire, and sexual identity. Rather, by exposing the incoherencies and inconsistencies within and between these three terms, a queer analysis demands a much broader critique of culture and power that must be central to any discussion of the South's regional peculiarities. Indeed, it is precisely where gender and sexuality are most unstable that the wider complexities of culture and society within the South become most apparent."[3] In *The Queerness of Native American Literature*, Lisa Tatonetti makes a similar point: "queerness, as [Jasbir] Puar and Indigenous studies scholars such as [Daniel Heath] Justice, [Scott Lauria] Morgensen, [Mark] Rifkin, Andrea Smith, and [Craig] Womack have shown us, provides an analytic, a way of seeing, a path to understanding (some part of) our ever-shifting contexts. . . . Queer practices or desires and concepts like the heteronorm or queer imaginary necessarily work within and/or against a settler-defined sex/gender dichotomy."[4] As both Bibler and Tatonetti demonstrate, a queer lens sharpens, expands, and clarifies the dimensions and dynamics of sociocultural power structures that, all too often, go unquestioned. Bibler builds on E. Patrick Johnson's important argument for a "quare" approach that understands sexual difference in relation to other kinds of difference, including racial, and also in relation to specific historical situations, the oppressive workings of colonial power, and more.[5] Indeed, Bibler presents "queer/quare" as conjoined keywords for Southern Studies and contends: "Rather than a stable identity, 'queer' is . . . better understood as an active denaturalization of identity categories and an unsettling of the power structures that support them."[6] Tatonetti argues that "queer Native literature comes from a space of *opposition* (to dominant settler norms, to normative neoliberal agendas, to heteronormative resistance movements) *and* a space of *relationship and coalition* (with other Native queers, with other queers of color, with other Indigenous peoples),"[7] a point Bibler also broaches, particularly in his discussion of a "quare" attentiveness to nonwhite southernness and queerness.

In *The Doe Boy*, tensions between predictable, ready-made identity categories and exploratory identities-in-the-making destabilize both. Of the three identities I discuss in this essay—queer, Native/Cherokee, and southern—the film remains most steadfastly silent about "southern."[8] Northeastern Oklahoma as Redroad represents it is southern by implication: verbal and visual cues allow viewers to see and hear southernness, or perhaps more accurately to hypothesize southernness, in characters' speech, dress, possessions, habits, and other trappings. Even more implicitly, *The Doe Boy* takes its place in a Cherokee cultural and historical continuum profoundly disrupted and violated, although not destroyed, by Indian removal, the forced migration of Cherokees and other tribes from their southeastern homelands to "Indian Territory," present-day Oklahoma. This history of settler-colonial violence and dispossession does not simply or easily go away when it passes largely unmentioned in a given text. It quite literally carries the South to a new place, for "the South" itself is a non-Native regional construction retroactively imposed on Cherokees and other tribes and also presented, by non-Native settlers, as a coherent, cohesive, developing, but largely stable non-Native identity that motivates and even justifies the dislodging of Cherokee from their southeastern homelands. As Bibler observes, Southern Studies scholars are busy "reconsidering the gaps and fissures that emerge where Southern regional differences intersect and overlap with national (or global) normativities."[9] Redroad does not for the most part hit these historical questions and patterns head on and, as a result, his film is not overtly political; nonetheless, as I have begun to suggest, it is not exactly apolitical either, as the questions he raises about normative personal and cultural identities and relationships lay the groundwork for decolonizing.

The Doe Boy is a compact, eighty-seven-minute film set entirely in Tahlequah, Oklahoma. It begins in 1977, when Hunter is eleven, but takes place primarily in 1984. In its opening shot, a deer runs through woods, presenting a strong visual cue that the woods serve as an important setting and that, as the film's title also intimates, the first identity viewers are invited to think about is a four-legged one. Indeed, as the film unspools, deer figure prominently as local residents, topics of conversation, hunters' quarries, subjects of stories, and often comic images on yellow-and-black road signs. *The Doe Boy* makes clear from the opening moments that its protagonist's life is marked and measured by the presence of deer. The first human figures we see are three Indian boys; one pulls up and uses his inhaler, and another, as it turns out, is Hunter. But viewers do not know this at first. Not until several minutes later does the film identify Hunter not as the boy with the inhaler but as the one nicknamed Band-Aid Boy because of his hemophilia. The opening sequence introduces a world but does not map or otherwise caption this world.

That said, the film's narrator, who we later learn is Hunter's grandfather Marvin, says early on, "There was a boy who followed in the deer's footsteps, instead of his father's." With this line, Marvin introduces Hunter to viewers by explicitly linking the boy and the deer. Although he bears the almost excessively obvious name Hunter, perhaps a wish fulfillment on the part of his father, and although Hunter himself enthusiastically walks that path, he follows the deer rather than his father. In Marvin's phrasing, the word "in" makes all the difference, as it opens up the possibility that Hunter seeks to emulate, not to shoot and kill, the deer. In all, the design of the opening minutes complicates the protagonist's identity in ways that are entirely in keeping with the film's major thematic through-lines. Marvin confidently transmits information that keeps some questions unanswered—for example, why does he follow in the deer's footsteps rather than in his father's?—and that might or might not suggest a veiled critique of the father and possibly of Euro-American settler-colonial approaches to the natural world.

The 1977 scenes center on the story of Hunter's first, fumbled hunting expedition with his father Hank. For Hank, lineage and legacy boil down to hunting—"We're gonna try Hunter's hand this year. See if he's got any of his old man in him"—a paternal transmission fantasy that raises a question no one has asked and that is accompanied by only the thinnest amount of actual hunting instruction. Hank also notes: "They raised the limit this year. Damn deer about to run us out of the state." Deer are not just for food or sport; in Hank's view, they pose a problem verging on a threat, as if these deer would do to white Oklahomans what white settlers did to southeastern Indians. Here it is also worth noting that Hank has nailed deer heads to the walls of the family living room and of his garage. Hunter's dad holds particular notions about what constitutes normative masculine behavior and hopes to transmit these notions to his son. But, in bed with Maggie, Hank acknowledges, "He ain't your usual chip off the old block." A little later he elaborates: "can't play sports, can't work with tools . . . damn sure never take him in the military . . . I'm afraid he's gonna end up a nurse, too." Maggie, who is a nurse, retorts: "Ain't nothing wrong with a boy taking after his mother." Hank snuggles up to Maggie and makes what he sees as his strongest argument in favor of letting Hunter go hunting with him in spite of his hemophilia: "There's nothin' like killin' your first buck, Mag. . . . Never forget the look in my dad's face when I killed mine. The only other time I saw that look was when I got into flight school. He was dead before I ever made him proud again." When this appeal falls short, Hank tries shame: "You want to tell him that he's gotta be the first man on either side of the family that don't hunt? Be my guest." Throughout this conversation, Hunter eavesdrops outside his parents' bedroom door and silently celebrates when Maggie finally relents. Only when he raises his arms in triumph do we understand that he really does want to go hunting with his father. At the same time, this shot of the son standing in a dark hallway with a wall between him and his parents stands as a strong visual metaphor: he is alone and in the dark as his parents debate his normativity.

While Hank is prone to say things like "Sometimes I can't believe you sprung from my loins" when Hunter doesn't know what a crescent wrench is, Hunter's grandfather Marvin offers other ideas about what masculinity is and how it works. In addition to critiquing Hank's notions and his hunting method, Marvin comfortably enjoys pastimes that neither Hank nor his own grandfather would dream of doing, like playing the flute in a downtown park. Hunter even asks his grandfather if he "got Granny" by playing his flute. Intriguingly, Marvin, who jokes about being disowned by his granddaddy for his flute playing, whether because it seems emasculating or because he plays for food or perhaps both, and who stands in sharp contrast to Hank's blunt and predictable masculinity, is the person Hunter wants to talk with about heterosexual courtship. Further, in his voiceover narration Marvin remarks: "A buck with a broken or damaged rack is seen as inferior by other bucks. A strong buck won't hesitate to attack a weaker one and run him out of his territory." While this is unmistakably a comment about male behavior, it is as much about the value of understanding deer. In this vein, Marvin's statement meshes with a line spoken by the aptly named Cheekie (Kody Dayish), a boy Hunter's age, who says to his Cherokee father that when it comes to hunting deer, "Mom says you're cursed. Mom says they hold a grudge against you because you hit too many with your truck." From both an elder (who, I assume, conveys this knowledge to his grandson as well as to viewers) and a boy, Hunter gleans that deer have reasons for doing what they do. The repetition of "Mom says" offers another salient reminder, one that Hank, to his credit, typically heeds when he talks with his wife about their son and listens to her words.

Redroad makes clear that the sharp differences between Marvin's and Hank's approaches to deer and hunting are not only stylistic and pedagogical but also cultural: Hank's perspective is Euro-American while Marvin's is Cherokee. Marvin encourages Hunter to think about how he stands in relation to other Cherokees such as Tommy Deer-in-Water, a skilled hunter, not a "warrior like your daddy." Tommy "always hunts alone. Only takes one arrow" because "that's all a real hunter needs." Marvin adds that "a good hunter always gives the deer a chance. You don't have to dress up like a tree and then sit around and wait for one to walk by." However, when Hank and Hunter go hunting, they follow Hank's usual practice of toting guns, dressing like trees, and sitting around. When Hunter repeats Marvin's remarks about the folly of hunting like Hank does, Hank dismisses them; then, while Hank dozes beneath a tree, Hunter sees the buck that, after he shoots and kills it, lies on the forest floor as a doe. The difference between what he sees before he shoots and what he sees afterward uncomfortably juxtaposes gender change (or confusion or misperception) with the generational and transcultural tension between his grandfather's views about hunting and his father's. Displeased, Marvin faults Hank for the mistake, saying that Hunter "wanted a story to tell for the rest of his life. You napping while he shoots a woman. Probably don't cut the mustard." The problem, as Marvin points out, is that the mistake was avoidable and that it creates a failed transmission, not the story Hunter hoped to be able to tell and to transmit, in turn, to future generations. Hank's rejoinder goes where he ordinarily does not go, as he draws a starkly racist distinction between Cherokee "magic" and Euro-American settler-colonial "real life": "You ain't helping him any. Filling his head full of stories of magic beads and magic hunters. There ain't no magic around here, Marvin. It's just real life."

The majority of *The Doe Boy* takes place in 1984, seven years after Hunter shoots the doe. Early in the 1984 part of the film, we see him in his high school's nurse's office, receiving an injection as other students look in through the door. The point is clear: his hemophilia separates him from his peers and in a sense quarantines him. His nonnormativity defines him and makes him a spectacle. Meanwhile, his father's habit of getting quietly drunk and watching old war movies appears to be at least as entrenched in 1984 as it was in 1977. In a parallel to Hunter's isolation in the nurse's office, Hank sits by himself in the living room and eventually recites a Chuck Yaeger speech, which Maggie overhears and mouths, confirming that she has heard this set piece before. Hank is not isolated, but he seems trapped. Although father-son tensions loom, I want to underscore that Redroad also suggests, compositionally and visually, a shared loneliness or isolation that connects them but that proves difficult to bond over.

Indeed, Hank exacerbates the tension by making fun of Hunter's red-and-black plaid pants, one of the staples of early 1980s New Wave fashion: "You gotta be pretty brave to sport a garment that sweet," he says, and, more provocatively, "I know a neighborhood in Dallas where everybody dresses like that. If you want, Hunter, I can drive you down there and leave you for a week. You might fit right in." It is not clear whether Hank has a specific gay district or enclave in mind, but it is abundantly clear that his son's colorful and snug-fitting pants unnerve him. Hank also foresees his son staying at home and mooching off his parents: "If you're out of here by the time you're thirty, I'll give you a thousand bucks." Hank's language here is both oddly ornate—"sport a garment"—and insensitive, as when he proposes giving his doe-burdened son "a thousand bucks." After this argument escalates and Hunter storms out of the house and drives off into the night, he sees another deer sign along the road, this one with a front hoof clad in a cowboy boot. In the film's 1977 backstory, a sign for "Upper Shit Creek" portended trouble ahead; the deer sign in 1984 glosses a confrontation that just happened. Accused by his father of dressing funny (borderline gay), Hunter sees an image of a deer who dresses funny (borderline camp). The point is not so much to pin down Hunter's sexuality as it is to juxtapose his connection to deer with his relationship with his father and to suggest that things as familiar, normative, and regulatory as road signs can also enter into a more subjective, surreal, mysterious realm in which they comment, queerly, on both past and future occurrences.

This realm resurfaces in a more pointedly sexual way in a subsequent scene. Sitting in class, Hunter leans forward to smell the female student sitting at the desk in front of him. Then he lays her hair on his desk and bends over to smell it. The scene depicts a decidedly nonnormative interaction as well as a nonnormative way of occupying time and space. His grandfather Marvin, who is not there, narrates this encounter as Hunter acts it out. Says Marvin, "To a buck, every doe smells unique." Here Hunter leans forward and breathes her in. "When hunting with doe scent," Marvin continues, "it's best to use the scent of one doe instead of a mixture of lots of does." After Hunter smells his classmate's hair, he develops a bloody nose and must let go of her hair and leave class. The female student, who does not react when he plays with her hair, watches him leave with concern. Has she allowed him to play with her hair? Is he fantasizing or daydreaming rather than actually doing what the camera shows him doing? Does Marvin know what his grandson is doing, and if yes, how does he know? Does Marvin's voiceover narration endorse the idea that Hunter's fetishistic act is natural? Does it explain (away) an act that, if actually happening, could be prosecutable? Does it open up necessary space for Hunter to learn to be both a buck and a deer hunter (and to shed his Doe Boy identity)? In raising complicated questions about a scene that remains a mystery, Redroad depicts an apparently nonnormative act visually and also through an omniscient narrator who does not witness what he so accurately describes, while at the same time suggesting that this act might in fact be natural, as well as more pedagogically necessary to Hunter's growth than whatever the class is studying.

As Hunter's eighteenth birthday approaches and he prepares to make the transition into adulthood, his father circles back to the plaid pants and relents: "I don't hate them pants—just don't understand 'em." Then, when Marvin gives Hunter a wooden flute that he has made himself, Hank gracefully concedes that it's a nice one. Marvin declares, "That's the first one I made since your mama passed on," and adds, "I figure if Hunter learns to play, I won't have to take my one skill to the grave." However, when Hunter goes out to a bar later that night, he tries to pick fights and insists that he isn't afraid of anything. And when he returns home, he has a loaded exchange with his father:

> HANK. Most guys your age are looking at titties on the toilet, not quail and pheasant.
> HUNTER. That supposed to mean I'm gay or something?
> HANK. What it means are that guys like you are why plumbers can charge an arm and a leg to replace a washer, 'cause you read about stuff and never learn to do it.

While Marvin's narration presents Hunter in the process of becoming both a deer and a deer hunter, Hank suggests that he should by now be well established as a heterosexual masturbator. Hank also yells that he "ain't gonna beg you to hunt with me. My dad never had to beg me." Then, after Hunter criticizes his hunting methods, Hank retorts: "I hunt like every other man in the goddamn state." In other words, Hank insistently sees masculine behavior as a matter of alliances among men; acting as other men do is his benchmark for normativity. Hunter responds: "It's probably your blood that ruined me . . . goddamn white disease," at which point Hank strikes him and Hunter bleeds (see figure 9.1). Then, when Hank offers to get Hunter's mother (who, again, is a nurse), Hunter one-ups him in performing normative masculinity, saying, "If you need her, you go get her." I recapitulate this scene at some length because it is such a grab-bag of unresolved father-son tensions. While many of the recriminations and accusations spoken here in anger concern transmissions, the argument also shifts its focus several times, most notably when Hunter says "gay" out loud and Hank is unable to respond directly, opting instead to suggest that Hunter is nonnormative because he is not much of a handyman around the house. For a man so anxious about patriarchal lineage, the worst insult his son can fling is that he, Hank, has transmitted a

FIGURE 9.1. After the hemophiliac Hunter angrily tells his father, Hank, "It's probably your blood that ruined me . . . goddamn white disease," Hank strikes his son and draws blood. Earlier, Hank insults Hunter by accusing him of being queer, but neither father nor son resorts to physical violence until one of them activates racial anxieties. Immediately after Hank's punch lands, the camera deletes him from the frame and focuses on Hunter, who stares at both his bloody hand—which appears in close-up—and his skin. The scene is dimly lit, but the minimal lighting illuminates Hunter's shocked, absorbed, contemplative face and signals that this moment is really about him.

disease through bad white blood. (Hemophilia is, they both know, an inherited condition, though they both seem foggy as to how this inheritance actually works.) Far from being the reliable marker of normative masculinity that Hank so wants it to be, he fears—wrongly, but the anxiety is very real—that his y-chromosome might well be a toxin, while Marvin's is not.

Hank and Hunter's relationship improves from here. As they work through their differences, the film skillfully interweaves several narrative threads even as Hunter continues to feel compelled to keep secrets and set himself apart until he resolves, or comes to a better understanding of, his shooting and killing of the doe. In brief, Hank and Hunter reconcile just before Hank dies (ironically, in a hunting accident); Hunter meets his next-door neighbor Geri (Jade Herrera), who is Pueblo, Navajo, Mexican, and Spanish, and romantic sparks fly between them; Hunter sees his doctor, learns about AIDS, and fearfully awaits the results of his blood work; Marvin continues to guide Hunter along a Cherokee path; and Hunter eventually goes back to the woods, alone, to hunt deer while wearing face paint and carrying a bow. Taken together, these interrelated narrative threads reinforce the idea that much depends on how Hunter navigates his relations with other people while he focuses intently on his own body, blood, and being. In various ways, he is working toward knowing his own blood better and cutting through fears and secrets to learn, unmute, and release his own transmissions, his own stories. For example, before he returns to the woods to hunt deer, he goes to bed with Geri for the first time but quickly removes himself, telling her that he wants to sleep with her but cannot yet do so. After his journey into the woods, he knocks on her door and falls, weeping, into her arms. Redroad thus gives viewers two bookended Hunter-and-Geri scenes without explicitly articulating how they bookend what happens in the woods. Further, all the couple do in the latter scene is hug on her porch, on a threshold they do not (yet) cross. Redroad neither confers a conventionally romantic Hollywood ending nor answers hanging questions. The ways these various interconnected narrative threads braid and unbraid, and evoke powerful emotions without neat resolutions, creates new spaces for queer Native southern transmissions.

Indeed, much of the second half of *The Doe Boy* explores challenges, problems, and possibilities having to do with transmission. Soon after meeting Geri, Hunter visits Dr. Moore; their conversation centers on failures of transmission. For instance, when the doctor tells him that Jimmy Littlejohn, "the only other Indian hemophiliac in the state," has recently died of AIDS, he also queries Hunter: "You haven't heard of AIDS? From your mom or on the news?" He has heard of it, but he does not really know what it is. "It's that gay disease, right?" he asks, to which the doctor responds: "There's no such thing as a 'gay disease.'" Jimmy, who was only thirty-four years old, contracted AIDS through his infusions. Although the doctor assures Hunter that "he had a much more severe case than you," Hunter is understandably shaken, unsure whether his own infusions have been free of the virus. With AIDS, the terms and the dangers of his hemophilia shift. He becomes more at risk. Faced with these frightening possibilities, Hunter opts to shut down transmissions, to carry the burden alone and to keep his blood test a secret until he learns his results. As Marvin says later, "A deer is a perfect hiding machine. It can disappear in any terrain, in any season." But Marvin's aphorisms are not always reliable; Maggie (his daughter and Hunter's mother) rejects the keeping of family secrets and, throughout the film, brings things out in the open, including her son's AIDS scare.

Geri studies linguistic pathology at Northeastern Oklahoma State University because she wants to help people work through speech impediments due to strokes and such so that they can communicate better. Hunter jokingly asks her whether she likes "dudes with medical problems," but just as Hunter and Geri grow closer and seem to be on the verge of intimacy, the film cuts to

Hunter and Marvin, who take up another kind of transmission. Hunter asks, "Granddaddy? How come out of all your kids and grandkids, you pick *me* to pass your flute on to?" to which Marvin responds, "Because you're the one I trust to pass it on again, when you're an old man." While Marvin, Maggie, and Geri encourage transmission, and more particularly want to help Hunter, he is not yet ready to step inside their visions, to assume the romantic, conversational, and Cherokee normativities they offer. True, he gradually draws closer to readiness as the film unspools. But anxieties linger:

HUNTER. When I was little, I used to think my blood was bad because I wasn't a full blood like you.

MARVIN. Ah, you're lucky. Sometimes I feel like a tick that ate too much. Like I'm gonna blow up!

Both laugh at Marvin's words, but both also admit to worrying that there is something wrong with their blood, that it might be contaminated or self-destructive. Finally, their interactions do not include Geri much, just as Hunter and Geri's interactions do not include Marvin much. The spaces between Marvin and Geri loom large.

In subsequent scenes, Hank proves himself to be much more than a cartoon bad guy; he demonstrates patience, good will, and effort in his dealings with Hunter and is generally kind and honest with Maggie. He pays Hunter a friendly visit at his new apartment, buys groceries for him, and says to Maggie, "Any kid that survived this long with that mouth must have magic powers. Cut that boy open, a bunch of four-leaf clovers would probably pour out." Hank confides to his son, "I always admired you." Hunter confides in turn that he is "so scared" about his blood test, and Hank reassures him that "we're gonna stand by you no matter what happens." Hank moves beyond homophobic discourse not long after he most openly expresses it, as if the very act of giving voice to it allows him to purge it in favor of love and admiration for his son. But shortly after this scene, Hank dies while hunting, accidentally yet symbolically shot by two Cherokees who are also out for deer.

With so much happening and so much still unresolved, Hunter goes hunting, perhaps for the first time since 1977, bolstered by Marvin's words: "You don't need practice for what you're looking for, Hunter. Just courage. And you're full of that." En route to the woods, he passes a deer sign along the road, this one featuring a deer with red wings. With paint around his eyes, he enters the woods, having left behind for Geri the bracelet he wore in case of emergencies. He sights and gives chase to a male deer, then trips and falls, momen-

FIGURES 9.2 and 9.3. Hunter has gotten up after tripping and tumbling down; he sees the deer, which has come back to him rather than taking the opportunity to escape. The deer's red and black necklace matches Hunter's red and black flannel shirt. This connection serves as a visual metaphor of a deeper connection between them, one that transmits a new story to supplant the story of Hunter as Doe Boy.

tarily loses sight of his quarry, picks up his bow, turns around, and finds the deer standing very near, wearing a red and black necklace that matches Hunter's shirt (see figures 9.2 and 9.3). When Hunter prepares to shoot his arrow, the deer seems to shake his head as if saying no, yet remains standing just a few yards away. As Hunter's hand bleeds, he and the deer look into each other's eyes until the deer looks down and starts sniffing the ground and Hunter lowers his weapon. Then Marvin offers a valedictory voiceover: "There was a boy who was part deer and part bird, part science and four-leaf clovers. There was a boy who dreamed of becoming a good story and made it happen." Marvin's words echo Hank's earlier remark that his son must be full of four-leaf clovers, suggesting a sort of peace between the two men. But Marvin adds "science" to the mix and, more important, Indigenous self-determination: "and made it happen."

After plunging his bleeding hand into a river and finding the deer's necklace on its bank, Hunter comes back, hand wrapped, goes to Geri, and weeps in her arms. The implication is that their relationship is alive and growing, but Redroad (still) does not treat this narrative thread as the most important one. Instead, he again leaves viewers with questions: Why does Hunter weep? What, if anything, is transmitted here? Perhaps he resolves the 1977 doe incident by going into the forest in the way he does and then by coming to a face-to-face understanding with a deer that he does not kill. A brief shot of eleven-year-old Hunter walking out of the woods and holding his bow up in triumph supports this interpretation, but it also revises what actually happened—the 1977 Hunter hunted with a rifle, not with a bow.

At film's end, Hunter is still navigating various transitions and moving toward figuring things out. As I have argued, reading *The Doe Boy* with an eye to its productive, supple queer temporalities and spatialities suggests that queer Native southern transmissions have less to do with actual gay (or southern) identity than with identity transformations that are no less important for being less than perfectly clear. In some ways, Hunter gains power as the film unspools; throughout, though, he also finds himself unsure how much power he holds and how viable, healthy, bridled, or unbridled that power might be. The film gradually destabilizes some of the forces that found the derogatory nickname Doe Boy compelling and also grants Hunter and Hank the chance to reconcile and recalibrate their relationship before Hank dies. Promising as these developments are, Redroad mainly gives viewers something like a snapshot of one difficult yet also partially and potentially transformative part of his main character's life. While he resists imposing a neat resolution, he presents Hunter's various challenges and choices as progressively more relational than oppositional. Visually and structurally as well as thematically, the film indicates that Hunter stands in relation to people, places, and histories in ways he is only just beginning to realize. His sexual choices and his path toward Cherokee identity work more in tandem than not.

The Doe Boy's queerness works similarly, as a state or condition or experience of becoming, a receptivity to transmissions and transformations that propose alternatives to the normal, or, perhaps more accurately, alternative normativities. *The Doe Boy*, in this light, offers a meditation on forms of power and on the challenges and possibilities inherent in losing or lessening particular kinds of power in favor of others. Throughout, the film spotlights the great, at times crushing, weight of expectations, particularly expectations keyed to entrenched, firmly held, yet in some ways also competing notions of the normal. While "queer" in the context of *The Doe Boy* does not mean "gay" or even "sexual," it has much to do with navigating and when necessary challenging a "normal" that operates both as a sociocultural grid used against anyone who exceeds or challenges the grid and as a weight that descends especially heavily on those who do something other than simply perpetuate sameness. As Lisa Tatonetti emphasizes, "Importantly, *queer* names a subjectivity or practice that diverges from *dominant* norms."[10] At this point in his young life, Hunter wants to figure out what the yardsticks, the gauges, the frames and contexts for his life are; he wants to know *how* to gauge himself, *how* to connect or arrange different, sometimes competing, cultural contexts and other pressures, tensions, and desires. In other words, he is still learning and working out the guidelines, cultural and otherwise, that he wants to live by. He might well end up opting for some version of normativity, but the point is that he has not yet figured out his own relations to the normal.

The Doe Boy sets in motion an intricate and powerful network of fears, anxieties, uncertainties, and possibilities having to do with queer Native southern transmissions. Hunter's story plays out on land that is itself a field and a transmitter of both Cherokee and non-Cherokee cultural forms, practices, and desires, land specifically situated in linear time and grounded in Indigenous stories/affiliations, and (more in the background) contextualized by Indian removal. Questions of lineage, ancestry, and inheritance offer Hunter connections to earlier southeastern Cherokee practices and also intensify because they speak to his futures: his emerging identities as a Cherokee, an Oklahoman, an adolescent coming of age in the context of HIV/AIDS, a young man possibly on the verge of a relationship with a Pueblo/Navajo/Mexican/Spanish college student, and a hemophiliac. And while hemophilia's conditions—easy bruising, sudden and prolonged bleeding—serve Redroad well as metaphors for Hunter's sensitivity and struggles, questions of blood also point toward the impossibility of taking blood for granted and toward the ways transmissions in *The Doe Boy* are both silenced and articulated, both normative and, however modestly, queered. Transmissions are potentially deadly; they are also indispensable to personal and cultural relations and relatedness as well as to survival.

The Doe Boy closes with the hope, however tentative and fragile, that Hunter might be moving toward a more stable identity, one that weaves queer, Native, and southern together and creates possibilities for new transmissions. Here I take to heart Kevin Ohi's engagement with "queer theory's exorbitant potential,"[11] alongside Carolyn Dinshaw's joyful confidence in "queer potential." As Dinshaw explains: "In my theorizing of temporality I explore forms of desirous, embodied being that are out of sync with the ordinarily linear measurements of everyday life, that engage heterogeneous temporalities or that precipitate out of time altogether—forms of being that I shall argue are queer by virtue of their particular engagements with time. These forms of being show, in fact, that time itself is wondrous, marvelous, full of queer potential."[12] In strong intertextual, transdisciplinary, queer support of this point, much of what Dinshaw says here rings as true for Native American and Indigenous Studies as it does for her field of medieval studies. Whether it rings as true for the U.S. South, and for Oklahoma, considered as part of the South, is an open, complicated question. But the queer Native southern transmissions that flow through *The Doe Boy* ultimately help Hunter change his nickname and help viewers understand that the title of the film is one such transmission precisely because it tells a story about personal and Cherokee self-determination across pasts, presents, *and* future.

NOTES

1. *The Doe Boy*, dir. Randy Redroad (2001; Santa Monica, Calif.: Genius Products, 2006), DVD.

2. Different as our projects are, I have found Kevin Ohi's work on queer transmission useful in helping me to think through my argument, particularly his insight that "*queer* also resonates because it has come to signal—at least for queer theoretical discourse—an anarchic troubling of heteronormative lines of cultural transmission, and because it indicates, paradoxically, a tradition of such troubling" (7, emphasis in original). See Kevin Ohi, *Dead Letters Sent: Queer Literary Transmission* (Minneapolis: University of Minnesota Press, 2015).

3. Michael P. Bibler, "Queer/Quare," *Keywords for Southern Studies*, ed. Scott Romine and Jennifer Rae Greeson (Athens: University of Georgia Press, 2016), 200–12, at 200.

4. Lisa Tatonetti, *The Queerness of Native American Literature* (Minneapolis: University of Minnesota Press, 2014), xix.

5. E. Patrick Johnson, "'Quare' Studies, or (Almost) Everything I Know about Queer Studies I Learned from My Grandmother," *Text and Performance Quarterly* 21 (2001): 1–25.

6. Bibler, "Queer/Quare," 200.

7. Tatonetti, *The Queerness of Native American Literature*, xvii.

8. For a fuller discussion of the ways southernness, Indigeneity, and silence intertwine, and for an indispensable reading of *The Doe Boy*, see Melanie R. Benson, "The Native Screen: American Indians in Contemporary Southern Film," *American Cinema and the Southern Imaginary*, ed. Deborah Barker and Kathryn McKee (Athens: University of Georgia Press, 2011), 253–76.

9. Bibler, "Queer/Quare," 201.

10. Tatonetti, *Queerness of Native American Literature*, xix, emphasis in original.

11. Ohi, *Dead Letters Sent*, 9.

12. Carolyn Dinshaw, *How Soon Is Now? Medieval Texts, Amateur Readers, and the Queerness of Time* (Durham, N.C.: Duke University Press, 2012), 4.

Chapter 10 ▸ Down South at Peckerwood: Mom, Anti-Mom, and Queer Pedagogy in *Auntie Mame*

JEFF SOLOMON

A Climax in North Hollywood

On June 16, 2016, a warm Thursday night, I saw the 1958 film *Auntie Mame* at the Laemmle North Hollywood, where it had been featured as part of a Summer Camp series.[1] The film sold out unexpectedly and was moved to a larger theater—221 seats—that sold out as well. The film is frequently programmed in Los Angeles, and Outfest, the Los Angeles LGBTQ film festival, shows *Auntie Mame* during the holidays each year. Since 2002, these shows have been in concert with the American Cinematheque, which usually sells out the 616-seat Lloyd E. Rigler Theatre. Often, extra holiday screenings are added. All this *Auntie Mame* is not the work of one rabid fan on a programming board: there is an annual "Homo for the Holidays" showing in Seattle, where the Three-Dollar Bill Cinema not only shows *Auntie Mame* but also offers an annual "pre-film soirée." A cursory search finds *Auntie Mame* programmed in many American cities, usually in the context of a gay series, or for the holidays, or both. In short, *Auntie Mame* still holds a queer audience, more than sixty years after its premiere. What may be said about this continued appeal besides its association with homosexuality and the holidays? And why is the South essential to this movie otherwise set in New York and environs, and why is the South integral to its use for a queer audience?

Novel, play, movie, musical, movie musical: men who had sex with men were essential to all five versions of *Auntie Mame*, except for the second movie, a notorious flop, and I am tempted to see the relative dearth of queer men among its creators as a proximate cause of its failure. Although the original author, Edward Everett Tanner III, is often called bisexual, he called himself homosexual, and he eschewed female partners after he left his wife for a man. Jerome Lawrence, half of the team who wrote the play, most of the first screenplay, and the book of the musical, was a self-identified gay man, as was Jerry Herman, who wrote the music and lyrics for the musicals. Morton DaCosta, who directed both the play and the first movie, was gay,[2] as was the costumer for this extremely fashion-conscious movie, Orry-Kelly, and the set decorator, George James Hopkins. These queer men created a multivalent text that never directly features male homosexuality but works as a type of gay fairy tale that could both find mass-market success and still appeal to gay viewers to this day.

The film is a close adaptation of the original novel, *Auntie Mame: An Irreverent Escapade*,[3] and many viewers had been readers. The book topped the *New York Times* best-seller list for five weeks in 1955, spent more than two years in the top fifteen, and was one of the ten best-selling novels of both 1955 and 1956. *Auntie Mame* itself was an adaptation of a collection of short stories about "Patrick Dennis," the narrator, who writes a "memoir" of his relationship with his aunt. Tanner was so frequently taken as the hero of *Auntie Mame* that he often took his character's name as his own.[4] To spare my reader, I shall refer to the author as "Tanner" and the character as "Patrick."

In 1955, as now, short story collections were hard to sell, and Tanner's editor suggested that he link the stories into a novel through the conceit of comparing Auntie Mame to a more traditional "auntie," supposedly from *Reader's Digest*'s "Admirable People I Have Known." Each chapter/story now began with a description of the "sweet little New England spinster" who had found a baby on her doorstep and proceeded to raise him,[5] with her good works then countered with Mame's escapades. These adventures were broadly queer—not necessarily in terms of sexuality, but contrary to hegemonic values—while illustrating the principle at hand, such as "charity." Mame offers a fabulous alternative to traditional parenting, and her greater success repudiates the traditional values that the spinster represents.

Throughout his career, Tanner either actively resisted or crumbled under the strain of novelistic structure, and more than once he left the final pages of his novels to others. These difficulties prevented him from successfully adapting *Auntie Mame* into a play, and the job fell to Jerome Lawrence and Robert E. Lee, best known today for the 1955 play *Inherit the Wind*, a dramatization of the Scopes trial. Lawrence and Lee retained aspects of almost all the chapters, but they do excise two: "Auntie Mame in the Ivy League," in which Mame has a torrid relationship with Patrick's college friend, and "Auntie Mame and the Call to Arms," a World War I episode during which Mame fails to mother some horrible children. These cuts correspond with Lawrence and Lee's reshaping of the novel, which dampens Mame's sexuality and heightens her maternity. Their 1956 stage play *Auntie Mame* earned two Tony nominations and enjoyed a long run on Broadway, followed by a national tour. The play was quickly followed by the 1958 film, which shared the same director, Morton DaCosta, and many of the same actors, especially Rosalind Russell as Mame and Jan Handzlik as young Patrick. Notable additions to the film cast include Fred Clark as Mr. Babcock, Coral Browne as Vera Charles, Forrest Tucker as Beauregard Burnside, and Brook Byron as Sally Cato MacDougal. Almost all of the playscript remains unchanged, but Russell, furious that producers Lawrence and Lee did not close the play after she left it, insisted that the screenplay be credited to Adolph Comden and Betty Green, although their contributions were slight.[6]

Auntie Mame was the highest-grossing film of 1958 at nine million dollars, and was nominated for six Academy Awards. When the film came out, the play was still running on Broadway, and the novel remained on the bestseller list, as was the limp 1958 sequel, *Around the World with Auntie Mame.* All made a great deal of money and spurred each other's consumption. Lawrence and Lee would then write the book for the 1966 musical *Mame*, with music and lyrics by Jerry Herman. The musical, which is largely beyond my scope here, was filmed in 1974, with Lucille Ball as Mame.[7]

While the novel *Auntie Mame* is episodic, the play, the 1958 film, and the musicals are neatly halved between Patrick as a child and Patrick as a young man. The southern fantasia that is the climax of the first half makes the strongest case for the film's attraction to queer audiences.

All versions begin after ten-year-old Patrick is orphaned and taken in by his aunt. Mame shares responsibility for Patrick with the trustee of his estate, the conservative Mr. Babcock. As the banker who enforces normativity, Babcock embodies masculine hegemony, and his and Mame's quarrels over Patrick's future provide the narrative spine of *Auntie Mame*. In all versions (except perhaps the filmed musical), Little Patrick is easily read as a queer boy through his preternatural sophistication (he makes perfect martinis), his fussy dress (he favors short pants and suits), and his sensitivity, self-control, and general lack of hegemonic little-boy-ness.[8] He is never dirty or mean, never in trouble, and apes Picasso rather than plays sports (see figure 10.1). All correspond to the powerful nexus of homosexuality, effeminacy, sophistication, decadence, the arts, and wealth at midcentury—a time when (1) gender and

FIGURE 10.1. Little Patrick (Jan Handzlik) and his Christmas gift for Auntie Mame.

sexuality were strongly associated, (2) rich men were understood as less masculine than working-class men, and (3) the arts were not seen as masculine—and thus gay men were understood as effeminate, arty, sophisticated, and rich. In short, Little Patrick's half of the novel, play, and movie feels like an extended fantasy for a gay boy (or, if you will, proto-gay boy) who wishes that his staid Midwestern parents would leave him to a glamorous, fun-loving aunt in Manhattan. Patrick's sexuality was obvious to a queer audience, and perhaps to a straight one, but was publicly unspeakable due to the censorship that demanded the denigration of gay men but did not acknowledge gay children per se. The sexuality of Little Patrick is therefore unusually legible for a midcentury mass-market product.

Some readers may be taken aback by the term "gay boy." The specifics of psychosocial development into mature homosexuality have been theorized by psychoanalytic practitioners and theorists such as Beverly Burch, Ken Corbett, Teresa de Lauretis, and Richard Isay. All subscribe to a model of psychosexual progression that allows for (but does not mandate) an ordered and organized sexuality. Kathryn Bond Stockton augments this discussion by suggesting that the proto-gay child may exist only retrospectively, after gay identity or desire is realized. Stockton's "growing sideways" allows for a proto-gay adult as well as a proto-gay child, which is helpful. In practice, however, Stockton's thesis of retrospection—which, of course, applies to *all* children—is much more likely to be applied to the proto-gay than the proto-straight, just as the mandate for historical specificity when discussing sexuality is much more likely to be applied to homosexuality than to heterosexuality. Both instances exemplify how the precepts of queer theory, determined to destabilize the normal, may, in a case of putatively friendly fire, be used to deny specific queer identities, even though such identities and subjectivities tend to be hard won, rather than "normal." Stockton herself makes the interesting claim that the proto-gay child "makes *gay* far more liquid and labile than it has seemed in recent years, when queer theory has been rightfully critiquing it. Odd as it may seem, *gay* in this context, the context of the child, is the new *queer*—a term that touts its problems and shares them with anyone."[9]

Certainly the gay men who created the various iterations of *Mame*, as well as its generations of gay fans, validate a gay teleology of *Auntie Mame*. Just as certainly, Patrick Dennis is a boy made of art rather than a boy filled with blood—a boy who in all forms of *Auntie Mame* grows up to marry a woman, as did his primary progenitor, Edward Everett Tanner. The novel's Patrick, as an adult, lives in suburbia with his wife and child; by the sequel, he speaks openly of his boredom and frustration. He tells the stories that compose the novels to escape his present. The example of Tanner himself, who came both to embrace his homosexuality and to take Patrick's name, as well as adult Patrick's disposal of his present in favor of his past, indicate that Patrick/Tanner, as an adult "straight" man, has grown *in the wrong direction*—or, more precisely, has not grown straight but has not been able to realize his homosexuality amid the homophobia of his culture. To willfully ignore this puts one in league with Tanner's and *Auntie Mame*'s contemporary sexual theorists, who would have viewed Patrick's proto-gayness, via the interpretations of Freud at large in the mid-1950s, as a mistaken understanding of his "true" self: a developmental disability to be corrected, rather than a healthy, organized, psychosexual stability, not yet entirely embodied but present.

Little Patrick's perceptible gayness is echoed in the party scene by the appearance of Alice B. Toklas and Gertrude Stein, who may be identified by their clothes, their age, and their pairing (see figure 10.2). Henry Brandon, who played headmaster Acacius Page in the movie, reports on this open secret: "I would not advise filmmakers to preview a picture in Westwood. Those UCLA kids . . . laughed through every word of my dialogue because they were watching two ladies in the corner of the screen! I never noticed while we were shooting, but in that corner of the film frame, just off to my left elbow, were two lesbian ladies. Their purses didn't have lipstick or powder, it was chains and wrenches and steam hammers. I've seen the film four or five times since then with an audience and nobody notices them, just those sharp kids from UCLA."[10]

FIGURE 10.2. Mame and Patrick at the party, with lesbian guests.

While Little Patrick, Gertrude, and Alice are easily seen by the initiated, the gay content of the second half is necessarily coded, as Little Patrick has become Big Patrick, and a gay adult man could not be featured as a sympathetic character in a mass-market film. Even so, the gay concerns are easily seen. Consider Mame's fervent assertions that racially and ethnically "exclusive and restricted" circles are abhorrent. May they be read as a closeted plea for sexual tolerance? Yes, they may. All these allusions are expected for a mass-market work created by gay men in the 1950s. What is unusual about *Auntie Mame* is the presence of a gay child, Patrick, and how his presence allows the closer than usual exploration of queer childhood issues.

For an eager queer audience, Mame fruitfully combines an idealized mother of a gay child with an avatar of the gay man this gay child will become. In this light, *Auntie Mame* is a series of pedagogical moments. Both by example and by lecture, Mame instructs Patrick how to resist the normative policing of Mr. Babcock and the interpellation of a repressive ideology. The climax of Little Patrick's story comes when Mame, who has lost all her money in the Depression and who faces ceding control over Patrick to Babcock, must maneuver Beauregard Burnside, a Georgia millionaire, into marriage. In the southern scenes, the young hero is peripheral to the plot, but he is shown to exult in Mame's union with Beauregard, which both coincides with and embodies his own sexual maturity. Her success and the onset of Patrick's adolescence effectively end Little Patrick's queer story, because the adult Patrick can only "be gay" in a more closeted register.

The southern setting helps constitute this first, gayer climax. In all versions we are at Peckerwood, a fantastic southern plantation. Fox hunts and mint juleps, the sidesaddle and the southern belle: most hoary tropes are here, without much concern for the actual South. "Peckerwood" itself is an insulting southern black inversion of "woodpecker" that contrasts with a racialized "blackbird" and means "a poor, rural white." Tanner characteristically disregards these specifics and privileges the phallic sense of the term. These southern scenes are the most dynamic in the movie: only here does *Auntie Mame* make notable use of techniques essential to cinema but unavailable to theater—close-ups, tracking shots, zooms, panoramas. These are the only moments in the movie that do not seem like a filmed play, and this sudden liveliness grants "the South" a heightened order of cinematic being. My point is not that a Hollywood "southern imaginary" should be contrasted with the historical South, but that the hyper-vivid faux southernness of Peckerwood is essential to this scene's function as a useful allegory for gay men. In a film composed of pedagogical moments, the South offers the most potent lesson.

How to find and keep a sugar-daddy-cum-lover-cum-husband, how to navigate between the open secret and the closet, and how to fight a hostile community and secure a happy union—it all comes down to Peckerwood.

Anti-Mom and Auntie Mame

Auntie Mame is not usually described in terms of maternity. The original trailer barely shows Patrick's face but focuses on the adventures of the "wacky and warm, wild and wonderful Auntie Mame."[11] Nonetheless, *Auntie Mame*, as titled, is the story of an orphan taken in by his aunt.

AUNTIE. "Auntie" is an affectionate diminutive of "aunt." Some women are called "auntie," and some women are biologically related to those whom they *aunt*, but the term was in use at midcentury for a middle-aged or elderly gay man, as Tanner, Lawrence, and DaCosta well knew. "Aunties" are effeminate, gossipy, and maternal (although, like aunts, they are not usually mothers per se), and the term is affectionate when those attributes are good and insulting when they are not. Aunties are known for drinking—and the alcohol flows in *Auntie Mame* like nobody's business. Mame has "thirteen cocktail parties in two weeks." A scene is built around the correct way to make martinis, and another around the proper ingredients for a daiquiri. Even for the 1950s, the discussion and consumption of alcohol is remarkable. For "aunties" at the bar, where the stereotype places them, this runs true to form.

AUNTIE MAME. Soften the long *a* to a schwa *o*, and "Mame" is "Mom"—a harder, grander Mom, as suits a former chorine in *Chu Chin Girl* and current society hostess who is installed in a luxury townhouse in midtown Manhattan. "Mame" reiterates "auntie": maternity is queered with a specifically gay valence. Thus Edmund White titles his review of his nephew Keith Fleming's memoir, *The Boy with the Thorn in His Side*, which concerns White's own "mothering" of Fleming, "Uncle Mame."[12] White offers no explanation for the reference: "Uncle Mame" means queer male maternity. For a reader or viewer who intuits such matters or knows the argot, "Auntie Mame" oscillates between an older, somewhat feminine gay man and Mame herself, who is written and played as a woman with specific characteristics that allowed gay men to easily identify with her via the midcentury self-construction, at least in fantasy, of the urban gay man. Mame is rich, sophisticated, and urbane. Mame does not possess conventional seductive traits but is the focus of male desire. Mame has a wicked sense of camp humor, and she couples this frivolity with fierce politics as she pits herself against Babcock for the life and future of Little Patrick.

Such closeted expressions and understandings were standard for gay artists and their audiences in the 1950s. Auntie Mame is not complicated in her being but in her apprehension.

ANTI-MOM. Through one eye, gay and gay-attuned audiences see Auntie Mame as a "gay auntie"—and through the other, anyone may see that the character puts natural femininity, including the femininity usually associated with good mothering, in doubt. As written by Tanner, Mame is self-contained and somewhat selfish, which often conflicts with her "mothering." Lawrence and Lee orient her affections and attention more firmly around Patrick until she can say "I don't know what I would do without him," but she still has an unusual amount of agency for a "good" mother. In all her forms, Mame is responsible for none of the discipline or drudgery of raising a child: the servants do that. She is similar to the stereotype of a divorced father, or queer aunt or uncle, whose weekly outings are looked forward to with excitement by the children and with resentment by the stay-at-home parent who creates the mundanity that the nonresident parent explodes. Such explosion is what Mame *is*.

In all versions, Mame's femininity remains an overt, self-conscious performance. Dress, hair, and makeup are a major concern, on a plot as well as a comic or ornamental level. Mame's jangling bracelets drive the plot in one scene, and we shall see how her southern costume is essential to the southern scenes. As Mame's townhouse is regularly done over to accord with the fashions of the day, so Mame has three hair colors in the course of the film. The artificiality of female appearance is constantly referenced.

This artificiality includes maternity. When Mame and her best friend Vera Charles scheme for Mame to appear as a conventional mother to win the approval of Patrick's trustee, they overtly treat such motherhood as a matter of costume: a black switch to create a halo, a conventional suit, pearls. Mame only seems like a "natural woman" next to La Charles.

Vera (for "truth") is an old-school "romantic" actress who plays properly feminine heroines, and we see her play the Princess in *Midsummer Madness*. Vera is actively false, so much so that the destruction of her femme pretensions *is* her surface. Despite her romantic fame, she is sexually outspoken and ravenous, often drunk unto unconsciousness, and remarkably self-obsessed and self-promoting. Much is made of her hailing from Pittsburgh. Coral Browne, who plays Vera in the film, is made up to be less hegemonically attractive than Russell, who herself shares in the drag that all older women sport in a society that defines sexual appeal through youth. As he discusses *Mame* the musical, D. A. Miller notes how "every woman must always seem to be harboring a gay man. . . . The frankly mannish Vera . . . is only the most ostentatious signal of an all-inclusive camp."[13] If Auntie Mame is the Anti-Mom, then Vera Charles is the Anti-Heroine, and she serves to make Mame less extreme.

Anti-Mom Meets the False Boy

Auntie Mame begins after the death of Patrick's father in a Chicago steam room; his biological mother goes unmentioned. (We are left to wonder what happened in that steam room to bring on a heart attack.) After the credits, Patrick, aged ten and still in short pants, reads a newspaper headline about his father's death but shows neither grief nor any other emotion. He and his nanny, Nora Muldoon, travel from the Midwest to New York City to meet Mame. The initial meeting between little boy and aunt resonates with childhood fears of abandonment. Patrick and Nora, lost in a confusing city, come to a home in the midst of a chaotic—and, in every sense, fabulous—party. Mame's house is decorated in an "exotic" Chinese motif, and the guests include a Russian composer and his wife, a Lithuanian archbishop in full regalia, a turbaned man with a monkey, motley bohemians, and an older female couple in men's suits. Foreigners, artists, nonwhites, Stein and Toklas: in 1958 this was the cutting edge for the mainstream audience, as queer as you could be without posing a threat to the established order. We see here both the quiet yet direct reference of homosexuality, through Stein and Toklas, and the more usual broad queerness of ethnicity and nationality, which in the WASPy confines of *Auntie Mame* is conflated with everything else that is not entirely acceptable. Three years later, Blake Edwards would shoot a very similar party for *Breakfast at Tiffany's* to telegraph Holly Golightly's sophistication and broad queerness.[14]

Mame herself may be surrounded by exotica, and she is certainly exotic to Little Patrick and Nora, but she reads more as regal than as colorful comic relief, unlike, say, the archbishop in his costume-shop cassock. She may wear pants, but they are part of an Orry-Kelly beaded crepe cocktail outfit, and her long cigarette holder adds grandeur, as such holders do. Mame is very much in charge of the party, shaking hands with the monkey with aplomb. She does not recognize her nephew but assumes that Nora is the new cook and that Patrick is her son: "He looks like a nice enough little boy, and if he misbehaves, we can just toss him in the river." Despite Nora's protests, Mame does not grasp the relation, and Patrick starts to tear up. But once she finally understands Patrick's identity, she says, with great brio, a famous line from the movie: "But darling, I'm your Auntie Mame!"

This line remains in all five versions of *Auntie Mame* and is frequently quoted. Often, in my experience, the audience claps or shouts along. The line is in the trailer, and Richard Tyler Jordan uses it as the title for his *Auntie Mame* compendium, though the line itself is neither clever nor lyrical. I can only explain the audience response through its projection upon Patrick: he is the little boy who has learned to project a false self and hide his real feelings, for he has no parent who can see him. The line relieves the mounting tension that Patrick's "mother" will not know him—a tension made even greater by Patrick's stolid refusal to react. Patrick is both literally and experientially an orphan, which explains his dull response to his father's death. Later he tells Mame what home was like:

MAME. Didn't your father ever talk to you?
PATRICK. Hardly ever. I only saw him at breakfast time.
MAME. And what did he say then?
PATRICK. He usually said, "Pipe down, kid, the old man's hung."

Thus Mame's recognition has great power. For a gay boy who has not been seen for who he is—who carefully censors his expression of his thoughts and feelings, recognizing their impropriety—this *seeing* and the public announcement that follows have resonance. For not only does Mame announce her new motherhood, she makes it public: "Quiet! Quiet everybody! I have an important announcement to make. This is my little boy."

Mame has not prepared for Patrick's material needs and scrambles to find him food and a bed. What she does do is instruct him to mingle with party guests, to try caviar, sushi, and other "exotic" foods, and to increase his vocabulary: she suggests that he write down every word that he hears but does not know. Later, when she asks Patrick to read his list, his words include "psychoanalysis," "neurotic," "squiffed," "stinko," and "heterosexual"—at which point Mame stops him. Patrick's new vocabulary includes unconscious desires and the perils of their repression, intoxication, and sexuality. "Heterosexual" is an especially queer word: heterosexuality becomes something to comprehend, rather than an unquestioned sexual essence. Furthermore, Mame stopping Patrick short emphasizes the unspoken "homosexual." This word would roil the surface of a film that was appropriate for children, while "heterosexual" does not—which, too, is something that Patrick must learn. Clearly, for the anti-mom, maternity equals providing knowledge—a particularly sexualized and sophisticated knowledge, oriented toward pleasure. Patrick thrives: in his next scene he is a happier, more open, ebullient little boy.

Auntie Mame vs. the Bad Cock: WASP vs. WASP

As Auntie Mame is Patrick's maternal figure, so the Pater is Dwight Babcock, or, as Dennis loudly signals, the "Bad Cock." Like action figures animated by Little Patrick, Anti-Mom and the Bad Cock fight over Patrick's future throughout the movie. Mame and Babcock's two great battles arise over Patrick's education and his choice of spouse; each conflict anchors one half of *Auntie Mame*. The will of the late Mr. Dennis dictates that Babcock is in charge of the money and Patrick's education, and Mame is in charge of everything else. As Mame says, "I have the responsibility and he has the authority." This aligns with 1950s gender roles, as do Mame's weapons when she battles with Babcock. As she has no legal power, she can defeat Babcock only through seduction, wiliness, or the assistance of another man. If she accepts Babcock's money, her power is even less.

To see how the South figures into this conflict, note that Mame and Babcock agree on their field of battle: the culture and mores of well-to-do WASPs of New England and New York, the traditionally dominant socioeconomic group of the United States. For instance, the two agree that Patrick must attend prep school: the fight is between *types*, rather than whether to go at all. Should Patrick enroll at a traditional same-sex boarding school or a trendy coeducational day academy? In her arguments with Babcock, Mame fights against repression and exclusion. She argues against Babcock's desire to keep Patrick's acquaintance "exclusive and restricted" and not from the "wrong side of the tracks." Nonetheless, this remains a world where only WASPs matter; where the multicultural guests at Mame's party are not characters but exotica; where the Irish hover at the edge of acceptability, adorned with a brogue and stereotyped as a nanny or poet; where discrimination against Jews is deplored while Jews themselves go unseen; where the Asian avatar is the effeminate, giggling houseboy; and where African Americans are entirely absent except in the South, where they are portrayed as grooms, silent servants in livery, or traditional lawn statues of jockeys—except for one unnamed man, presumably a butler, with one line of incidental dialogue, which we will see in context later: "Look at her ride! She's passin' everybody!"

The otherwise broad stereotyping of the South in *Auntie Mame* makes this representation remarkable, and the liberal politics (for their day) of Tanner, Lawrence and Lee, and DaCosta, as well the economic ramifications of African American representation in the 1950s, dictate intentionality here. The speaker is not dressed as a groom or house servant, and he stands on the veranda next to the matriarch of the plantation without the cringing that marks almost all to whom she speaks. His long white linen coat, black tie, and black trousers mark him as a butler to those who know this code, as does his receipt of a stallion and direction of other servants concerning it, but to an average viewer (certainly to me, the first few times I watched this scene) he reads as just another partygoer in "southern" dress. He is clearly of a higher class than the other servants, all male, who, per Hollywood tradition, all pass as African American though some are more easily read as Native American, Filipino, or Latino.

The butler's presence addresses civil-rights-era concerns that not all African Americans in the South be represented as menial (though, again, the man *is* a servant), yet the brevity of his appearance keeps him from challenging those viewers who support such stereotypes. In this way, his appearance may be compared to the lesbians in the party scene: a nod to those who can read the broadly queer. And though this man is not in livery, he, like all denizens of Peckerwood, is defined by his southerness. Other southerners may be WASPs, but they are not from the Northeast.

Before we go south, however, let us quickly note that the character in the movie with whom Mame experiences the greatest sexual tension is the poet Brian O'Bannion, who springs, Irish eyes a-smiling, from the Dell of Sexiness in the movie's second half. The Mame of the novel has a much greater sexual presence and practice, and has many more romantic and sexual partners, but she too prefers non-WASPy men. Throughout Tanner's corpus, the sexiest men are not exactly white, or at the least not exactly WASP. This is yet another iteration of the usual positioning of sexuality in the cultural Other.

Santa from the South

Mame's money, which she inherits rather than earns, funds her fabulous lifestyle, her enjoyment of culture, her concatenation of cocktails, her and her townhouse's frequent costume changes, and her resistance to Babcock and all that he stands for. Her wealth gives her resistance brio, and in the gendered realms of soft power where Mame operates—where the vectors of force are charm, confusion, attraction, and style: in other words, glamour—brio is power. Mame does not need the money put aside for Patrick's care in her brother's will, and so Babcock lacks many of the hard weapons used to control women. She may not be able to confront him directly, but he may neither beat her nor starve her. He can only use the power of law to tell her what to do.

This balance is threatened when Mame loses her money in the Crash and has to support two servants and a child. No version of *Auntie Mame* reflects the actual costs of such a ménage, but all clarify that Mame must now go to work, and that only work that is gendered female is available to her: model, actress, shopgirl, telephone operator. (Note, too, that these forms of employment are very much those that a child—especially a female or a queer child—might imagine as fun, glamorous work in the city.) Alas, Mame's glamour does not equip her for workplace success, and the money she earns cannot keep her household afloat. And so Mame must marry.

Both book and movie treat these circumstances ruefully. In the novel, after Mame is fired for slapping a man who pinches her, Henri Bendel, the famed founder of the women's specialty store where Mame has been modeling, writes her in a letter that "the best career for Auntie Mame would be marriage."[15] When Nora has to pay the household bills herself, she tells Mame, "What a pretty lady like you needs is a nice *man*."[16] These statements hang above white space, which stands out in a novel careful to subvert any homilies at play, whether they come from Mame's foil the "sweet little New England spinster" or Mame's nemesis Mr. Babcock or Mame herself. "You must do this" directives invariably are made ridiculous, and so the lack of comment about the marriage mandate stands out.

Does Mame agree? If so, she acts uncharacteristically. When Mame accepts a suggestion, she takes it up wholeheartedly, even foolishly, yet here no scheme ensues. Mame's history also makes agreement unlikely. Patrick notes in the novel, "I suspected she was between thirty-five and forty, and she seemed a lot younger."[17] Russell was fifty-one when *Auntie Mame* was filmed, and although she might look a decade younger, she was not young. Mame's appeal to men, and her constant suitor Lindsay Woolsey's many proposals, prove that she has been single by choice. Now that she must marry for financial reasons, she cannot, for she cannot accept that motive. In the movie, Mame clarifies why she cannot marry Woolsey: "I said 'no' so many times when I had money, I couldn't say 'yes' when I went broke!" Yet Mame must marry a rich husband if she wants to remain Mame.

If not Woolsey, then who may Mame marry? Such dilemmas require a fairy-tale ending, which Mame receives. Her final job is as a salesgirl, the "roller skate lady" during the Christmas rush. Her inability to keep the order forms in order both charms her last customer and gets her fired. Mame returns home in despair and then decides to celebrate Christmas early to lighten the gloom. The decision to celebrate Christmas based on the need for an "up," rather than holding to a set schedule (much less the birth of Christ), exemplifies how *Auntie Mame* combines the heartwarming with the subversive. The scene ends with the appearance of a symbolic Santa, in the person of Mame's last customer, who declares, "It's a miracle! That's what it is! It's—it's a good old-fashioned Christmas miracle!" Beauregard Burnside has found Mame, after searching the ninety-seven Dennises in the Manhattan phone directory. He feels obliged to apologize for her losing her job. And so we enter a higher, southern order of fantasy.

Beau Regard and Ideal

There is not much to Beauregard Jackson Pickett Burnside besides his name, which contains his essence: his "beau regard," which does not mean his own good looks or beautiful eyes, but rather a beglamoured male gaze firmly centered on Mame. In his view, Mame is not incompetent but ill placed: "Why, a woman of your culture and refinement: why, you should have an executive position." Such regard makes him a beau ideal for such a self-dramatizing, theatrical woman, so much so that in an echo of the fey origins of "glamour," his focus on Mame leads to his demise. On their round-the-world honeymoon, Beau insists on photographing Mame at every possible opportunity—and falls to his death while trying to properly frame her on the Matterhorn, after which she inherits all his money and lives as a merry widow. Beau ideal indeed!

The name Beauregard Jackson Pickett Burnside also alludes to Beau's southernness, which is more "otherness" than southernness per se. Consider Mame's description of him in the novel, which also serves the film: "'Patrick, darling,' she said, 'you haven't asked me about my Southern gentleman.' Then she told all. 'He's a lovely man. We went to Armando's and had steak and then we talked and we talked and we talked. His whole name is Beauregard Jackson Pickett Burnside and he's descended—one way or another—from *four* Confederate generals! Oh, the gallant old Southland! He's *very* nice and he owns this big oil company and he has lovely eyelashes.'"[18] One general is not enough. He is descended from four Civil War generals, after three of whom he is named: P.G.T. Beauregard, Stonewall Jackson, and George Pickett. Note, however, that the fourth general in his name, Ambrose Burnside, was not a Confederate but a Union general, whom Tanner, who favored a beard, presumably included either as an homage to his sideburns or by mistake—or because a Union general is not a mistake, exactly, as the important signifier is "Civil War general" rather than any southern particular. For the South here functions as a counter to the Northeast of *Auntie Mame*, rather than as itself. Beau's purpose is to gaze at Mame, and to offer her an appropriately expensive frame—and his southern heritage and the South itself is the setting for the frame, just as her "exotic" party guests set off Mame's fabulousness but never threaten her social standing as a "lady." Here subjectivity belongs to the object, not to the subject of desire.

Note, too, Beau's oil. Stereotype marks him as western, or at least Texan; the few oil wells in the South are not in Georgia. But as both the South and the West are neither in New York nor in the Northeast, they may be safely conflated, for from *Auntie Mame*'s perspective, one province is much like another. Does it matter where Prince Charming rules? In the novel, his money is literally magic: "Everything Uncle Beau touched seemed to turn to gold, and he was constantly amazed and delighted by his good fortune. 'Just luck, sugar,' he'd say to Auntie Mame. Money meant little to him except the pleasure it could give to others."[19]

The pleasure it could give to others. To belabor the obvious, Beau's funds keep Peckerwood flush, and those gushers spouting from the ground allow him potency, unlike Lindsay Woolsey, who, with his perfect manners, his job in the arts, and his deference to Mame, reads, via the nexus discussed earlier, as gay, or at least as a sexual nonentity. Preppy Woolsey is too presentable for sex, because Tanner configures sexual potency in an inverse relationship to social acceptability. Woolsey's nominal derivation from the cheap fabric linsey-woolsey, something Mame would never wear, echoes his poor fit. In the circle that places the Dennises and Babcocks at the center and the Irish at the edge, the South is just far enough away to leaven Beau's class and let sex rise.

In short, Beau is ideal, the good cock to Mr. Babcock's bad. For a contemporary queer audience, Beau's charge may be problematic, as potency and masculinity are equated with straight men, but in 1958 he could be read easily as both a "sugar daddy" and "trade." Arguably, the perfect partner for many midcentury queer men was a straight, adoring, aristocratic millionaire. The novel addresses this perfection, prefacing the film: "A few uncharitable people have said that Auntie Mame married Mr. Burnside for his money. I will concede that Mr. Burnside's being the richest man under forty south of Washington, D.C., may have influenced her. But she really loved him. He was her father, brother, son, Santa Claus, and lover."[20] But for Mame to truly win her southern (western) millionaire Prince Charming, she must first brave the plantation.

Plantation Follies

The great difference between the chapter "Auntie Mame and the Southern Belle" and the southern scenes in the film is that Lawrence and Lee delay Mame's marriage until after her trip to Peckerwood. In both, Beau's ex-belle, Sally Cato MacDougal, connives to win him back, but in the film the stakes are higher and cruder. In the novel, Mame is faced with the loss of Beau's interest rather than his hand, which Tanner, no great lover of institutions, presents as the greater loss. In the film, marriage is presented as the happy climax of Mame's romance and the end of her financial troubles: the proposal *means* something. Sally Cato's suit is aided by Mother Burnside, who wants her son to marry within his tribe. In the film, she lectures her son within the first minute of her appearance: "Son, we got our sweet Georgia peaches right here—don't know why you had to go up to the land of the enemy and bring back a Northern lemon."[21] The contest between Sally Cato and Mame is one between a culturally appropriate and inappropriate partner—a conflict that speaks to queer viewers.

In the novel, Mame assumes southern stereotypes before she ever sets foot in the South: "Her speech grew slightly blurred, softer and less staccato. She called me Honey a great deal and used You-all both in singular and plural."[22] Throughout the novel, Mame assumes and discards roles, but her southern aping reads differently because she is married to, in love with, and financially dependent upon Beau. She is no longer an independent woman amusing herself, but a wife pleasing her man. Her transformation is complete by the time of Patrick's grade-school graduation:

> She was a triumph of Southern Womanhood at the commencement exercises. She wore a fluttering white garden party dress—it looked as though it were made of spun sugar—lace gloves, lace hat, lace parasol which she twirled coquettishly, and a lace fichu which she kept dropping to be retrieved by the pimpled gallants of St. Boniface. I won the composition prize for the Lower School and she said to the English master, "Ah vow, Ah'm so proud of that child Ah could just *bust!* But then, his daddeh was one of the most literareh boys down home."[23]

Typically, the satire is blurred. Is Mame mocked, or is the South itself reduced to costume and dialect, in which case Mame is no more superficial than the region?

The film retains this question. When we first see Mame in southern drag in the movie, at Peckerwood, over a banjo-and-strings arrangement of "Old Folks at Home," she looks no less "authentic" than anyone else. Orry-Kelly outdoes himself with Mame's pouffy white dress, which falls on the border between costume and fashion (see figure 10.3). While there are no hoops, the nipped-in waist and wide hips reveal a corset—but hidden in the many layers and weights of artificial white net is an unexpected, 1950s-fashionable layer of key lime green, which rhymes with the mint green ribbons worked into the bodice and attached to her bonnet, which she dangles from its broad ribbons like a purse. Mame's hair has been dyed champagne beige and is carefully waved, and the entire ensemble is so 1950s-fashionista that even the white lace butterfly worked into the waves does not tip her into parody.

Mame's dress suits the setting, which itself seems to quote rather than embody the South, and suits the ersatz banjo stylings. Take away the outrageously abundant wisteria and artfully arranged Spanish moss, and viewers are left with a typical 1920s Hollywood Regency mansion that still might be seen in the Hollywood Hills. When, in a long shot, the mansion—painted on

FIGURE 10.3. Sally Cato (Brook Byron) tells a horrified Mame (Rosalind Russell) about tomorrow's hunt.

glass? as a matte painting?—is situated in a fantastical southern Arcadia, the representation seems no less real. In his autobiography Orry-Kelly claims that he, not the set designer, coordinated the color, and certainly the lilac, dusty rose, and shades of green that carry from Mame's and Sally Cato's dresses through the rest of the costumes into the plantation house and out into the garden increase the sense of artificiality and play that pervades the southern scene.[24]

In fact, the "southernness" of Mame's dress is incidental, for its primary register is *bridal*. In a nuptial light, the crowd of Jacksons, Picketts, and Burnsides read as wedding guests—and Mame's counter, Sally Cato, as a bridesmaid in her lavender and lilac ensemble, grander than the guests but not so grand as Mame. The dress is only part of Mame's innocent-maiden performance, the humor of which is heightened by Russell's age, strong personality, and contralto voice. (Even as a starlet in the 1930s, Russell was more classically beautiful than sweet and cute, and she tended to be cast as an aristocratic beauty rather than a fresh-faced virgin: as, say, Lady Sybil Barclay, or Lady Venetia Cunningham, or Countess Zarika Rafay.)[25] In her first scene at Peckerwood, Mame comes running to Beau holding her full skirts like a young belle. When Beau leaves her with his relatives to fetch drinks, Mame heightens her performance by falling into a southern accent: "Well, I . . . I cain't tell you how charmin' it is to meet all of you-all!"[26]

Auntie Mame now seems to punish Mame for her pretension; if we interpret her actions as a metaphor for closeting, then she has gone too deep inside. Till now, Mame's mimicry—the "Chinese" costuming of herself and her flat, for instance—has been purely a manner of style; Mame herself has been easily detectable beneath. At Peckerwood, however, Mame claims that she "is" southern, and Sally Cato uses her own authenticity to trap Mame in her foolishness. When Sally Cato asks, "Was it *horses* brought you and Beauregard together?" Mame chirps, "Oh, I just love riding. Why, up in New York hardly a day goes by I don't have the sadd—um, *boots* on. Up every morning at the crack of dawn for a brisk canter through Central Park." As Mame flounces in equestrienne pantomime, her southern audience stands in silent judgment. The true and false southern belle speak over each other:

> SALLY CATO. Listen, evabodeh! Beauregard's gone and *surprised* us all! It seems Miz Dennis here is a prominent North'n horsewoman.
>
> MAME. Well, I wouldn't say *prominent*—No, I'm not prominent.
>
> SALLY CATO. So natcherly, we've got to have a hunt! Listen! Dawn, tomorrow morning! And evabody's invited! Won't we have a lark though, all of us—at sunup—leapin' over those hedges, jumpin' over those river gaps, and the hounds yappin' around those boulders—I tell you, Mame, every eye in the county is going to be on you tomorrow mornin'![27]

Mame, who does not know how to ride, attempts to avert humiliation with "If I'd only *known*. You see, I didn't bring any of my ridin' togs." When Sally Cato offers to lend a habit, and Mame lies that her shoe size is the tiny 3B, Sally Cato says, "Marvelous. Same as I wear"—highlighting her greater delicacy. When Sally Cato asks if Mame rides astride, Mame claims the more "feminine" option: "Sidesaddle—always. Daddy, the Colonel, insisted that I learn it. He said it was the only way for a true lady to ride. So graceful. Silly of him, of course, because *nobody* rides sidesaddle these days, but it's the only way I know how." Sally Cato of course has a sidesaddle to lend: "Beau darlin,' we're havin' ourselves a hunt! . . . Your sweet little Yankee girl is ridin' side-saddle." When Beau says this is too dangerous, Sally Cato protests, "But, darlin,' she's insisted."[28]

Mame has met her match. Unlike the bamboozle-able Babcock, Sally Cato meets Mame on "female" ground. Beau is the focus of their conflict but is a noncombatant: as emotions and love are gendered feminine, the battle is waged through the women. Later, when Mame carefully sets the scene for a proposal—she places Beau's hand in hers, then girlishly shrinks away—Sally Cato, listening at the door, bursts in and gets Beau off his bended knee. As a hegemonic midcentury man, Beau has potency and power but is as perceptive as stone.

Mame's future now depends on her performance in the fox hunt, a traditional ritual predicated on the destruction of an attractive, colorfully dressed animal at the hands of a bloodthirsty mob with traditional values. Again, the situation is familiar to a queer audience, many members of which have been hounded and run down by normativity.

Lady into Fox: A Queer Primer

To the hounds! In short, Mame, despite her ill-fitting boots and her inability to ride, and despite Sally Cato's selection of the mad stallion Meditation as her mount, captures the fox. Beau is overwhelmed by the triumph of his "little Yankee Valkyrie! . . . Look here, everybody! I want three cheers for—for the future Mrs. Beauregard Jackson Pickett Burnside!" The proposal is made in public, as suits a union whose primary obstacle is Mame's public acceptance. No wedding ceremony is needed, for "three cheers" *is* the ceremony. Furthermore, Mame's performance reveals that the South itself has no essence beyond theater. Performativity is all, and Mame's triumph in the fox hunt upends any sense that she is punished for her pretension. This great feat is a primer for successful homosexual coming of age in a hostile environment.

GRIT. Mame does not back down, even when she approaches the stallion with great trepidation, and Patrick suggests, "I can trip you! You'd only break a leg." For queer folk in a homophobic environment, the successful performance of hegemonic romantic and sexual rituals often requires great courage and nerve. At Peckerwood, Mame illustrates how to successfully perform a ritual for which she is unsuited by either experience or desire. (It's not like Mame *wants* to hunt fox.) Furthermore, she succeeds despite the grueling public scrutiny of those who want her to fail because they believe that she is unsuitable—which also speaks to the twentieth-century queer experience.

RIDING THE HORSE. For heterosexuals at midcentury, the relationship between private sexual pleasures and hegemonic rituals such as dating and marriage was well established; they were supposed to be sides of the same coin. This was not true for queer men, who were well advised to have and enjoy sexual and romantic experiences outside of the public gaze or, indeed, of cultural understandings of what sex and love *were*. Mame's successful ride on the mad stallion—that traditional symbol of uncontrolled male sexuality—points the way.

Note, before the hunt, Mame's Freudian slip when she says that "hardly a day goes by I don't have the sadd—um, *boots* on." Wearing the saddle humorously makes Mame the ridden horse rather than the rider—but, at least in the context of the movie, Mame's sexual experiences are securely hidden, although if they were not somehow apparent, the line would not receive the laugh that, in my experience, it always does. Note too how, après-hunt, handsome Cousin Jeff exclaims, "What a seat that woman has! What a magnificent seat!"—to which a startled Russell smoothes down her skirt. Clearly, Mame's sexuality is an open secret, admirable and apparent, and yet not.

In terms of the action itself, how *does* Mame stay seated on her raging stallion? When Patrick asks, Mame, referencing an earlier scene when her bracelets get stuck to Vera on stage, explains that "I got stuck but at the other end." In other words, she did not *stay* on the horse but was *stuck*. What then is this horse that the veterinarian yells is "a killer! I got to stop this!"? A mad stallion, charging the wrong way: that sounds like gay adolescent sexuality circa 1958 to me, especially if one is attached to said stallion by one's ass and cannot let go. Yet Mame rides the stallion to victory. The sexual metaphor comes to a climax when Meditation, in yet another sexual metaphor, is spooked by a gunshot and throws Mame—and who is not thrown by an unbridled orgasm? Nonetheless, Mame is unharmed and wins the hunt.

CAMOUFLAGE. The southerners do not understand what is happening, and Mame uses their ignorance to her advantage. Consider this running commentary:

> EXTRA. Look at her ride! She's passin' everybody!
> MOTHER BURNSIDE. She's passin' the Mastuh of the Hounds! Mighty bad form, passin' the Mastuh.
> PATRICK. She's passing the dogs!
> MOTHER BURNSIDE. Mother of Jefferson Davis, *she's passin' the fox!*

Mother Burnside never considers that Mame is not in control of her mount; her nonnormative actions are unreadable. Mame is smart enough neither to ask for help nor to admit how she wins. Such talents for camouflage were essential for a queer population in the era of the open secret, when every gay man who was not otherwise empowered had to be careful not to drop hairpins in a straight context. The skills that Patrick learns from the steeplechase are skills that he will need for successful closeting—for hiding in plain sight when danger may rear at any time.

EMBRACE THE SEXUAL ANIMAL WITHIN. Mame wins the hunt but does not kill the fox. When Mame is thrown, Beau runs up to her and finds the fox cradled in her arms. This follows, as Mame and the fox are one. Both are known for their remarkable dress, and both are viewed by the southerners as lesser orders of being and targeted for destruction. Instead of destroying her animal nature, her sexuality, she becomes one with it and is embraced by her lover. While her attempts to ape southern normativity land her in trouble, her embrace of her wildness—her helpless, hapless riding of the wild horse—leads to a successful union with Mr. Goodcock.

MATERNAL IDENTIFICATION AND RELEASE. After her engagement, and Beau's suggestion that he and Mame "take a trip around the world for a couple of years, just you and me," she notices Patrick tearing up—"I won't see you for a long time"—just as he teared up at the start of the film when Mame did not know him. Mame jollies and reassures Patrick until he is comforted: "You will always be my little love." After offering a working demonstration of how to ride a bucking sex drive into a publicly celebrated union, Mame reclaims her pedagogical, maternal role. What more could a queer child want or need?

Patrick at Peckerwood

In every other scene in the first half of the movie, Patrick is essential to the action. Why not at Peckerwood? He approves of the match—"I *like* Beau"—but does little else. In his most active moment, he reads to Mame from *How to Ride a Horse*.

Patrick is largely absent from Peckerwood because he *is* Mame at Peckerwood: Mame's pursuit of Beau is Patrick's own imagined pursuit of a man. The projection is called back only after she rides the horse to the climax and resumes her maternal role. Patrick himself is on the brink of sexual maturity; just before Peckerwood, at the nonce Christmas, he receives his first pair of long pants. Very soon after the southern scenes, Jan Handzlik is replaced by Roger Smith, and Little Patrick becomes Big Patrick, postcollegiate and looking to marry. His is the erection that "Peckerwood" engenders.

Mame's union is Patrick's union, but not as in a more conventional film, such as *The Parent Trap* or *The Courtship of Eddie's Father*, both great successes released within five years of *Auntie Mame*.[29] These films are complex variations on identity and desire in a heterosexual matrix, as understood through the simplified version of the Freudian family romance at large in the

American midcentury. In both films, children project their desires upon their parents: through the child's identification with the parent of the same sex, their parent's coupling is their own. In *The Courtship of Eddie's Father*, Little Eddie (Ron Howard), who looks about nine years old and who is still experiencing disassociated, violent episodes of grief over his mother's recent death, works first to make his father marriage-minded and second to steer him toward the nice lady across the hall (Shirley Jones) rather than toward a socialite (Dina Merrill). The climactic marriage both fulfills Eddie's need for a mother and consummates his crush on the neighbor—and furthers his identification with his dad. His heterosexuality is doubly bolstered.

The psychological stylings of *The Parent Trap* are more baroque but equally straight. Hayley Mills plays twins Susan and Sharon, separated as babies after their parents' divorce and unaware of each other until, at what in 1961 would be called "the cusp of womanhood," they meet at summer camp. Susan, more properly feminine, lives with her repressed Bostonian mother (Maureen O'Hara), while tomboy Sharon lives on a ranch in Monterey with Dad (Brian Keith). Clearly, Susan/Sharon is one girl split in two. She cannot reconcile her parental identifications: she must be either Mommy's or Daddy's girl. After a physical fight, the girls discover their sisterhood, express their sadness at being kept from the other parent, and agree to switch places after camp. In other words, the girls merge, and the different identifications are reconciled. Susan/Sharon then works to remarry her parents, which requires her both to melt her mother's romantic reserve and to defeat her father's sexy fiancée. Susan/Sharon must have her cake and eat it: the Boston mother must be made more sexually receptive for the parents to reconcile, but the mother's sexuality, as symbolically externalized in the person of the fiancée, must also be defeated. Competition with the mother is thus reconciled, and her union with the father is the girl's own. The heteronormative nuclear family metabolizes an inherent conflict and stands firm.

By contrast, Beauregard is never Patrick's parent in any but the most remote way. Throughout Beau's brief marriage with Mame, he is *literally* across the world from Patrick, on the honeymoon from which he never returns. Instead, Patrick enters into Mame's own romantic fantasy of a wealthy hunk who worships her, appreciates her merits despite her misfortunes, marries and enriches her, and takes her off on a world tour during which she remains his center of attention—unto death! Patrick's pleasure comes from vicariously "appreciating" Mame's southern triumph and then her and Beau's honeymoon in letters, in the montage that follows Peckerwood. In all forms of

Auntie Mame, the actual marriage is a lacuna: when it's over, Patrick is grown. As an adult male hero in a family-friendly 1950s movie cannot overtly interest himself in men, queer pedagogy is now closeted within Mame's attempt to persuade Big Patrick to come to his senses and ditch vapid, preppy princess Gloria Upson—Babcock's choice—for Mame's assistant, the Irish (of course) Pegeen.

In the second half of the book, play, and movie, the South is replaced by Mountebank, Connecticut, the home of Gloria and her parents. "Mountebank," of course, means charlatan, and through the Upsons, *Auntie Mame* attempts to distinguish between different stripes of WASPiness. The Upsons' crime is embodying the ruling class so poorly. Much is made of their lack of sophistication. Their home is called, regrettably, Upson Downs, and Mr. Upson is damned for the secret ingredient in his daiquiris, strained honey. The more substantial fight between Mame and the Upsons, however, takes place over what might become Gloria and Big Patrick's home as newlyweds, next door to the Upsons. Mountebank is a restricted community that does not allow Jews to buy property within town limits—but Upson Downs is at those limits, and Mame's gift of the property would keep the Upsons safe from Jews. In the novel, play, and movie, Mame ends up buying the property for a home for Jewish war refugees; in the musicals, for a home for unwed mothers. In both cases, the Upsons' discrimination leads Patrick to reject Babcock and the Upsons and to marry sensible Pegeen.

The film's Pegeen, in her tasteful skirt suit, is poised on the very edge of WASPiness, a delicate balance that makes her suitable for love, sex, and marriage. Compared to Nora Muldoon and Brian O'Bannion, she is deracinated. The novel's Pegeen, daughter of Mickey the Mick, is a redheaded barmaid, secretly a scholar of French, who gets into a catfight with a trio of heiresses,[30] but there is nothing Irish about the film's Pegeen but her name. Still, her name signifies that nominally "ethnic" Pegeen is an acceptable marital partner while echt-prep Gloria is not. Yet Pegeen's boring propriety is presumably why she receives only a few moments of screen time. Neither Lawrence and Lee nor DaCosta show any interest in fleshing out Big Patrick's sensible marriage.

In this contest of "appropriate" versus "inappropriate" choice of intimate partner, questions of gender and sexuality are mapped upon questions of class and ethnicity, and there is no heightened cinematic equivalent to Peckerwood and the Queer South. This may be why the film's second half, despite its virtues, feels less vivid and more protracted. Its queer pedagogy has gone deep in the closet until the very end of the film, when Patrick and Pegeen's son is taken up by Auntie Mame, and the queer mothering of Mom and Anti-Mom begins again. Then it is time for queer audiences to restart the ritual of rewatching *Auntie Mame* as well.

NOTES

1. *Auntie Mame*, dir. Morton DaCosta (Warner Bros., 1958).

2. As was common for midcentury queer men, DaCosta left no biography, and his press, including his obituary, mentions no personal life. His homosexuality is asserted in Charles Higham's *In and Out of Hollywood: A Biographer's Memoir* (Madison: University of Wisconsin Press, 2009), 124.

3. Patrick Dennis, *Auntie Mame: An Irreverent Escapade* (New York: Vanguard, 1955).

4. Tanner, who enjoyed disguises, ended his life not as "Patrick Dennis" but as butler to the very rich, including Ray Croc, the CEO of McDonald's.

5. Dennis, *Auntie Mame*, 4.

6. *Auntie Mame* [play], dir. Morton DaCosta, 1956, published as *Auntie Mame: A New Play by Jerome Lawrence and Robert E. Lee* (New York: Vanguard Press, 1957). See the excellent *Uncle Mame: The Life of Patrick Dennis* by Eric Myers (New York: St. Martin's Press, 2000), as well as Richard Tyler Jordan's *But Darling, I'm Your Auntie Mame* (Santa Barbara, Calif.: Capra, 1998), for the history of the five versions. Myers and Jordan agree that Russell's autobiography *Life Is a Banquet* (New York: Random House, 1977) is inaccurate in terms of *Auntie Mame*.

7. Patrick Dennis, *Around the World with Auntie Mame* (New York: Harcourt, Brace, 1958). *Mame* [musical], dir. Gene Saks, 1966; *Mame* [film], dir. Gene Saks, written by Paul Zindel, 1974.

8. I use "hegemonic" to indicate those qualities and practices that are dictated and enforced by the hegemony, and whose lack is punished. "Conventional" lacks sufficient force.

9. Kathryn Bond Stockton, *The Queer Child, or Growing Sideways in the Twentieth Century* (Durham, N.C.: Duke University Press, 2009), 4. Also see, especially, Ken Corbett, *Boyhoods: Rethinking Masculinities* (New Haven, Conn.: Yale University Press, 2011); Teresa de Lauretis, *The Practice of Love: Lesbian Sexuality and Perverse Desire* (Bloomington: Indiana University Press, 1994).

10. Jordan, *But Darling, I'm Your Auntie Mame*, 119–20. In *So Famous and So Gay: The Fabulous Potency of Truman Capote and Gertrude Stein* (Minneapolis: University of Minnesota Press, 2017), I discuss Stein's mass-market celebrity and its visual signifiers.

11. *Auntie Mame*, movie trailer (1958; Warner Home Video, 2010), DVD.

12. Edmund White, "Uncle Mame," *BOMB* 72 (Summer 2000): 24–26; Keith Fleming, *The Boy with the Thorn in His Side* (New York: Morrow, 2000).

13. D. A. Miller, *Place for Us: Essay on the Broadway Musical* (Cambridge, Mass.: Harvard University Press, 2000), 122. *Mame* differs from *Auntie Mame*, but Miller's point about Vera holds.

14. *Breakfast at Tiffany's*, dir. Blake Edwards (Paramount, 1961). Also see the echoes of Mame's cigarette holder and Japanese houseboy.

15. Dennis, *Auntie Mame*, 48.

16. Dennis, *Auntie Mame*, 55.

17. Dennis, *Auntie Mame*, 67.

18. Dennis, *Auntie Mame*, 60.

19. Dennis, *Auntie Mame*, 63.

20. Dennis, *Auntie Mame*, 63–64.

21. See Adolph Comden and Betty Green, *Auntie Mame*, revised final script with changes, February 24, 1958, Story Department file 1721A (F008788), Warner Bros. Archives, School of Cinematic Arts, University of Southern California, Los Angeles, page 68. Both Mame's false southern accent and the "real" accents in this scene are intentionally extreme. This extremity begins with the novel and carries through the Lawrence and Lee playscript, which is incorporated almost whole cloth into the screenplay. In this essay, all "dialect" spellings and punctuation are from the Comden and Green script. When the playscript and the film differ, as scripts and performance often do, the quotes reference the film.

22. Dennis, *Auntie Mame*, 64.

23. Dennis, *Auntie Mame*, 64–65.

24. Orry-Kelly, *Women I've Undressed* (London: Allen & Unwin, 2016), 392–93.

25. *China Seas*, dir. Tay Garnett (MGM, 1935); *Under Two Flags*, dir. Frank Lloyd (Twentieth Century Productions, 1936); *The Night Is Young*, dir. Dudley Murphy (MGM, 1935).

26. Comden and Green, *Auntie Mame*, 70.

27. Comden and Green, *Auntie Mame*, 71–72. See note 21.

28. Comden and Green, *Auntie Mame*, 72.

29. *The Parent Trap*, dir. David Swift (Disney, 1961); *The Courtship of Eddie's Father*, dir. Vincente Minnelli (MGM, 1963). Joanna Barnes, who played Gloria Upson in *Auntie Mame*, plays a nastier, smarter foil in the *The Parent Trap*.

30. Dennis, *Auntie Mame*, 266.

PART V

CAMP AND COMEDY WITH SOUTHERN QUEERS

Chapter 11 ▸ Southern Manners and Camp Cannibalism in Tennessee Williams's *Suddenly, Last Summer*

TISON PUGH

Veering wildly between searing realism and torrid grotesquerie, Tennessee Williams's *Suddenly, Last Summer* (play 1958, film 1959) ends with the horror of cannibalism and, all too frequently, the damnation of critics.[1] An exploration of southern manners and illicit queer desire, of a mother's attempt to preserve the bowdlerized memory of her gay son from the chatter of gossips, both the play and the film flabbergasted contemporary reviewers. Anthony West decried the play's "grotesque and humorless enormity," Tom Driver denigrated it as "shock material," and Brooks Atkinson, in his *New York Times* review, concluded, "What Mr. Williams has to say is in essence repugnant"—although he softened this sentiment by noting that Williams "says it with awareness, sentience, musical grace and conviction."[2] More than forty years after the play's debut, Alan Sinfield witheringly dismissed it as "Williams' most homophobic play,"[3] and Michael Paller has more recently compared it to Shakespeare's anti-Semitic *The Merchant of Venice*, recognizing both as problematic plays that trouble modern audiences' appreciation of their authors' genius.[4]

Unsurprisingly, the play's 1959 cinematic adaptation—directed by Joseph L. Mankiewicz, with a screenplay by Williams and Gore Vidal—generated a firestorm of controversy even prior to its release. The film's sordid themes of repressed memory and unsuppressed desire clashed with Hollywood's Production Code, evident in Code enforcer Geoffrey Shurlock's complaint: "We also felt that the ending—cannibalism with its sexual overtones—was so revolting, that we did not feel justified in giving the Code seal."[5] Moira Walsh documents that the film was "originally denied a seal by the Production Code Administration," noting as well that, when eventually approving its release, the Code Administration's Review Board simply overlooked its "provision forbidding the screen treatment of 'sex perversion or any inference of it.'"[6] In a statement of moral distaste, the National Legion of Decency labeled it "inappropriate for exhibition to general audiences."[7] Upon the film's release, reviewers were virtually unanimous in their scathing reactions. Writing for the *Observer*, C. A. Lejeune fulminated, "I loathe this film. I say so candidly. To my mind it is a decadent piece of work, sensational, barbarous, and ridiculous."[8] One can hear John McCarten's sheer exasperation in the *New Yorker*: "the picture is a preposterous and monotonous potpourri of incest, homosexuality, psychiatry, and, so help me, cannibalism."[9] Even critics who admired the film's technical artistry deplored its story line, as is evident in Arthur Knight's conclusion to his review, cheekily subtitled "Eating People Is Wrong": "It is, in short, a wholly admirable rendering into film of a work that is at once fascinating and nauseating, brilliant and immoral."[10] To argue against these reviews would in many ways amount to little more than a fatuous gesture: Lejeune's adjectives—"sensational, barbarous, and ridiculous"—accurately capture the narrative's excesses, but, as I hope to show, critics such as Lejeune also, if inadvertently, captured in their litany of horrors its lasting appeal as a camp and queer meditation on southern manners.

For *Suddenly, Last Summer* revels in excess, and by appreciating rather than denigrating this quality, one can enjoy the film for its mercurial yet submerged camp humor as an exposé of the pretense of decorum: it is in many ways an unrecognized comedy of manners in a southern setting. Moe Meyer's succinct definition of camp as "the total body of performative practices and strategies used to enact a queer identity, with enactment defined as the production of social visibility,"[11] captures the paradox of the film's outré style, for it produces a vision of queer identity in its margins while simultaneously refusing to depict homosexuality. Viewers hardly see Williams's enigmatic Sebastian Venable—except in flashbacks while shot from behind—because he has been consumed prior to the narrative's beginning, yet his queer (un)presence campily subverts the film's halfhearted flirtations with realism.[12] In looking through *Suddenly, Last Summer*'s reception history, it becomes apparent as well that some critics recognized, even if they did not appreciate, this decadent comic ethos. The *New Republic*'s Stanley Kauffmann states that Williams "has created an exercise in Grand Guignol" and then extends this critique: "To make it worse, he has plunged with such blind fervor that he has not composed a good Guignol."[13] (Within this theater of excess, "good Guignol" often verges on camp itself, with Kauffmann apparently missing this irony.) William Whitebait, in a caustic *New Statesman* review, nonetheless hints at *Suddenly, Last Summer*'s hidden appeal—"If we wanted a parody of Tennessee Williams, where should we go but to Tennessee Williams?"[14]—and Isabel Quigly similarly declares that the film is "not admirable or deplorable, but absurd. The sort of *jeu d'esprit* someone might think up for a literary competition, a story in the *manner* of Tennessee Williams."[15]

In this light both the play and its cinematic adaptation offer themselves to camp interpretations that prize their ostensible failures, for numerous viewers have found reason to laugh heartily at this story of the decadent yet mannered South. The plot features Violet Venable (Katharine Hepburn) desperately seeking to maintain her sense of maternal propriety by bribing the honorable lobotomist Dr. Cukrowicz (Montgomery Clift) to purge her niece, Catherine Holly (Elizabeth Taylor), of memories of her son Sebastian's gruesome demise, yet she must accomplish this cruel objective while outwardly presenting herself as if butter wouldn't melt in her mouth. Indeed, in documenting the humor that some audience members enjoyed during its screening, Whitebait skitters near an alternative interpretation: "The plot is so absurd that one couldn't seriously set it down on paper. Even a publicity-stunned audience stirred at times to laughter."[16] On a similar note, Gore Vidal recorded his belief that Williams had transgressed the limits of theatrical and cinematic decorum, declaring that "Tennessee Williams is the best of American playwrights, but he has gone overboard."[17] He later, in his 1995 memoir, also documented the pleasure found by some audiences in this so-called travesty: "I should note that whenever *Suddenly, Last Summer* appears on Italian television, the local boys find it irresistibly funny."[18] Horrifically demented for many, *Suddenly, Last Summer* is humorously demented for many others, and the adaptation's camp sensibility—evident in its exaggerated symbolism, lurid story line, and uneven performances—illuminates the possibility of finding treasure in a cultural artifact dismissed as trash by so many of its contemporary reviewers. Digging in the junkyard of southern culture, unexpected pleasures can often be found, particularly when the region's famed celebration of good manners and hospitality is skewered on a campy spit.

Williams, Vidal, and Camp Symbolism

Camp frequently springs forth in an audience's interpretation of a given work, not necessarily as a result of the artistic vision of its creator(s). Yet as mid-twentieth-century gay men, Williams and Vidal were widely exposed to camp and camp humor.[19] Camp percolated throughout midcentury American and European queer subcultures, notably documented in such texts as Christopher Isherwood's novel *The World in the Evening* (1954) and Susan Sontag's landmark essay "Notes on 'Camp'" (1964), as well as in camp films penned or inspired by queer southern authors, including Truman Capote's screenplay for John Huston's *Beat the Devil* (1953) and William March's novel adapted into the Mervyn LeRoy film *The Bad Seed* (1956). Williams and Vidal had known each other personally and professionally for more than a decade by the time of their collaboration on *Suddenly, Last Summer*, and for the most part their friendship ran smoothly (in contrast to Williams's on-again, off-again acquaintanceship with Truman Capote, with whom Vidal feuded publicly for decades). To a notable degree Williams and Vidal appreciated each other's sense of humor. In letters to Donald Windham penned in 1948, Williams praised Vidal's good looks—"Gore is a beauty"—while also acknowledging his endearingly madcap mannerisms: "He is such a lunatic that anything he says is partly discountable. I liked him but only through the strenuous effort it took to overlook his conceit." Williams also enjoyed Vidal as a kindly misanthrope, as recorded in a letter to Windham the following year: "I miss him, for it is comforting to know somebody who gets along worse with people than I do, and I still believe that he has a heart of gold."[20] As the years passed and their friendship deepened, Williams's assessments of Vidal's writing, initially disparaging, notably improved. In a 1948 letter to Carson McCullers, he dismissed Vidal's *The City and the Pillar*: "I have just read [it] and while it is not a good book it is absorbing. There is not a really distinguished line in the book and yet a great deal of it has a curiously life-like quality. The end is trashy, alas, murder and suicide both."[21] Moving from this unfavorable appraisal of Vidal's style and plotting, he later wrote, in a 1952 letter to Oliver Evans, "I am impressed by Gore's new book [*The Judgment of Paris*]. . . . I am deeply impressed by the cogency of the writing and the liquid smooth style."[22]

From this friendship and an admiration of each other's literary talents grew their collaboration on *Suddenly, Last Summer*, with Williams receiving co-credit for the screenplay, although they both, on numerous occasions, admitted that Vidal undertook the lion's share of the writing. As Vidal recalls, Williams and producer Sam Spiegel expressed high ambitions for the artistic and commercial success of *Suddenly, Last Summer*'s cinematic adaptation:

> In 1958 I went down to Miami to meet Tennessee and the film producer Sam Spiegel. Would I write the screenplay for *Suddenly, Last Summer*? The Bird [Vidal's

> nickname for Williams] was manic that season and Sam more than usually devious. I agreed to write the script if Tennessee would have no hand in it. Later, Sam would talk him into taking co-credit for my screenplay on the ground, "Baby, it will win the Academy Award." As the Bird was ravenous for prizes, he put his name alongside mine on the script. Happily, the reviews were so bad that he immediately regretted what he had done; later, he was less disturbed as the press proved to be so bad that the public was driven to see what *The New York Times* shrieked was a celebration of sodomy, incest, cannibalism, and Elizabeth Taylor at her most voluptuous.[23]

Williams conceded that "the screenplay was mostly written by our wonderful new playwright, Gore Vidal," as he further affirmed his preference for his drama: "Of course I prefer the play, naturally."[24] The Williams-Vidal collaboration, then, was largely one in name only, yet it is nonetheless clear that Williams believed Vidal capable of successfully transmuting his play into a film—if not that the result would (d)evolve into a camp classic of southern cinema.

Key to a camp reading of *Suddenly, Last Summer* is the observation that Williams moved from the wrenching emotional drama of *A Streetcar Named Desire* (1947) and *Cat on a Hot Tin Roof* (1955) to a play only tenuously anchored to any sense of realism. He stated that *Suddenly Last Summer* is "not a realistic play," labeling it instead a "moral fable of our times" and praising it, in a 1961 interview with Studs Terkel, as "perhaps the most poetic" of his works.[25] Further along these lines, Williams argued that realism frequently hampers an artist's vision of truth: "Sometimes the truth is more accessible when you ignore realism, because when you see things in a somewhat exaggerated form you capture more of the true essence of life. The exaggeration gets closer to the essence. This essence of life is really very grotesque and gothic. To get to it you've got to do what may strike some people as distortion."[26] Certainly, one can view *Suddenly Last Summer* from a realist perspective, as its events all fall within the realm of, if not the plausible, the nonetheless possible, and key elements of Williams's life—his overbearing mother, his psychologically troubled sister, and even his sex life—invest autobiographical elements into its story line. As John Lahr observes in his magisterial account of Williams's life, "*Suddenly Last Summer* was a sort of autobiographical exorcism that worked through Williams's grief and guilt over his sister, Rose, as well as his anger at Edwina for deciding to allow a bilateral prefrontal lobotomy to be performed on her without informing him in advance about the procedure—an omission for which Williams never forgave his mother."[27] Furthermore, Sebastian Venable's use of his European travels as an opportunity to sate his rapacious sexual appetite mirrors Williams's own journeys. Albert Devlin and Nancy Tischler note that Williams "used 'Cabeza de Lobo' as fictional shield for the Barcelona scenes in *Suddenly Last Summer*,"[28] and Williams, in a letter to Donald Windham, voices sentiments he later ascribes to Sebastian: "We were both getting an appetite for blonds as the Roman gentry are all sort of dusky types,"[29] a line echoed in Catherine's cry, "We were going to blonds next. Blonds were next on the menu. All next summer, Sebastian was famished for blonds. Fed up with the dark ones." But the simple fact that the play and film contain realist edges and hints of Williams's autobiography does not necessitate that they be assessed against the criteria of psychological realism, and this disjunction between critical expectations and grotesque excess has dogged their critical history.

Williams insisted his narrative should be read symbolically, stating that Sebastian "is completely enslaved by his baser nature and this is what destroys him. His death is a ritualistic death, symbolic. And when he fails, when he is unable to write his poem that summer, then he is completely lost."[30] Ironically, in a 1960 interview with Edward R. Murrow, Williams criticized cinematic adaptations that hew too closely to their source: "I think they should create something entirely new in a cinematic form, you see. . . . But they stick too close to the stage play and a stage play is not always effective on the screen, you know."[31] Then, in a double irony, he faulted the adaptation of *Suddenly, Last Summer* for failing to adhere to his symbolism, stating that "Sebastian's death is treated realistically on the screen, which was deplorable. Actually, cannibalism was simply a dramatic metaphor. It's never been accepted as such because people have seen the picture and not the play."[32] Here Williams locates the film's failure in its ostensibly realist depiction of his symbolism, yet Mankiewicz stages this climactic scene not with the boys literally devouring Sebastian but with Sebastian being pulled down by them as his hand reaches out to escape (see figure 11.1). It is indeed a metaphoric staging of Williams's key symbol, but one in which this symbolism cannot hide the outré possibility of cannibalism that Williams seeks to camouflage. In many instances a camp sensibility cannot be purged from a story line so drenched in excess, as this telling controversy about the staging of cannibalism makes clear. Williams may have focused his critique on the fact that the cinematic adaptation of *Suddenly, Last Summer* turns cannibalism-as-symbol into cannibalism-as-act, yet numerous other camp elements, many of which appear in the play as well, render the narrative queerly amusing and apt for humor, particularly in its seriocomic treatment of southern manners and mores.

FIGURE 11.1. Sebastian's hand reaches out to the sky in a mostly metaphoric rendering of a scene of cannibalistic consumption, yet Williams blamed this scene for failing to capture the essence of his play.

Southern Manners and Camp Cinema

Camp indulges in excess, and excess defines the stereotypes of the South as a land of gentility, hospitality, and manners. These traditions can be traced throughout various cultural artifacts, which collectively depict the South as fastidiously concerned with respecting social protocols and etiquette. In contrast to the stock figure of the brusque Yankee, the genteel southerner hyperbolically represents the manners of the region, yet this excessive performance cedes in numerous instances to virtual parody. In his deflation of the southern hospitality myth, Anthony Szczesiul argues, "Today we recognize southern hospitality not from having experienced it so much as from having heard about it repeatedly in this long history of repetition and citation, and in most instances, this discourse today seems entirely emptied of any real meaning or higher ethical or moral significance."[33] The emptiness and exaggerations concomitant with southern myths of manners frequently devolve into comedy: the devolution from Vivien Leigh's dramatic performance as Scarlett O'Hara in *Gone with the Wind* to Carol Burnett's famed parody ironically testifies to the many parallels of these performances. When madness, lobotomies, and homosexuality enter the dramatic scene, any pretense of southern decorum is almost immediately dismissed, with camp stagings undercutting any purported emotional resonance of southern manners.

Suddenly, Last Summer begins with the dramatic excess of a lobotomy, and thus it begins humorously. Some readers might vehemently disagree with this pat statement, and I offer it not as a definitive account of one's viewing of the film but as a potential interpretation aligned with the narrative's dark and campy comedy. Within much of popular culture, lobotomies are simply *beaucoup trop*—not just surgery but brain surgery, not merely a rehabilitative treatment for an ill patient but for a mentally deranged one. Certainly, lobotomies were a subject of great seriousness for Williams, given his sister Rose's psychiatric problems, yet in the wider cultural imagination they often elicit humorous responses, such as in a (likely apocryphal) quip attributed to Dorothy Parker ("I'd rather have a bottle in front of me than a frontal lobotomy") and in the stock figure of mad lobotomists who appear in horror films (a tradition that Williams's Dr. Cukrowicz helps inaugurate).[34] Some might decry the concept of brain surgery serving as the foundation for comedy, yet reimagining horror as humor is common within a camp sensibility. Catherine's frantic cry to Dr. Cukrowicz—"Where will you cut my brain, doctor?"—can be interpreted both as the film's dramatic apex and as the campy failure of its drama to cohere within the expected paradigms of realism.

The marketing of *Suddenly, Last Summer* sought to capitalize on its sensationalistic story line of lobotomies and cannibalism, giving titillating hints about its content that nod to its camp potential. In the trailer, text splashes across the screen, stating, "Suddenly You are Face to Face with a New Emotional Peak in Motion Picture Making!" and declaring as well that the film is based on "The World's Most Provocative Play."[35] The trailer's narrator tantalizingly acknowledges the film's taboo subject matter: "This generation's great author and poet, writer of *A Streetcar Named Desire* and *Cat on a Hot Tin Roof*, unashamedly writes of a woman's strong wants and a man's strange needs." The adverb "unashamedly" tacitly implies that perhaps Williams should indeed be ashamed of his shocking narrative, with the telling allusion to a "man's strange needs" hinting at his (and Sebastian's) homosexuality. Again, Meyer's declaration that camp humor makes queer identities visible is relevant, for the trailer acknowledges the film's queer heritage while at the same time disavowing it.

The film's opening scenes at Lion's View asylum feature madness on display: a knitting woman scares off an older woman in a rocking chair, while another woman fetishistically holds up a doll. Dr. Cukrowicz soon lobotomizes this latter inmate. A foreshadowing of Mrs. Venable's nefarious plan for Catherine, this operation illustrates Dr. Cukrowicz's dedication to curing the mentally ill, yet Catherine is not insane and thus never in need of a lobotomy. As the conclusion makes clear, a single session of Freud's talking cure, administered through a magic potion in the form of a truth serum, suffices to heal her psychic scars. The threat of her lobotomy nonetheless escalates the film's emotionalism to a fevered, overwrought pitch, such as when Catherine learns her brother George and mother have agreed to Mrs. Venable's extortion, and a comedy of southern manners ensues:

GEORGE. But, Cathie, the way Aunt Vi put it, there was no choice at all. Mama's got to sign.

MRS. HOLLY. Besides, honey, it's not like it was for always. In fact, they say in no time after the little operation you'll be able to . . .

CATHERINE. What "little operation"?

MRS. HOLLY. Oh, Cathie! Oh, Cathie!

CATHERINE. There's only one "little operation" they perform here! It's on the brain! It's called a lobotomy! You may have heard of it, or read about it. I have. It's that nice, young doctor's specialty! In cases of hopeless lunacy—he bores holes into the skull and operates on the brain!!

MRS. HOLLY. Oh, honey, please don't talk about it. Please!

In the ensuing family tempest, George adds unconvincingly, "They say it don't hurt at all . . . No worse than having your tonsils out." Mrs. Holly's and George's paper-thin loyalty to Catherine wavers at the promise of cash, with Catherine's outburst prompting Mrs. Holly, in a virtual parody of the self-martyring mother, to cast herself as the victim ("Please don't talk about it. Please!"). Moreover, in comparing a lobotomy to a tonsillectomy, George diminishes Catherine's suffering and proves the expendability of her brain when opposed to his pecuniary desires. An over-the-top presentation of venality, Vidal's depiction of the Holly clan teeters near the edge of humor, and for many viewers totters over.

Violet Venable's dark obsession with preserving Sebastian's reputation against aspersions concerning his homosexuality—truthful though they may be—overshadows other aspects of her character, yet her shallow vanity paints her as deserving of viewers' laughter as well, for she enacts the maternal role of southern manners only to mask her steely, cruel determination. Her secretary, Miss Foxhill, primly and ridiculously chastises Dr. Cukrowicz for arriving early to his appointment—"You are twenty-three seconds early. Sit down, please"—with her words preparing viewers for an exaggerated vision of southern propriety. Descending in her baroque elevator to meet her guest, Mrs. Venable plays her patrician charm as a facade, yet the facade cannot hide

FIGURE 11.2. Violet Venable stages quite an entrance for herself, descending from above and unsubtly hoping to seduce Dr. Cukrowicz.

the frailties underneath, both maternal and amorous (see figure 11.2). As she meets Dr. Cukrowicz, she asks in response to his stare, "Am I only wearing one earring? Have I forgotten my lip rouge?" testifying to her continued attention to her appearance despite her advanced years. Furthermore, her erotic interest in young, alluring Dr. Cukrowicz is evident: "I must say, you're much handsomer than your photograph in the paper without that awful paraphernalia you doctors wear." The stock figure of an older woman seeking to hide the ravages of time and desperately pursuing younger men appears in many comedies of manners (e.g., Lady Wishfort in William Congreve's *The Way of the World*), and in this scene Mrs. Venable aligns with other aging belles in Williams's work who invite camp stagings, such as Miss Collins in *Portrait of a Madonna*. This connection is heightened by the fact that Mrs. Venable in the film, like Miss Collins in the play, is last seen succumbing to madness. Miss Collins teeters between tragic and comic valences in the loneliness of her life and in her refusal to accept her fading looks, which Williams stages for a grotesquely comic effect: "*Self-consciously she touches her ridiculous corkscrew curls with the faded pink ribbon tied through them. Her manner becomes that of a slightly coquettish but prim little southern belle.*"[36] A flirting youngster in the body of an aged woman, Miss Collins subverts the foundational image of southern women's sexual allure. Along similar lines, Mrs. Venable's queries about her earring and lip rouge precede her statement "I'm in mourning," suggesting that she privileges her vanity over her devotion to her son's memory.

More than merely an aging debutante, Mrs. Venable adheres to the archetype of camp femininity, the bitch—a role of paramount significance to southern literature and film—with her bitchiness evident in her scathing assessment of her niece. Dr. Cukrowicz warns her, "You must realize the operation I do is only for the unapproachable, for the hopeless," to which she callously replies, "If she isn't unapproachable and hopeless, I don't know who is," a line that elicits laughter, even if unintentional. Seemingly showing concern for Catherine, she observes, "She's mad as a hatter, poor child." She then glibly redirects the conversation to her true interest: "Would you like to see Sebastian's studio? It's at the end of the jungle," thus disproving the tender concern she sought to portray and reminding viewers of the outlandish setting in which the action unfolds, a tropical jungle transported into a New Orleans home. In another line with humor humming underneath its surface, she bitterly declares of Sebastian's relationship with Catherine, "How he must have loathed being touched by her," which reveals more of her blistering, bitchy character. The bitch figure rewrites the traditionally gendered scripts of femininity, with her callousness and brazen style often evoking laughter both despite and due to her sharp tongue, besides contrasting with the image of honeyed southern femininity promulgated by the myths of the South.

Camp humor flourishes in melodrama as well, particularly when an ostensibly realist portrayal of heightened emotions reaches beyond its expected registers. When Dr. Hockstader, the hospital administrator, proclaims of Dr. Cukrowicz's plan, "This is very unorthodox," Dr. Cukrowicz replies, "So is insanity. That's why we're here." Montgomery Clift's delivery of his lines cements his character's earnestness, if also his exaggerated naiveté. For all of Dr. Cukrowicz's appealing characteristics in his role as the concerned physician, his unflappable calm merges disjointedly with his insistent innocence: "What would attraction have to do with a son and a mother?" he obliviously wonders, blind to the blatant psychosexual dynamics of an over-the-top Oedipal complex unfolding before him. In a camp reading of *Suddenly, Last Summer*, it is one of the film's funniest lines, showing the expert in the workings of the human mind unable to decipher what is apparent to all. As his last name implies—he explains to Mrs. Venable that it comes from the Polish word for "sugar"—Dr. Cukrowicz is an outsider to New Orleans's aristocratic society of French descent, and so he inevitably fails to understand the mores of southern culture in which he is ensnared.

But most ridiculous in *Suddenly, Last Summer*'s transition from play to film is the introduction of romance into a story of lobotomies and southern sexual secrets. Catherine continually flirts with Dr. Cukrowicz, such as when she pretends that she will sexually assault him (but then redirects her attention to his cigarettes). As their first session together winds down after she initially confronts the traumatic memory of Sebastian's demise, she kisses the doctor, but he simply brushes it off as a "friendly kiss"—a bizarrely inappropriate response for a medical professional, particularly as Catherine admits, "Maybe it wasn't." Certainly she is concerned about her appearance: "I want you to know that I can look attractive, if I had my hair done and if . . . When I'm at Lion's View, may I wear a pretty dress?" Their romance deepens as they prepare for her to divulge the truth of Sebastian's death. Dr. Cukrowicz asks her not to resist him and to tell him the complete story, and she agrees as they clasp hands—"Here are my hands. But there's no resistance in them." They soon kiss as she cries, "Hold me. I've been so lonely." In the film's dénouement, Catherine is cured: "Miss Catherine's here," she proclaims as she walks away with him in a symbolic staging of their budding love. By merging Williams's darkly symbolic play with a romance, Vidal upends expectations based on genre and source text, resulting in a disjointed film humorous in its unexpected courtship scenes, particularly as Miss Catherine seems perfectly content to exploit her condition if, in the final act, she finds herself a suitable beau. Southern manners, after all, are so frequently deployed with a specific goal in mind.

Camp Casting

In casting Hepburn, Taylor, and Clift in the adaptation's lead roles, Spiegel generated buzz for *Suddenly, Last Summer* through their combined star power, and these actors, overwhelmingly admired for their distinguished careers, mostly escaped censure for their performances.[37] With sentiments representative of the critical consensus, Peter Baker praised the threesome in *Films and Filming*, suggesting that they "combine to give one of the most perfectly balanced pieces of teamwork we have seen in the cinema for many years."[38] Both Hepburn and Taylor received Academy Award nominations for Best Actress—although Simone Signoret won for Jack Clayton's *Room at the Top*—with Hepburn's imperious, cruel, and ultimately vulnerable realization of Violet Venable receiving particular praise. Albert Johnson raved of Hepburn that she is "absolutely magnificent. She creates a completely villainous, hawklike creature of . . . elegant abstrusity and affectation."[39] Taylor also received plaudits, such as Arthur Knight's assessment that "hers is unquestionably one of the finest performances of this or any year."[40]

At the same time, casting decisions are notoriously subjective and routinely generate controversy, and Williams admitted his doubts about Spiegel's choices:

> When Sam Spiegel bought *Suddenly Last Summer*, we agreed on the casting. At first, I wasn't sure about Katharine Hepburn as Violet Venable. I thought she was quite too young to play such an older woman, as I visualized the part. In the stage production, Hortense Alden played the part in a wheelchair. But I admitted that casting Miss Hepburn might be daring, and it took me a while to get accustomed to the idea. Now, of course, I know she was brilliant. So was dear Monty Clift as Dr. Cukrowicz. But while Elizabeth Taylor was very good as Maggie in *Cat on a Hot Tin Roof*, she simply wasn't right as Catherine Holly in *Suddenly Last Summer*.[41]

Given the legendary status in Hollywood history enjoyed by Hepburn and Taylor, it is not easy to question their performances, yet I too find them curiously off, both in Hepburn's restrained demeanor and in Taylor's excessive emotionality, and off as well for their skewed southern style. The reviewer for *Time*, while conceding that Hepburn "does an intelligent job portraying the devouring mother," suggests amusingly that she is "dolled up like a cross between Auntie Mame and the White Queen"—a drolly apropos assessment of the decadence repressed under her exterior of southern manners.[42] Bosley Crowther similarly snipes: "Katharine Hepburn plays the arch and airy dowager with what looks like a stork's nest on her head and such bony and bumptious posturing that she acts a Mary Petty caricature."[43] Vidal mentions that Bette Davis was his first choice to play Violet Venable,[44] and in light of her gleefully demented roles in subsequent years—*What Ever Happened to Baby Jane?* in 1962 and *Hush . . . Hush, Sweet Charlotte* in 1964, both directed by Robert Aldrich—it is easy to imagine an even campier version of *Suddenly, Last Summer*, one in which Hepburn's restrained patrician facade gives way to Davis's raw passion of a woman on the edge of sanity.

In a similar vein, the *Time* critic berated Taylor's performance: "Actress Taylor's inability to reproduce a recognizable emotion becomes almost an advantage in a role that contains no recognizable emotions."[45] The paradox of Taylor's performance is that she must play, as this reviewer points out, unrecognizable emotions, for what performance can adequately capture the horror of witnessing one's cousin devoured by child cannibals? Taylor's delivery of key lines—such as "He was lying naked on these broken stones. And this you won't believe. Nobody, nobody, could believe it. It looked as if . . . as if they had devoured him!"—ranges within the possible registers of human expression, but given the ludicrousness of the story line, coupled with her dire situation, they will almost of necessity conflict. Another scenario that evinces either Taylor's brilliance or her incompetence arises when Catherine defends herself against aspersions on her sexual morality: "You see, I'm classified as violent, which means I'm apt to attack you physically and then accuse you of rape. . . . I molested an elderly gardener of great virtue." A decadent comedy of southern manners in such moments as this, *Suddenly, Last Summer* appropriates Wildean wit for a narrative on the edge of the macabre, mixing radical tenors of expression and emotion in ways that cannot be contained by its overarching dramatic form.

One of the odder defects in both Hepburn's and Taylor's performances is that they play southern women who speak with southern accents only when insulting or imitating other southerners, thus undermining the coherency of their portrayals and the film's construction of the South. In her simmering distaste for her nephew George, Mrs. Venable archly states, "I said take the clothes, George. Don't flaunt them in my face." She then shifts into a cornpone dialect and continues, "Why don't you both kindly let yourselves out?" and then returns to her normal timbre: "Get the rest of the clothes another time." Similarly, Catherine impersonates Sebastian's southern accent while speaking to Dr. Cukrowicz: "Mr. Venable was a good man, but dull to the point of genius," she says, and then continues in her usual tone, "That was Sebastian you just heard talking." Notably, Mrs. Venable uses her exaggerated southern accent to insult despised George, whereas Catherine mimics esteemed Sebastian; these varying southern accents, then, are markers not so much of the characters' social classes as of the actors' regional roots, which Hepburn and Taylor do not modulate for their roles. Camp often emerges in failed performances, and Hepburn's and Taylor's unsteady play with dialect imbues *Suddenly, Last Summer* with an ironic distance between the non-southern actors—Hepburn was raised in Connecticut, Taylor in London and Hollywood—and their characters.

With Hepburn's and Taylor's performances receiving outsized attention, many reviews simply overlooked Clift, yet the emotional range of his Dr. Cukrowicz is strangely stilted and off-balance. Kauffmann observes that "Montgomery Clift, as the young doctor, is present a good deal of the time, but his contribution is small" and then derides him as "a husk that once contained a small kernel."[46] Albert Johnson describes him simply as "extra-numb in

[a] numb role,"[47] and Henry Hart gripes that he "is completely impossible."[48] Clift's 1956 car accident is often seen as the turning point in his career, as he increasingly turned to drugs and alcohol to mute the residual pain, and his performance in *Suddenly, Last Summer* suffers from an eerie lack of affect. Yet this stiff performance, as suggested previously, imbues the film with an edge of laughter, for Dr. Cukrowicz is simply too slow to grasp the grotesque twists of southern familial desire surrounding him. A camp sensibility often embraces the performative and narrative lapses that arise when a production fails to reach the rarefied emotional heights to which it aspires, and Hepburn, Taylor, and Clift collectively contribute to *Suddenly, Last Summer*'s downfall in this regard, thus also contributing to its apotheosis as a queer, southern, and camp classic.

A Camp Conclusion

In the year of its release, Williams endorsed *Suddenly, Last Summer* enthusiastically, praising Spiegel for his efforts and predicting their long-standing alliance: "This picture filled out on the screen. The first two-thirds had more dimension than the play had. Sam Spiegel . . . is one of the greatest producers in movies today. If there were faults, they weren't his. I want him to do all my plays in the movies from now on. Sam and Gore Vidal plotted the play structure and did a fabulous job."[49] In later years, however, he spoke more openly about his distaste for it, as in a 1974 interview with Cecil Brown: "It horrified me, the film; Sam Spiegel made the mistake of inviting me to a private screening of it in his apartment and I walked out in the middle of it. I was so offended by the literal approach because the play was metaphorical; it was a sort of poem, I thought—I loved Katharine Hepburn in it but I didn't like the film, to be honest."[50] Also, Williams recalls that, in his deal with Spiegel, he requested $50,000 and 20 percent of the profits; Spiegel agreed, but Williams noted ironically, "the profits were as good as the movie was bad.—that figures."[51]

But even if one agrees with Williams that the film of *Suddenly, Last Summer* is bad, it is one of the more enjoyably bad films of midcentury queer cinema. Its flaws—stylized and overdetermined acting, a ludicrous and lurid plotline, southern family ties predicated on the roles of bitchy dowager and traumatized innocent—are its most compelling features, ones that dazzle with their sheer outrageousness. In describing the lush set he created as Sebastian's garden, designer Oliver Messel admitted that many of the flowers were fakes, but tellingly suggested, "The artificial might do even better than the real."[52] Indeed, sometimes the artificial is better than the real, the failures more interesting than the successes. As Cukrowicz's colleague Dr. Hockstader concludes of Catherine's disturbing tale, "There's every possibility that the girl's story could be true," and from a camp perspective that prizes artificiality over genuine emotion, one should consider the very real possibility that the film is a black comic masterpiece—one unrecognized by its creators and unappreciated by most critics. And in this light even some critics give the film's queer fans ample opportunity to laugh, such as in Peter Baker's unintentionally hilarious declaration "If Mr. Williams chooses to be sensational about homosexuality (and heaven knows, it's as old as Man himself), then at least he should find out more about his subject."[53] Truly, Mr. Williams knew a thing or two about homosexuality, but perhaps Mr. Baker—and Mr. Williams, too—should have learned a thing or two about camp humor before decrying the melodramatic horrors of *Suddenly, Last Summer*, celebrating it instead as a misunderstood masterpiece of southern cinema.

NOTES

This chapter was previously published as "Camp Cannibalism in *Suddenly Last Summer*," *Tennessee Williams Annual Review* 15 (2016): 21–34. The author gratefully acknowledges the permission granted by the journal to reprint an adapted and expanded version.

1. Williams's play title *Suddenly Last Summer* does not include a comma, whereas the film title places one between *Suddenly* and *Last*. When the title appears in a direct quotation, original punctuation has been retained. Quotations are taken from the film *Suddenly, Last Summer*, with the screenplay serving as the default for the spelling of character names and locations; Gore Vidal borrowed many lines directly from the playscript in his adaptation. For the play, see *Suddenly Last Summer*, in *The Theatre of Tennessee Williams*, vol. 3 (New York: New Directions, 1971), 343–423. For the film, see *Suddenly, Last Summer*, dir. Joseph L. Mankiewicz, screenplay by Tennessee Williams and Gore Vidal, perf. Elizabeth Taylor, Katharine Hepburn, and Montgomery Clift (1959; Sony Pictures Home Entertainment, 2006), DVD.

2. These reviews are compiled in George W. Crandell, ed., *The Critical Response to Tennessee Williams* (Westport, Conn.: Greenwood, 1996), 211, 166, 165.

3. Alan Sinfield, *Out on Stage: Lesbian and Gay Theatre in the Twentieth Century* (New Haven, Conn.: Yale University Press, 1999), 192.

4. Michael Paller, *Gentlemen Callers: Tennessee Williams, Homosexuality, and Mid-Twentieth-Century Broadway Drama* (New York: Palgrave Macmillan, 2005), 145–46.

5. Geoffrey Shurlock, quoted in R. Barton Palmer and William Robert Bray, *Hol-*

lywood's Tennessee: The Williams Films and Postwar America (Austin: University of Texas Press, 2009), 154. Palmer and Bray address *Suddenly, Last Summer*'s code violations in greater detail (152–57).

6. Moira Walsh, "Films," *America* 9 January 1960: 428–30, at 428–29.

7. "Legion Labels Film: *Suddenly Last Summer* Is 'Separately Classified,'" *New York Times* 4 December 1959: 36.

8. C. A. Lejeune, "Deep in the Heart of Tennessee," *Observer* 15 May 1960: 21.

9. John McCarten, "The Current Cinema: Meagre Merriment," *New Yorker* 9 January 1960: 74–75, at 75.

10. Arthur Knight, "*SR* Goes to the Movies: Eating People Is Wrong," *Saturday Review* 2 January 1960: 31.

11. Moe Meyer, ed., *The Politics and Poetics of Camp* (London: Routledge, 1994), 5.

12. For a study of the significance of Sebastian's absence, see Andrew Sofer, "Self-Consuming Artifacts: Power, Performance, and the Body in Tennessee Williams' *Suddenly Last Summer*," *Modern Drama* 38 (1995): 336–47.

13. Stanley Kauffmann, "Arty Horror, Straight Suspense," *New Republic* 18 January 1960: 20–21, at 20.

14. William Whitebait, "Aftermaths," *New Statesman* 21 May 1960: 753.

15. Isabel Quigly, "Neither Here nor There," *Spectator* 20 May 1960: 736–38, at 736.

16. Whitebait, "Aftermaths," 753.

17. Gore Vidal, "Vidal Admires Tennessee—But," *Variety* 29 August 1960: 55.

18. Gore Vidal, *Palimpsest: A Memoir* (New York: Random House, 1995), 152.

19. For analysis of Tennessee Williams and camp, see William Free, "Camp Elements in the Plays of Tennessee Williams," *Southern Quarterly* 21.2 (1983): 16–23, and "Camp Sadomasochism in Tennessee Williams's Plays," from my *Precious Perversions: Humor, Homosexuality, and the Southern Literary Canon* (Baton Rouge: Louisiana State University Press, 2016), 19–42.

20. Donald Windham, ed., *Tennessee Williams' Letters to Donald Windham, 1940–1965* (New York: Holt, Rinehart and Winston, 1976), 211, 216, 255.

21. Albert J. Devlin and Nancy M. Tischler, eds., *The Selected Letters of Tennessee Williams*, vol. 2, *1945–1957* (New York: New Directions, 2004), 170–71.

22. Devlin and Tischler, *Selected Letters of Tennessee Williams*, 2:421.

23. Vidal, *Palimpsest*, 335.

24. Edward R. Murrow, "Interview with Tennessee Williams, Yukio Mishima, and Dilys Powell," *Conversations with Tennessee Williams*, ed. Albert J. Devlin (Jackson: University Press of Mississippi, 1986), 69–77, at 70.

25. Don Ross, "Williams on a Hot Tin Roof," Devlin, *Conversations*, 50–53, at 52; Studs Terkel, "Studs Terkel Talks with Tennessee Williams," Devlin, *Conversations*, 78–96, at 86.

26. Cecil Brown, "Interview with Tennessee Williams," Devlin, *Conversations*, 251–83, at 264.

27. John Lahr, *Tennessee Williams: Mad Pilgrimage of the Flesh* (New York: Norton, 2014), 347.

28. Devlin and Tischler, *Selected Letters of Tennessee Williams*, 2:13n.

29. Windham, *Tennessee Williams' Letters to Donald Windham*, 215.

30. Jeanne Fayard, "Meeting with Tennessee Williams," Devlin, *Conversations*, 208–12, at 210.

31. Murrow, "Interview," 71.

32. Charles Ruas, "Tennessee Williams," Devlin, *Conversations*, 284–95, at 287.

33. Anthony Szczesiul, *The Southern Hospitality Myth: Ethics, Politics, Race, and American Memory* (Athens: University of Georgia Press, 2017), 13. On the dissemination of these myths of the South, see also John Bush Jones, *Reinventing Dixie: Tin Pan Alley's Songs and the Creation of the Mythic South* (Baton Rouge: Louisiana State University Press, 2015), esp. 91–111.

34. Jenell Johnson calls lobotomists "a familiar monster in the American imagination" (153) and traces their pop-culture portrayals to *Suddenly, Last Summer*; see her *American Lobotomy: A Rhetorical History* (Ann Arbor: University of Michigan Press, 2014), 153.

35. This trailer is available on the DVD of *Suddenly, Last Summer.*

36. Tennessee Williams, *Portrait of a Madonna*, in *The Theatre of Tennessee Williams*, vol. 6 (New York: New Directions, 1981), 107–27, at 114.

37. Montgomery Clift's role, Dr. Cukrowicz, was initially offered to William Holden; see Thomas M. Pryors, "New Movie Role for Miss Taylor," *New York Times* 31 October 1958: 33. Vidal reports that Elizabeth Taylor insisted on Clift for the part (*Palimpsest*, 399).

38. Peter Baker, "*Suddenly Last Summer*," *Films and Filming* June 1960: 21–22, at 21.

39. Albert Johnson, "Review: *Suddenly Last Summer*," *Film Quarterly* 13.3 (1960): 40–42, at 41.

40. Knight, "*SR* Goes to the Movies: Eating People Is Wrong," 31.

41. Don Lee Keith, "New Tennessee Williams Rises from 'Stoned Age,'" Devlin, *Conversations*, 147–60, at 154.

42. "The New Pictures," *Time* 11 January 1960: 64+, at 66.

43. Bosley Crowther, "*Suddenly Last Summer*: Movie from Williams Play at Two Houses," *New York Times* 23 December 1959: 22.

44. Vidal, *Palimpsest*, 319.

45. "The New Pictures," *Time*, 66.

46. Kauffmann, "Arty Horror, Straight Suspense," 20.

47. Albert Johnson, "Review: *Suddenly Last Summer*," 41.

48. Henry Hart, "Film Reviews: *Suddenly Last Summer*," *Films in Review* January 1960: 39–41, at 41.

49. Joe Hyams, "Tennessee Williams Turns Critic," *New York Herald Tribune* 23 December 1959: 13.

50. Brown, "Interview with Tennessee Williams," 274.

51. Tennessee Williams, *Memoirs* (1975; New York: New Directions, 2006), 176.

52. Oliver Messel, quoted in Hollis Alpert, "In a Messel Garden," *Films and Filming* January 1960: 8+, at 8.

53. Baker, "*Suddenly Last Summer*," 21.

Chapter 12 ▸ "Vienners" at Odum's: DeAundra Peek and the Atlanta Televisual Drag Scene

MARGARET T. MCGEHEE

> We have given it a try, we southerners, even though we were skeptical and never really believed our freedom would amount to much. We stuck our noses out of the closet and took a look around at one another. Liking what we saw, what we still see, we set about the business of making a place for ourselves out in the open, in sunshine, in our city.
>
> —JIM GRIMSLEY

> If it's not fun, don't do it.
>
> —Motto of Funtone USA, Dick Richards's Atlanta-based recording label

With her signature exclamation of "Yeaaaaaa!" the forever-sixteen-year-old DeAundra Peek served as an enthusiastic emcee for several variety shows on Atlanta's public access channel from the late 1980s to the early 2000s. With curly blond locks affixed with a large glittery D barrette, bright blue eye shadow reaching far above the natural brow line, patches of heavily applied rouge on her cheekbones, dark eyeliner, pink lips outlined in black, empire-waist polyester gowns and flouncy bows at the neckline, purses seemingly constructed out of a child's stuffed animals, and a rural Georgia drawl, the lovable DeAundra broadcast Friday and Saturday evenings from Odum's Trailer Park in Palmetto, Georgia—in actuality, from the Atlanta home of producer Dick Richards (see figure 12.1). In each episode, she engaged her sidekicks Duffy Odum and Candi Suntop in humorous banter, offered cooking demonstrations featuring her favorite ingredient of canned Vienna sausages (pro-

FIGURE 12.1. DeAundra's most popular publicity photo, taken by Dr. Michael Pelligrinon. Photo courtesy of Rosser Shymanski.

nounced "vy-enners"), and showcased her singing talent in music videos such as "Losing My Vienners" (set to the tune of R.E.M.'s "Losing My Religion").[1]

Rosser Shymanski (b. 1957), a former production manager at Georgia Public Broadcasting, performed as DeAundra for almost twenty years.[2] Shymanski came to Atlanta in 1983, a few years after graduating from the University of Florida, and he made his first appearance that same year on *The American Music Show*,[3] a variety program produced by Atlanta local Dick Richards. Richards helped to launch RuPaul's career, signing RuPaul to his label, Funtone USA, and producing his first two albums, *Sex Freak* in 1985 and *RuPaul Is Star Booty* in 1986. Shymanski already knew of RuPaul, whose posters he had noticed around Atlanta, but when a friend introduced him to *The American Music Show*, he states, "I went, 'I gotta know these people, I gotta work on this show.'" Shymanski continues, "So I wrote them a letter and sent them my résumé and everything. And the next week went to watch the show at my friend Richard's house because you had to have cable and there they were reading my résumé and making fun of my cover letter. So they were making fun of me because of my naiveté, and I was mortified."[4] Richards soon invited Shymanski for an interview and then began offering him roles every few months. In 1986 Molli Worthington, who played Wanda Peek on *The American Music Show*, wanted to reunite the Singing Peek Sisters, but the performers who had played her sisters Starla and LaShonda wanted to move on

FIGURE 12.2. DeAundra Peek with RuPaul. Photo courtesy of Rosser Shymanski.

to other roles. So DeAundra Peek, their little sister, stepped forward to fill their shoes, and Shymanski devoted hours over the years to crafting her image, making her a sweet girl who loved and was loved by everyone (see figure 12.2).[5] Applying DeAundra's makeup and getting into costume could take up to two hours. Shymanski shopped for dresses at thrift stores, opting frequently for old bridesmaid dresses or dresses that could be cinched with a belt. He made her D hair bob from foam core and glitter. He and friends created the backdrops that appeared on DeAundra's multiple cable-access shows throughout the 1990s and into the next decade, including (but not limited to) *Teenage Music Club, DeAundra Peek's Video Funhouse, Most Fun Summer Playhouse, Ultra Style Bin,* and *Hi Class Hall O' Fame Theatre.* (Episodes may be seen on YouTube.) These shows followed a certain formula, according to both Richards and Shymanski, but they were unscripted.[6] Shymanski performed on screen as DeAundra until 2006, and he has continued to make occasional private appearances as Miss Peek since that time.[7]

Most likely it will come as no surprise to readers that very little scholarly attention has been paid to DeAundra Peek or to Atlanta's televisual drag programming of the late twentieth century. LGBTQ+ history—especially in southern locations, both urban and rural—remains severely understudied. Groundbreaking works like E. Patrick Johnson's *Sweet Tea: Black Gay Men of the South* (2008) and John Howard's *Men Like That: A Southern Queer History* (1999) have filled some gaps, revealing the value of oral history for reimagining the lives of historically marginalized populations for whom archival materials are scant. Edited collections such as Howard's *Carryin' On in the Lesbian and Gay South* (1997), Carlos L. Dew and Carolyn Leste Law's *Out in the South* (2001), and Reta Ugena Whitlock's *Queer South Rising: Voices of a Contested Place* (2013) also contribute significantly to southern LGBTQ+ historiography, but more work is needed to bring to light the complexities and particularities of the lives of gay individuals and of the drag scenes in such a conservative region. Southern literature and southern literary studies have faced similar issues, as this volume's editor, Tison Pugh, notes. While some works of southern literature indulge in "derogatory treatments of homosexuality," in general there is "an extensive silence" and a "virulent miasma of nothingness" on the topic within the works of southern writers.[8] So it is no wonder that campy DeAundra Peek has not yet received the full spotlight she deserves, with the exception of Tara McPherson's astute analysis of Peek in *Reconstructing Dixie: Race, Gender, and Nostalgia in the Imagined South* (2003).

McPherson contends that DeAundra Peek offers a different South to viewers as she challenges tropes of southern white femininity—namely, the figure of the southern belle. In turn, Peek—along with contemporary Ruby Ann Boxcar, author of a series of "trailer park cookbooks," who is frequently referred to as "the Dame Edna of the double-wide world," and members of the Atlanta Feminist Lesbian Alliance (AFLA)—can "offer models for a politics of engagement, working nationally and globally (via mediated information streams and organized campaigns) while also building vibrant local communities underwritten by a slightly utopian hope in other possible Souths."[9] Peek, Boxcar, and members of the AFLA are not closed off from networks beyond the perceived borders of "the South," McPherson claims, and their local efforts work against limited definitions of what the region is and could be. Peek's shows "envision new counterpublics that link local communities to broader spheres, competing with the neo-Confederates and the Christian Right over the meaning of the South." "It is possible to be of a place and apart from it," writes McPherson, "creating new modes of southern identity, sketching the contours of a critical regionalism."[10] Through her use of a "white trash veneer" and her "parodic excesses," DeAundra serves "to destabilize southern standards of taste, femininity, and decorum," bringing to the fore "strategies, imperfect yet viable, for troubling the normalizing power of iconic southern femininity."[11] Peek symbolizes a "move toward an *expansive southernness* in Atlanta (and beyond)," claims McPherson, as her performance "unmoors southern identity from a fixed relation to certain icons of southern history and tradition."[12]

McPherson's analysis is spot on, for DeAundra Peek certainly challenges "iconic southern femininity." However, in examining DeAundra Peek's "shows" within a broader context of LGBTQ+ entertainment, social life, activism, and politics in Atlanta during the late 1980s to early 2000s—which McPherson alludes to but does not spend a great deal of time unpacking—it becomes clear that what DeAundra Peek (as well as other Atlanta-based drag queens) expanded was not so much southernness as *gayness*, or more specifically gay visibility, in the United States to include LGBTQ+ populations within Atlanta. They were, in effect, "unmooring" Atlanta from its associations with southernness (conservatism, whiteness, elitism, heteronormativity, and more) and essentially undoing the construction of southernness (along with race, gender, class) in the process. Appearing on public access television in a southern city as well as in clubs in New York, Minneapolis, and other cities around the country during the era of the AIDS crisis, DeAundra Peek used camp—defined by theorist Moe Meyer as "the process of the *social signification* of gayness—the production of gay social visibility"—to make known and give voice and vitality to gay identities within an urban center in the South, all the while signaling to her audience that Atlanta was a great place to be gay.[13]

It is important to keep in mind the particular context in which DeAundra and her counterparts thrived—specifically, Atlanta of the late 1980s to early 2000s. Historian James Sears reminds readers that there is not one gay identity or region: "Localities from Atlanta to Charlotte . . . are better understood as local queer ecologies: queer spaces occupied by various groups with differing beliefs, symbols, identities, lifestyles, languages, and interests operating inside a common border and within a cultural context of homophobia and heteronormativity."[14] As Wesley Chenault and Stacy Braukman write in the introduction to *Gay and Lesbian Atlanta*, the narratives of gay and lesbian Atlantans "were all shaped in part by the experience of living in Atlanta. Indeed, the histories of these men and women are inseparable from the history of the city itself."[15] From such scholarship, and from a memoir like *Lettin It All Hang Out* by Atlanta native RuPaul Charles, it is clear that it would have been an exciting time to be out and to be a drag queen in the city. Shymanski states, "We really had a great time in the '80s and '90s because Atlanta had a *fantastic* club scene back then. There were clubs in several different areas of town where you could [go] for shows—if not you, then someone you knew. Color-box, 788, Velvet—and the upstairs area Mr. Chuck Brand called the Popcorn Lounge."[16] According to Sears, nearly two dozen gay clubs existed in Atlanta in the 1970s, some of which "catered to black gays (although these were seldom listed in bar directories, gay newspapers, or entertainment magazines)." The drag scene had been growing since the mid-to-late 1960s, thanks to performers like Diamond Lil (Phillip Forrester) and Phyllis Killer (Billy Jones).[17] Atlanta was the "Hollywood of drag" in that era, Sears asserts, with "the preeminent showplace in the South" being Sweet Gum Head on Cheshire Bridge Road.[18]

It took several decades for Atlanta to emerge as a gay mecca. Despite its location "in the nation's most conservative region," Atlanta appealed to gay transplants because of its "economy and progressive image," an image cultivated over the decades by city leaders as they worked to make Atlanta understood nationally and internationally as "The City Too Busy to Hate."[19] The period of 1940 to 1970 was one of "quiet accommodation" as "quiet social networks" formed and grew.[20] There were female impersonators, such as Guy Dobbs, who performed at the Five O'Clock Supper Club as Little Gwendolyn, but drag shows happened mainly in "straight venues" during the 1950s and 1960s.[21] In these early years, gay Atlantans shared a fear of coming out, and for good reasons. Georgia's sodomy law was not ruled unconstitutional until 1998; in the Atlanta Library Perversion Case of 1953, police pursued men engaging in sexual acts at the Atlanta Public Library and then published their names in the city newspaper; police raids made Piedmont Park unsafe; and *Atlanta Constitution* editor Ralph McGill campaigned in print for "tougher sex crimes legislation as well as psychiatric treatments for offenders."[22] The "cultural configuration unique to the Bible Belt South," according to John Howard, led to such responses to homosexual activity in Atlanta just after World War II. "Elected officials, concerned with the state's expanding role in policing social morality, relied on religious precepts as guides to constructing public policy," he writes, while "law enforcers and judicial interpreters enlisted religious leaders in their campaigns to eradicate deviant sexualities."[23]

After the Stonewall Riots in 1969, a shift away from "quiet accommodation" occurred in Atlanta—more precisely, a shift from an "assimilationist homophile movement" to "gay liberation, gay pride, and diverse sexual and gender radical movements," marked in part by the emergence within the city of formal organizations devoted to improving the rights of LGBTQ+ individuals, an increase in the number of clubs for and events focused on gay and lesbian Atlantans, and the proliferation of magazines and newspapers cen-

FIGURE 12.3.
Atlanta's Pride 1992 parade featured DeAundra riding on the custom-made float for *Southern Voice*, painted by DeAundra's friend Quinn. Photo courtesy of Rosser Shymanski.

tered on gay life and social issues in Atlanta and the South more broadly. "The line between socializing and politics blurred during the 1970s," state Chenault and Braukman.[24] Publications such as *Southern Voice* were crucial for producing the "imagined communities," to borrow Benedict Anderson's phrase, of gay Atlantans—although these communities and the sense of belonging to and within them turned out to be quite real, evidenced in part by the growth of Pride Atlanta over the years from 250 attendees in 1971 to an estimated 200,000 in 2007 (see figure 12.3).[25] From 1990 forward, gay Atlantans began to gain more formal power in politics and through protests, such as the protests against Cracker Barrel in the metro area, in which DeAundra Peek participated, and against Cobb County for an antigay resolution, the latter resulting in no athletic events being held there for the 1996 Olympics.[26] Former mayor Shirley Franklin (in office 2002–10) was known for including gay advisers in her inner circle; Atlanta employers began to sponsor Pride Week; and the city began offering same-sex partner benefits to employees in 1993.[27]

The creation of gay spaces contributed to the success of the gay rights movement in Atlanta and to the flourishing of gay life in the city. The demographic shift of conservative whites to the suburbs during a period of "white flight," according to McPherson and others, "facilitated a thriving gay and lesbian culture" in Atlanta, with Midtown "emerg[ing] in the 1970s as ground zero for a nationally recognized gay community."[28] Shymanski says that he moved to 14th Street in Midtown in the early 1980s because it was the "hotbed of gay activity." "Midtown Atlanta was probably the closest thing to

Haight Ashbury I've ever seen," writes RuPaul, who at one point lived with fellow drag queens Lady Bunny and Floydd on the corner of 10th and Juniper. "It was a place where the misfits of [the Civil War], the lost and the wounded, would wind up. It was Misfitsville, and I fit right in. The gay community was also there, and all the artists too, because of the affordable housing."[29] According to Chenault and Braukman, a 1971 article in the national publication *David* included a map of "Gay Atlanta," highlighting areas in Midtown, on Ponce de Leon Avenue, and in Little Five Points.[30] Arnold Fleischmann and Jason Hardman mention these spaces as well, terming them "gay ghettos or safe havens" that became voting blocs with "political clout."[31]

It was in these areas that the drag scene thrived. RuPaul mentions having the clubs Cheetah 3, TV Dinner, Weekends (where he was a go-go dancer), Illusions, and Backstreet "within a four-block radius" of his apartment in Midtown.[32] Atlanta drag also traveled. Not only did RuPaul, perhaps the most widely known drag star, come out of Atlanta, but Lady Bunny (Jon Ingle) and Floydd (Bryan Chambers), who became popular drag performers in New York City, also got their start there. Shymanski traveled widely as DeAundra Peek while remaining based in Atlanta. He states, "us Atlanta folks would go visit everyone else. We went out to Los Angeles for SPEW 2, this underground fanzine fest, and then Pride in San Francisco and of course Lady Bunny's Wigstock [annual drag celebration in New York City] for years in the '90s. We'd go to Wigstock for four or five days, book some gigs at a couple of clubs—the Limelight, the Pyramid Club." Shymanski claims that "long-lasting friendships" were created at SPEW 2, and he emphasizes the significance of the underground zine movement in helping to create networks of performers across the country and to put Atlanta on the map. The summer 1992 issue of the Chicago-based black-and-queer-focused zine *THING* (tagline: "She Knows Who She Is") advertises an upcoming appearance by DeAundra, "Georgia's peach," at Chicago's Hothouse for a fundraiser for Illinois senatorial candidate Carol Moseley Braun (see figure 12.4); in the fall 1991 issue, editor Trent Adkins mentions running into DeAundra after her performance at the Limelight in New York the week after Lady Bunny's annual Wigstock extravaganza.[33] In Chicago, Shymanski says, he and others from Atlanta were "welcomed like superstars," as Dick Richards had entered videos of DeAundra and other Atlanta performers into gay film festivals around the country, including Chicago, and underground zines were spreading the word about Atlanta's scene. Back in Atlanta, DeAundra appeared at events around the city, including performing with the Peek Sisters as the final act at the twentieth anniversary of

FIGURE 12.4. Mona Foot, Joan Jett Blakk, and DeAundra at a 1992 Chicago benefit for the campaign of Carol Moseley Braun for U.S. Senate. Photo courtesy of Rosser Shymanski.

the Atlanta Gay Pride Festival in 1991, riding on *Southern Voice*'s Pride float in 1992, and serving in 1994 as emcee of the local Wigwood event, "a gender-bending block party that pays homage to the wig and raises funds for ACT UP Atlanta."[34]

The mention of the organization ACT UP Atlanta—the AIDS Coalition to Unleash Power, formed in 1988—is a potent reminder that with this period of excitement and liberation came fear and persecution. As Jim Grimsley poignantly writes of AIDS in the South, "The plague changed our bars, closed our sex rooms, made us learn how to put on condoms, changed our mating habits, infested our art."[35] The emergence of AIDS on the national and local scenes led to significant activist efforts on the part of Atlantans, including the formations of AID Atlanta, Project Open Hand, a chapter of People with AIDS, ACT UP, and Queer Nation, as well as the participation of many Atlantans in the 1987 March on Washington and the unfolding of the Names Quilt.

In the 1980s, the local press did nothing to alleviate the stigmas associated with homosexuality and/or having HIV/AIDS. Meredith Raimondo details the ways in which coverage of AIDS in the *Atlanta Journal-Constitution* was similar to that of other urban locales, noting further that "two specifically regional factors: a strong influence of religion and the state sodomy law" framed how the newspaper addressed the disease. That law, which the Supreme Court upheld in the 1986 case *Bowers vs. Hardwick*, created for activists "a barrier to the efforts . . . to educate Atlantans about safer sex"; "to identify as a gay man with AIDS," she writes, "was to admit breaking the law."[36] In the face of such prejudice, gay Atlantans persisted while resisting the narratives placed upon them. And one way many of them did so was through drag. A drag troupe known as the Armorettes, for example, was initially formed to entertain patrons during halftime of football games at the Armory, one of Midtown Atlanta's gay bars. During the height of the AIDS crisis, the Armorettes began focusing on educating patrons and continued to do so after AIDS receded from the forefront of public discussion. According to Jeffrey Bennett and Isaac West, these performers used "tactical repertoires of resistance, reminding patrons of the need to practice safe sex and proactively protect themselves from sexually transmitted diseases," which "provide a ritualized reminder of the communal obligations created by illnesses that quietly continue to kill men and women in the South." Bennett and West define the group's work as a form of "political intervention" and locate them within a historical lineage of drag performers who "gave voice to the injustices perpetrated on queers, publicly flaunted their queerness and lent their talents to raising funds for political causes."[37]

Bennett and West further claim that camp drag functions as a way to hit people from the side, getting an audience to laugh, which better allows its members to receive the message being sent. It also enables performers to say things that they might not say out of character. As Shymanski stated in an interview with Jarboe of the group Swans, "I think I get to burn to a crisp things from behind the façade of a character that maybe I keep to simmer as myself."[38] It would seem then that the Armorettes and DeAundra Peek both complement and contradict what Pugh warns against in *Precious Perversions*—that is, the limits of humor in producing significant social change. While he argues that humor in the South "assists in establishing gay and lesbian subcultures" and "a transgressively ironic, often mordant, comic sensibility served as a subcultural shibboleth to distinguish friends from foes," he also points to the limits of humor in "eradicating injustice or achieving the desired ends of social integration." He further warns—particularly in terms of camp—against being "excessively optimistic . . . about humor's seditious force. Camp humor reimagines possibilities of gender and culture, yet . . . a man putting on a dress and a tiara does not a revolution spark."[39]

While it is difficult, perhaps impossible, to measure the extent to which the camp drag performances of DeAundra Peek effected political or social change, her performances contributed to a larger movement toward increasing gay visibility, resistance, and pride, especially in the South of the 1980s and 1990s. Theoretical and historical scholarship on camp and drag (and camp drag) in recent years has shown it to be a political means for certain forms of activism, for sparking a sense of communal identity, and for bringing about emotional catharsis in the face of persecution. This holds true for camp drag in Atlanta. For while Atlanta was reputed to be a progressive urban environment during the late twentieth century, it was still located within a conservative region, as Raimondo and others remind us. Tara McPherson points out that Cobb County "sent Newt Gingrich to Washington in 1983"—the year that Shymanski arrived in the city—"and came to national prominence in 1993 by passing a resolution condemning the 'gay lifestyle.'"[40] Camp drag became a way for many gay Atlantans to find solace, escape, and community in an era of persecution from multiple sources. For performers, camp drag empowered them, giving them a form of agency and voice that can only be described as political. When asked during our interview about whether he conceived of DeAundra as political, Shymanski initially responded that anything political was "pseudo-accidental." Later on, he returned to this idea, stating:

> I guess we were kind of political just because we existed in the first place. We just said screw it, we are gonna do this, and we're gonna have a good time while we're doing it. And we aren't going to let anyone get us down. And that was not only just us, but there were several troupes of performers around town that we joined up with at various points. . . . The great thing was that what we found was that instead of competing against these other groups for the attention or the club gigs or whatever, we all approached it, all of us approached it, from a teaming up and a getting together and a joining forces sort of situation. . . . And that was a very powerful thing, to find such a great community of people. . . . Especially in the '90s and the real early 2000s, but especially the '90s, was a time in Atlanta when there was a show every single weekend that you could go to that either you were in or somebody you knew was in. It was very powerful because we were able to just go out and express ourselves and just be ourselves and be super-queer.

In this way, camp drag in Atlanta during the 1980s to the early 2000s (and perhaps beyond) was restorative. In his book *Camp Comforts: Reparative Gay Literature in Times of AIDS*, Christian Lassen discusses how ACT UP used camp "to cause a storm of protest and to draw attention to the disease and to the innumerable casualties and losses it has brought about."[41] Lassen understands camp as geared toward "both social change . . . and personal healing"; as subversive and restorative; as a "mode of enjoyment," as Susan Sontag first posited in "Notes on Camp" in 1964; and as "reparative," an adjective borrowed from Eve Kosofsky Sedgwick.[42] Jack Babuscio claimed in his 1977 essay "Camp and the Gay Sensibility" that camp serves as "a means of undercutting rage by its derision of concentrated bitterness. Its vision of the world is comic. Laughter, rather than tears, is its chosen means of dealing with the painfully incongruous situation of gays in society." "Usually overlooked by critics of the gay sensibility," writes Babuscio, "is camp's strategy of irony. Camp, through its introduction of style, aestheticism, humor, and theatricality, allows us to witness 'serious' issues with temporary detachment, so that only later, after the event, are we struck by the emotional and moral implications of what we have almost passively absorbed."[43]

Add to the mix that Shymanski and others were performing camp drag *on public access television* in Atlanta throughout the 1980s into the early 2000s. Here was the queer South on screen—or at least a few queer southerners—appearing on television Fridays and Saturdays at 10:30 p.m. DeAundra's shows were not limited to the space of a gay club in Midtown; rather, they were available to the masses—on Atlanta's PeopleTV channel (and in New York and Minneapolis, according to DeAundra herself); on videotape (available for purchase at one point through a companion website); and, in more recent years, on YouTube. It was through the public access medium that RuPaul Charles and Rosser Shymanski came to find a place of belonging in Atlanta. In his autobiography, RuPaul writes that when he first saw *The American Music Show* during the summer of 1981, he thought, "'That's where I belong.' I knew these were the people who would get my sense of humor and understand what I was doing."[44]

Through public access television, Dick Richards and his team broadcast queerness locally and, later on, thanks to the technological innovation of the internet, to the nation and the world. In so doing, they and the performers on screen were not expanding southernness per se, as McPherson argues, but rather expanding gayness—giving visibility to it as well as confirming camp drag's worth as a cultural reflection and production of queerness. Laura Linder confirms the role of public access programming in giving voice to marginalized groups. Because media outlets are driven by profit, larger companies opt for shows that will attract a large audience, and "in their quest for the largest audience, most media tend to omit or marginalize the people who are not in the broadest majority audience."[45] Public access television, however, allows "ordinary people with something to say" a space in which they can share their message, essentially offering groups or individuals an "electronic soapbox" from which they can offer "alternatives to the concentrated, commercial messages that dominate the mass media."[46] Linder claims that "for minorities this is especially important" because it allows them, as Jesikah Ross and Aaron Spitzer put it, to "represent themselves the way they choose to be represented."[47] In effect, public access television sought "to create community," "to empower people by . . . providing a form (video) and an outlet for their messages," "to encourage public discourse and diversity awareness," and "to use film and video technology to bring about social change."[48]

This certainly seems to have been true in Atlanta, where PeopleTV, founded in 1986, provided—and continues to provide today—an outlet for multiple populations' self-expression.[49] Perhaps RuPaul puts it best: "I am sure that the bright spark in Washington who thought up [public access television] imagined an endless series of worthy but dull shows about local rotary meetings. The last thing he would have imagined would have been a bunch of old hippies and drag queens seizing the airwaves."[50] According to Gabriel Gomez, while gay and lesbian "activists continue to seek greater representation in mainstream film and television products," public access television at that time already provided a space for "Queer centered programs" in the form of "Drag queen TV"—including *The Brenda and Glenda Show* in New York, *Decoupage* in Pasadena, and *DeAundra Peek's Hi Class Hall O' Fame Theatre* in Atlanta (which Gabriel Gomez labels—unfairly, I feel—as "cable access grunge").[51] In all of these shows, Gomez claims, drag performers "create forms of expression where the overtly political and the cultural coalesce in Queer identity that is visible, open, and powerful."[52] Visibility seems key: by virtue of these programs being public, shows like *DeAundra Peek's Teenage Music Club* or *DeAundra Peek's Youth Explosion* had the chance to reach a larger audience than a bar-based drag show might (although how widely viewed the show was at the time, and by whom, is impossible to determine). In turn, according to Shymanski, the show made getting gigs within the Atlanta bar-based drag scene easier for him and others because so many people had seen DeAundra and her friends on screen.

Beyond the cable access shows, Peek's column, titled "DeAundra's Dixie Diary," appeared in several issues of *THING*, the black queer zine published by Robert Ford in Chicago in the early 1990s.[53] In writing that column, which he and Ford and Ford's coeditor Trent Adkins conceived together, Shymanski states, "I got a chance to be a voice for Atlanta in Chicago for this segment of the population down here that needed to be told up there." In each "entry," DeAundra describes recent events in Atlanta's drag scene while further developing her character with anecdotes from the fictional trailer park. In the sixth issue, she introduces herself and the Atlanta drag scene to readers outside the region. DeAundra uses the column to highlight the drag stars who came out of the Atlanta scene, including RuPaul. "Me and my sorry sisters taught him everything he knows about make-up," she writes, "and he looks real pretty now that he's done fixed himself up and got that big hi-style recording contract on Tommy Boy."[54] In later issues, while highlighting what was happening in Atlanta's drag scene, she added to the fictional narrative of her life in Odum's Trailer Park: "Competition is fierce a 'tween T. O. Captain Duffy Odum and Sonya LaTrail Stubbs of Team Del Vista Ray Mar. Last time, durin' the three-legged vienner toss, Sonya LaTrail missed Duffy an' flew into the security ditch out back, flinging them vienner cans all over Rango Fain's Snack Shed's parkin' lot. Luckily, Nurse MacWorld was there an' got them splints on all them vienners so's they could finish playin,' an' a course Team Odum won, yeaaaaa!"[55] Included in each entry was always a recipe, whether it was Holiday Vienner Popcorn Balls, Twice Baked and Fried Vienners, or Vienner Roll Ups. According to producer Dick Richards, "Through her run on public access TV, DeAundra gained a loyal following. She did many personal appearances and charity events, became a darling in the gay punk zine culture, appeared on commercial television on *The Best of the Worst Show* on Fox, became a regular on *TV Pizza* on Channel 4 in London, and performed many times at Lady Bunny's Wigstock Festival in New York."[56] Although not as well known among mainstream audiences as RuPaul or Divine, DeAundra was legendary in her own right.

All of this brings us, finally, to the character of DeAundra Peek with her self-described "makeup philosophy" of "blue to the brow 'til death" and "do like me, y'all—don't wear too much makeup or you'll look cheap."[57] John Walker describes Peek as "sporting Farah Fawcett feathering and minty Karen Carpenter couture" and having "the infectious charisma of Tammy Faye Bakker and the naively self-assured conviction of Florence Foster Jenkins."[58] DeAundra, in fact, claimed her singing voice and "natural blonde hair" as her God-given gifts.[59]

Journalists and others often use the term "white trash" to describe DeAundra's appearance. A 1993 article in the *Atlanta Journal-Constitution* describes DeAundra as "the ever-gracious princess of trailer trash."[60] Tara McPherson writes, "It's a class-based performance, deploying a white trash veneer to mock the etiquette-driven, rule-bound fixation of southern culture and 'hospitality.' DeAundra Peek and Ruby Ann Boxcar are Mary Kay gone bad, trumping even Tammy Faye Bakker in their cosmetological finesse and retooling the image of both the redneck and dominant white femininity."[61] The mention of whiteness here is critical, and McPherson suggests that Peek's performance works to disrupt "regionally reified notions of whiteness, gender, and class."[62] In the words of Ragan Rhyne, white drag queens "denaturalize" whiteness. The "veneer" thus represents a means for questioning the politics not only of gender but of class and race. Simply put, camp drag is intersectional, as Rhyne claims, and "the codes of gender can be read only through these other axes." White drag queens, in particular, "might challenge the hegemony of whiteness through a complication of idealized femininity" as the "performance of imperfect femininity and imperfect class implies an imperfect whiteness."[63]

Rhyne sees this best demonstrated in Divine's performances in the films of John Waters, including *Pink Flamingos* (1972), *Female Trouble* (1974), and *Polyester* (1981); her performance of working-class, "white trash" femininity, Rhyne argues, reveals the excesses of whiteness.[64] Similar claims may be made about DeAundra Peek. While her blue eye shadow, rouge, and lipstick may be what first catch viewers' attention, Peek's foundation makeup is also significant. It often appears bright white—not cream or light beige but copy paper white. Although one might view it as clownish in style and although Shymanski says he used whatever makeup was around, the makeup often reads as "whiteface"—a means of highlighting whiteness as both performative/unreal and really not all that attractive. Such use of whiteface, in others words, preempts a successful performance of elite southern white femininity. The lovable DeAundra tries to embody the belle, through appearance and action. But every episode reminds viewers that she is from a trailer park southwest of Atlanta; that she consumes Vienna sausages from a can, as seen in many a cooking demo and in her song/video titled "I Eat Out of Cans" (to the tune of "I Am What I Am" from *La Cage aux Folles*); that she does not apply her makeup well; that she cannot sing on key; and (we are always aware, as is the case in most drag performances) that underneath, DeAundra is Shymanski, a man performing as a woman.[65] The appearance of DeAundra's column titled "DeAundra's Dixie Diary" in *THING*—geared toward a black queer audience in Chicago—suggests a deliberate attempt on the part of Shymanski and editor Robert Ford to disrupt racial norms and regional boundaries.

Peek destabilizes southern white femininity, as McPherson argues, but I do not see her "figuring different Souths" per se or serving as a representative of an "expansive southernness."[66] In other words, she does not break down some constructions (gender, race, class, sexuality) only to create new ones ("the South" and "southernness"). DeAundra's performance—relying on an affect that would indeed read as "southern" to most—is not about expanding southernness as much as it is about producing *an expansive queerness*, making at least part of "gay Atlanta" visible on screen in the midst of thriving gay rights activism in the southern metropolitan region. DeAundra's incorrect grammar and accented speech, her celebratory "Yeaaaaa," and her frequent use of "y'all" combine linguistically to reinforce viewers' perception of her southern identity, at the same time signaling that identity as a performed fiction. What emerges as real in the process is *queerness in the South*—on screen and beyond.

With her ritualized appearance on public access television every Friday and Saturday night, DeAundra Peek offered a representation of gay vitality and endurance in an era marked by AIDS-related loss and fear *and* by the ongoing homophobia and discrimination coming from multiple directions, including evangelicals and lawmakers in the conservative South. Perpetually confident, forever young, always positive, DeAundra Peek stood tall, singing her heart out, enjoying life to its fullest, with good friends and some "vienners" by her side. She and her show were something devoted viewers could count on.

Through highly entertaining campy scripts and performances, Peek's various shows regularly offer a celebration of gay identity and sexuality while subtly (and sometimes not so subtly) presenting alongside such celebration a critique of religious, evangelical, and conservative norms. RuPaul and DeAundra emerge out of these shows as heroines, stars, and role models while those typically held up as emblematic of "hi-class" social norms—Christian elites in certain parts of Atlanta, for example—are taken down a notch. In an episode of *Salon de Odum's*, after DeAundra covers RuPaul's "House of Love," Candi Suntop announces in the Current Events segment that, first, trailer park owner Maxine Odum has proclaimed her "top three choices, in no particular order, for Grand Marshal of Odum's Founder's Day Parade—Starbooty [RuPaul's character in a film of the same name], Lassie and Timmy, Michael Jackson," and, second, at Snopes's Evangelical Mobile Home Park in Buckhead, a wealthy area of Atlanta, a woman had her trailer pulled over because of a septic tank overflow. Duffy Odum, the "facilitator" of the salon, then introduces a video of "an interpretative dance of arts and crafts"—which turns out to be a risqué clip from a RuPaul film. "Wrong tape," says Duffy Odum.[67] Here DeAundra and her sidekicks poke at various hierarchies of class (as linked to religiosity) and propriety. The typically chaotic nature of the show often masks what is really being shared: DeAundra and friends rapidly deliver their quips using erratic grammar; they regularly talk over one another, loudly; one person is usually yelling "Yeaaaaaa!" while another is speaking; and all seem to possess a certain kinetic energy, meaning that one or more is always moving on screen.

When a viewer breaks through the noise, it is impossible to miss the references to gay male sexuality, in particular. The cooking demos, consistently featuring an innovative combination of the phallic Vienna ("vienner") sausages with creamy white Miracle Whip and O'Boisies (oh-*boy*-zees), alone provide sexual innuendo. When asked about the choice to use Vienna sausages and their potential phallic implications, Shymanski said it was more about choosing a disgusting, inexpensive food commodity and making the recipes as gross as possible. At shows in Atlanta and elsewhere, DeAundra would prepare a recipe on stage but have prepared in advance a tray of samples to hand out to audience members. Also, part of the formulaic aspect of each episode involved Candi's opening the can of Vienna sausages during the cooking demo segment, at which point DeAundra would put her microphone next to the can and say, "There's nothing like the sound of a can of vienners openin' up."

DeAundra and her sidekicks regularly contribute to such undertones. In an episode of *Hi Class Hall O' Fame Theatre*, for example, DeAundra and Duffy "sing" a duet, which consists of a conversation about "vienners" and trailer underpinnings, the sexual "underpinnings" of which are fairly blatant.

DEAUNDRA. Say, lookahere, Duffy Odum, I bet you don't know whether you got more vienners than me or not.
DUFFY. I bet I got more vienners than you because that's really hi-class.
DEAUNDRA. I tell you what.
DUFFY. What?
DEAUNDRA. Lookahere, Duffy Odum. Ain't you gonna show me all those vienners?
DUFFY. I don't know whether I want to show you them vienners or not.
DEAUNDRA. Well, I tell you what.
DUFFY. What?
DEAUNDRA. I betcha I got more underpinning down there on my trailer at Odum's than you has got.

DUFFY. I bet you don't. I bet my underpinning is more hi-class than yours cuz I got more of it. More acreage.

DEAUNDRA. I bet you ain't.

DUFFY. I bet you I got more hi-class than you.

DEAUNDRA. More hi-class what?

DUFFY. Stuff!

BOTH. Yeaaaaaaaa![68]

They quickly move on to the Duffy Odum Parable Segment, in which Duffy shares an allegedly biblically inspired lesson. DeAundra pronounces, "Y'all know it's real hi-class on account of cuz them parables is something's come out of the bible, and that's about as hi-class as you can get." Duffy's parable, titled "Hi-Class Videos" and written by Rev. J. T. Stovall (a character from *The American Music Show*), informs listeners that if someone has DeAundra's or RuPaul's videos, it is because "sometimes these video help us," reads Duffy. He continues, "When a boy is thinking about doing something he knows is wrong, one look at a picture of RuPaul in his video may decide for him to do something right." "Yeaaaaaaaaaaaa!" screams DeAundra. Duffy continues to read the parable, stating that pictures from RuPaul's videos "are meant to influence us sometimes to fight or work a little harder or to gain sympathy. I hope in every little boy and every little girl's room you have a picture of RuPaul . . . and it would be nice to see a picture of DeAundra there as well." Again, DeAundra and RuPaul emerge as the paragons of virtue, as aspirational figures to be admired, as symbols of goodness and righteousness rather than as sinners or abominations.

In general, DeAundra's shows and segments exude a particular kind of carnivalesque joy. Carnivalesque, in the Bakhtinian sense, is summarized by Peter Stallybrass and Allon White as "a potent, populist, critical inversion of *all* official words and hierarchies," "a festive critique, through the inversion of hierarchy, of the 'high' culture."[69] Critics of Bakhtin point to the fact that carnival is "a *licensed* affair" (that is, those in power allow it to happen for a finite period of time). Stallybrass and White acknowledge that carnival may have "no noticeable politically transformative effects" for a period of time, but they conclude that "it may often act as *catalyst* and *site of actual and symbolic struggle*."[70] Essential to the ritual of carnival was the grotesque body of the participants—"the marginal, the low and the outside from the perspective of a classical body situated as high, inside and central"—which often reflected a Foucauldian "transgression," or "a kind of reverse or counter-sublimation, undoing the discursive hierarchies and stratifications of bodies and cultures which bourgeois society has produced as the mechanism of its symbolic dominance."[71] Along these lines, DeAundra and her gang offered representations of the grotesque often associated with southern literature, but *without* the implication of moral or spiritual incompleteness that a writer like Flannery O'Connor signaled via her characters' physical oddities. Quite the opposite in the case of DeAundra and her friends, as they were manifestations of joy, pride, and completeness in the face of a world trying to silence them. Perhaps instead, with all their quirks—the often hard-to-follow banter between DeAundra and her costars, the endearing awkwardness of the childlike Duffy Odum (and his piercing stare), the ever-present petite and phallic Vienna sausages mixed with Miracle Whip and O'Boisies, music videos featuring DeAundra's loud and off-key singing of parodies like "Losing My Vienners" or her remake of RuPaul's "Supermodel"[72]—they served up for viewers one delicious dish of grace. Every week for almost twenty years, Rosser Shymanski and friends brought their "transgressions" to Atlanta viewers via their cast of characters, breaking out of the closet to which gay Atlantans and southerners more broadly had been confined and rejecting cloaks of invisibility in favor of organza gowns. In turn, they brought visibility to gay life in the South, claiming camp drag and the space of public access television as their own. And for that, we should all yell, "Yeaaaaaa!"

NOTES

The epigraphs are from Jim Grimsley, "Myth and Reality: The Story of Gay People in the South," *Out in the South*, ed. Carlos L. Dews and Carolyn Leste Law (Philadelphia: Temple University Press, 2001), 229–35, at 235; and "The Funtone USA Museum," www.funtone.com/index.html.

1. The sidekicks did not perform in drag, although they were in costume. Duffy Odum—described by Dick Richards as "a learning-challenged little boy"—was played by Paul Burke, who went on to play the character of Ralph Bailey, Fred Willard's cohost on the Comedy Central show *Access America*. Candi Suntop was played by Potsy Duncan, girlfriend of Atlanta City Council member James Bond, brother of Julian Bond. According to Richards, he and Bond started *The American Music Show* on radio station WRFG and in 1980 began to produce the television show in the basement of Bond's mother's home, soon after Bond had helped to negotiate a contract with Cable America that included "a generous public access component"; see Carolyn Rivera, "Nelson Sullivan, Funtone USA and *The American Music Show*," nelsonsullivan.com/more-about-nelson.html.

2. Georgia Public Broadcasting Creative, "Your GPB Rosser Shymanski," 2014, vimeo.com/89615532; RuPaul, *Lettin It All Hang Out* (New York: Hyperion, 1995), 58. Shymanski says that the moniker "the fabulous Rosser" came from Fabulous Rosser

Originals, the name of his company at the time. In his early days in Atlanta, Shymanski created splatter-painted T-shirts and other artwork on the patio of his Midtown apartment and would occasionally showcase his work on *The American Music Show*.

3. John Walker, "The (Drag) Queen of '90s Public Access TV Is Ready to Reign Once More," *Splinter*, splinternews.com/the-drag-queen-of-90s-public-access-tv-is-ready-to-re-1793860128. For more information on the origins of *The American Music Show*, see nelsonsullivan.com/more-about-nelson.html. All episodes of *The American Music Show* are archived in the Stuart A. Rose Manuscript, Archives, and Rare Book Library at Emory University.

4. Rosser Shymanski, personal interview, 10 August 2017. All quotations of Shymanski are taken from this interview, unless otherwise noted.

5. DeAundra was one of many characters that Shymanski performed over the years; others included Your Aunt Roz and Nurse MacWorld. According to Shymanski, Richards "asked me to do some characters onscreen. I started creating characters based on need. One week, they might need a farmer. The next week, a mailman. One week, they decided to do the Peek sisters, and so I picked a name, put on the makeup, and DeAundra was born. We became this overnight sensation in Atlanta, and by 1988 we were doing a bunch of gigs at Club Rio downtown" (John Walker, "The (Drag) Queen of '90s Public Access TV"). Dick Richards offers a similar narrative about DeAundra's "birth" (Carolyn Rivera, "Nelson Sullivan").

6. Carolyn Rivera, "Nelson Sullivan"; Shymanski, personal interview. Shymanski describes the shows as much like a "video playback show" of the 1980s and 1990s. DeAundra and friends would engage in banter and introduce videos to viewers throughout the show, including work by artists out of San Francisco as well as videos from *The Now Explosion*, Atlanta's music show from the early 1970s (predating MTV).

7. Shymanski stopped performing as DeAundra following his partner Rodney's death from liver cancer. However, he says that he has not completely sworn off show business or performing as DeAundra in the future.

8. Tison Pugh, *Precious Perversions: Humor, Homosexuality, and the Southern Literary Canon* (Baton Rouge: Louisiana State University Press, 2016), 6. Scholars such as Pugh, Michael Bibler, Pippa Holloway, and Gary Richards have made significant contributions to the field of queer southern studies and have paved the way for further examination of LGBTQ+ lives and identities within southern literature and history.

9. Tara McPherson, *Reconstructing Dixie: Race, Gender, and Nostalgia in the Imagined South* (Durham, N.C.: Duke University Press, 2003), 202. See also Ruby Ann Boxcar's blog at http://rubyannboxcar.blogspot.com/.

10. McPherson, *Reconstructing Dixie*, 196, 203.

11. McPherson, *Reconstructing Dixie*, 243, 196, 202.

12. McPherson, *Reconstructing Dixie*, 195 (emphasis mine), 203.

13. DeAundra Peek, "DeAundra's Dixie Diary," *THING* 6 (Summer 1992): 51; Moe Meyer, *An Archaeology of Posing: Essays on Camp, Drag, and Sexuality* (Madison,

Wisc.: Macater Press, 2010), 4. My thanks to Elliott Kuecker, formerly at the Oxford College Library, for helping me track down Peek's "DeAundra's Dixie Diary" entries. In this column Peek indicated that her shows appeared not only on public access television in Atlanta but in New York and Minneapolis as well.

14. James T. Sears, *Rebels, Rubyfruit, and Rhinestones: Queering Space in the Stonewall South* (New Brunswick, N.J.: Rutgers University Press, 2001), 319.

15. Wesley Chenault and Stacy Braukman, *Gay and Lesbian Atlanta* (Charleston: Arcadia, 2008), 8.

16. Walker, "The (Drag) Queen of '90s Public Access TV," emphasis in original.

17. Sears, *Rebels, Rubyfruit, and Rhinestones*, 286, 81–82.

18. Sears, *Rebels, Rubyfruit, and Rhinestones*, 153.

19. For an extensive discussion of LGBTQ+ Atlanta history, see Wesley Chenault's doctoral dissertation, "An Unspoken Past: Atlanta Lesbian and Gay History, 1940–1970" (University of New Mexico, 2008). For more on the efforts of Atlanta's business and political leaders to shape Atlanta's post–World War II development and reputation, see Clarence N. Stone, *Regime Politics: Governing Atlanta, 1946–1988* (Lawrence: University Press of Kansas, 1989); Ronald H. Bayor, *Race and the Shaping of Twentieth-Century Atlanta* (Chapel Hill: University of North Carolina Press, 1996); Charles Rutheiser, *Imagineering Atlanta: The Politics of Place in the City of Dreams* (London: Verso, 1996); Frederick Allen, *Atlanta Rising: The Invention of an International City, 1946–1996* (Marietta, Ga.: Longstreet, 1996); Larry Keating, *Atlanta: Race, Class, and Urban Expansion* (Philadelphia: Temple University Press, 2001); and Kevin M. Kruse, *White Flight: Atlanta and the Making of Modern Conservatism* (Princeton, N.J.: Princeton University Press, 2005).

20. Chenault and Braukman, *Gay and Lesbian Atlanta*, 29.

21. Chenault and Braukman, *Gay and Lesbian Atlanta*, 47.

22. John Howard, "The Library, the Park, and the Pervert: Public Space and Homosexual Encounter in Post–World War II Atlanta," *Carryin' On in the Lesbian and Gay South*, ed. John Howard (New York: New York University Press, 1997), 107–31, at 117; Arnold Fleischmann and Jason Hardman, "Hitting Below the Bible Belt: The Development of the Gay Rights Movement in Atlanta," *Journal of Urban Affairs* 26.4 (2004): 407–26, at 413–14.

23. Howard, "The Library, the Park, and the Pervert," 108.

24. Chenault and Braukman, *Gay and Lesbian Atlanta*, 59.

25. "History of Atlanta Pride," AtlantaPride.org, atlantapride.org/about/history. On imagined communities, see Benedict Anderson, *Imagined Communities: Reflections on the Origin and Spread of Nationalism* (London: Verso, 2016).

26. Chenault and Braukman, *Gay and Lesbian Atlanta*, 103–7.

27. Fleischmann and Hardman, "Hitting Below the Bible Belt," 421–22.

28. McPherson, *Reconstructing Dixie*, 193.

29. RuPaul, *Lettin It All Hang Out*, 74–75.

30. Chenault and Braukman, *Gay and Lesbian Atlanta*, 60, 65.

31. Fleischmann and Hardman, "Hitting Below the Bible Belt," 418–20.

32. RuPaul, *Lettin It All Hang Out*, 75.

33. "Every Thing to Go," *THING* 6 (Summer 1992): 6; Trent Adkins, "Parties and Other Tee," *THING* 5 (Fall 1991): 40.

34. Paula Crouch Thrasher, "Gay Pride Festival Has Reunion, Parade," *Atlanta Journal-Constitution* 22 June 1991; DeAundra Peek, "DeAundra's Dixie Diary," *THING* 8 (Winter 1992/93): 45; "Peach Buzz," *Atlanta Journal-Constitution*, 20 May 1994. DeAundra Peek came to life in a city seemingly welcoming of a diversity of LGBTQ+ populations, but it is also worth acknowledging that DeAundra and her drag counterparts performed in a social scene dominated by white men (even as images from the era suggest that interracial interaction occurred within drag clubs). A full history of gay men and women of color in Atlanta (and in many places throughout the United States) and of interracial social networks among LGBTQ+ populations has yet to be written.

35. Grimsley, "Myth and Reality," 234.

36. Meredith Raimondo, "Dateline *Atlanta*: Place and the Social Construction of AIDS," in Howard, *Carryin' On*, 331–59, at 355–56.

37. Jeffrey Bennett and Isaac West, "'United We Stand, Divided We Fall': AIDS, Armorettes, and the Tactical Repertoires of Drag," *Southern Communication Journal* 74.3 (2009): 301–6.

38. For this interview, see Dennis Cooper, "DeAundra Peek Teenage Superstar Day," 2 September 2016, denniscooperblog.com/deaundra-peek-teenage-superstar-day.

39. Pugh, *Precious Perversions*, 9–10.

40. McPherson, *Reconstructing Dixie*, 195.

41. Christian Lassen, *Camp Comforts: Reparative Gay Literature in Times of AIDS* (Bielefeld: Transcript-Verlag, 2011), 12.

42. Lassen, *Camp Comforts*, 13, 26–31.

43. Jack Babuscio, "Camp and the Gay Sensibility," *Camp Grounds: Style and Homosexuality*, ed. David Bergman (Amherst: University of Massachusetts Press, 1993), 19–38, at 28.

44. RuPaul, *Lettin It All Hang Out*, 58.

45. Laura R. Linder, *Public Access Television: America's Electronic Soapbox* (Westport, Conn.: Praeger, 1999), xxiii.

46. Linder, *Public Access*, xxvi–xxvii.

47. Jesikah Maria Ross and J. Aaron Spitzer, "Public Access Television: The Message, the Medium, and the Movement," *Art Papers* 18.3 (May 1994): 43, quoted in Linder, *Public Access*, xxvi.

48. Linder, *Public Access*, xxvi.

49. PeopleTV, "About Us," www.peopletv.org. PeopleTV's mission "is to provide the Atlanta Community a voice through Public Access to Media Technology. . . . We are strong advocates of the right of Public Access and freedom of speech as provided by the First Amendment of the U.S. Constitution." From the highlights reel that appears on the channel's website, it appears that PeopleTV has been widely used by people of color in Atlanta.

50. RuPaul, *Lettin It All Hang Out*, 58.

51. Gabriel Gomez, "DQTV: Public Access Queers," *Fuse* 17.1 (1993): 8–11, at 8–9.

52. Gomez, "DQTV," 11.

53. For more information on Robert Ford, see the website for the exhibition titled "THINGS: A Queer Legacy of Graphic Art and Play," *ONE Archives at the USC Libraries*, one.usc.edu/things-a-queer-legacy-of-graphic-art-and-play/. See also Holland Cotter, "Art of the AIDS Years: What Took Museums So Long?" *New York Times* 28 Jul. 2016.

54. DeAundra Peek, "DeAundra's Dixie Diary," *THING* 6 (Summer 1992): 51.

55. DeAundra Peek, "DeAundra's Dixie Diary," *THING* 9 (Spring 1993): 42.

56. Rivera, "Nelson Sullivan."

57. Richard Gincel, "Quickies: Peeking at the Roots of a Hip Singer/Model," *Atlanta Journal-Constitution* 20 August 1993.

58. Walker, "The (Drag) Queen of '90s Public Access TV."

59. Gincel, "Quickies."

60. Gincel, "Quickies."

61. McPherson, *Reconstructing Dixie*, 195.

62. McPherson, *Reconstructing Dixie*, 202.

63. Ragan Rhyne, "Racializing White Drag," *The Drag Queen Anthology: The Absolutely Fabulous but Flawlessly Customary World of Female Impersonators*, ed. Steven P. Schacht and Lisa Underwood (Binghamton, N.Y.: Haworth, 2004), 181–94, at 187–88.

64. Rhyne, "Racializing White Drag," 190.

65. "I Eat Out of Cans" is available at www.youtube.com/watch?v=uktMXuSC5Ro. Many episodes of DeAundra's various shows may be found on misterrichardson's YouTube channel (presumably posted by producer Dick Richards).

66. McPherson, *Reconstructing Dixie*, 195.

67. "House of Love," *Salon de Odum's*, www.youtube.com/watch?v=sTkx50Z9mNQ, posted 19 January 2017.

68. Untitled episode of *DeAundra Peek's Hi Class Hall O' Fame Theatre*, www.youtube.com/watch?v=tggMqvwppb4, posted 2 February 2011.

69. Peter Stallybrass and Allon White, *The Politics and Poetics of Transgression* (London: Methuen, 1986), 7.

70. Stallybrass and White, *Politics and Poetics*, 14.

71. Stallybrass and White, *Politics and Poetics*, 23, 200–201.

72. DeAundra's version of "Supermodel" appears to have been shown alongside RuPaul's original and Jennie Livingston's film *Paris Is Burning* at the Whitney Museum of American Art in January 1995 as part of the film and video program of an exhibition titled *Black Male: Representations of Masculinity in Contemporary American Art*. See archive.org/details/blackmalebrochur2123unse.

Selected Bibliography

This selected bibliography compiles major works related to queerness, queer theory, Southern Studies, and southern cinema, television, and other media, primarily those cited in this volume. See each essay for additional sources relevant to its specific critical intervention.

Abley, Sean. *Out in the Dark: Interviews with Gay Horror Filmmakers, Actors, and Authors.* Maple Shade, N.J.: Lethe Press, 2012.

Ahmed, Sara. *The Cultural Politics of Emotion.* 2nd ed. Edinburgh: Edinburgh University Press, 2014.

Altman, Dennis. *AIDS in the Mind of America.* Garden City, N.Y.: Anchor Press/Doubleday, 1987.

Anderson, Eric Gary, Taylor Hagood, and Daniel Cross Turner, eds. *Undead Souths: The Gothic and Beyond in Southern Literature and Culture.* Baton Rouge: Louisiana State University Press, 2015.

Balio, Tino. *The Foreign Film Renaissance on American Screens, 1946–1973.* Madison: University of Wisconsin Press, 2010.

Barker, Deborah E. *Reconstructing Violence: The Southern Rape Complex in Film and Literature.* Baton Rouge: Louisiana State University Press, 2015.

Barker, Deborah, and Kathryn McKee, eds. *American Cinema and the Southern Imaginary.* Athens: University of Georgia Press, 2011.

Bassett, John E., ed. *Defining Southern Literature: Perspectives and Assessments, 1831–1952.* Cranbury, N.J.: Associated University Presses, 1997.

Benshoff, Harry M. *Monsters in the Closet: Homosexuality and the Horror Film.* Manchester: Manchester University Press, 1997.

Bergman, David, ed. *Camp Grounds: Style and Homosexuality.* Amherst: University of Massachusetts Press, 1993.

Berlant, Lauren, and Lee Edelman. *Sex, or the Unbearable.* Durham, N.C.: Duke University Press, 2014.

Bersani, Leo. *Homos.* Cambridge, Mass.: Harvard University Press, 1995.

Bibler, Michael P. *Cotton's Queer Relations: Same-Sex Intimacy and the Literature of the Southern Plantation, 1936–1968*. Charlottesville: University of Virginia Press, 2009.

———. "Introduction: Smash the Mason-Dixon! or, Manifesting the Southern United States." *PMLA* 131.1 (2016): 153–56.

———. "Queering the Region." *The Cambridge Companion to the Literature of the American South*. Ed. Sharon Monteith. New York: Cambridge University Press, 2013. 188–203.

Bingham, Shawn Chandler, and Lindsey A. Freeman, eds. *The Bohemian South: Creating Countercultures, from Poe to Punk*. Chapel Hill: University of North Carolina Press, 2017.

Bone, Martyn. *The Postsouthern Sense of Place in Contemporary Fiction*. Baton Rouge: Louisiana State University Press, 2005.

Botting, Fred. *Gothic*. New York: Routledge, 1996.

Brasell, R. Bruce. *The Possible South: Documentary Film and the Limitations of Biraciality*. Jackson: University of Mississippi Press, 2015.

Brim, Matt. *James Baldwin and the Queer Imagination*. Ann Arbor: University of Michigan Press, 2014.

Brode, Douglas. *Dream West: Politics and Religion in Cowboy Movies*. Austin: University of Texas Press, 2013.

Brooks, Peter. *The Melodramatic Imagination: Balzac, Henry James, Melodrama, and the Mode of Excess*. New Haven, Conn.: Yale University Press, 1976.

Brown, Trent, ed. *Sex and Sexuality in Modern Southern Culture*. Baton Rouge: Louisiana State University Press, 2017.

Butler, Judith. *Gender Trouble: Feminism and the Subversion of Identity*. New York: Routledge, 1990.

Cagle, Chris. "Imaging the Queer South: Southern Lesbian and Gay Documentary." *Between the Sheets, In the Streets: Queer, Lesbian, and Gay Documentary*. Ed. Chris Holmlund and Cynthia Fuchs. Minneapolis: University of Minnesota Press, 1997. 30–45.

Campbell, Edward D. C., Jr. *The Celluloid South: Hollywood and the Southern Myth*. Knoxville: University of Tennessee Press, 1981.

Caserio, Robert L., Lee Edelman, Jack [Judith] Halberstam, José Esteban Muñoz, and Tim Dean. "Forum: The Antisocial Thesis in Queer Theory." *PMLA* 121.3 (2006): 819–28.

Cash, W. J. *The Mind of the South*. New York: Knopf, 1941.

Chamberlin, J. Edward, and Sander L. Gilman, eds. *Degeneration: The Dark Side of Progress*. New York: Columbia University Press, 1985.

Chenault, Wesley, and Stacy Braukman. *Gay and Lesbian Atlanta*. Charleston: Arcadia, 2008.

Clover, Carol J. *Men, Women, and Chain Saws: Gender in the Modern Horror Film*. Princeton, N.J.: Princeton University Press, 1992.

Courtney, Susan. *Split-Screen Nation: Moving Images of the American West and South*. New York: Oxford University Press, 2017.

Cox, Karen L. *Dreaming of Dixie: How the South Was Created in American Popular Culture*. Chapel Hill: University of North Carolina Press, 2011.
Davis, Angela Y. *Blues Legacies and Black Feminism: Gertrude "Ma" Rainey, Bessie Smith, and Billie Holiday*. New York: Vintage, 1998.
Dean, Tim. *Beyond Sexuality*. Chicago: University of Chicago Press, 2000.
DeAngelis, Michael, ed. *Reading the Bromance: Homosocial Relationships in Film and Television*. Detroit, Mich.: Wayne State University Press, 2014.
Deleuze, Gilles, and Félix Guattari. *A Thousand Plateaus: Capitalism and Schizophrenia*. Trans. Brian Massumi. London: Bloomsbury, 1987.
Demory, Pamela, ed. *Queer/Adaptation: A Collection of Critical Essays*. New York: Palgrave Macmillan, 2019.
Dews, Carlos L., and Carolyn Leste Law, eds. *Out in the South*. Philadelphia: Temple University Press, 2001.
Dinshaw, Carolyn. *How Soon Is Now? Medieval Texts, Amateur Readers, and the Queerness of Time*. Durham, N.C.: Duke University Press, 2012.
Dollimore, Jonathan. *Sexual Dissidence: Augustine to Wilde, Freud to Foucault*. New York: Oxford University Press, 1991.
Douglas, Mary. *Purity and Danger: An Analysis of the Concepts of Pollution and Taboo*. New York: Routledge, 1966.
Duck, Leigh Anne. *The Nation's Region: Southern Modernism, Segregation, and U.S. Nationalism*. Athens: University of Georgia Press, 2006.
Duggan, Lisa. "Down There: The Queer South and the Future of History Writing." *GLQ: A Journal of Lesbian and Gay Studies* 8.3 (2002): 379–87.
Edelman, Lee. *No Future: Queer Theory and the Death Drive*. Durham, N.C.: Duke University Press, 2004.
Elliott-Smith, Darren. "The Homosexual Vampire as a Metaphor for . . . the Homosexual Vampire? *True Blood*, Homonormativity, and Assimilation." *True Blood: Investigating Vampires and the Southern Gothic*. Ed. Brigid Cherry. London: Tauris, 2012. 139–58.
———. *Queer Horror Film and Television: Sexuality and Masculinity at the Margins*. London: Tauris, 2016.
Fleischmann, Arnold, and Jason Hardman. "Hitting Below the Bible Belt: The Development of the Gay Rights Movement in Atlanta." *Journal of Urban Affairs* 26.4 (2004): 407–26.
Freeman, Elizabeth. *Time Binds: Queer Temporalities, Queer Histories*. Durham, N.C.: Duke University Press, 2010.
French, Warren, ed. *The South and Film*. Jackson: University Press of Mississippi, 1981.
Gilbert, James. *Men in the Middle: Searching for Masculinity in the 1950s*. Chicago: University of Chicago Press, 2005.
Goddu, Teresa A. "The Ghost of Race: Edgar Allan Poe and the Southern Gothic." *Criticism and the Color Line: Desegregating American Literary Studies*. Ed. Henry B. Wonham. New Brunswick, N.J.: Rutgers University Press, 1996. 230–50.
———. *Gothic America: Narrative, History, and Nation*. New York: Columbia University Press, 1997.

Graham, Allison. *Framing the South: Hollywood, Television, and Race during the Civil Rights Struggle*. Baltimore: Johns Hopkins University Press, 2001.
Greeson, Jennifer Rae. *Our South: Geographic Fantasy and the Rise of National Literature*. Cambridge, Mass.: Harvard University Press, 2010.
Grosz, Elizabeth. "Experimental Desire: Rethinking Queer Subjectivity." *Supposing the Subject*. Ed. Joan Copjec. New York: Verso, 1994. 133–58.
Guerrero, Ed. *Framing Blackness: The African American Image in Film*. Philadelphia: Temple University Press, 1993.
Halberstam, Jack [Judith]. *In a Queer Time and Place: Transgender Bodies, Subcultural Lives*. New York: New York University Press, 2005.
———. *Skin Shows: Gothic Horror and the Technology of Monsters*. Durham, N.C.: Duke University Press, 1995.
Haritaworn, Jin, Adi Kuntsman, and Silvia Posocco, eds. *Queer Necropolitics*. New York: Routledge, 2014.
Harker, Jaime. "'And You Too, Sister, Sister?': Lesbian Sexuality, *Absalom, Absalom!*, and the Reconstruction of the Southern Family." *Faulkner's Sexualities*. Ed. Annette Trefzer and Ann J. Abadie. Jackson: University Press of Mississippi, 2010. 38–53.
———. *The Lesbian South: Southern Feminists, the Women in Print Movement, and the Queer Literary Canon*. Chapel Hill: University of North Carolina Press, 2018.
Hill, Mike, ed. *Whiteness: A Critical Reader*. New York: New York University Press, 1997.
Hinrichsen, Lisa, Gina Caison, and Stephanie Rountree, eds. *Small-Screen Souths: Region, Identity, and the Cultural Politics of Television*. Baton Rouge: Louisiana State University Press, 2017.
Hocquenghem, Guy. *Homosexual Desire*. Trans. Daniella Dangoor. 1978. Durham, N.C.: Duke University Press, 1993.
Holland, Sharon Patricia. *The Erotic Life of Racism*. Durham, N.C.: Duke University Press, 2012.
Holloway, Pippa. "Manifesto for a Queer South Politics." *PMLA* 131.1 (2016): 182–86.
Howard, John, ed. *Carryin' On in the Lesbian and Gay South*. New York: New York University Press, 1997.
———. *Men Like That: A Southern Queer History*. Chicago: University of Chicago Press, 1999.
Johnson, E. Patrick. *Black. Queer. Southern. Women.: An Oral History*. Chapel Hill: University of North Carolina Press, 2018.
———. "'Quare' Studies, or (Almost) Everything I Know about Queer Studies I Learned from My Grandmother." *Text and Performance Quarterly* 21 (2001): 1–25.
———. *Sweet Tea: Black Gay Men of the South*. Chapel Hill: University of North Carolina Press, 2008.
Johnson, E. Patrick, and Mae G. Henderson, eds. *Black Queer Studies: A Critical Anthology*. Durham, N.C.: Duke University Press, 2005.

Jones, Anne Goodwyn, and Susan V. Donaldson, eds. *Haunted Bodies: Gender and Southern Texts.* Charlottesville: University of Virginia Press, 1998.
Jones, John Bush. *Reinventing Dixie: Tin Pan Alley's Songs and the Creation of the Mythic South.* Baton Rouge: Louisiana State University Press, 2015.
Jones, Suzanne W., and Sharon Monteith, eds. *South to a New Place: Region, Literature, Culture.* Baton Rouge: Louisiana State University Press, 2002.
Kimmel, Michael. *Manhood in America: A Cultural History.* New York: Free Press, 1996.
King, Richard H. *A Southern Renaissance: The Cultural Awakening of the American South, 1930–1955.* New York: Oxford University Press, 1980.
King, Richard H., and Helen Taylor, eds. *Dixie Debates: Perspectives on Southern Cultures.* New York: New York University Press, 1996.
Kirby, Jack Temple. *Media-Made Dixie: The South in the American Imagination.* Rev. ed. Athens: University of Georgia Press, 1986.
Kreyling, Michael. *The South That Wasn't There: Postsouthern Memory and History.* Baton Rouge: Louisiana State University Press, 2010.
Langman, Larry, and David Ebner, comps. *Hollywood's Image of the South: A Century of Southern Films.* Westport, Conn.: Greenwood, 2001.
Lassen, Christian. *Camp Comforts: Reparative Gay Literature in Times of AIDS.* Bielefeld: Transcript-Verlag, 2011.
Lechner, Zachary J. *The South of the Mind: American Imaginings of White Southernness, 1960–1980.* Athens: University of Georgia Press, 2018.
Leiter, Andrew B., ed. *Southerners on Film: Essays on Hollywood Portrayals since the 1970s.* Jefferson, N.C.: McFarland, 2011.
Lewis, R. W. B. *The American Adam: Innocence, Tragedy, and Tradition in the Nineteenth Century.* Chicago: University of Chicago Press, 1955.
Linder, Laura R. *Public Access Television: America's Electronic Soapbox.* Westport, Conn.: Praeger, 1999.
Lloyd, Christopher. "Southern Gothic." *American Gothic Culture: An Edinburgh Companion.* Ed. Joel Faflak and Jason Haslam. Edinburgh: Edinburgh University Press, 2016. 79–91.
Love, Heather. *Feeling Backward: Loss and the Politics of Queer History.* Cambridge, Mass.: Harvard University Press, 2007.
MacCormack, Patricia. *Cinesexuality.* London: Routledge, 2008.
Marshall, Bridget M. "Defining Southern Gothic." *Southern Gothic Literature.* Ed. Jay Ellis. Ipswich, Mass.: Salem Press, 2013. 3–18.
Martin, Robert K., and Eric Savoy, eds. *American Gothic: New Interventions in a National Narrative.* Iowa City: University of Iowa Press, 1998.
McCarroll, Meredith. *Unwhite: Appalachia, Race, and Film.* Athens: University of Georgia Press, 2018.
McPherson, Tara. *Reconstructing Dixie: Race, Gender, and Nostalgia in the Imagined South.* Durham, N.C.: Duke University Press, 2003.
Meyer, Moe, ed. *The Politics and Poetics of Camp.* London: Routledge, 1994.

Miller, D. A. *Place for Us: Essay on the Broadway Musical*. Cambridge, Mass.: Harvard University Press, 1968.

Morris, Charles E., III, ed. *Remembering the AIDS Quilt*. East Lansing: Michigan State University Press, 2011.

Muñoz, José Esteban. *Cruising Utopia: The Then and There of Queer Futurity*. New York: New York University Press, 2009.

———. *Disidentifications: Queers of Color and the Performance of Politics*. Minneapolis: University of Minnesota Press, 1999.

Murphet, Julian, and Stefan Solomon, eds. *William Faulkner in the Media Ecology*. Baton Rouge: Louisiana State University Press, 2015.

Nama, Adilifu. *Race on the QT: Blackness and the Films of Quentin Tarantino*. Austin: University of Texas Press, 2015.

Ohi, Kevin. *Dead Letters Sent: Queer Literary Transmission*. Minneapolis: University of Minnesota Press, 2015.

Orry-Kelly. *Women I've Undressed*. London: Allen & Unwin, 2016.

Paller, Michael. *Gentlemen Callers: Tennessee Williams, Homosexuality, and Mid-Twentieth-Century Broadway Drama*. New York: Palgrave Macmillan, 2005.

Palmer, R. Barton, and William Robert Bray. *Hollywood's Tennessee: The Williams Films and Postwar America*. Austin: University of Texas Press, 2009.

Pugh, Tison. *Precious Perversions: Humor, Homosexuality, and the Southern Literary Canon*. Baton Rouge: Louisiana State University Press, 2016.

———. *Queer Chivalry: Medievalism and the Myth of White Masculinity in Southern Literature*. Baton Rouge: Louisiana State University Press, 2013.

Punter, David, and Glennis Byron. *The Gothic*. Malden, Mass.: Blackwell 2004.

Richards, Gary. *Lovers and Beloveds: Sexual Otherness in Southern Fiction, 1936–1961*. Baton Rouge: Louisiana State University Press, 2005.

Rogin, Michael. *Blackface, White Noise: Jewish Immigrants in the Hollywood Melting Pot*. Berkeley: University of California Press, 1996.

Romine, Scott, and Jennifer Rae Greeson, eds. *Keywords for Southern Studies*. Athens: University of Georgia Press, 2016.

Russo, Vito. *The Celluloid Closet: Homosexuality in the Movies*. New York: Harper & Row, 1987.

Savran, David. *Communists, Cowboys, and Queers: The Politics of Masculinity in the Work of Arthur Miller and Tennessee Williams*. Minneapolis: University of Minnesota Press, 1992.

Schacht, Steven P., and Lisa Underwood, eds. *The Drag Queen Anthology: The Absolutely Fabulous but Flawlessly Customary World of Female Impersonators*. Binghamton, N.Y.: Haworth, 2004.

Sears, James T. *Rebels, Rubyfruit, and Rhinestones: Queering Space in the Stonewall South*. New Brunswick, N.J.: Rutgers University Press, 2001.

Sedgwick, Eve Kosofsky. *Between Men: English Literature and Male Homosocial Desire*. New York: Columbia University Press, 1985.

———. "Queer and Now." *The Routledge Queer Studies Reader*. Ed. Donald E. Hall and Annamarie Jagose. London: Routledge, 2013. 3–17.

Sinfield, Alan. *Out on Stage: Lesbian and Gay Theatre in the Twentieth Century*. New Haven, Conn.: Yale University Press, 1999.
Slade, Alison, Dedria Givens-Carroll, and Amber Narro, eds. *Mediated Images of the South: The Portrayal of Dixie in Popular Culture*. Lanham, Md.: Lexington, 2012.
Slotkin, Richard. *Regeneration through Violence: The Mythology of the American Frontier, 1600–1860*. Middletown, Conn.: Wesleyan University Press, 1973.
Solomon, Jeff. *So Famous and So Gay: The Fabulous Potency of Truman Capote and Gertrude Stein*. Minneapolis: University of Minnesota Press, 2017.
Sontag, Susan. "Notes on 'Camp.'" *Partisan Review* 31 (Fall 1964): 515–31.
Stallybrass, Peter, and Allon White. *The Politics and Poetics of Transgression*. London: Methuen, 1986.
Stewart, Jacqueline Najuma. *Migrating to the Movies: Cinema and Black Urban Modernity*. Berkeley: University of California Press, 2005.
Stockton, Kathryn Bond. *Beautiful Bottom, Beautiful Shame: Where "Black" Meets "Queer."* Durham, N.C.: Duke University Press, 2006.
Sullivan, Nikki. *A Critical Introduction to Queer Theory*. New York: New York University Press, 2003.
Szczesiul, Anthony. *The Southern Hospitality Myth: Ethics, Politics, Race, and American Memory*. Athens: University of Georgia Press, 2017.
Tatonetti, Lisa. *The Queerness of Native American Literature*. Minneapolis: University of Minnesota Press, 2014.
Watkins, Jerry T., III. *Queering the Redneck Riviera: Sexuality and the Rise of Florida Tourism*. Gainesville: University Press of Florida, 2018.
West, Isaac. "Queer Generosities." *Western Journal of Communication* 77.5 (2013): 538–41.
Wexman, Virginia Wright. *Creating the Couple: Love, Marriage, and Hollywood Performance*. Princeton, N.J.: Princeton University Press, 1993.
White, Patricia. *Uninvited: Classical Hollywood Cinema and Lesbian Representability*. Bloomington: Indiana University Press, 1999.
Williams, Linda. *Playing the Race Card: Melodramas of Black and White from Uncle Tom to O.J. Simpson*. Princeton, N.J.: Princeton University Press, 2001.
Williams, Tennessee. *Memoirs*. 1975. New York: New Directions, 2006.
Wise, Benjamin E. "Sideways, Backwards, and Queer: Toward a New Southern Studies." *Journal of American Studies* 48.3 (2003): 719–22.

Contributors

ERIC GARY ANDERSON is associate professor of English at George Mason University, where he teaches Native and Southern Studies and directs the interdisciplinary minor in Native American and Indigenous Studies. In addition to his book *American Indian Literature and the Southwest: Contexts and Dispositions,* he has published more than twenty essays in edited volumes and journals. With Taylor Hagood and Daniel Cross Turner, he edited *Undead Souths: The Gothic and Beyond in Southern Literature and Culture.* He served as the 2012–14 president of the Society for the Study of Southern Literature.

TED ATKINSON is associate professor of English at Mississippi State University and editor of *Mississippi Quarterly.* Atkinson is the author of *Faulkner and the Great Depression: Aesthetics, Ideology, and Cultural Politics.* He has published numerous essays in journals and edited collections; his current book project is a cultural history of the Tennessee Valley Authority.

R. BRUCE BRASELL is the author of *The Possible South: Documentary Film and the Limitations of Biraciality* and articles in *Cinema Journal, Film History, Journal of Film & Video, Wide Angle, Jump Cut, Mississippi Quarterly,* and several anthologies. He has taught film and media studies at New York University, Sarah Lawrence College, Vassar College, Brooklyn College, Hunter College, Manhattanville College, the University of Alabama at Birmingham, and Oklahoma State University.

SCOTT COMBS is associate professor of film and English at St. John's University. He is the author of *Deathwatch: American Film, Technology, and the End of Life,* the first book-length study of the ways in which cinema has grappled with the moment of death. He has also published on silent film melodrama, American film history, and the cultural work of "white trash."

DARREN ELLIOTT-SMITH is senior lecturer in film and gender at the University of Stirling. His research focuses on representations of queerness, gender, and the body in horror film and television and extends to cult and trash cinema and film exhibition and programming. He is the author of the 2016 monograph *Queer Horror Film and Television: Sexuality and Masculinity at the Margins,* and he has contributed to several edited collections on horror and melodrama.

JOE EDWARD HATFIELD is a PhD candidate in the Department of Communication at the University of Colorado, Boulder. Hatfield's research integrates rhetorical theory and cultural studies in examinations of queer communication and social practices. The chapter included in this volume originates from an award-winning master's thesis titled "Southerners and the City: Queer Archives, Backward Temporalities, and the Emergence of AIDS" completed at Syracuse University. Another article on backwardness and queer southern identity can be found in *Text & Performance Quarterly.*

DAVID MARKUS is a language lecturer in the Expository Writing Program at NYU. His writing about art and contemporary culture appears in *Frieze, Art in America, Art Journal,* and *FlashArt.* At present, his academic research is focused on spatiality in contemporary art and literature and on late capitalist cultures of excess. His book project, *Anti-Orpheus: Modern Love and the Myth of the Artist,* centers on alternative masculinities and the conflict, expressed by numerous modern writers, between artistic ambition and intimacy.

MARGARET T. MCGEHEE is associate professor of American Studies and associate dean for faculty development at Oxford College of Emory University. Her research and teaching focus on twentieth-century southern women writers, the Atlanta imaginary in fiction, and multiethnic U.S. literature. Her work has appeared in *Southern Quarterly, Cinema Journal, Southern Spaces, North Carolina Literary Review,* and *Studies in American Culture.*

TISON PUGH is Pegasus Professor of English at the University of Central Florida. His monographs in Southern Studies include *Queer Chivalry: Medievalism and the Myth of White Masculinity in Southern Literature, Truman Capote: A Literary Life at the Movies,* and *Precious Perversions: Humor, Homosexuality, and the Southern Literary Canon.*

D. MATTHEW RAMSEY is chair of the Department of English, Communications, and Media and coordinator of the Film Studies program at Salve Regina University in Newport, Rhode Island. He has written and presented extensively on William Faulkner's relationship with Hollywood, covering such Faulkner-related films as *The Story of Temple Drake* (1933), *Today We Live* (1933), *The Road to Glory* (1936), and *The Tarnished Angels* (1957). He is currently working on articles addressing Howard Hawks's epic *Land of the Pharaohs* (1955) and Edgar G. Ulmer's *Moon over Harlem* (1939).

JEFF SOLOMON is assistant professor of English and Women, Gender, and Sexuality Studies at Wake Forest University. His book *So Famous and So Gay: The Fabulous Potency of Truman Capote and Gertrude Stein* was published in 2017. His current book project investigates camp films of the mid-twentieth century.

JESSICA WALKER is assistant professor of English at the University of North Georgia, where she teaches courses in Renaissance literature. Her publications include essays on appropriations of Renaissance literature in pop-culture texts and several forthcoming articles on *True Detective*. With editors Francis Teague and Margaret Ezell, she is associate editor of *Educating English Daughters: Late Seventeenth-Century Debates*.

Index

The South on Screen

Truman Capote: A Literary Life at the Movies,
BY TISON PUGH

William Faulkner in Hollywood: Screenwriting for the Studios,
BY STEFAN SOLOMON

Unwhite: Appalachia, Race, and Film,
BY MEREDITH MCCARROLL

Queering the South on Screen,
EDITED BY TISON PUGH

CPSIA information can be obtained
at www.ICGtesting.com
Printed in the USA
LVHW111334030320
648844LV00002B/244

9 780820 35672